We'll All Go Home In The Spring

Personal accounts and adventures
as told by the pioneers of the West

We'll All Go Home
In The Spring

Collected and Compiled by
ROBERT A. BENNETT

 Pioneer Press Books
Walla Walla, Washington
U.S.A.
1984

Library of Congress Catalog Number 83-063182

Pioneer Press Books
37 South Palouse
Walla Walla, WA 99362

Cover art by Norman Adams

*Dedicated to the memory of
the pioneers of the Inland Empire*

Peace and rest at length have come,
All the day's long toil is past,
And each heart is whispering, "Home,
Home at last."

Thomas Hood

Acknowledgments

Projects such as this could not be attempted without the existence of libraries, the repositories of mankind's knowledge. With the assistance of dedicated librarians, I have been able to explore the fascinating records of the Old West.

My appreciation is extended to the many people who have contributed their assistance. Thanks to the staff of Whitman College's Penrose Library, especially to Lawrence L. Dodd, curator of the Eels Northwest Collection; and thanks to the staff at the Walla Walla Public Library.

Many of the stories reprinted here were generated at the request of local, state and regional historical societies. First-person accounts were also produced by magazines and newspapers, written by interviewers such as Fred Lockley, C.S. Jackson and Nellie G. Day. Those of us who love to read pioneer stories owe a debt of gratitude to all who were involved in gathering and preserving these accounts of human history.

Table of Contents

Indian Wars

Settlers and Frozen Dreams

The New Eldorado-Sports, Vigilantes and Pony Express Riders

Building and Civilizing

Indians' Last Stand

Epilogue

Freedom. More than any other nation in the world, America values this right above all others. America's War of Independence fought with England, and in fact, all of its wars have had freedom, either its own or others', as the underlying and fundamental cause. Freedom of religion, a free press, freedom to choose where to live, freedom of association, and all of the freedoms contained in the Bill of Rights were revered and cherished privileges.

The lack of restraint associated with freedom implied to many Americans that they had the prerogative of "Manifest Destiny", that obvious and unmistakable right to inhabit the whole of the American continent. Even before the American Revolution was settled, emigrants had started moving west from the original thirteen colonies. Through the gaps of the Appalachian mountains they filtered into Kentucky and Tennessee and into the Ohio river valley. From there the tide of emigrants pushed ever westward into the old Northwest and across the Mississippi river into Missouri and Iowa. After the settlers had reached this point, many felt that they would be unable to move further west, as the next great barrier was a vast unhospitable land, full of nothing but savage Indians, wild buffaloes, and prickly pears, and labeled by the early explorers as the 'Great American Desert.' Surely no one could settle in this barren land.

Americans, however, were not to be denied their manifest destiny, for in 1843 a large wagon train traversed the supposedly uncrossable desert, journeying to a faraway land known as Oregon. When fur trader John McLoughlin, Chief Factor of the British owned Hudson's Bay Company at Fort Vancouver, heard that the first large group of Americans had crossed the Rocky Mountains and reached Whitman's Mission at Waiilatpu, he was heard to exclaim, "Tut-tut-tut, the damn Yankees will get to China with their ox wagons, yet!" Not quite--but it was the start of an epic immigration that wouldn't end until the United States stretched from the Atlantic to the Pacific.

All kinds of people and conditions of humanity surfaced in the Pacific Northwest. The first whites to come who were to stay, were the fur traders-- next came the missionaries, then the settlers. Gold was the magnet that drew the greatest diversity of people to the West, first to California then to the Northwest. By the tens of thousands they came, prospectors, adventurers, drifters, grafters, and all sorts of men and women. Some came intending to stay, more hoped to make their 'poke' and return home to family and friends with their newly gained wealth. Settler or adventurer though, they were all seeking prosperity, and the West held out to them a promise of individual opportunity. Hardships yes, obstacles many--yet those who survived and endured generally found life better in the West than their place of origin. Thus, many stayed to become the first builders of the Pacific Northwest.

This book is a collection of reminiscences, letters, and biographies as told and written by these pioneers. Each storyteller played a role in conquering the vast wilderness. They overcame obstacles that seemed insurmountable and, as their hair turned to gray and their children bore children, they paused to look back at their accomplishments and they were proud. Their venture to the West was a risky leap in the dark, so to speak, and their gamble was handsomely repaid. More so than accounts written from the historian's point of view, these stories are rich in detail, creating a vivid picture of life in the Old West, as no one else can tell it.

Biographies and stories by the pioneers are important tools used by historians to interpret historical events and distill the pertinent facts. Source documents such as diaries, letters, journals, and official reports contribute additional facts which help to expand the story. The material presented in this book is for the most part accurate. What must be remembered though, is that many of these articles were written years after the events had taken place, and often supporting diaries and documents had been lost or destroyed. The passage of time and later circumstances in a person's life also influenced the recollection of an event. Sometimes names are misspelled and dates mixed-up or misremembered. The notorious outlaw Bill Bunton becomes Bill Button or Bill Bunting or any number of other spellings. These small errors do not interfere with the flow of the story, but the serious scholar would be wise to check facts against other sources.

A great deal of thought was given to selection of the sub-title for this compilation. Selecting *Personal Accounts and Adventures ...* was an easy task, but defining a geographical area was more difficult. Almost all of the letters and stories in this book were written by men and women who eventually settled in the Inland Empire of Eastern Washington. All of this group traveled through or lived in other areas of the West before finally settling down. Their westward journey often took circuitous routes that involved them in many facets of the West's history, from the Mormons of Utah to the 49er's of California. They traveled over the Oregon and Santa Fe trails; prospected for gold in California, Colorado, Oregon, Idaho, and Montana; fought with Indians to protect their families; and when they finally found an opportunity that suited them, they settled down. Even though most of these pioneers lived in the Inland Empire, their stories are a microcosm of the history of the entire West, and contribute to the colorful essence of the Old West.

Robert A. Bennett

Chapter  1

Passages West

"I was a poor, homeless, youth destitute alike of friends, money and education. Actuated by a reckless spirit of adventure, one place was to me the same as another. No tie of near kindred or possessions bound me to any spot of the earth's surface. Thinking my condition might be bettered, and knowing it could not be worse, I took a leap in the dark."

J.W. Nesmith

*B*ound for a new land called Oregon, the first large wagon train, containing one thousand men, women and children, left from Indian Territory (Nebraska) in the spring of 1843. They had been preceded a year earlier by a smaller train of some one hundred people who had established a rude trail through to Fort Hall where they had left their wagons. The 1843 train was the first to bring their stock and wagons all the way to the Willamette Valley. At their destination they found a land blessed with a mild climate, fertile soil and an abundance of natural resources. Letters were sent back home encouraging their relatives, friends and former neighbors to make the westward journey.

The next year, three separate trains with over fifteen hundred pioneers made the overland trip. By 1847 over five thousand people were on the trail heading for what they hoped would be a fresh beginning in a young land. Lured by the thought of prosperity the pioneers expected at the very least sufficiency.

As more settlers arrived in the Willamette Valley, communities started to form, and farms, hewn out of virgin forests, began to checkerboard the fertile valleys and rolling hills. Most commerce was by barter as money was scarce, and buckskin and calico were the common dress of the day.

In December of 1847 the settlements along the Willamette were thrown into an uproar. Word was received that Doctor Marcus Whitman and his wife Narcissa, missionaries located near Fort Walla Walla, a fur trading post on the Columbia River, had been slain along with several others in an unprovoked attack by the Indians. In addition there were several hostages taken by the slayers. A contingent of mounted volunteers was quickly raised and sent to the Walla Walla country to recover the hostages and punish those responsible for the foul deed.

The Whitman massacre signaled an end to an era in the Northwest -- an end to a time that saw a peaceful if somewhat tenuous co-existence between the whites and the native population. It was the start of a series of Indian wars, spawned by an encroachment on the Indians' ancestral land, that didn't entirely end until the late 1870's.

Just why the pioneers made that first great migration across the trackless plains and mountains has been an often posed question. There were just about as many reasons as there were pioneers. Let's join a young adventurer now, who is writing his mother from Indian Territory prior to his departure for Oregon, his only writing implement being a charred stick.

W. C. Dement

*A letter written to his mother in the spring of 1843
just before leaving for Oregon territory
in the first large western emigration.*

Headquarters, Indian Territory, May 18, 1843. Mrs. Julia Dement,
Geo. Town, D.C.,

Dear Mother: — I have waited until the very last moment before starting
to hear from some of you; but have not. I have now just time to write a few
lines as the company is now striking tents, and must be off in five or ten
minutes. I have no doubt but that you will think this a dangerous trip and a
wild freak of mine; but I can assure you there is nothing to be apprehensive
about. Our company consists of five hundred men with one hundred and
twenty wagons commanded by Capt. Burnett. My expenses will be but little. If I am pleased with the country I will remain and if not I will return next
spring. I saw Aunt L. some two weeks ago; they are all well. We have been
camped here several days waiting for part of our company which has just
arrived.

I am now compelled to close this short letter and bid you farewell.

W.C.D.

P.S. — Give my love to all my sisters and brothers. I shall write when I get
to Oregon. I must apologize for not writing you before but I have been so
much engaged in assisting and getting ready for the trip that I really had not
time to do so. This is written with a stick; I fear you cannot make it out.

J.A. Stoughten

*J.A. Stoughten, a resident of Spokane County,
wrote this piece in 1899. Another version of his story
appeared in the* Walla Walla Union *in 1924 which was
subsequently reprinted in* Told by the Pioneer,
*a W.P.A. project by the State of Washington
published in three volumes in 1938.*

"In March 1843 I was in a little town in Missouri called Weston. And there
heard a speech by Dr. Whitman which gave the Oregon fever. In support of
the speech a noted lawyer, named Peter Burnett, (afterwards Governor of

California) took up the cause and canvassed several Counties trying to get emigrants to go to Oregon.

"As a reward for his efforts, we in the latter part of March gathered together about twenty wagons, to start for a rendezvous, where we were to meet others attracted by speeches of Dr. Whitman, from the different States visited by him.

"We met about 75 miles south of Ft. Levensworth in the Indian territory and there gathered together about 200 wagons averaging about five souls each which were drawn by oxen.

"On about the 20th of April we made the start, and then began an experience of hardships which in my experience has never been equaled. Our first difficulty was with the soft ground, and I remember seeing as many men as could get hold of a wagon working at the wheels to get it out of the mud, the oxen having to flounder out as best they could; I have seen them up to their sides in the mire.

"In fording streams we sometimes had as many as 20 wagons fastened together. And I remember in crossing the Platt River our hind wagons worked down stream until they reached deep water and then rolled over and over costing us much loss and trouble.

"We seldom got across a stream without trouble as we had to swim our cattle and to make matters worse we did not have any road or trail and crossing the sage brush country we had to cut our way through.

"Our lives were greatly endangered by Buffaloes having seen them thousands upon thousands of them and we had to send out guards ahead to shoot into the herds as we could see them stampeding for miles in advance.

"We had to keep a close lookout to keep from getting trampled under foot by the maddened animals.

We also had great trouble with the Indians, stopping us and making us pay tribute.

"One morning we came upon a body of Indians who had just finished a battle, the dead still lay on the ground with arrows sticking in the bodies and some of them scalped.

"The Indians who had won the battle halted us and demanded some of our cattle. We finally compromised by giving them a number of cattle which they killed on the spot and proceeded to make themselves merry over their success.

"Everything went well for about a week when we were halted again by Indians and just at that time Kit Carson, under the control of Col. Fremont, who was sent out by the government to report the best locations for posts came up. The Indians wanted more tribute for the privilege of crossing their country.

"We told Kit Carson about our being stopped before and he advised us to go out and investigate, saying the Indians were full of tricks and that it might be the same band.

"Accordingly some of our men went out with him and found to our surprise that it was the same band of about 800 strong who had stopped us before.

"When Kit Carson saw that it was a trick he had every man take his rifle. Confronting the Indians he demanded that they let us pass saying that they had been payed once and would get no more.

"As a result of our stand they opened their lines and let us pass through and we did not see them any more.

"As we got into the alkali desert the cattles' feet began to wear out and they died from the alkali. My father lost two yoke of oxen. Whitman let the party scatter out more to get feed and at times it was 100 miles from front to rear of the train.

"Upon our arrival at Ft. Hall we found it in charge of the Hudson Bay Co. Mr. Grant, the President of the company, tried to discourage us in every way. Saying that we could not get through and that we had better stop there.

"Failing to influence us he next proposed that we trade our cattle and wagons for pack horses. He and his under men almost insisted that we trade them. But Dr. Whitman who came in a little late told us not to pay any attention to Mr. Grant but to rely on him and he would pilot us through in safety.

"An amusing incident occurred when we were within about 100 miles of Whitman Mission.

"I had a sister who was a very lovely girl with long golden hair, and it appears an Indian chief had been informed of her, as one afternoon he rode up and asked my father how many horses he would take for her and my father in a joking way told him that he would take 1000. The Indian disappeared and in the morning we heard an awful noise and to our surprise found that the Indian chief had returned with the 1000 horses to purchase my sister.

"When he found out that my father would not trade he was awful mad and no doubt would have done us harm if he could.

"Having great confidence in the man who had been the cause of our starting on the journey we did his bidding and moved on a couple of miles and camped for three days in order to let all catch up and rest our tired animals.

"We were well organized from the first having a Captain, Corporal and Sentries, who stood guard all the time and one who was found asleep on duty was hauled up and court marshalled and a verdict of guilty would deprive him of his gun.

"We traveled on to Snake River Falls.

"In crossing Snake River we chained together about ten wagons. There were two islands and we had to cross from one to the other. In crossing Dr. Whitman rode beside the wagon I had charge of which was the hindmost wagon and kept punching the cattle in the sides to keep them from getting into deep water. The current was terrible strong and came against the bank below with terrible force.

"Before we were across I had got so far below that my horse got into deep water and Dr. Whitman seeing the dangerous position I was in wheeled round and left the wagons and the cattle to look after themselves. He grabbed my horse by the bridle hollering let go of the reins and pulled him so that we reached the island in safety. Otherwise I would not have been alive to write this story.

"After we had crossed Snake River Dr. Whitman left us and came on to Whitman's Mission.

"We followed and when we were within about 150 miles of the Mission, we ran short of food and had to send men ahead to Dr. Whitman to get food (the Doctor having a little pair of burrs with which to grind wheat). After getting their supplies they came back and met us.

"When we arrived at the mission we lay there three weeks and made canoes by digging out the big cottonwood trees and floated them down the little Walla Walla river to Ft. Walla Walla (now Wallula Junction) and was in charge of The Hudson Bay Co. The Officers of the Company after inspecting our Canoes told us that it would be suicide to start in such Canoes as we had and advised us to get Canoes of the Indians which we did (I must say our three weeks work was wasted as the Canoes we made would turn over so easy) and we had to hire an Indian in each canoe to pilot us as we did not know how to mannage such frail crafts and did not know the character of the water we had to pass over.

"My father traded a beautiful hand-made quilt for a canoe and as our party started to leave the squaw came and wanted her canoe back.

"I can see them standing there yet, the old squaw with knife in hand and my father armed with a rock. Douglas, commander at the post, came out and advised father to give the squaw her canoe, otherwise it would cause trouble. So he took the quilt and bought another canoe.

"Just before we reached Ft. Vancouver we encountered a terrible wind which caused us to lay up. We had no provisions and our party was forced to eat an old beef hide which had layed in the bottom of the canoe and was watersoaked so that the hair was falling off. Some of them burned it to a crisp and ate it. But the next day we were able to proceed and reached Ft. Vancouver in the evening and were supplied with food; Doctor McLaughlin was very good to us.

"It was Dr. McLaughlin, who when he heard that we had got over the plains as far as Whitman's Mission said, 'tut-tut-tut, the Dam Yankees will get to China with their Ox wagons yet'.

We went up the Willamette River and got as far as where Portland now stands and camped. At the time there was nothing but timber, not even a sign of civilization.

"From Portland we went to Oregon City, our destination, and were received very kindly by the Missionaries who showed us every favor and we stayed with them until we could branch out and get our land. At Oregon City we found a grist mill belonging to the Hudson Bay Co., a sawmill and a store, all supplies coming from England.

"Thus ended my first experience crossing the plains which lasted a period of about eight months."

Jesse Looney

A letter written by Jesse Looney, an immigrant of 1843,
explains to his brother what to expect
on the overland passage.

Waiilatpu, October 27, 1843. Jesse Looney to John C. Bond, Greenbush, Warren County, Ill.

Dear Sir: I embrace the opportunity of writing to you from this far western country, afforded me by the return of Lieutenant Fremont to the States this winter. He thinks he will be at Independence, Mo., by January next, which will be in time for those who intend coming next season to this country to get some information about the necessary preparations to be ready for the journey.

It is a long and tiresome trip from the States to this country, but the company of emigrants came through safely this season to the number of 1,000 persons with something over 100 wagons to this place, which is 250 miles east of the Willamet (sic) Valley, and, with the exception of myself and a few others, have all gone on down there, intending to go through this winter if possible. About half of them have traded off their stock at Walla Walla, twenty-five miles below here (he means the Hudson's Bay fort) and are going by water. The balance went on by land to the Methodist Mission, 175 miles below this, intending to take to the water there.

I have stopped here in the Walla Walla Valley to spend the winter, in order to save my stock. This is a fine valley of land, excellent water, good climate, and the finest kind of pine timber on the surrounding mountains, and above all a good range for stock both summer and winter. The Indians are friendly and have plenty of grain and potatoes, and a good many hogs and cattle. The missionaries at this and other missions have raised fine crops of wheat, corn, potatoes, etc., so that provisions can be procured here upon as good or better terms than in the lower settlements at present. Cattle are valuable here, especially American cattle. Things induced me to stop here for the winter, save my stock and take them down in the spring.
spring.

In preparing for the journey of Rocky Mountains, you cannot be too particular in choice of a wagon. It should be strong in every part and yet it should not be very heavy. The large size, two-horse Yankee wagons are the most substantial wagons I have seen for this trip. You should haul nothing but your clothing, bedding and provisions. Goods are cheaper here than in the States. Let your main load be provisions — flour and bacon. Put in about as much loading as one yoke of cattle can draw handily, and then put on three good yoke of cattle and take an extra yoke for change in case of failure from lameness or sore necks, and you can come without any difficulty. The road is good, much better than we had expected, but is long. Bring all the loose cattle you can, especially milk cows and heifers. Do not attempt to bring calves. They will not come through, and by losing them you will be in danger of losing their mothers.

I cannot urge you too strongly to be sure to bring plenty of provisions; don't depend on the game you may get. You may get some and you may not. It is uncertain. We were about five months on the way to this place, and I had plenty of flour, etc., to do me, but most of the company were out long before they got here, and there is little or nothing in the way of provisions to be had at the forts on the way. I would advise you to lay in plenty for at least five months, for if you get out on the way you will have trouble to get any till you get here. I would advise you to start as soon as the grass will admit. We might have started near a month sooner than we did, and then would have been here in time to have gone through with our cattle this winter. We left Independence, Mo., the 22nd of May and we are just about a month too late. Myself and family were all sick when we left and continued till we left Blue River, and the rain and wind, but when we reached the highlands along the Platte we began to mend. My health is better than for years, and so far as I have seen this country I think it is very healthy. There was five or six deaths on the road, some by sickness and some by accident, and there were some eight or ten births. Upon the whole we fared much better than we expected. We had no interruptions from the Indians. Our greatest difficulty was in crossing rivers. Mrs. L. says prepare with good strong clothing or sage brush will strip you.

This shrub is very plenty, and was hard on our teams, especially those that went before, but it will not be so bad on those that come next year, for we have left a plain, well beaten road all the way. I will have a better opportunity of giving you accounts of this country next spring, and I want you to write the first chance and to direct to the settlement of Willamet.

So no more, but remain,

Your brother till death,
Jesse Looney.

W.S. Gilliam

Thoughts by W.S. Gilliam, pioneer of 1844,
regarding his early experiences
in Oregon and the Northwest.

Having been requested by Mr. W.D. Lyman, President of the Inland Empire Pioneer Association to write some reminiscences of my trip across the plains and also of my early experiences in Oregon and the Walla Walla country, I commence by stating that we left our home in Western Missouri on the 24th of February, 1844, that being the fifteenth anniversary of my birthday. We started thus early for the reason that our feed was exhausted and with the view of crossing the Missouri river into what was then Indian Territory, but now State of Kansas where we could graze our stock on rushes which were very abundant. We crossed the river the 2nd of March at a point about six miles above St. Joseph, then know as Capless Landing. I think it is now known as Amagonia. That being the place designated as the place of rendezvous of the emigration and expecting to be detained there sometime we built comfortable camps in which we could live fairly comfortable. We remained here preparing, organizing and waiting for the arrival of fellow emigrants until some time in May. We then went out to a distance of about twenty five miles to the Nermaha Agency where a stop of two or three days was made with a view of having some blacksmithing done, it being the last point where we could have that privilege. According to my recollection and my ideas of the points of the compass we traveled from there about due west over a trackless country. The first or second night out the Indians followed us from the agency and stole several head of cattle. A hot pursuit was made next morning which resulted in trailing them back to the Agency. It did not take long to fasten the deed upon the guilty ones. The affair was amicably settled by the Agent making restitution out of the annuities of the perpetrators. We pursued our western course until we struck the trail leading from Independence to the Rocky Mountain region. The emigration of the previous year had followed this road, we in turn followed it, immediately after this the great rains overtook us and our worst troubles commenced. We camped about 1½ miles from a small stream called the Vermillion. It rained heavily during the night, by the time we got hitched up and drove to the ford, it was impassable and rising rapidly. The rain continued to fall in torrents for days and the stream to rise correspondingly until it got into the boughs of the trees and when it commenced falling it was several days before it got into its banks so we could ferry it and swim the stock in safety. The earliest possible advantage was taken of these latter conditions. This little stream that at low water could be stepped across detained us seventeen days in one camp. The Big Blue, the next obstacle that detained us was about twenty-miles from the Vermillion, but we found it well in its banks and also had the good fortune to find a couple of large canoes with a platform between which had been left by a party immediately ahead of us, so all we had to do was to ferry our wagons over and swim the stock, which occupied three days. These rains of which I have been writing caused the highest waters that had been known up to that time in that region and that high water mark has never been reached since, so I feel that I have a fair claim to the distinction of being out in and enduring the heaviest rain of the 19th century, be this a distinction or honor. It is an experience that I do not care to have repeated in my life time. After we crossed the Blue we were not troubled with high water to any extent worth mentioning. Our worst obstacle was mirey roads but every days travel the road improved in this respect. We traveled across the country to the Republican Fork. We journeyed up this stream several days and before we left it we celebrated the fourth of July by stopping over and drying our baggage and hunting. On the 7th we struck Platte at a point where I am told Fort Kearney was afterwards built. Our route lay up the Platte and in some two or three days travel we sighted the first buffalo. The hunters were soon out in force. They laid low 22 monarchs of the plains in a short time and it is estimated that there was but about one consumed all the balance wasted. I in company with several others went out to the nearest slain buffalo to procure what meat we wanted. It was the first one that any of the crowd had seen. They are about as ugly animals as ever graced our continent. There was a minister in the crowd who expressed himself by saying that if he had seen it without knowning what it was he would have thought that he had met "old nick" himself. Shortly after this the company being large and cumbersome, dissatisfaction arose which resulted in the dismemberment of the train into smaller companies, which proved very advantageous to all concerned. About this time our smaller company fell in with Andrew Sublette a noted mountaineer who accompanied us as far as Fort Laramie. We traveled several days up the Main Platte before we came to the forks. We traveled several days up the South Fork and then crossed it to the north side where we camped. The next morning a sight opened up to us that can never be seen again by mortal man. As far as the eye could reach up the valley of the South Platte and as far on the bluffs as we could see was black with buffaloes. The quantity of buffalo was one thing that the early travelers could not exaggerate. Under the guidance of Mr. Sublette we struck across the country from the last mentioned camp to North Platte. In the course of the day we descried a large band of buffaloes under full headway making directly for the train. We hastily gathered our guns and put ourselves in position and as soon as the head of the herd came in shooting distance we commenced firing on them and succeeded as we thought luckily in turning them around the rear of the train. I think I may safely say that while we were in the buffalo country we were hardly ever out of sight of the animals. We struck the North Platte the next day and traveled up the stream most the way to Fort Laramie where we laid by a day. We met Mr. Joseph

Walker who was a noted mountaineer and also an old friend of my fathers. He happened to be going our way as far as Fort Bridger and made a very acceptable guide for us. The day we laid by I was taken with a very violent fever and remember but little that happened till we got to Sweet Water where I became convalescent. I remember seeing Independence Rock covered with names innumerable, and the Devils Gate where the river had cut its way through a hill, leaving perpendicular banks perhaps a hundred feet high and a gorge not any wider than the stream. We followed up Sweet Water several days to a point where we left it to our right and took in to the South Pass across the Rocky Mountains. After a moderate days travel we camped at the Pacific Springs, the first water that we had encountered that flowed westward. I remember that we felt jubilant over the affair and thought that this was quite a circumstance in our journey. In passing over the country from there to Fort Bridger we crossed the two Sandies, Green River and Hams Fork. We stopped a day at the Fort and next day it being the first day of September we started a northerly course across the country to Bear River. We followed down this stream to the Soda Springs which was a great wonder to us. On an area of perhaps one hundred acres, hundreds of springs boil up. Many in the bed of the river. We camped here and next morning when we started we left the river and after traveling some sixty or seventy miles we reached Fort Hall, then a Hudson Bay Co. trading post. When Mr. Grant was Chief Factor, here a circumstance occured that has caused me throughout life to regard Grant as a bad hearted man. Peter H. Burnett a noted man of the previous emigration had written a letter of instruction and encouragement and sent it to Grant with instructions that he should read it to the emigrants when they reached Fort Hall. When we arrived there the letter was called for and Grant read it to us. It was a very welcome note giving us useful instructions about the route and strong encouragement about the country we were going to, but you can scarcely conceive of the barrels of cold water that he poured on to Mr. Burnett's words of encouragement. The circumstances were such that such a proceeding was of no profit or benefit to him or the company he was serving for it was next to impossible for us to turn back. We were from the very nature of our situation compelled to go ahead and he well knew that his discouragements could avail nothing towards stopping us. I have never been able to regard him as a good man. When we left Fort Hall we entered the country of the Snake Indians. We traveled about 150 miles down the South Side of the Snake River then over to the north side at a point now known as Glenns Ferry, then traveled a northerly course for about seventy miles and we came to Boise River at a point a few miles above where Boise City now stands. We followed the river down to its mouth where it enters the Snake River which we recrossed at this place. Not far from this place we left the country of the Snake Indians.

It is perhaps well enough for me to state the kind treatment we received from them while in their country especially after so many massacres perpetrated on succeeding emigrations. I can most emphatically say that their treatment of us was of the most friendly kind. They seemed to welcome us and I think regarded us as curiosities. Anything we possessed was of value to them for a pin or a rag we could buy a large Salmon. When we came to the first crossing of Snake River they volunteered their assistance to us. It was a dangerous crossing, deep swift and the bar upon which we crossed somewhat narrow. A man had been drowned the previous season by getting off of the bar into deep water. The Indians assisted by one of them going ahead of the point team thereby showing where the bar or shallowest water was and others who were dressed in the same fashion mother was before she ate of the forbidden fruit took positions below each team to prevent them from being beat down by the strong current in the deep water. They signified to us by signs to get into the wagons. They performed their tasks faithfully and took us over safely, for which we felt very grateful; but there was a couple of gamblers that followed in our wake from whom the Indians stole a horse. They followed them up, overtook one of them and killed him and ever after that they were hostile.

After crossing Snake River the second time in two or three days travel we reached Burnt River. Here we encountered decidedly the worst road that we had traveled over. For about twenty miles we passed the narrow canyon of the river over large stones and up and down steep banks with frequent crossings of the stream made it very lively for us but when we got through the canyon on better road we felt a sigh of relief. About the time we reached the better road we had the good fortune to meet James Waters an old friend of my father and also an acquaintance of several persons in our party, who had gone to Oregon the year before and had kindly come to meet us and help us in. I well remember that he was plied with many questions. One question was asked with some solicitude that was if there was sufficient food for the incoming immigration. His answer was that there was enough for several such immigrations. His services were valuable to us especially in locating camps and in many other ways.

We pursued our way until we reached the Blue Mountains and camped at the foot of them where La Grande now stands. In crossing the mountains I saw the first tall timber that I had ever seen. All the timber that I had seen before being the spreading or umbrageous varieties. On discussing the height of the trees one party remarked that it took three looks to see the top. We crossed the mountains in about three days travel and camped about a mile below where Pendleton stands. At this camp a circumstance occured which was recalled rather vividly to my mind while passing over the scene a few weeks since on the train. The next morning when we gathered our stock we found a horse of one of the party was missing. After a little searching we were satisfied that he was stolen. After hunting till nearly noon that noble red man, Esticus, came to camp telling us to go our way and assuring us that he would see that we got the horse. We broke camp about noon that day and while we were nooning the next day Esticus rode up with the stolen horse and without hinting about a gift or present mounted his horse and rode off like a king. In the course of a day or two after the delivery of the horse we reached the Columbia River. We thought the distance from where we struck the river to the mouth of the Umatilla about two miles being able to trace the course of the stream by a fringe of willows on its margin. We considered reaching the Columbia River another important event in our journey. The Indians between this point and the Dalles we found to be the most insolent and thieving ones that we had met in our travels. Their insolence was met on more than one occasion with a good sound thrashing. From this point to the Dalles our route lay principally along the South Bank of the Columbia River although at places the abrupt bluffs closed in to the river and forced the road out onto the highlands. We reached the Dalles about the first of November and camped there preparatory to "taking water" as some of them characterized it.

The boats were supplied by the Hudson Bay Co. The wagons had to be taken to pieces, the boats not being large enough to take them any other way. The wagons and household goods were loaded onto the boats and women and children and some of the men also took the boat and were landed at Linnton a point a few miles below Portland that was expected at that time to be the future metropolis of Oregon. Most of the men and some of the larger boys took the task of driving the livestock over the trail that led down the Columbia River. The snow on the mountains having fallen so deep as to preclude the possibility of passing that way I was assigned to the task of assisting in driving the stock down the trail. For the first few days the weather was good, but before we reached the Cascade Falls the gates of heaven seemed to have opened and the rain came down in torrents. The stream near where we camped raised in the course of the night so as to make it impossible to cross it. There we were with very little to live on. Our situation was becoming acute, but about the third day late in the evening we got provisions from the Falls and the next morning the water had fallen so that we could cross. We at once availed ourselves of this favorable condition and crossed and pursued our journey to the Falls a distance of about ten miles where we found plenty of food awaiting us. When we arrived here the oxen were taken to haul the wagons around the portage which detained us probably two days after which we resumed our journey and enduring hunger, drenching rains and traveling over the worst roads that I ever saw we reached Vancouver early in December. In taking a retrospect of my life I regard this trip from The Dalles to Vancouver as the severest hardship that it was ever my lot to endure. For days and nights my clothes were never dry. That coupled with starvation and the frightfully terrible roads over which we traveled combined to make it such, yet this occured when I was only 15 years old. Mr. Douglas who was chief Factor at Ft. Vancouver received father very kindly and treated him splendidly. We were there several days in crossing the river; during our stay here we were the guests of Mr. Douglas who was kindness personified and whom I shall always remember with gratitude. Before we got the stock ferried over a boat loaded with immigrants on its way to Linnton stopped at Vancouver. I suppose father thought I had had about enough for one of my age so he put me aboard of the boat and in a few hours I landed at Linnton. The next morning a team went out so I went along with it and by night I reached the place where the family had preceded us. Father had to come around by Oregon City with cattle and in a few days he joined us and our long and tedious journey was ended.

It may be well enough to take a retrospect of things as they were then and compare them with things as they are now. We traveled through the Territory that now constitutes the States of Kansas, Nebraska, Wyoming, Utah, Idaho and well through Oregon and in all this vast region we did not find one single home unless you by a strained construction call a mission or trading post a home--a thousand miles of this journey which required six months time to perform it we stood guard to protect our lives and property from hostile Indians. This being the year that Polk was elected President. The earliest news that we got of it was in July following and considered ourselves rather fortunate in getting it thus early, it having come via ship when in fact we did not expect to get it until the arrival of the immigrants in the fall. When a presidential election occurs now if we do not get the news the next day we feel that we are unfortunate in being deprived of the news so long. I took my first trip back three years ago. I was three days in making it and on the route found two large cities (Salt Lake and Denver) and seemingly happy homes everywhere and made the trip in a comfortable manner that was undreamed of in those early days.

Well to return. We wintered where the town of Cornelius now stands about 80 rods south of the Depot with Messrs. Waters & Emerick who were keeping batch at that time. The winter was very mild which impressed us favorably with the climate. In February father went up the country to select a land claim. I think his was the first claim taken south of the Rickreall. The town of Dallas stands on part of it. He came back with a glowing account of the country he had seen and particularly of the place that he had selected for a home. So we got ready and as early in March as traveling was good we started for our new home. We arrived there the 16th of March, it being Sunday. The whole country was a natural park and combined with the ideal spring day that we reached there made it seem to me like dream land. We went to work in good earnest building a log cabin but before we could complete it we were overtaken by the equinoctial storm which gave us some very serious discomfort. The next thing to do was to put in some garden and sow some wheat. Will say that nature gave us a bountiful yield in both field and garden. During this season we suffered some privations in food, for instance at times we had to substitute boiled wheat for bread. It is hardly necessary to say that we did not do this from choice, but having plenty of wild meat, milk and butter we could have a meal that would hardly pass muster now but I can assure you that a person would be a long time starving to death on it. We never had any shortage of breadstuff after the first season, for there was a grist mill built in the immediate neighborhood the next year where we could get flour any time. A large share of the immigrants who wintered at Dr. Whitman's during the season settled in our immediate neighborhood and I learned a great deal about the Dr's. character from them. It seemed as if he had made a deep impression on them for they talked a great deal about him and from their talk I came to have a high regard for him. They told me that he would come home from Wallula a distance of twenty-five miles before breakfast or if necessary go up to where they were building the saw mill, a distance of eighteen miles before breakfast, in fact his energy seemed to have no bounds and no obstacle with him seemed insurmountable. It was this summer of 1845 that he visited the Willamet (sic) Valley and while there he called on my father and as it happened I was away from home and therefore failed to see him, a circumstance that I have always regretted. More especially since he has become such an important figure in history.

The way we cut and threshed our wheat would seem primitive indeed alongside of our steam threshers and combines of today. We prepared what we called a threshing floor by smoothing off the ground and firming it the best we could and then spread sheaves down and then ride and drive the horses over them until the grain was threshed out of the straw, then rake off the straw and put another lot down and when the chaff and wheat got too deep on the floor we would rake it to the center of the floor into a heap where it would remain until we finished threshing. The next step would be to winnow the grain from the chaff which we did with the wind there being no Fanning Mills at that time in that part of the country. Two years later in 1847 the neighborhood got the loan of a fanning mill for a limited period of time. It was considered such a boon that it was run day and night so that all of the wheat fanning might be done by the time the mill had to be returned. Notwithstanding the serious deprivations like the above that we were subjected to, we were in part at least compensated by having a country to live in that was fresh from the hands of nature. Our only ways of traveling were by horseback or ox wagon. If more than one person were going sometimes a wagon was brought into requisition but most generally horses were used in getting about. Saddle horses were cheap and the keeping of them cost nothing for the abundant wild pasture furnished a varied bountiful and rich supply of feed. It was truthfully said in those days that it cost less to raise a cow or a horse than it did to raise a chicken. The above being the conditions, horses were not spared and treated as kindly as humanity would dictate for they were generally ridden in a gallop which was faceiously called the "missionary lope" from the fact I suppose that they generally rode in that gait.

This spring (1845) there was a company went overland from Oregon to California. The rendezvous was near our place. Quite a sprinkling of our immigration joined the company and among them was James W. Marshall who three years later discovered the gold mines in California. It was my good fortune to travel in company with him the entire trip. Father had procured the irons of a plow made in the missionary balcksmith near Salem, but before it could be used the woodwork had to be put on it. Marshall being a carriage builder and expert in working wood generally volunteered to stock the plow as we called it. He went to work on it and did a good job. So we had a plow that was stocked by a man who afterwards became famous the world over as the discoverer of the gold mines in California and from which the impulse to gold hunting was given that has resulted in all the rich discoveries since. The immigration of 1847 brought from Washington City Father's appointment as Postal Agent with instructions from Post Office Department concerning the same. On a recent visit with my sister at Dallas, Oregon who has all the papers I had the pleasure of inspecting them anew. I found them queer reading from our standpoint. In the fall of 1847 father disposed of the place we settled on and moved up the country about twelve miles and bought a place on Pedee. This fall one of my sisters married. In the meantime some Indians had become acquainted with us and were living in the immediate neighborhood. They took some interest in the wedding and were very curious to know what her husband gave for her, it being their custom to sell their daughters in marriage. They were surprised beyond measure when told that she was given to him. It was November of this year that the Whitman massacre occurred. Father was at once notified that he was requested to take command of the volunteers that were to be raised to march against the hostile Indians. He left home abruptly early in December never to return. His death was the heaviest blow that has ever befallen me.

The next year was one long to be remembered in Oregon. It was the year of the discovery of gold in California. It was late in August that reports of the discovery begin to reach Oregon. They reported the mines to be so rich that at first they were discredited but they were soon confirmed in such a way as to relieve all doubts. It would be hard to exaggerate the excitement that was raised upon the confirmation of the news. In fact it would be hard to excite a community in any other way to the pitch ours was on this occasion more especially when we consider how small it was. Everybody that could get away dropped their business and left. My brother-in-law and I rigged ourselves out with a saddle horse and pack horse apiece and started. We had to travel through the Rogue river and Klamath countries in considerable bands to protect ourselves against the hostile Indians but by the time we got to where it was dangerous we had fallen in with plenty of company so we had no trouble on that score. We passed through the hostile country without being attacked or having any horses stolen. In fact to me it was a trip that afforded me some of the keenest kind of pleasure, new scenery every day and some of it (for instance Mt. Shasta) was of the grandest kind.

It was the first time I had left the parental roof. When we got well into the Sacramento valley just after we had struck Camp an acquaintance rode into camp with his pack horse and proceeded to camp with us. He had a thrilling story to tell of his previous nights experience. It seems that the company he traveled with through the hostile country were highly disagreeable to him so when they reached the Sacramento Valley where the Indians were friendly he tore himself away from it and was traveling alone. During the first day of his own travel he bought a salmon of the Indians. When he camped that night he cooked part of his salmon for supper and laid the balance within a few feet of where he made his bed. After retiring while looking out into the increasing gloom he saw approaching him a form that looked as large as a covered wagon. His bearship (for such it was) very cooly and unconcernedly appropriated the remainder of the salmon and sat down within a few feet of him and quietly ate it. After eating he still sat there seeming to ponder on what to do next. In the meantime the campfire got into the dry grass and burnt towards where Mr. Bear was sitting. When it got unpleasantly near him he slowly moved away and disappeared. Some Indians were at the camp in the morning and were shown the track. They assured him the best they could that he was very fortunate in not being served up for a supper for Mr. Bear. When he reached our Camp and narrated the circumstance he remarked that he had concluded that he would not camp alone any more.

I went into the mines and worked with only fair success until late next spring when I became home-sick and not appreciating the opportunities as I would have in later life, I returned home where I arrived the 16th of June, 1849. After resting a few days I visited a camp meeting that was in progress near Salem. I had visited the meeting at the same grounds the year before. I was very forcibly impressed with the difference in the dress of the people in the two years. The first year before California had poured her wealth of gold into the country the people were dressed in very plain pioneer style. The men in buckskin pants with the balance of the suit corresponding. The women in calicoes and muslin, but this year it was very evident that they had freely availed themselves of the privilege that the great quantity of gold that had found its way to Oregon gave them to improve their attire, for in case of the men broadcloth had taken the place of buckskin, and in the women, silks and satins had replaced calico or gingham.

In 1851 there was a vacancy in the Sheriff's office and I was appointed by the County Commissioners to fill the vacancy. During my incumbency in the discharge of my duty as Sheriff, it fell to my lot to execute a death warrant by hanging a man by the name of Evesman who had committed a very foul murder. It was not a very pleasant duty to perform and most certainly one that I never wanted to be called on to repeat. This was the first execution for murder in Polk County and I think the second in the Territory excepting the Indians that were hung at Oregon City for the murder of Dr. Whitman and others. There was another circumstance that grew out of the above murder case that gave me the unenviable distinction of being the only man that ever put up a white man at auction and sold him to the highest bidder. The man in question was a brother of the above murderer. He was found guilty of being accessory to the murder after the fact, which would entitle him to a term in the penitentiary. There was no penitentiary in the territory at that time and the Judge in sentencing him to a term made the provision in the order that in default of there being a penitentiary that he be sold to the highest bidder for the same term that he was sentenced to the penitentiary. Some of my lawyer friends tell me that the Judge assumed a very doubtful right in so sentencing the culprit, but no legal move was made to invalidate the judge's order so the matter rested. The above execution occured on the 11th of May, 1852.

That year my future wife crossed the plains and settled in the neighborhood where I lived. After a year's acquaintance we were married and moved onto a donation claim that I had three miles northwest of Dallas. At this time I was engaged in cattle raising. We lived here till 1859 when we became disgusted with the long wet dreary winters that coupled with the growing shortage of the public pasturage caused us to sell and seek a country with less winter rains and more public range. From what we could hear of the Walla Walla Country we concluded that the winter weather and range were about what we wanted so we at once decided to migrate thither. In July I gathered up the cattle and started. The journey was somewhat tedious, a part of it being over dusty roads and the weather at times hot. I reached Dry Creek at Mr. Aldrich's place early in August. I bought a mans claim just above Mr. Aldrich's place. I stayed some two weeks getting the cattle settled on the range. I started back for the family the first day of September traveling with saddle and pack horse. On my way back I had the good fortune to fall in with an immigrant who had been in Oregon and knew the locality where my land was to sell him my farm and thus relieved me from being detained on that account. I reached home in twelve days after leaving Dry Creek and found the folks all well. We hurriedly made our arrangements for our departure to the place that I had selected for our new home. We bundled our household goods into a wagon, bid good-bye to our friends and started. We drove over the country to Portland where we put the wagon and team on the boat and got on ourselves and finally landed at the Dalles. From there we took the wagon to Walla Walla arriving at our new home the 23rd of October. There was nothing there in the shape of a house but a miserable hut that would neither protect us from the rain or cold, therefore it was very important to build a house at the earliest possible time. I took a man with me into the mountains to assist me in getting out the timbers and put another one to hauling them as fast as we got them out, so it was not but a few days till we had the material on the ground with which to build a cabin. We at once put it up and finished it so as to make it endurable for the winter. This was a tolerably severe winter, a good deal of cold and snowy weather, but the stock got through in good shape for the reason that the grass was fine in the late fall which put them in good shape to withstand bad weather and the country was all open so that they could range on to the creeks and brouse when the grass was covered with snow.

As to ourselves we got along fairly well in the line of provisions but I can assure you that we did not enjoy any delicacies. We had plenty of bread, meat and potatoes, but as to the bread, I remember that at times I had to work for it. When the flour ran low I had to take corn to neighbors who had a steel hand mill and grind it into meal. I think any person who has ever had the experience of grinding on a hand mill in the matter of recollection will be like myself, that is, he will remember it. When spring came the first I did was to gather up the cattle that had got considerably scattered, when that was attended to we went to seeding and planting garden. The season being very favorable everything planted grew luxuriantly. I have never seen such a crop of potatoes as we raised that year. We estimated the crop at six hundred bushels per acre and I am inclined to believe that it was over rather than under the estimate. I often hear people remark that it rains more now than when the country was first settled. I can confidently say that there has never been a season in which more rain fell in summer season with possibly the exception of 1862 than fell this season of 1860. I heard remarked that had it not been for the peculiar nature of our soil that readily absorbed it, the crops would have been generally drowned out. I look back upon this season as being one of the most enjoyable of my life. The summer was all that we could want it to be. I heartily enjoyed looking over the beautiful country, fresh from the hands of nature and unmarred by the hands of man. Everything seemed to smile. The country became endeared to me and I have never seriously thought of making any other place my home.

To give an idea of how little people then in the country knew of its value, when it was being surveyed it was talked among the people that it was a waste of government money to survey it for the reason that there was so little of it fit for settlement and today you could not get an acre of that ground for less than forty dollars. It was universally believed that all the country was worth anything for was its grazing qualities, excepting the low bottoms which were known to be very productive. Everybody who came to the country then came with the intention of raising stock on the fine pasturage that the country afforded. Nobody came with the intention of farming for the reason that it was thought that a very small part of the country would produce grain.

In 1861 I was elected a member of the Territorial Legislature which I have always thought was unfortunate for me for the reason that the following winter was *the* hard winter and my presence at home would have been very desirable and beneficial to my interests. As soon as the Legislature adjourned, although the severe weather was still in evidence, I started at once for home. We traveled in public conveyance as far as Monticello. We found the Columbia thoroughly frozen up and waited a few days hoping that there might be a break up but as the bad weather continued and showed no signs of a change, Mr. Moore, a member of the legislature and I concluded to start on foot for the Dalles. It was one of the hardest trips I ever had. We traveled mostly on the ice but at times would take to the land where trails were beaten between neighbors in the snow, who lived along the shore. We were fortunate enough to find lodging every night and to procure meals when we wanted them.

After about a week of weary treading we reached the Dalles where we got saddle horses. Wells Fargo and Co. Messenger fell in with us here which swelled our company to three. We had traveled a couple of days when my two comrades became badly afflicted with snow blindness. The road had been broken through the snow, but had later filled up with fresh snow. It took the practiced eye to follow it. My comrades being snow blinded, it devolved on me to lead and break the way. The weather at times was intensely cold but we found lodging every night except one. Luckily for us it happened to be one of the mildest nights we had and some blankets, we passed the night fairly comfortably. We reached Walla Walla about the last of February. The war was raging then to such an extent had travel been impeded that we brought news that was six weeks old. I found my folks all well and hearty but the destruction of our stock was frightful. When I looked them up later I found about ten percent of them alive, but being in the prime of life and enjoying perfect health, I was not discouraged. This season the Oro Fino and Florence mines poured wealth into the country to such an extent that money was very plentiful and produce very high. I succeeded in a large lot of potatoes and vegetables and some grain. The season being highly favorable everything grew splendidly and produced abundantly and brought a very high price. Potatoes selling four and one-half cents per lb., and other things in proportion, so at the end of the year I had to a large extent retrieved my losses that I had sustained by the severity of the winter. Ever since I had heard so much about Dr. Whitman from the immigrants who wintered with him in 1844 and especially after his tragic death I had become interested in him and in the site of his Mission but had never visited it. In June this year I took a day for it and got on my horse and rode to the old site. Father Eells was occupying it then. I told him the object of my visit. He was very kind indeed and took a great deal of pains in showing me about the place and explaining things the best he could. He took me to the ruins of the old adobe building and explained the plan of it and showed me the spot where Dr. Whitman according to reports must have fallen. He then took me to where the victims of the massacre were buried and while standing there one of us kicked the loose dirt and turned up the lower jaw bone of one of the victims. One of the teeth in the bone was filled with gold. We buried it as well as we could without tools and inferred from the circumstance that they had been buried in shallow graves or been dug up by badgers. I went home feeling that I had been well rewarded for my ride.

The next year 1863 I was elected Sheriff. I have nothing to report that was unusual during my term. The usual routine of business incident to the office and nothing, no executions for murder or anything else worth speaking about. At the same I was appointed Deputy Collector of Internal Revenue under Phillip D. Moore. The duties of this position was simply collecting revenue that fell due to the government. The most unpleasant part of the duties was my responsibility for the considerable sums of money that I had in my possession. After the expiration of my term I returned to the farm and entered into the usual humdrum routine pertaining to farm life. In 1869 for the first time since leaving, I took a trip to Oregon. The election occurred the day before I started. The telegraph line had reached Umatilla when the boat landed there the messenger went immediately to the telegraph office with the election news. This was my first contact with the telegraph and it was hard for me to realize the fact that while the operator was sending the dispatch that at that very moment it was being received in Portland. At the Dalles we met the first tourists who had come on the newly completed transcontinental railroad to San Francisco and from thence by steamer to Portland and from Portland by river Steamers to the Dalles. I went to Dallas where most of my people lived. I had a very enjoyable visit, having been away ten years. In due time I returned home and found the folks all well.

My reminiscences having come down to and partly including the year 1869, the year that the transcontinental railroad was completed, I think about this time they should lose their character as pioneer reminiscences and thus far their interest to the public, for I think the future historian will draw the line between those who came in ox teams and those who came on the railroads. So I feel that my task is done and when a person's work is finished it is a good time to quit.

March 8, 1904

W.C. Dement

A letter written by W.C. Dement
to his mother in the year of 1845
telling of his marriage and new life in Oregon.

Oregon City, July 25th, 1845
Mrs. Julia Dement, Geo. Town, D.C. Care of John Smoot

Dear Mother: As I have written you in some of my former letters, I arrived here in the year 1843 after a long and tedious journey across the mountains; found a few whites settled here and a great number of Indians in the country. The latter we had some difficulty with, though finally subdued them with a loss of some of our men. Since we have had but little trouble with them, except when they occasionally steal a few horses, etc.

The emigration from the states has been pouring in every year since I came; the country is improving rapidly; it already appears like an old settled country to me; the climate I consider good was it not for the rains of winter which last from three to six months. I have never known a shortage of animal feed in winter until last winter which was unusually cold, so much so, that one-half of the horses and cattle died for want of food; the farmers not expecting such a severe winter did not prepare ahead for the care of their stock.

I have been engaged in different kind of businesses since I came here, of late principally farming. I have a farm six miles from this place situated on the Clakimas (sic) river and considered valuable — at least it will be so if Uncle Sam will give me a deed for it. The laws of this country allow us 640 acres of land but whether we will get it or not I can't say. Last year I raised a fine crop of wheat, oats and potatoes, though received but little for it considering the prices of goods here. We have to take goods in exchange for our produce. With the rest I lost part of my stock during the cold weather.

This year I have rented my farm and am living in town. Spiritous liquors we have not had in the country until very lately; some of hitherto peaceable and quiet citizens have become outlaws.

I suppose you will be somewhat surprised to learn that I have taken a wife in Oregon as you expected to see me at home first. A visit back home is what I have intended every year since I have been here but circumstances were such that I found it impossible to get off. The spring after landing I had sufficient means to have paid my passage home. I waited some time for a vessel but none arrived. I then concluded I would go the following spring but was again disappointed. Since I have accummulated some little property which I could not dispose of for money as there was none in the country. And so I have been kept from year to year; but I yet hope to see you all again.

I was married last July to Miss Olivia Johnson, the daughter of a Baptist preacher, formerly of Kentucky. Mr. Johnson was sent to Oregon as a missionary in 1844. We are keeping house; her father lives a few doors from us and is preaching in this place. There are few Baptists here though increasing in number some. Olivia is not yet sixteen; you will think her rather young to marry; yet the girls think nothing of getting married here at from twelve to fourteen. If any of the young men at the old home think of coming to Oregon I would advise them to bring wives as there are none here.

Your loving son,
WILLIAM C. DEMENT

Lucie Fulton Isaacs

Childhood memories and
musings as told by Lucie Fulton Isaacs, pioneer.

An emigrant train that had left St. Joseph, Missouri, in April 1847, reached the Willamette Valley by the recently opened "Barlow's Gap road" through the Cascade Mountains, and Lucie Fulton arrived at her father's Donation Claim near Lafayette, Yamhill County, Oregon, a child of six.

"We were met a day's journey out, by Dr. McBride, a friend, who had preceded us, and who entertained us until our log house was built beside some lovely oaks that had dropped their leaves before we had moved in. Oh! how it did rain that first winter, and mother often had tears in her eyes, and child though I was, I think I realized something of the sick longing she had for her old home.

"In November there was wild fright for a few days over exaggerated stories of the Whitman Massacre and the fear that the Indians would continue their raids into the "Valley," but nothing happened and presently I was going to school three miles away (it was a church on Sunday), riding across lots on my mother's pet mare "Zilfa," with our neighbors children, quite bravely, for I had ridden many a mile on the journey across the plains and had no fear of a horse; if I shivered sometimes in riding through a woodsy place, at the memory of some lurid fireside tale of Indians I never told it, for fear I should be kept at home," said Mrs. Isaacs to the writer, in one of her reminiscent moods.

"Harpers was our only magazine in those days; how I revelled in the 'easy chair' essays of George William Curtiss; my father rather looked askance at first, a monthly periodical was such a new idea, he was sure it was frivolous and that I had much better be reading the Bible or Shakespeare.

"After some years at the Portland Academy, that pioneer 'finishing institution' for so many of the west, we removed to Wasco County, Oregon, near The Dalles where the dryer climate was more suited to the business of farming and stock raising. The Pioneer Spirit, that wander-lust so largely responsible for the development of our country was a matter of heredity in my father, who combined the Scotch-Irish blood of his father's people with Hugonot and English of his mother, developed through the vicissitudes of two generations of frontier life, in North Carolina and Kentucky with Daniel Boone and George Rogers Clark."

In 1860 Lucie Fulton married Henry Perry Isaacs, a native of Philadelphia, an Oregon pioneer of 1852, and a merchant of Walla Walla from 1862. A tract of land in the east portion of the town of Walla Walla became their home, Brookside being built in 1867 and here for just fifty years the subject of this sketch made her home. It was a home in every sense of the word for combined with the beauty of trees and flowers, of the garden and the brook from which it takes its name, was the atmosphere of hospitality which welcomed new ideas as well as people. Mrs. Isaacs accorded a special welcome to the stranger within the city's gates, and many a lonely one, thousands of miles from his home found sympathy and friendly cheer within those walls.

Nancy Osborn (Kees) Jacobs

Early days in Eastern Oregon and Washington and first hand telling of the Whitman Massacre by Nancy Osborn (Kees) Jacobs.

When asked to write of the scenes and memories of the early days of our beautiful Eastern Oregon and Washington, I shrank from the task, for I felt incompetent and I feared the criticisms that one gets when writing of the past, especially when telling of the days of their childhood. Yet I realize that, at best, but a few years more can elapse until those who know at first hand of these stirring events will have passed on to that undiscovered country from whose bourne no traveler returns, and then only hearsay evidence of those times will be available, unless those who do know shall leave a written record.

I am not ashamed of the name Pioneer, neither am I ashamed of the part that fell to me as one of their number. But who is able to tell of the heroes and heroines who came to this coast. Shakespeare said "The World is a stage and we are all actors", and well did many a man, and woman too, act their part.

And now you will pardon me if I use in my story the names of Josiah Osborn, who was my father, and Margaret Findley Osborn, my mother. Father was born in Connecticut May 1, 1809. His mother was Annie Lyon, a cousin of the General Lyon who was killed at the battle of Springfield, Missouri, during the late Civil War. Mother was born January 30, 1817, in Clark County, Indiana, and emigrated to Illinois when fourteen years of age. They were married June 6, 1834. Both now rest in the McHargue Cemetery, near Brownsville, Oregon. It was more than interesting to me, when a child, to hear father tell of hearing the roar of the cannons when Commodore Perry fought his famous battle on Lake Erie, and also to hear my mother relate the brave deeds and hardships of the Revolutionary War, as told to her by her grandsires, both of whom were soldiers during that war.

It seems a part of God's great plan that some people are born to go out ahead to blaze the trails and fight the battles of life so that the flag of freedom may be planted in new places.

During the autumn of '44 and the spring of 1845 some letters were published in the newspapers telling of the Oregon Country, its fine climate, plenty of fish and game, wild berries in abundance and everything nice. No place like the West,--and you know the sequel.

The doctor advised father to take the trip because of a tendency to tuberculosis, so on the 12th day of April, 1845, we bade adieu to our home and friends in Henderson County, Illinois, and started Westward to the setting sun. How vivid to me yet are some of those scenes; the silent clasping of hands, the falling tear. Once do I remember the voice of father's brother as he said, "God bless you on your journey". 'Twas thus we started on our way, not with the puffing of the stately engine or scream of the whistle, as when an emigrant train starts west today, but it was "Come Boys! Gee Dick! Haw Tom! the pop of the whip, and we were off for Oregon. Oh how much it meant to each of us who were in that wagon then.

At Oquawaka, over four miles from our old home, we crossed the Mississippi River on a small steamboat. We took dinner that day with Grandmother Findley and stayed all night with John P. Courtney, who, with his family, joined our party the next day.

In our prairie schooner we carried all of our provisions for the six months trip, father's chest of tools, a box of books, mostly histories of Greece and Rome, etc., Bibles and a few miscellaneous ones, and all of our clothes, bedding and household equipment. The wagon box was arranged so that the upper part projected over the wheels. We had a corded bedstead arranged so that mother could lie down and rest any time that she wished. This she frequently did as the rough jolting of the dead ox wagon was very tiresome. We had two yoke of oxen and one cow. Together, with a small amount of money realized from the sale of things which we could not bring with us, this equipment constituted our material wealth as we began our long and tiresome journey on the great trail to the West. But if aught were lacking in equipment, it was abundantly replaced by courage and faith that God would care for us, no matter where we wandered.

As I remember, the emigrants that year were mostly from Illinois and Iowa. On May 24, 1845, we crossed the Missouri River on a ferry. I well remember how frightened was I when, as we were about mid-stream, a yoke of grandfather's cattle became unmanageable and jumped overboard and swam to the shore. We crossed the river at St. Joe, then an Indian Agency and the western limit of civilization. Here was the rendezvous for forming trains for the long westward hike and we met a number of other emigrants and formed a train. Mr. Abner Hackleman was elected captain of the train, and we remained under his charge until a few days after crossing Snake River near the end of our journey. The Indian Agent at St. Joe, a Mr. Rubydeau, told the emigrants that the Indians were all ready for their summer buffalo hunt except for the corn which he was to grind. He promised to put off the grinding as long as possible. His plan was to detain the Indians as he feared trouble for the emigrants if the Indians overtook them. The Indians did overtake us later, while we were camped on the Big Blue River.

They stampeded our stock during a severe hail storm and killed one of Grandfather's cows. She had 14 arrows in her. Some of the horses were lost but most of the stock was recovered.

With neither roads, bridges nor ferries, our train began its journey toward the land of promise in the New Oregon, and we forded every stream from the Mississippi to the Columbia. As soon as we had crossed the Missouri River we were in Indian Territory and had to stand guard each night to prevent our stock being stampeded and stolen. To the right of the trail just after crossing the Green River was the open grave of Mr. Sager who had been buried there the year before. The Indians had opened it and I remember the small poles with which the body had been covered, as they were standing upright in the grave. The train stopped a few minutes while we looked at the gruesome reminder that we knew not when we would have to leave some of our loved ones to this same fate. Another time I recall was when a stampeded buffalo herd threatened our train. The wagons were quickly halted and every man grabbed his gun. The great fear was of stampeding our oxen as well as danger of being trampled by the hordes of buffalo. The leader of the herd was shot just before reaching the head wagons of the train and the herd was thus divided and scattered. Guarding against such attacks as these, as well as Indians, selecting camping places, feed, water, etc., were some of the various duties of the captain.

There was no settlement until we reached the Willamette Valley. There were some Hudson Bay forts or trading posts at Laramie, Hall, and Fort Boise, and those who occupied them were not in favor of Americans coming to this coast to spoil their trade with the Indians. There were two mission stations, one at Waiilatpu, the home of Dr. Marcus Whitman and his noble wife, and one at the Dalles, then occupied by Father Waller and Rev. Brewer of the Methodist Episcopal church. There was no place on that long journey over mountains and plains and deserts to get provisions except at Waiilatpu, and that near the end of our journey, and in a limited amount.

There were a number of accidents and many incidents during our trip. Some of the latter I shall mention. On the morning of the 5th of August, the water at our camp ran east. When we camped at night the water ran west. We had crossed the divide of the Rocky Mountains. A young man by the name of Andrew Rogers, of whom more will be said later, was helping drive the loose cattle that day. He left the cattle and assisted father, who had dropped out of the train during the day because of mother, to get our wagon into camp that evening. That night a young chap came to our camp and he came to stay. He weighed about twelve pounds, and later persisted in calling me sister. I called him Alexander Roger Osborn. There was one wedding in our train—a Mr. Scott and Rebecca Cornelius were married as we descended the western slope of the Rockies. I remember how, as they stood in front of their tent by a small fire, my father came up with an armful of sage brush and threw it on the fire. Instantly the whole scene was lighted so that the entire camp could witness the ceremony which was being performed by Mr. Evans, a Baptist Minister.

Soon after reaching Snake River the emigrants felt safe from the dangers of the plains and the train split up into small divisions on account of the greater ease of procuring food and water for the stock. With father was Grandfather Courtney with two wagons, and Elisha Griffith. While along the North bank of the Snake River we met Dr. White who told us of Dr. Whitman at Waiilatpu where we could get some provisions. When we reached the Grande Ronde Valley, John B. Courtney and his son John were sent ahead with a little gray mare to secure provisions from Dr. Whitman. On their return to our party they told us of the need of a mill-wright at Waiilatpu as the Indians had burned the mill which Dr. Whitman had erected there. They had told the Doctor of my father as a man who would suit his need, and so we parted from our friends at the foot of the Blue Mts. near the old Cayuse station and wended our way to Waiilatpu, our first camp being near where Athena now is. That was about the middle of October, 1845. Later Isaac Cornelius and Tom Summers came with their families to the mission and stopped for the winter. Summers as a blacksmith and worked for the Doctor. Jacob Rynearson taught the Indian School and Andrew Rogers, a young man from Illinois taught the mission school for the white children that winter. The latter school was small, but a number of the pupils are living yet. I am one of them. You will find the name of Andrew Rogers on the marble slab with Whitman's. They also had a Sunday-school for the Mission children. This was my first Sunday School and Mrs. Whitman was my teacher. The twenty-third psalm was my first lesson. How I love to think of that school.

March of '46 found us again on the road to the Willamette Valley. We drove overland to the Dalles where we stopped and whipsawed lumber enough to make a flat boat and shipped the wagons and outfit. The four wagons in the party belonged to Messrs. Rynearson, Cornelius, Summers and Osborn. It required several days to saw the boards and build the boat. My father had his tools along and was chief builder of this craft. We drove the stock along the trails and swam the fork cattle across the river just above the Cascade falls. There we unloaded the boats and made a five mile portage. So far, father had steered the boat and Cornelius and Summers had done the rowing but they did not fancy the undertaking of shooting the Cascade Falls in that unwieldy vessel so hired some Indians to take it out and turn it loose in mid stream above the falls. Other Indians caught it when it came to the eddy below the rapids. Here we reloaded and resumed our journey to Oregon City, which was then the headquarters of the American settlers. There we spent the summer and made the acquintance of Geo. Abernathy, the first Governor of Oregon, Dr. McLoughlin of historic fame, Wm. McKinley, also of the Hudson Bay Company and Dr. McKay. In the fall of '46 we moved to Salem, now the capitol of Oregon, where stood the old Institute, the pride of the Methodist Missionaries. Judson and McLain were two of the leading men there at that time.

Dr. Whitman came to Salem in the fall of 1847 and purchased the Dalles Mission for the Presbyterian Board of Missions and put it in charge of his nephew, Perrin B. Whitman and Mr. Hinman. Father met the Doctor while he was at Salem and contracted with him to go back to Waillatpu and take charge of the work at the mission for two years, this giving him more time to devote to his work with the Indians. Father was to receive three hundred dollars per year, either in stock or money, besides living for himself and family. We children were to be in the Mission School.

We left our cattle and chickens and most of our belongings with grandmother Courtney and taking only father's tools and a few household necessities we made the trip up the Columbia River in a batteau with an Indian crewl. At Vancouver, Mr. Ogden sold us tea, coffee, sugar, tobacco and other supplies for the trip, all of the order of Dr. Whitman. We left our boat at the mouth of the Walla Walla River and sent word to Doctor that we were there. We waited three days and were camped near some Indians who had the measles. I well remember the death of a little papoose and the mourning of its parents, particularly, the father.

Early on the morning of the third day, Crockett Beaula, (Bewley) who was massacred with Whitman, came to our camp with a large wagon and provisions from Waillatpu. As soon as we could cook a meal we started on our way to the Mission and arrived there the following day in time for dinner. As we were crossing the Touchet River the oxen, which were quite wild, started up the stream and got into deep water. Mr. Beaula stopped them by jumping out and wading ahead of them. Father carried us children from the back end of the wagon to land and then assisted in getting the wagon and cattle out of the river. We had been at Waiilatpu just five weeks when the fatal 29th of November came. A number of emigrant families had stopped for the winter, expecting to go on in the spring to the Willamette Valley. They brought the measles with them. That year the Indians had been more troublesome than usual. Many of them had the measles and their mode of treatment was nearly always fatal to the patient. They would take a sweat bath and then jump into the cold water. Of course, death was the result. We also had the measles. My mother came near dying and we buried her babe on the 14th of November. My sister, in her sixth year, died on the 24th. Her memory brings to my mind a scene which I cannot forget. An Indian came into the room where the form of my sister lay. Mrs. Whitman asked leave to show him the dead child. She wanted the Indians to know that the measles were killing the white people as well as the Indians and thus hoped to allay the growing distrust of the red men. The Indian looked long at my sister, then how cruelly he laughed, to see the pale face dead. The good Doctor and his noble wife were kept busy night and day to care for the sick and dying.

At last came the fatal 29th. The school, which was taught by Mr. Saunders a lawyer from Wisconsin, and which had been closed on account of sickness, was reopened that day. Three men, Messrs. Kimball, Hoffman and Canfield, were dressing a beef. Father, who had been out to get a bucket of water, remarked that there were more Indians about than usual but thought it was because they had killed a beef. Mother had gone in to Mrs. Whitman's room to see Hanna Sager and Helen Meek who were sick with the measles. Both girls died a few days later. It was the first time that Mother had walked across the room for three weeks. The Doctor who was sitting by the stove reading, was called into the kitchen to give a sick Indian some medicine. The sudden and continuous firing of guns was the first alarm. Mrs. Whitman began to cry and the children to scream. Mother said, "Mrs. Whitman, what is the matter?" She replied, "The Indians are going to kill us all." Mother came back into our room and told us what was being done. Mrs. Whitman called out to fasten the doors and father took a flat iron from the fireplace and drove a nail above the latch on the outside door of our room. Then he seated himself on a box by the foot of the bed on which lay my brother, John, sick with the measles. Mother sat near the head of the bed and I was between them. Mrs. Whitman came in soon after for water. Mr. Kimball had been wounded and had fainted. She came back a second time, asked for my father and said, "My husband is dead and I am left a widow." She returned to her room wringing her hands and saying, "That Joe! That Joe! He had done it all." This Joe Lewis was a half breed Indian of ill repute who had crossed the plains that year from the Red River Country. He it was, instead of Mr. Rogers, who told the Indians that the Doctor was poisoning them. Some late writers claim that Mr. Rogers made this statement to save his life at the time of the massacre. They base their claims, as also in other instances, upon unreliable Indian testimony and the statement of a priest who did not even claim to be a witness of the events narrated. None of the whites present at the time the statement was claimed to have been made have ever made such an assertion. Joe Lewis and an Indian named Cup-ups came around the house and broke our window with the butts of their guns. Mrs. Whitman and those in her room had gone up stairs. I had spoken twice to father and said, "Let's go under the floor." He did not answer me but when the Indians began breaking in the doors of the adjoining room he opened the floor, which was made of loose boards, and we were concealed beneath. In a few moments our room was full of Indians, talking and laughing as if it were a holiday. The only noise we made was by my brother Alex, two years old. When the Indians came into our room and were directly over our heads he said, "Mother, the Indians are taking all of our things." Hastily she clapped her hand over his mouth and whispered that he must be still. I have often been asked how I felt when under the floor. I cannot tell but I do remember how hard my heart beat, and how large the ventilation holes in the adobe walls looked to me. They were probably only three or four inches wide and a foot long, but they seemed very large to me when I could see the Indians close on the other side. The Indians tried to follow those who had gone up stairs but were kept back by a broken gun being pointed at them. They then persuaded them to come down, saying that they were going to burn the house. Mrs. Whitman fainted when she came down and saw the Doctor dying. She was placed on a settee and carried by Mr. Rogers and an Indian. At the door Mr. Rogers saw the circle of Indians with their guns ready to shoot and dropping his end of the settee exclaimed, "My God we are betrayed." A volley from the waiting savages was his answer and both he and Mrs. Whitman were mortally wounded. The Indians then told Joe Lewis that if he was on their side he must kill Francis Sager to prove it. Francis was my school mate and about fourteen years old. We heard him cry to Lewis, "O Joe, don't shoot me," then the crack of the gun as Lewis proved his loyalty to the red men.

As soon as it became dark the Indians left for their lodges of which a number were near. Everything became still. It was the stillness of death. All we could hear was the dying groans of Mr. Rogers who lay within six feet of us. We heard him say, "Come Lord Jesus, come quickly." Afterward he said faintly, "Sweet Jesus." Then fainter and fainter came the moans until they ceased all together. Thus dies my first teacher.

We lay beneath the floor until about ten o'clock that night, then came out and tried to find some wraps and something to eat. We could find but little and did not linger long. Hanging by the window was a small bag with my childish keepsakes in it. When we came from under the floor I started to get this and stumbled over a small tin cup. I asked mother if I could take this and having her consent placed it in my little reticule. Later father split a stick and fastened to this cup so that mother was able to get water from the river while he was gone up to the fort for aid. It was cold in death. There was only star light to guide us and as we came out of the house we turned west, went down through fields and crossed the Walla Walla River near the mouth of Mill Creek. Father made three trips to carry us across, first taking my two brothers, then myself, and lastly mother. We then secreted ourselves the best we could in the bushes. When daylight came we found that we were near a trail and we could hear the Indians pass and repass, laughing and talking as they carried the plunder from the Doctor's house. Our thought was to go to Fort Walla Walla on the Columbia River near what is now known as Wallula, which was about thirty miles distant.

Tuesday night we were able to get but a short distance before mother gave out. When she could no longer stand, she tried to persuade father to leave us and go to the fort to try to get help. At first he would not. He said, "I cannot leave you, but I can die with you." Mother waited until he became more calm and then pleaded duty. How often that word has helped a faint and faltering heart. When darkness came again and each had lifted their hearts to God in prayer, for they were praying people, he made ready to go. They knew that he could take but one of us with him. Which should it be? Finally he took my little brother John, who was sick and weak, hoping to leave him at the fort to be sent to our friends in case the rest of us should be lost. Such a parting as that was. I hope I shall never witness the like again. How we listened to his footsteps as he slipped away in the darkness. Just think of that lone man carrying a sick child nearly four years old, and he had never been over the way but once. He was nearly drowned while attempting to cross the Walla Walla River, but managed to get out on the same side he went in and continuing on, finally crossed near Wallula and arrived at the fort just at day break. He was put into a room where there was nothing but a fire and given a cup of tea and a few scraps to eat. He asked for help to get us in and was told that his wife would surely be dead and that he had better not try to get us children. He replied to McBain that he would save us or die in the attempt. Fortunately for us, an American artist by the name of Stanley, who was out painting and sketching for some company in New York and had been out in the Colville country where Rev. Eells and Walker had their mission station, came to the fort the same day father got there. He offered his horses and what little provisions he had left and made the sick child as comfortable as he could, for they would not keep him at the fort. A Walla Walla Indian was secured as a guide and they came back to us. He had left us in the dark and was not familiar with the locality so of course it was difficult for him to locate us when he returned. Finally he called my mother and when she answered the Indian jumped from his horse and came to us. He had his hand in his blanket and we thought he would kill us but he raised his hand and said "Hia Klatawa," meaning "Hurry and go." Then we knew that he was of the Walla Walla tribe and not a Cayuse Indian for they did not use the jargon. Father said, "My God, Margaret, are you still alive?" and fell across us. Such a meeting as that was. But here is where I must draw the curtain.

It was now getting light and we were soon on our way. McBain had ordered father to go to Chief Five Crows on the Umatilla River, as he was still friendly to the whites. We started and soon came to what is now known as Mud Creek. The banks were steep and we had to unsaddle the horses to get them across. The Indian bent willows down to form a bridge over the creek and carried all of the things and us children across on it. While he was saddling the horses we saw a Cayuse Indian about a half a mile away on a little knowl. Soon he came to us with his hand on his gun and told our guide, who was unarmed, to be still while he killed that white man. The Walla Walla Indian shamed him out of this by telling him that it would not be a brave act to kill a sick man who had his sick family with him. The Cayuse replied that he had never killed a white man and was not anxious to do so and would let him go for the rest of the Cayuses would soon get him anyway. Father had heard that if an Indian accepts tobacco from anyone he would not injure him, so he offered this warrior a piece of his tobacco. With a laugh, the Savage accepted it and placed it in his bosom, and turning, rode off toward Waiilatpu.

We kept on to the Hudson Bay Farm where a Frenchman with his Indian wife was in charge. There we secured a change of horses as the ones we had were worn out. I found out later that these horses belonged to Rev. Eells and had been loaned by him to Mr. Stanley. A friendly Indian secured them and returned them to Mr. Eells later. The Frenchman told father that he would never live to get to the Umatilla as the Indians were hunting him like bees to kill him, and advised us to go to Fort Walla Walla and demand admittance as American citizens, and if they refused protection to go to the mercy of the friendly Yakima Indians on the North side of the Columbia River.

Father asked the Frenchman to conceal us there but he refused and told us to hurry away. We started again and reached the top of what is now called the "Oregon Hills." Here mother asked where we were going and upon father's replying, "To Umatilla", she slipped from her place behind him and said that she would go no further, adding, "If I have to see you murdered, it will be here." Father told her that McBain had told him not to come back and he did not know what to do, She pleaded with him to follow the Frenchman's advice so father called to the Indian that we would turn and go to the fort. His only comment was "close", meaning "Good". After a short rest we changed and I rode with father and mother was placed behind the Indian and tied to him as she was too weak to stay on the horse. He also fixed rope stirrups to hold her feet and make it easier riding for her.

Our guide then took us over into what is now called Vancycle Canyon. We then traveled down toward the Fort and after some very narrow escapes reached it in the night. McBain's first words to us were, "Why have you not done as I bid you and gone to the Umatillas?" He was told that my mother would not go there and we were then taken into the Fort, but they wanted father to leave that night. He told McBain that he would not go until he could take his family with him. He said, "I demand protection as an American citizen. If you turn me out I will die by the walls of your fort." He was then told that he should be protected. We remained at the Fort until Mr. Ogden, one of the men of the Hudson Bay Co., at Vancouver, came up and bought us and the prisoners who were yet among the Indians. Paying for all in trade, 50 blankets, 50 shirts, 10 guns, 10 fathoms of tobacco, 10 handkerchiefs, 100 balls of powder. For Spaulding and family he gave 12 blankets, 12 shirts, 12 handkerchiefs, 200 balls and powder, 5 fathoms of tobacco, and some knives.

The night after the Indians received their pay they took a war dance in the Fort, and I do not think that any one who has ever heard the savage yell when he is hungry for blood will ever be mistaken when he hears the genuine chorus as we heard it that night. On the 3rd of January, 1848, we left the Fort in batteaus to go down the Columbia. The ground was frozen and it was snowing some when we left. We had not been gone an hour when the Cayuses, hearing that the Volunteers were on their way up, came to re-take us. The boats had to be unloaded at night and drawn ashore to keep them from freezing fast in the ice. You can imagine something of the trip. When we arrived at the Dalles, we met some of the Volunteers for there were no soldiers on this coast then. We met more at the Cascades. They helped us make a five mile portage. The boats had to be carried on men's shoulders.

Every child that could walk and carry a bundle had to do so. (I carried a bag.) Not much of a pleasure trip you will say. But there was gladness in our hearts when we had made that portage. We were out of reach of the hostile foe. And now remember, we were prisoners of war and had to be kept together until we were given over to the Governor of Oregon. When we arrived where Portland now stands, for there were but few cabins there then, Gov. George Abernathy with 25 Volunteers stood on the sloping bank where the street dock now is, to greet us. They stood with arms presented until our three boats came under their guns, their flag floating over them. They fired over us, took off their caps and gave three cheers. I wish that I could picture to you as I saw it when Mr. Ogden stepped ashore and he and the Governor of Oregon clasped hands. He took out his papers, handed them to the Governor, and turning to us said, "Now you are a free people. You can go where you please."

Oscar Canfield

William Canfield's son, Oscar, was a lad of 10 at the time of the Whitman massacre and retained many vivid memories of the horrors of that terrible day. Here in an interview in 1909 he gives some interesting facts in connection with the massacre and the experiences of his family.

William Canfield, who was born in Vermont, moved West and settled at Oskaloosa, Iowa. Receiving a letter from a friend who came with one of the early immigrations to Oregon, that the place had a mild climate, fertile soil and abounded in game and fish, Mr. Canfield, dissatisfied with the cold climate of Iowa, decided on the receipt of this letter to sell out and move to Oregon. An interesting fact about this letter in this time of lightning expresses, is that it was ten months coming from Portland to Mr. Canfield. It went on a sailing vessel around Cape Horn to New York, thence across the continent westward, the last part of its journey was made by the pony express.

In the Spring of 1847 a train of 100 wagons and 1,500 loose horses and cattle started for Oregon and Mr. Canfield and family were members of it. Mr. Canfield often remarked that he did not know what was before him or he never would have undertaken the journey. Yet he never regretted the move and ever thanked the Providence that brought him to the Pacific Coast. He was bound for the Willamette Valley, but Dr. Whitman, wanting a blacksmith and a teacher, went to, or near the present sight of Pendleton, met the wagon train and induced Mr. Canfield and a Mr. Sanders to come to the Mission, where they arrived just two weeks before the massacre. They had not yet unloaded their wagons. Mr. Canfield stood in front of the blacksmith shop, November 29, 1847, at half past 1 o'clock. The signal gun of the massacre was fired by one of a group of six Indians who were sitting on a rail pile watching Mr. Canfield and two others, dress a beef. One of Mr. Canfield's helpers was killed and the other wounded. He ran to the wagon and picked up his youngest that was playing around it, while Oscar came out of the blacksmith shop and took another. Both ran for the Mission house where the family was domiciled in one room. Oscar avers that at least 20 shots were fired at his father, only one striking him.

He saw one Indian near him drop down on his knee and take deliberate aim at his father. He is firmly of the opinion that it was mostly due to poor guns and ammunition that any of the white men escaped.

Once in the building which was an adobe Mr. Canfield and son went up into the loft and seem to have been forgotten by the Indians, as that part of the house was not searched. That night he came down and he and his wife had a long conference in which she urged him to try to make his way to Lapwai, the home of Rev. Spaulding, and save his life for his children's sake. The Indians had quieted down and there seemed no immediate danger to the women and children, as no women but Mrs. Whitman had been killed and no children but the Sager boys who were wards of Dr. and Mrs Whitman. He yielded to the earnest entreaties of his wife and children and stole out in the darkness to a spot of underbrush on Mill Creek northeast of the mission houses and not far from the present site of the grave in which are buried Dr. Whitman and Mrs. Whitman and the others who were killed. At daylight of the following morning he returned to the hill near the mission and stood about where the monument now stands, to see if the Indians were making any kind of hostile demonstrations. His last words to his family the night before were, "If I see anything in the morning to make me think the Indians intend to kill the women and children, I shall return and defend you as long as my life is spared," but all was quiet. The savage appetite for blood seemed satisfied and he started on the Nez Perce trails for Lapwai.

A few days before, he had made some cinch rings for a Nez Perce Indian, and from him had learned the route to the Lapwai. He followed the trails cautiously by night and hid in the daytime until he reached an Indian camp on the Tukanon. He had traveled about 5 miles and had had nothing to eat but a few biscuits and the Indian food which is not appetizing under many circumstances, was relished and gave him strength.

These Indians had not heard of the massacre, and had no suspicion concerning their guest when he told them, he was one of St. George's men. He offered the chief a buffalo robe if he would take him on a horse to the crossing of Snake River. The offer was gladly accepted. At the river he gave his vest to Chief Timothy for taking him across the river in a canoe. Soon after he reached Lapwai and was the first to break the news of the massacre to Mrs. Spaulding.

When the news of the massacre was received at Vancouver, Chief Factor Ogden of the Hudson Bay company lost no time in coming to Wallula, to rescue the captive women and children and in about two weeks he had ransomed all the captives for blankets, handkerchiefs, rounds of ammunition, guns, shirts and tobacco. The tobacco was braided into ropes then and was sold by the fathom, a length of six feet. All amounting in value to about $500.

Agents were sent to the Mission. The oxen were yoked to the wagons and what few belongings the robber bands of the Indians had spared, were hastily thrown in and the helpless band of women and children that had lived in hourly terror of the savage's tomahawk for two weeks, started on their way to freedom. The distance was over 20 miles and the drivers were boys, none of whom were over 10 years of age. The train might be attacked any time, for it was a well known fact that some of the Indians were fiendishly angry because the women and children were not to be killed and they could scarcely be restrained from indulging their savage desire. The boys, frightened as they were, goaded the oxen on to their greatest speed and the journey was probably accomplished in the shortest time of any ever made with oxen. Wallula reached and they were turned over to Mr. Ogden, thus becoming hostages of Great Britain.

The Indians seemed to be greatly rejoiced over their wealth acquired by the ransom. The squaws began bringing up drift wood and piled it high within the walls of the fort. At dark it was lighted and all the Indians gathered around, and began singing. As the flames rose skyward the singing grew louder and soon the warriors began to dance. The dance merged into the war dance. Mr. Ogden was quick to see that these demonstrations meant danger to the occupants of the fort, and gave orders to let no Indian inside the fort building on any pretense whatever and armed every one that could use a gun and told them if an attack was made to sell their lives as dearly as possible. There was little sleep at the Fort that night and the Indians were the first to enjoy the rest of slumber as they sank exhausted from their orgies.

Mr. Ogden had sent Nez Perce escorts to bring the refugees to Lapwai. Rev. and Mrs. Spaulding and family, Mr. Canfield, Rev. Gray and others.

New Year's Day, 1848, the ransomed and few others in all nearly a hundred, embarked in batteaux, belonging to the Hudson Bay Company and rowed out into the Columbia, leaving the Indians and danger behind and this time fate befriended them, for no sooner had they reached the middle of the river than the Indians hearing that Colonel Cornelius Gilliam with volunteer troops was on his way from the Willamette Valley to punish them, rode in great numbers to the bank and demanded that they return, but the redmen were too late, the prey had eluded their grasp and was gone forever. No, not forever, for Mr. Canfield returned later to help the volunteers chastise his enemies.

The journey to Vancouver in an open boat in winter, was attended with much suffering and many hardships. The portages at The Dalles and Cascades were made, by the men carrying the boats on their shoulders and the women and children walked. In the latter case the distance is six miles. The endurance of those people is almost incomprehensible. Soon after reaching Oregon City, Mrs. Canfield gave birth to a child, but it lived but a few days.

Not withstanding all the hardships endured by this couple, they both lived to a good old age in their California home in Sonoma County and strange as it may seem, Mr. Canfield carried the bullet in his back that he received at the massacre, all his life and it was not the cause of his death.

Many years later Oscar Canfield returned here and went to see Chief Timothy.

"Do you remember, long time ago, taking a man across Snake River, who had no money and gave you his vest?" he asked him.

"Dr. Whitman man?" he asked.

"Yes."

"Timothy remembers."

"Well that man was my father, and you saved his life. If you will tell me how much you charged for taking a man across the river at that time, I will pay it and interest up to today."

"Halo," the chief replied.

"Me, close tum tum," he said placing his hand on his heart.

"Do you know that you would get a whole lot of money?" Mr. Canfield asked.

"Hi-you! yes," he said. "But Dr. Whitman my close friend. Me close tum tum. Man my friend." And no amount of urging could induce the Indian to take pay for his service.

"Well then," said Mr. Canfield, "I would like to make you a present," and offered him a gold piece.

"My friends give me present yes, but pay halo."

The amount seemed insignificant to Mr. Canfield and he offered him some tobacco and as long as Timothy lived he always received a present of tobacco once a year or oftener.

Catherine Sager Pringle

Massacre survivor tells about
her 1847 Christmas dinner,
held captive in a Cayuse Indian village.

"The Christmas of 1847," said Mrs. Pringle, "was celebrated in the midst of an Indian village, where the American families who kept the day were hostages, whose lives were in constant danger. There is something tragically humorous about that Christmas, and I laugh when I think of some of the things that I cried over on that day.

"When the survivors moved to the Indian village, a set of guards was placed over us, and those guards were vagabond savages, in whose charge nobody was safe. Many times we thought our final hour had come. They ordered us around like slaves, and kept us busy cooking for them. Whenever we made a dish, they compelled us to eat of it first for fear there was poison in it. They kept up a din of noise that deprived us of peace by day and sleep by night. Some days before Christmas we complained to the chief of the village, who was supposed to be a little generous in our regard, and he gave us a guard of good Indians, under command of one whom we knew as 'Beardy.' The latter had been friendly to Dr. Whitman; he had taken no part in the massacre, and it was claimed to be through his intercession that our lives were spared.

"We hailed the coming of 'Beardy' as a providential thing, and so, when the holiday dawned, the elder folks resolved to make the children as happy as the means at hand would allow.

"Mrs. Sanders had brought across the plains with her some white flour and some dried peaches, and these had been brought to our abode in William Grey's mission. White flour was a luxury and so were dried peaches then. Mrs. Sanders made white bread on Christmas morning and then she made peach pie. 'Beardy' had been so kind to us that we had to invite him to our Christmas dinner. We had ever so many pies, it seems, and 'Beardy' thought he had tasted nothing so good in all his life. He sat in one corner of the kitchen and crammed piece after piece of that dried peach pie into his mouth. We were determined that he should have all the pie he wanted, even if some of us went hungry, because 'Beardy' was a friend upon whose fidelity our lives probably depended.

"And so we had our Christmas festival, and we sang songs and thanked Heaven that we were still alive. After dinner, and about an hour after 'Beardy' went away, we were thrown into an alarm by a series of mad yells, and we heard Indian cries of 'kill them!' 'Tomahawk them!' A band of savages started to attack the Grey residence and we saw them from the windows. Our time had come and some of us had begun to pray. The day that opened with fair promises was about to close in despair.

"To our amazement and horror, the Indian band was led by 'Beardy' himself, the Indian we counted upon to protect us in just such emergencies. He was clamoring for the death of all the white women.

"Fortune favored us at the critical juncture, for just as the Indians were entering the house, messengers arrived from Fort Walla Walla. The messengers knew 'Beardy' well and they advanced on him and inquired the reason of his wild language.

" 'Me poisoned!' cried 'Beardy;' 'me killed. White squaw poisoned me. Me always white man's friend; now me enemy. White squaw must die.'

"That would be a liberal translation of the Indian's words. Then followed a colloquy between 'Beardy' and the messengers, and from the language used we gleaned that 'Beardy' had suffered from an overdose of American pie, and not knowing of the pains that lie in wait after intemperate indulgence even in pie, he rushed to the conclusion that the pie had been poisoned.

"It required a long time for the messengers to convince 'Beardy' that the women were innocent of any intention to cause him pain, but that he was simply suffering from the effects of inordinate indulgence in an indigestible luxury.

"The messengers talked 'Beardy' into a reasonable frame of mind; he called off his horde of savages, and peace once more spread her wings over the William Grey Mission.

"We were all happy that night-happy that Mrs. Sander's pie had not been the means of a wholesale slaughter of white families on Christmas Day.

"The messengers I speak of brought good news from the fort. Succor was at hand, and on December 29 we were removed to the fort, and started down the river to The Dalles, January 3, 1848. The Christmas of the year 1847, as it was celebrated in this territory, offers somewhat of a contrast to the Yuletide merriment in all the churches and homes today."

Judge Thomas C. Shaw

Judge Shaw was a member of the
Oregon Mounted Volunteers,
citizens enlisted from the Willamette Valley
to punish the perpetrators of the Whitman Massacre.

"In December, 1847—when all the fall and early winter work had been completed and the crops sown, and the people were taking a little rest, the immigration of 1847 having all arrived in the Willamette Valley, except a few who had been compelled to stop at Dr. Whitman's mission on the Walla Walla river in eastern Oregon, and were employed by him in making improvements at the mission—our country was beginning to prosper and it was fast developing into a splendid stock and farming country. There being peace and plenty in the land, it was just the thing to expect that the residents of this beautiful country would be ready to say as one did of old, 'soul take thine ease.' While we were ready to do so and to enter into the full enjoyment of the fruits of the land, not knowing what had happened some 300 miles east of us, to our great surprise a courier arrived, bringing us the startling intelligence that Dr. Whitman, a missionary under the auspices of the Presbyterian church, his wife (who was a refined lady) and some twelve or fourteen American citizens (who were engaged at the mission) were, without any provocation whatever, on the 27th day of November, 1847, ruthlessly murdered in cold blood by the Cayuse Indians, who were then his charge.

"This news threw the country into a great fever and everything you could

hear was about the war which was inevitable. The Indians had not only killed the missionaries and those in their employ, but had taken several young
women and girls and abused them in a horrible manner. The first thing then
to be done was to get these girls and young women from the Indians.

"It was reported to us that the bodies had all been decently interred by
those sent to attend to this matter by the Hudson Bay Company, but I was
shocked when I went to the place called the grave of those worthy dead, and
found that the bodies had been disinterred by the wolves, and pieces of their
bodies were strewn around as if they had been of no more value than those
of wild beasts. Dr. Whitman's body was almost entirely disinterred, and
what shocked the writer most was to see the beautiful golden curls of Mrs.
Whitman scattered promiscuously over the ground as if the evil one had
done his best to destroy every vestige of what this good and noble woman
had done for the last ten years, and had succeeded in scattering her beautiful
golden hair as a trophy to the wind and sand of the Walla Walla Valley.

"I must be permitted right here to express my disgust at this, one of the
most revolting and blood-curdling scenes of my life. My blood first ran cold
then hot, and my rage, and that of my comrades, became almost
unbearable at times, and the only satisfaction that we could hope to attain,
was the pleasure of seeing in the engagements that followed with our
enemies that our unerring rifles had done their work well when we saw
some red men of the forest tumble to the ground. And we never saw such an
occurence as this without a sweet sensation of revenge. When we were in an
engagement we invariably thought of her who had worn that beautiful
golden hair, and took a great pride in avenging her wrongs, for we well
remembered that she was one of two noble women that left father, mother,
brothers and sisters and all else to them that seemed dear, and made the trip
across the plains in the year 1836, and all for the purpose of carrying the
good news of the gospel to those red men, who had at first received them
kindly, but by some unaccountable change in their minds had become the
murderers of those that would be their benefactors.

"We found everything around the mission in bad condition. Fences were
all down, and almost everything of value had been destroyed and appropriated and there was nothing left to represent the thrift that this mission
had in the year 1844 when our immigration came by on its way to the
Willamette Valley. As soon as our command arrived we took possession of
what was left and immediately commenced to build a fort out of the debris
that was left.

"Our officers found it too hard a task to fight and guard the stock that we
had taken, and they ordered it all turned out. This I hated, for I saw some of
the oxen in this herd that hauled the Sager family from the Missouri river to
Whitman station. This Sager family was a family that came across the
plains in the year 1844. They lost their father in Green river with the camp
fever and their mother near Fort Hall with the same dread disease. My
father, Capt. William Shaw, brought the family to Dr. Whitman's, and

their father and mother being Presbyterians, Dr. Whitman and wife kindly agreed to take the children and do the best they could for them, and when the massacre took place, John and Frances Sager were murdered, and the Sager girls, five I think in number, were taken prisoners by the Indians. Frances Sager was the only person in the whole number that was murdered that attempted to fight when the Indians set upon Dr. Whitman to murder him. This boy being about thirteen or fourteen years of age, drew a small pistol and would have dispatched an Indian with it but for the interference of some trackers who still had some hopes that they would be spared."

W.W. Walter

The personal experiences of W.W. Walter,
dealing with the Cayuse war
following the tragedy at Waiilatpu.

In December 1847, word reached the settlements in Oregon that the Cayuse Indians had killed Doctor Whitman and wife and twelve others. A runner carried the word to Vancouver, and a messenger was at once dispatched to Oregon City to Governor Abernathy, while Peter Skeen Ogden, factor of the Hudson's Bay Company, with a small company of Hudson's Bay men set out at once for the scene of the massacre — where he accomplished his wonderful work of ransoming the white captives held by the Indians.

"No other power on earth," says Joe Meek, the American, "could have rescued those prisoners from the hands of the Indians." And no man better than Mr. Meek understood the Indian character, or the Hudson's Bay Company's power over them.

The Oregon Legislature was in session when the message from Vancouver arrived, telling of the massacre. A call was made at once for fifty riflemen to proceed at once to The Dalles — to guard the settlements below from an invasion of the Indians. This company was known as the "First Oregon Riflemen."

Word came that the Cayuse Indians were coming to kill all the settlers in Oregon, and it was deemed best to meet the hostiles on their own ground.

After the first fifty men had started for The Dalles, five companies of volunteers were organized. I went from Tualatin County (now Washington) in Capt. Lawrence Hall's company of volunteers — every man furnishing his own horse and equipment — every one who could contribute a gun, or a little powder and lead — that was the way we got our munitions of war.

We rendezvoused (sic) at Portland, awaiting marching orders, which were given about January 1, 1848. We were in Portland a week or more, and I remember myself and some other lads made a ride back to the Plains to attend a dance — Christmas week.

About January 1, 1848, we started for the Cayuse Country, three hundred men, all told—we marched across the country and ferried over the Columbia at Vancouver. There the Hudson's Bay Company let us have a cannon, and it was an elephant on our hands.

From Vancouver we traveled up the north side of the Columbia (dragging that old cannon along) to a place above the Cascades where we built a ferry boat and crossed the river again to the south side and followed up the trails to the Dalles. We still kept our cannon, making portages with it, and at the Dalles we mounted the thing on a wagon. The fifty men stationed there to hold the Mission were greatly annoyed by the Indians, and just after we arrived a report was brought in that there were hostile Indians up the Deschutes River, and two of our men on horse guard were decoyed by the Indians and killed. It happened thus: the Indians stripped their horses and let them graze near the guards, giving the impression they were loose horses. Our men thought them their own horses and went after them, when the Indians, who were concealed in the grass with ropes on their horses, fired and killed the two men. Those were the first men killed in the war.

So when we heard of the Indians up the Deschutes we were anxious for a fight and started for them. The battleground was at the mouth of Tygh Creek on the ridge where we, as emigrants, had come down the Deschutes hill two years before. We met the Indians early in the morning. The first we knew of their whereabouts we saw them formed in line on the front of a high hill. To reach them we had to climb that hill, facing their fire. We left our horses and took it afoot up that hill, but they did not stand long—we soon routed them—we had but one man wounded. We followed up with continuous firing on both sides—then we had our horses brought up and gave chase. As the country was level on top the hill we followed them five or six miles—they outstripped us, as they had splendid fresh horses; we skirmished all that day—camped on the hill at night, then the next day followed on until we reached their deserted camp. There we found a very old and feeble Indian man and woman—too old to travel. They were deserted and alone, with a little pile of food lying by them. They refused to talk, so we learned nothing from them—so we left them undisturbed and returned to the Dalles, where we fitted up some old emigrant wagons and got some emigrant cattle and Mission cattle, and made up a train of wagons to haul what little supplies we had with us. We now started for the upper country, following the old emigrant road.

We had our next encounter with the Indians at Wells Springs between Willow Creek and Butter Creek. We camped there for the night—in the morning we had just gotten out of camp when we began to see Indians — Indians in every direction, in squads of ten and fifty, just coming thick. There were enough of them to eat up our little band of three hundred. We went only about a mile and a half when Col. Gilliam called a halt and we began preparations for a fight.

It was estimated over one thousand Indians were on the ground. A party of chiefs came out and called for a talk. Col. Gilliam, Tom McKay, Charlie McKay and Mungo, the interpreter, went out to meet them. When they met it was learned there were Indians from all the northern tribes besides the Cayuses. There were Coeur d'Alenes, Flatheads, Pend d'Oreilles and Spokanes.

The Cayuses had sent runners to all the different tribes telling them the Whites in Oregon had killed all the Catholics and Hudson's Bay men who were friends to these Northern Indians — they told them they had killed Tom McKay, their best friend, and were now coming to kill them and take their country. But when an old chief met the commission, he saw and recognized old Tom McKay and knew then they had been deceived and asked an explanation.

When Tom McKay, who was intimately acquainted with those northern Indians, and whose influence over them exceeded that of any other man in the country, told them the true story and that they were only up there to punish the murderers of Dr. Whitman and people, the old Flathead chief promised to take no part and to draw off all except the Cayuses. When the haughty Cayuse chief, named Grey Eagle, heard this he was so enraged he turned on McKay and said, "I'll kill you, Tom McKay," and drew his gun to fire, but McKay was too quick for him and fired first, killing the chief.

Grey Eagle was a great medicine man, and had boasted he could swallow all the bullets fired at him — and McKay shot him in the mouth. As the Indians turned to run, Charlie McKay shot Five Crows, breaking his arm, but he escaped. It will be remembered he was the Indian who held captive a girl from the Mission. Five Crows, however, shot the powder horn off McKay, so you can see they were in pretty close quarters.

We boys gave McKay great credit for the service he done us — for our little band of three hundred looked pretty small compared with the foe.

Now, the battle was fairly on. The Northern Indians drew off on a hill and the Cayuses made a dash on us, about six hundred strong, all well mounted, riding in a circle and firing whenever a chance came. The Indians never left their horses — if they dismounted, the horse was fastened to the rider. When an Indian was killed we would always find the horse standing by his fallen rider, usually tied by the hair rope to his wrist.

(The horse rode by Grey Eagle was a beautiful gray, and McKay's son Alec rode him many years.) The fight lasted the whole day long — that cannon that had caused so much vexation of spirit was of but little use, as the Indians scattered so — it was fired a few times at a squad of Indians at long range — it served more to terrorize them than to kill, as it made a tremendous noise and they no doubt thought it great medicine. It was an impressive sight to see those hundreds of Northern Indians, splendidly mounted and armed after the Indian fashion, sitting on their horses at one side all day long, watching the progress of the fight. What a picture that would have made!

We camped that night on the battleground, but the next morning the

Indians were gone. I think neither side could claim a victory. As we traveled that day Indians kept in sight all day, but did not interfere with us until we reached the Mission at Waiilaptu, where we performed the sad duty of gathering up the remains of the martyrs and burying them. We found parts of bodies lying around, scattered about. We found a skull with a tomahawk wound in it—we supposed it was that of Mrs. Whitman. We also found locks of her beautiful yellow hair in the yard. It was taken to Oregon City and placed among the Oregon State Documents.

We made a sort of stockade by building a wall breast high of adobe from the old building—also built a corral for the horses by placing rails end in the ground, and corraled the horses every night and guarded them by day. We slaughtered what cattle we could find and jerked the meat so we would have supplies in case we were corralled by the Indians. We subsisted on Indian and Mission cattle—no bread.

After getting settled in camp, parts of two companies, myself one of the number, escorted Joe Meek and his party to the snow line of the Blue Mountains as he started on his famous trip across the continent at midwinter, as an agent from Oregon, to ask protection of the United States Government for the suffering settlers in the wilds of Oregon. He was accompanied by Squire Ebbert and Nat Bowman, both mountain men, and three others. So we left the little party to pursue their journey amid untold perils while we returned to Fort Waters, as the Mission was now called. This was in February. About the first of March about eighty-five or ninety men were called to go out on a raid to gather up what cattle we could and learn what we could of the whereabouts of the hostiles. My company went, as we were the best mounted men in the command. Not thinking to be gone long, we rode light and took no provisions.

We traveled what was long known as the Nez Perce trails, across the country to Copeii, where we were met by two friendly Indians. They told us the Cayuses were camped at the mouth of Tucanon. Our interpreter, Mungo, said he could pilot us there. We concluded to hunt them up.

So at dark we started going down Copeii, then across the country to Tucanon to where Starbuck now is. There we crossed and followed down the creek, reaching the encampment just at break of day. Just as we crossed Tucanon we ran onto an Indian guard, but he got away and ran to camp—so when we got near camp two Indians came out with a white flag. I will state here that runners had been sent with word that if friendly Indians would raise a flag of truce they would not be molested, as we were only seeking to punish the Cayuses. So when they sent out the flag and asked for a talk, Col. Gilliam went forward. They claimed to be Palouses and friendly to the Whites. Said the Cayuses had gone across Snake River, but had left lots of stock behind which they would turn over to the volunteers, and that they would go out and gather them in for us. So they began running in horses and cattle, we helping—and all went merrily along. However, we soon noticed the lodges going down as by magic and the boys on the hill saw them busily ferrying their families over the river, and asked why they were moving. They said their women were afraid of the Whites and wished to go. So by their cunning manoeuvres they had detained us half a day, and we, without any food since the early morning before, were beginning to feel pretty hungry.

When they had delivered up all the stock, Col. Gilliam said we would drive out to grass and camp and eat. So we started out, but soon discovered we had been duped the worst way. They were the Cayuses — even the real murderers were there, and they were after us. Now there was no thought of eating. Indians on every side, yelling like demons, calling us women — afraid to fight. It was a running fight all day long and we were still holding the stock at night — in McKay Hollow, where we strung along the little hollow seeking shelter from the Indians by hiding behind the banks. We did not dare kindle a fire. On examination it was found thirty volunteers were wounded, but not dangerously. Our ammunition was about exhausted and we were half famished.

The older men and officers evidently realized we were in a pretty serious predicament, but we young boys had no idea of the danger we were in, not as I see it now. During the night Gilliam ordered the stock turned loose — as we were now about out of ammunition he hoped by turning the stock loose to get rid of the Indians. The boys objected to that move, but instead of the Indians leaving us that only renewed their courage. They thought we were giving up, and attacked us more savagely than ever. We were pretty well hidden and in no immediate danger, so we saved our ammunition and only fired when sure of an Indian — they frequently came in range when circling around us. In the morning they still hung on our heels. As we started out they followed us on — calling to Mungo repeatedly, asking why we did not stop to fight, while he abused them in return.

The Indians would drop behind until a bunch of us were a distance from the command, then make a dash, trying to cut us off, and we surely were not cautious. Tom Cornelius, Pete Engart and myself were a little behind when an Indian shot Engart in the calf of the leg. He fell from his horse, saying he was killed. Tom and I jumped from our horses and shook him up and told him he was not hurt — he gave up. We finally threw him up astride his horse — we cursed him and told him to ride — *and he rode.* By this time the Indian were on us and the boys ahead had not missed us. I tell you we made a race for it, one of us on each side of the wounded man, but we made it.

Another time that day Mungo's horse was shot from under him. Tom Cornelius and I saw him fall and ran back to him. He had stopped to take his saddle — we were just in time, as the Indians were coming pell-mell, shouting, "We've got Mungo." I took Mungo behind me and Tom took his saddle and away we went. This was the way we were at it all the way, some one in close quarters all the time.

Mungo told the Cayuses we would fight when we reached the Touchet and got water. Then began the race for the first stand at the Touchet. The

Indians beat us on the lower side, but we headed them off above the ford. Some Indians hid in the brush and shot at our men as they passed on the trail. We were trying to get our wounded men across, but the Indians were killing horses and men. I was in the company up the creek. When we came down, Col. Gilliam told Lieut. Engart to rout those ambushed Indians. Engart called for volunteers to go in after them. I was one with twenty others. We started for the hiding place, skirting along the brush, expecting any minute to run on them. When we did find them, not more than five or six of us were together in the lead, and the Indians were firing at another squad of men some distance away — we were within thirty feet of them. I fired and hit my Indian just as he turned to run, striking him in the back of the head. He fell and I stepped back behind a bush to reload, when another man ran in and stood in my place; as he did so the Indian rolled over and fired at him killing him. Just then Nate Olney, an old Indian fighter, ran in with a tomahawk and made a good Indian of him. He scalped him and I carried the grewsome trophy at my saddle horn when I returned home. We killed about sixty Indians there. It was hard to make an estimate of how many, as they carried their dead away unless too hard pressed.

All during this battle the chief sat on his horse on the rocky point just above Bolles Junction [the present junction] and gave command and encouragement in a loud and stentorian voice. He could be heard for miles. Finally a bullet sped his way and he was killed — and he being the medicine man, the battle ceased and a council was called. We were now across the Touchet. We were carrying our wounded men on litters made by stretching blankets on willow poles — taking turns carrying — that was a hard job. As we began to climb the hill beyond the Touchet we heard the Indians let up their death-wail — they were gathered together on those low hills just north the Bolles Junction depot.

We traveled on to Dry Creek that day; there we went into camp and spying some Indian horses on the prairie, myself with some others ran in a bunch, near some brush where some of our men were hidden, and as they passed, shot two. That was the first horse meat I had tried to eat, but it made me sick — though they were young unbroken horses. I was sure they tasted of the saddle blanket — suggestion, I suppose. When we awoke next morning there was four or five inches of snow on our blankets — we had no tents.

A runner had been sent on to the Mission and a wagon sent out for our wounded men. My bunkie and I got up early, mounted our horses and rode on to the Mission that morning. The boys soon were preparing provisions for the famishing troops, but after starving so long the smell of food cooking made me sick and I could not eat until the next morning. Some of the boys were so ravenous they had to be restrained or they would have killed themselves eating.

Now we laid around camp, getting into mischief, and I learned to smoke. The only regular rations issued us was tobacco — and the smokers seemed to take such comfort in the pipe, I too indulged.

When we came into the Indian country Gilliam told us we could have any Indian horses we captured. I was pretty handy with a rope and got away with three head from the battle at the Touchet. One, a fine horse rode by a chief, I was particularly proud of. A big burly Dutchman in another company also coveted that horse, so one morning he put his rope on him and led him into camp. I at once claimed the horse and proceeded to make good my claim. He resisted and we got into a "scrap"; he had friends, so had I. All took sides — it was decided we fight for possession; the winner to get him. That suited me all right — so at it we went. Men say it was a hard fight, but I won and took the horse to lead him off, when an under officer, a friend of the Dutchman, stepped up and took hold of the rope, saying "I'll take this horse." I was only a boy of nineteen years, but I did not intend to give up the horse without a struggle, and was considering the consequences of hitting an officer when Colonel Gilliam walked unobserved into the ring, cut the rope behind the officer's hand, handed the rope to me and walked away without a word. I tell you I was the proudest boy in that camp — and after the colonel was gone I could not resist crowing at the Dutchman in true boy fashion. This is just an example of how justice was meted out in the army of volunteers.

In the spring about two hundred recruits came. We now numbered about five hundred men. Then a party set out for north of Snake River to hunt Indians. I was with the company. We crossed the Snake at the mouth of the Palouse — we made a camp at Little Falls — were at Big Lake on Cow Creek and all over the upper country, but failed to find any number of Indians. We fired a few shots at stragglers now and then but had no regular engagement. The Cayuse warriors had scattered about among other tribes, many going over the mountains to wait until the soldiers left the country.

A detachment of men was sent to Walker's Mission, called Tshimakain, where Walker and Eells and their families were located as missionaries among the Spokanes. We got the families and brought them back with us. We came back across country, crossing Snake River at the mouth of Alpowa Creek to an Indian encampment known as Red Wolf's Land — then we returned to Waiilatpu. This expedition went out the first of May. Sometime in June we began our return trip to Oregon, having been out about six months.

I remember while camped in the Umatilla country I was breaking an Indian horse to ride — and he would throw himself whenever I mounted. I had become pretty mad at his persistence in lying down so concluded to tie him down until he would be willing to stand up. I did so and left him close to camp — but in the morning I was minus a horse — the wolves had eaten him up. We had much to learn in those days.

On this trip Colonel Gilliam was killed accidentally. In pulling a gun from a wagon it caught in a rope and was discharged, killing him. He was a good man and a good officer, well liked by all his men, as he was a friend to all.

We arrived at Oregon City a few days before the Fourth of July. The Governor rode out and reviewed the troops, as we were on parade. Every man had his horse decked out in Indian trappings and we were as wild as a band of Indians. Crowds of people had gathered to welcome us home. The Governor made us a short talk and dismissed us. Thus ended the organization of Oregon's First Mounted Volunteers—we all scattered out to our homes.

Chapter

Golden Adventurers

"I am in hopes that I will lite on
some place yet while I stay in
this country and make my pile
so as to live easy when I come home
which will be soon,
pile or no pile."
M.B. Ward

As the Oregon Volunteers were returning from fighting the Indians in the Walla Walla country, an event happened in California that shifted the spotlight away from the Northwest for a few years. Gold was discovered at Sutter's mill early in 1848 on the American River. A good share of the settlers, who had earlier migrated to Oregon, headed south to the goldfields and were among the first arrivals. By the Spring of 1849, as gold mania swept the nation and the world, thousands of '49ers were on their way by boat, wagon and any way possible to get to the new eldorado.

The majority of those who came were only interested in the riches, intending to return home after they'd made their pile. Roisterous mining camps sprung up along the gold-filled gulches and streams throughout the mountains of California as the wealth poured forth. Only a few really struck it rich, and what the majority found was a lot of back-breaking work. But the wages were good and those who didn't lose their gold by gambling, whoring or by becoming sick were able to bring home at least a respectable poke.

After the gold discovery, most Oregon Trail travelers took the California cut-off near Fort Hall. As the gold fever wore off in the early 1850's, more wagon trains once again started to travel to Oregon. Cholera outbreaks were at their worst in the 1850's and endless new graves marked the route between Missouri and Oregon. The trail through present-day southern Idaho was especially filled with terror for the pioneers. Indian attacks were common and not a few of the settlers were reduced to starvation rations as game was scarce and no provisions could be bought between Fort Hall and The Dalles, on the Columbia River. Ever so many of the travelers arrived at The Dalles penniless and near starvation, their families shattered by deaths along the way.

Today we are surprised if a letter sent even thousands of miles away isn't delivered within a few days. In 1851 mail took months to get from the mines to their faraway homes, and many times it didn't arrive at all. Mail, as you can imagine, was happily received from separated spouses and lovers. Now, fancy if you will, a lonely miner, his fingers carefully caressing a treasured lock of hair as he sits in his bunk writing his thoughts home to his young wife and adored child. We join him in his tent on Poorman's Creek, California . . . . .

Michael B. Ward

*Michael Ward, one of the many miners that flocked to California
after gold was discovered there in 1849, writes home to his wife and
daughter who he had left home in Illinois. The letter was written
in a Gregory's Express Pocket Letter Book (3" x 5", 48 pages)*

June 20, AD 1851

Most affectionate companion it is with good health that I take my pen in
hand to Rite to you & it is my Sincere Desire that thoes few lines May find
you the Same & Augusta M. Ward The Same & all the Friends likewise. I
Received a letter from you dated March which gave me much Satisfaction
to here that you was all well, It gives me much satisfaction to here from you
by Letter, as I can not See you but I feel as tho it would Not be long till I
will. We have bin doing well for Some time Back but the prospect is not
very good ahead but I am in hopes that I will lite on Some place yet while I
Stay in this Contry & Make my pile So as to live Easy when I come home
which will be Soon pile or no pile.

June 22, AD 1851

This day I went prospecting. Started of Poor mans Creek With my bed and
board on my back went to the North fork of Slate Creek & there camped for
the nite under the braud Canopy of hevon & Slept well with my boots for a
Pillow.

June 23 took the Middle fork of Slate creek up to the head to day & found
Nothing to pay & camp for the Nite in the Same house & had the Same fare
very Mountainous & lots of Shaperell Bushes to day.

June 24

This day we went to the North fork of Kanion creek & went down to the
forks & found Nothing to pay & then took the Midel fork of Kanion creek
to the head and found nothing & campt for the nite in the Same house & had
the same fare-- Snow--plenty on the Mountains.

June 25 Started for the head of the Urysha River Came there & found
Nothing & then went to Jimison's Creek Saw the Quart lead But found no
gould to pay so we camped for The nite on Jimison's creek.

June 26

Started for the head waters of Nelsons Creek & by hard work we made out
to clime the Mountains & wade the Brush & camped for the Nite in the
Same house but the fare was not the Same. Hour Provisions Was gon all but
a few bites of Bread & Coffee We drank some coffee & lay down for the Nite
& in the Morning we Made Some Coffee & Started for poor Mans creek.
Made it hungry & tired as dogs So that wound up the Prospecting for Mee
for awhile I Say we have bin to work on poor mans Creek & doing purty
well. The wether is could here Nites & Mornings & warm in the midel of the
Day.

July 1

Some of hour boys are on Fether River Wingdaming the bed of the Stream that is all but Mee & I am on Poor mans Creek working on a clame Making from & up to 12 dollars a day & Some times more & some times less.

July the 4

Worked till Noon & Made 13 Dollars & then played the balance of the Day. Not by spending money but by staing in the house & Writing to you of whom all of my Thauts & Mind is on all of the time.

I think that if I have good luck & dont loose any more money i will Make More money Than I could have Made iff I had Staid to home but the man that Comes to this Contry art to Make More money here than he could to home for he has to under go many ups & downs in this country that he would not in the States.

Harison William & my Self has got twenty Seven hundred Dollars by us Now & I own eight hundred of it & I have sent two hundred home which I hope you will get & Harrison Sent Home the same all in Fathers name I want you to do as you please with the money iff you get it & dont want for any thing that you want to eat & ware & take good care of your helth & take good care of Augusta hour only Joy & when you get this I want you to Rite Soon So as I can Send Some More Money iff that goes Safe to you I think I will be able to fetch one thousand home with me iff I keep my health but iff a man gets sick here he Spends money fast. I shall be contented to Stay with you iff I dont have any money when I come home & be well paid for my time.

July 8

This day I worked by the day for one of hour Neighbours in a very Rich clame for Six Dollars a day & board & we took out Six hundred & fifty five Dollars in the after Noon The boys have all left Fether River yesterday & gon to Kanion Creek they could Not get down for water on fether river & So they gave it up I am on poor mans Creek all alone working by the Waiting to Setel with Some men as Soon as it is Due & as Soon as that is done I am going to the boys if I dont See a good chance to Make Money here & iff I do I am in for that company or no company.

I come to this contry to Make money & calculate to make every edge cut that will cut honest for the Dishonest way is hard for Some they Shoot for Stealing & hang for Stealing. The other day they gave a man forty lashes for Stealing close to where I was working they made the blud run down his heals like Sap from Sap tree in the Spring of the year.

July the 9, AD 1851

I received a letter from you to day Rote April 13 which gave me much comfereit to here from you & Augusta & there was a small lock of Augusta Hare in it Which Made tears Stand in my Eyes to look at it & could not See you & her. I took a Braid that I Brot with me & put them to gether & the last Braid was as dark again as the first you have no Ideah how much darker it is. I am a fraid I shall not Now her when I come back to the States.

But tell Augusta to bee a good girl & learn fast & I will fetch her A presant home. You gave me a Small peace of advice in the Next to the last letter I got to Not Make money as Some was, Making it by Stealing & keep out of bad Company. The advise is all good But thank the Lord I have kept out of all Such Company as you had reference to Oliver Pearson has got maried to a grass widow in Mariesville he is a Preachers Son and that is all but as for him keeping a bad house I dont now that he ever did.

John Devine & Edward left us in the Mountains & went South we had one letter from them since they left & they was well & on the American River Mr Moay is with us & he is well.

I want you to Rite in your next iff Rhodes has got eney Letter from Morrison Robb & iff he has tell me where he is in Califonia I left him on the Midel fork of The American River last August the 12, 1850 & he said he would Rite to me but I have had no word from his since I left Nor John Tripp but I expect by the time you get this & Rite the letter & Mee will pass on the Pacific ocean I hope so at least.

July the 19, AD 1851 it has bin one month since I Rote to you lat the longest time Since I have bin in Califonia I shall Not Make the time So long again I hope you get My letters Regaler I cant complane for I get one every now & then John Ward has got but one Since he Landed in Califonia I dont think that his wife Rites meney.

There is some cases of aresipoles on the creek but not meney Most all of the Miners are well.

You gave me some Poetry in my last letter So I will give you one virce:

> Soon Soon will these dark Drearry days be gone by
> And hour hearts be lit up with a beam from the sky
> O let not our spirits embitered with pain
> Be dead to the Sunshine that comes to us then
> Heart in heart hand in hand let us welcome the wether
> and Sunshine or Storm we will face it together

When we get to gether again & that will be Soon I think & long before we part for gold again.

I want you to give my best Respects to David & Anderson & Mr. Poplin & all the friends & relations but Mayer I dont want to have any thing to do with him He is a rich Man & I am a poor Man but I am in a place where a man stands a Small chance to be Rich in one week that is worth More than he is & I Supose he thinks that he is Some Punkins the more I think of him the more I think he is a scoundrel.

I am going to Start home on the first day of January iff it is Sickley this fall & iff it is not I will Start Sooner you may look for me by the 1st day of March any how they say it is not good for a man to come home in the dead of the winter leaving a warm contry & going into a warmer won & then in to a coald contrey That it is likeley to kill a man & I do not want to die for along time after I come back to you & Augusta Melissa Ward I have given you a long letter now So I must Bring my letter to a close by subscribing my self your afectionate husbnd till Death this from Michael B Ward.

To
A E Ward
A M Ward
When this you See remember me
I have not Shaved since the 15 day of August 1850. So you may guess the girls would take quite a shine to me iff they Could See me but I have Not Saw one for 7 months & I dont care iff I dont See one till I see you & Augusta So good by Take care of things as well as you can Till I come back & then I will take some of the Trouble of your hands & be Shure to take good care of your Self & Augusta hour littel pet.

There is Some of my hare in this letter it is as long as the wandering Jews. I have got your hare yet in my pocket here I send Augusta a Mushmelon Seed Waing 55 cts. which I want her to keep to Remember mee & I send you 1 peace of goald which waid 105 cts which you have not goat as you have Said Nothing about you Said you had got the gould Dollar. I have sent Gould in Most all of the letters I have Sent but you have not got half of them. It's getting So Dark I can not see the lines & Candles So good by for a Short time.

Michael B Ward
To
Amelia E Ward
&
Augusta M Ward
Poor mans creek
July the 19 AD 1851

J.E. Berryman

J.E. Berryman tells an interesting story about his life in the California mines, plus a fascinating trip to the gold fields of Australia and then back to a newly discovered "Eldorado" in Idaho and Eastern Oregon.

A little of the history of the travels of J.E. Berryman, who was born in Cornwall, England, somewhere about the 18th of May, 1834.

My father Richard was a miner; therefore I was one also. I worked in the tin and copper mines with my father and brothers when only ten years of age. Wheeling ore for them was my first work. It was then two thousand feet under ground and I had to wheel about 7500 feet ten hours a day, and climb down and up every day, and I was too tired to walk home to supper, which was seven miles away, but I well knew I had to do it and do it over again the next day for one year.

Then I was put to work at breaking ground. At this I was getting five dollars per month, instead of $1.50, as before. I then began to feel as though I was a big man and here I continued until I came to the state of Wisconsin.

My father and one older brother came to Wisconsin in '48. My mother and the rest of the family, with me, six in all, came the next spring, 1849.

We left Liverpool about the first of March for Quebec, Canada, in a bark, and a very rough and wicked time we had of it, I assure you. For a week and five days we were rolled about in that old bark of about three thousand tons burden, as sick as death and praying that we might die, while others would be swearing at us for it. At last we got in the field ice on the bank of New-foundland, but I saw no land or anything else but ice, and about a dozen other ships frozen up in it. Here we stayed for six days before we got out, but got out all O.K. and all in good health.

So we got into Quebec and found things rather strange to us, but after a little we got on the boat going up the St. Lawrence river to Montreal. Here we found a large and beautiful city. Then in boats or canals again, drawn by oxen or horses on the river bank, sometimes on one side and then on the other; so in about three weeks we got into Milwaukee, Wisconsin. From there my mother hired a team of horses and driver to take us to Hazelgreen, Grant county, where we found father and brother to welcome us and a good home to go into, and it was needed, for mother was about worn out with fatigue, but I was full of mischief, fat and healthy.

This part of Wisconsin is a very pretty country. It was then a prairie country with very few settlers in it, lots of good grass, wheat and good corn and good lead mines. It was the lead mines that brought my father here and rest of us too. So we all were soon put to work digging out the mineral, and did well at it. Father also had a little farm, but he might as well have had a thousand acres as one.

In the spring of '51 my mother and younger brother died. That struck us a hard blow, but I kept on at work digging lead all the time.

In the spring of '52 one brother William went to California, and in the fall of '53 I began to think that I must go too; but I was not of age and my father said no. But I would not take no for an answer. So I found a friend to lend me the needed money, and when I told my father about it he said, "Well, if you are determined to go you can get the money of me." Of course he told me I was too young; only a little over nineteen years of age and I had better wait a while. But I said no and meant no too; and on the 4th of January, 1854 I bade my father and the rest of the family good-bye and left with two other boys by the name of Willcocks for New York city.

Now we had railroads and steamboats. We got to New York on the 10th, and took boat passage for Aspenwall on the U.S.M. Steamship Co. or in other words, for San Francisco by Aspenwall and Panama.

Here in New York we found a very tough place and I considered ourselves, three young lads, very lucky to get out of it with any money left with us, but, thank God, we did. We gave $150.00 for a passage in the steamer from New York to San Francisco, but we had to pay our passage then across the isthmus to Panama, which would cost then about fifty dollars more.

But on the tenth of January we all went aboard the Old George, which looked to be a good steamship. They told me there were twelve hundred and forty aboard the ship. There was hardly standing room, however. But I got a berth, not a deck passenger.

We had good luck in leaving New York, calm, beautiful weather, and I made some new friends and began to feel at home. Of course I did not like the grub any too well.

At last the passengers got stowed away and they made room for a dance on the main deck. They had a band playing and it sounded nice on the water. But the fun was short. The third night out on the Gulf of Mexico the wind began to blow and the sea began to rise and the breakers to roll over the ship's deck so no one could stand on it and some began to be afraid, and by one o'clock in the morning all were afraid. The skipper fired the gun of distress to call for help if any should be in sight or sound. But I stayed in my bunk. I did not believe there was any danger, until I was washed out of my bunk; or rather the bunk was washed out with me in it. The bullwarks had broken in and I was washing around there until I found the railing on the lea side that led up to the deck; then I got out of the water and was told to go aft on the poop deck, which I did. But here I could not stay, for I would soon be crushed to death with people on top of me. For all the passengers were driven aft to keep the bows of the ship above water, for the bows were smashed in and from here the ship was filling with water, and by getting the weight aft it took the stern up.

By this time I had life preservers put on me, but threw them away. If I was going to drown, all right; those things were in the way and too painful. But by this time it was raining very hard, just coming down in torrents, so it beat down the breakers, turned them into swells; and the wind had also ceased its fury and the big ship was rolling about on the gulf with no steam nor sails.

Women and children and men, who were merry and dancing the night before, were now on their knees and lying around praying for God to save them. Here I heard the most fervent prayers I ever heard in all my life, while some would swear and curse.

At this time I, with many others, were put to dipping water with cans and buckets out of the ship to try to keep her alive, and as day broke we saw a little steamship in sight, the Empire City, from New Orleans. She had heard the distress guns and had been following us up waiting for daylight to appear. As soon as it got calm enough she hove alongside and the U.S. mail was taken out, then the passengers, then the crew and the captain, and then the Old George went out of sight alongside us. It looked as though she stayed up just long enough for us to get off and no more. But we were horrified to find only 804 to get off instead of 1240, but the rest must have been washed overboard, or lost in the boats that left the ship in the night.

Then we were so crowded we could hardly get standing room. The Empire City was a boat of about 2,000 tons burden. And here I found myself nearly naked, nothing on but a pair of socks, drawers, and undershirt, not even a rag to wipe the sweat from my face. I had not ten cents left. But I did not run away and hide, either, but stayed just as though I were dressed in the best there was to be had. Yet I saw many of the ladies gazing at me sideways and some of the men of the new ship asked me where my clothes were. Of course I said, with the George. But I was not long without getting a coat from one, pants from another, and a hat from another. I did not mind my clothes, so long as I was left.

In about thirty-six hours we found ourselves in Norfolk living sumptuously on oysters and fish, waiting for another ship, which was very hard to get at that place. And after three days they hired the same little ship, Empire City, to take us to Aspenwall, where we arrived all O.K. in eight days, but there were only 850 passengers; the balance had backed out and gone home afraid of the water, and the two boys who came with me went back also from Norfolk. Therefore we got more room.

We found Aspenwall a canvas town and very little of that, and a railroad running out of it toward Panama for about 18 or 20 miles to Georgena. It took 12 dollars to pay passage on it. I did not have one cent, but in fooling around the station I found a half of a ticket. I put it in my hat band, which was given me by a preacher, and went aboard the train and came out all O.K., as though I had lots of money.

We found Georgena nothing but a mud hole with one big corral full of mules which the passengers were hiring to ride across to Panama, a distance of 20 or 22 miles more. But here I struck out to walk on foot, which I could do very easy, and as I got to the other end of the corral I happened to see a mule strike out in the mud among the other mules with a young girl on its back, and in the rush the young girl fell under foot in the mud. I believe she would soon have been tramped to death if I had not been at hand there and then. But I was not long in getting her up and getting the mud out of her neck, ears, eyes, nose and mouth, when a young man came up to me with ten thousand thanks for what I had done. He then hired a mule for me to ride with them to help them on to Panama, which I did gladly. I found they were man and wife, just come from New York city and had never seen a mule, either of them, and when we got to the hotel in Panama the lady could not stand nor walk. We packed her on the bed, which was the last I ever saw of them. The young man begged me to stay there, saying he would pay my board bill; but I went on board the old ship, which had been waiting for us for a long time.

Now Panama is a strange city. I could not describe it in twelve hours as it is; therefore I pass it by and go on to San Francisco. But it was not all fun on this ship either. There was lots of sickness on board, many died of cholera, or some said black fever. Most of them would not be sick more than from six to ten hours, then they would be put on a plank with a bag of sand tied to their feet and slid into the deep. There was also lots of trouble about the grub. Very poor meat and nothing but hard bread caused lots of trouble. But I was lucky as usual, while I was only a stray passenger and had a bunk to lie down in nights if I needed to. But I got hold of a mess ticket belonging to the first table in the cabin , and I took my meals in the cabin all the time and another young fellow too, on the same ticket. One of us would use it for the first table, then give it to the other for the second table; but only for a few days, until we became known, then we needed no ticket at all.

We also had very rough weather. It took us twelve days to get to 'Frisco instead of eight or ten but it was a glorious arrival. The whole country, as well as the city, was waiting and longing to see the ship and know what was the matter. We were nine days late and no one knew what was the matter until we told them. There was no telegraph there. So we lost no time in going ashore and my case was soon known. Although without money I was treated like a king and found 'Frisco on the boom. I was offered six dollars per day to work there, but I was bound for old Mangteman. We got in 'Frisco about ten o'clock in the morning and at four in the evening I was on the boat for Sacramento. Twelve dollars was the fare. I had no money as usual, but they let me pass because I was the naked boy from the Old George.

We arrived in Sacramento about four the next morning. There were stages going to every mining camp in the state, but I asked for the Mangteman road and struck out on it before breakfast. I walked five or six miles, came to a house, and asked for work to pay for breakfast. I was told to come and pay for it some other time. While I was there yet they happened to see something about the naked boy in the paper. They asked me if I knew anything about him. I said, "This is the boy." I was then offered money to take me to Mangteman. I thanked them and said breakfast was good enough for me. So with many thanks I struck out afresh and came that evening to the Marble Valley, thirty-five miles from Sacramento, rather tired and weary. But I went in and asked for supper and said I would pay him some day, for I was going to stop at Mangteman. He asked me where I was from. I said, "The Old George." "By----;" he asked, "are you the naked boy?" "Yes," I replied.

The house was full of men. They all jumped up to shake hands with me as though I were Horace Greeley. I was king again that night. They tried all they could to make me drunk, but could not; no, no.

In the morning I struck out for the Mangteman, got there about three o'clock in the afternoon, found those who knew me, but my brother was not there. They again had a big time; tried to get me to drink often with them, but no, sir, no more for me.

Here I went to work, the first gold mining I ever did. But my brother heard of me and then I went to him at French creek, a distance of ten miles. On the road I met the first Chinaman I had ever seen. There were hundreds of them packing with stick across their shoulders. I was really afraid of them. I met them in a narrow trail in the mountains and I was worse scared than I was on the George. Then I met a band of Indian bucks and squaws. Then I began to think I was cold for sure and that it was the longest road I ever walked on in my life. The Indians wanted to sell me a pony very bad, but I did not know it then. They saw I was on foot and that I ought to have a horse, so they would not let me pass. As this was the first I knew of Indians they scared me pretty bad and I felt good when I got away from them.

About four o'clock I got to Frenchtown, a good mining camp, full of young men, strong and good looking, I thought the finest lot of young men I had ever seen. I went to the claim where brother was at work, shook hands with him, and he went to work and worked on till night.

Then they had a lively time with champagne and oysters, cards, songs and whisky, but I did not drink enough to please them, and as they still insisted I was afraid of getting drunk, Will, my brother, said to me I would be as drunk as any of them soon. I told them they would never see me drunk in Frenchtown, — neither did they, not in the state of California. I was never drunk but once, and have always used very little liquor.

But to my work. One of my brother's partners wanted to sell his share of the claim, and Will told me to buy it. I told the man I had no money. "Never mind the money. Say if you want it or not." "Yes," I said, "I want it." "Well, say so." He jumped out of the hole and said, "Here is the pick and shovel; go to work" — and you bet I did go to work.

When night came I could hardly walk to the cabin. Big blisters were on my hands and knees where the shovel handle came and sore all over. That night I was too weary to rest. But the next morning I went at it again with renewed vigor. The work was very hard in those mines. They would go at it like men on a fight, one man on each side of the sluice box shoveling in gravel and one on the top of the box forking out the rocks. This is what is called sluice diggings, about four or six feet deep, with a little gold all through the gravel, but most of it in on the bed rock, which is generally very hard to clean. Some men will leave as much gold lying there sometimes as they take off it. They will keep up with each other if they can, and then work in summer time about sixteen hours a day. But we always ate five times, three meals and two lunches.

So I kept on three days the first week. I was glad when Sunday came, got a good wash and change, cleaned our gold and payed our bills; and in the three days I found I had made forty dollars clear, but my poor hands and knees were horrible. But on that day I put leather on my pant knees and got gloves for my hands and went at it again on Monday morning in good spirit and then began to recover and was soon as good as my partners.

In three weeks I payed 150 dollars for my diggings and the next three weeks I sent home 150 dollars to my father, the amount I got of him to come to the state with and about forty of which I lost in my clothes on the George. Now I began to make money for myself, and save it too.

On Sunday there were about 700 young men would come to that town who were at work up and down the creek. They were the finest looking lot of men I ever saw in one place at one time. And they would spend lots of money on that day, but not as much as they did in some towns. It was a very quiet place for California. There was not a woman in camp nor a real gambling house, but they would play cards, get drunk and have a fight once in a while, but on the whole it was pretty good camp for those days. The boys all appeared to have plenty of money. Liquor was $7.50 per drink, and when one would treat there would be from three or four to a dozen. There would be always a barrel of walnuts, cheese and seedy crackers open free for all in the store. And the store that would sell liquor would sell other things, in those camps, every thing the miner needed. But as the camp grew older things began to change.

Now this was a winter camp and we had to work when it rained. The more it rained the better we liked it. When it rained hard we would take the long tom on our shoulder and pick and shovel in hand, go up in those dry gulches, go to work like madmen and find course gold, as much as six ounces in a chunk, sometimes nothing.

I did well on French Creek, but when the water dried up we had to leave and hunt new diggings for some time. So we left French Creek and went to Weber creek, or river. Here we opened out a different kind of claim and a different mode of working it. But I shall not take time to say all about it now. It was not far from Coloma, Eldorado Co. It was very hard work, but we made about $16 a day to the hand.

There was no town here. Our goods was brought to us by express, also our letters and papers. Every letter and paper would cost us 75 cents to get, but they would take them away for nothing. We got our mails only every two weeks.

While here we went to Coloma one day to see two men hung, the first I ever saw, but not the last. They were Logan and Gipsey. Logan shot a young man about a claim, and Gipsey shot a man about a game of cards. There were thousands of people on the ground. They were put on the scaffold, had the ropes put around their necks and the noose tied on and they both fell to the ground when the trap was let loose. But they were taken back helpless and hung over again. I thought it was too bad.

There were many fights in Coloma that day. It was a large town and the county seat of Eldorado Co. We went there to sell our gold when we sold any. It was a rich town on the American river, and it was here where Mr. Sutter first found the gold, two miles below Coloma, while digging a mill race.

When water came I went back on French Town again, worked out a claim, then went out on the prospect for new digging, and found some in a new place about fifteen miles from French creek where we could kill rabbits by the score and not leave the tent door, and wild pigeons by the hundreds. They were so thick that they would fly in big clouds so as to darken the sun. By shooting two barrels of a shot gun into the cloud we could bring down a half bushel often. But I never like to kill more than was needed for use. We called this place Hungry Hollow, and it got to be a good camp, lots of gold taken out of it.

But when it got filled up I sold out and went to hunt more new diggings. I went to Mangteman and stayed there a week or two, but found that would not do for me, too much gambling and madness. So I left.

About this time my brother and partner went back to Wisconsin and I and my partner struck out to find some new country, and we did. We found some good diggings in Calveras Co. at a place now called Renestia. There we saw two men hanged by the mob. They had committed a lot of crimes and one of them said he felt bad because he had not killed more. They were hanged by the trail on a tree and left there until the sheriff came and cut them down. The crowd that was after them first came to me and my partner, and as we were away out of the road in a deep gulch to ourselves, some of them thought we were the ones they wanted, which scared us pretty bad for awhile.

Our water gave out there and we went back to old Weber creek again and opened up a claim at a place called Japeck, where we did well again, the summer of 1856, by very hard work and hard living. Again there were two men hanged at Coloma. One was J.M. Crane, for killing a young girl at Merango, Weber river, or as some call it, Weber creek. He and the girl were spiritualists and he said he shot and killed her to live happy in the next world together, because her parents would not let them live happy, but her parents told another story about it. The other was a highwayman. Both these men appeared glad and joyful over the matter. The highwayman sang and danced on the scaffold and talked quite awhile. Crane sang a song he composed himself and talked to the people for an hour and forty minutes and said, "This is the happiest day I ever saw in all my life." The song he sang was something like this:

"Come brothers and sisters, I bid you adieu;
This necklace and gallows will soon set me through.
Come friends and all others, I bid you adieu.
This body no longer my spirit can chain,
Soon I'll be free from sorrow and pain.
No valley of shame do I see on the road,
But angels are waiting to take me to God."

He made and sang fine verses, something like the above, and the last words he said were, "Susan, I am coming." That was the name of the girl he had murdered. Some said the man was crazy, others said no. But they both looked like men that were going to be crowned kings, not like men about to be hanged.

There was a crowd of Chinese mining near us on that creek the same summer, and a band of Indians ran down from the mountain on the poor Chinese and scared them to pieces so they ran away and the Indians got all John left behind. The siwash only meant to scare John a little. Poor John fared hard in California.

Another time a party of men let on to be drunk and had a big fight and blew out the lights in a Chinese store on purpose to steal and plunder the poor fellow's store.

Another time a Frenchman accidentally shot and killed himself at the same place. It was found he had no money and we went around and gathered a thousand dollars to send to his wife in about two hours. and some of the same crowd that stole things from the China store gave lots of the money to the Frenchman.

This was my last on Weber creek. In the winter of '56 I went out again to hunt new country and new diggings and after a long time we found some again way down below Marble valley. Here my partner, Forester, and I were alone again. We got good diggings and coarse gold, some as large as eight or twelve dollars. But we had very little water, only when it rained.

We boarded at the White Rock house on the Sacramento and Mangteman road. By this time there were lots of women and girls in the state, and two or three right here, and Forester, my partner, got acquainted with one and told her about our prospects, which caused a big stampede on the ground, which made it much the worse for us. But I did not blame him any for being free with a pretty young girl, and she was pretty too; but he did get her. And farther up the road I had got acquainted with a Morman family who kept a hotel. They had a beautiful girl, with whom I spent many a happy hour. The old gent tried hard to make a good Mormon out of me, but I could not see it that way. They were very fine people, and the girls were of the right stripe. I hated to leave that place. One Sabbath evening I was shot at by someone while leaving that place. The bullet went through my shirt and necktie right across my breast, and the old gent tried to make me stay with him that night very hard, so much so that I began to think that he knew something about it, but he said not.

As spring came we sold out our diggings for good money and then went on the prospect again and kept on it nearly all summer. We did not make much, but did lots of hard work and spent lots of money in the hard work. I held up at old Hangtown again and while there got acquainted with two young men that were going to Australia, and I made up my mind to go too, so I did. Now I leave the Golden state, but I have told very little of what I might have told and I may say more later on.

On the first of October, 1857, I left Hangtown with Happy Peadler and James Asson for San Francisco. In four days we were in the Bay city and stayed there three days, took in all there was in 'Frisco, had a jolly time, and bought a passage to Port Phillip on the clipper ship Ferdinand in the first cabin, only six of us in the first cabin, for only $150 each. It was a large, new, beautiful sailer, Captain Stout, skipper, Mr. Melley, first mate. They were good men and had a good crew. There were six other men in the second cabin and seventy-five in the steerage, but not one woman or child on board the ship.

About the tenth of October we sailed out of the Golden Gate with a fair wind and everything lovely. I got sick for two or three days, then began to feel good and light as a bird; nothing to do but go to the table and partake of the best victuals ever got up in the world. So we went gloriously on for about thirty-five days with good, fair wind. Then we struck a claim in about 21° south. Of course it was very hot weather here and it had been very hot for a long time. We did not feel it much, because we had a large awning stretched over the hurricane deck, which kept the sun away, and everyone who had not crossed the equator before had to pay a forfeit, and in about two days we could not see our shadow at noon day. We found ourselves in a calm for twenty days, but no one was in a hurry to get away. There were natives on the islands near and some of us wanted to go ashore, but the skipper would not let the boat go, so at last five of us offered the captain $150 to let us have the boat in case we never came back with the boat again; not for the use of the boat, but in case we were kidnapped. But at last the captain ordered a good boat lowered on the water. We soon got in it and to shore we went. As soon as we got to land the natives ran away. They would not come near us and if we went toward them they would run away. So we stayed on shore about three or four hours, and took a good survey of everything. It was a pretty place, everything green and full of tropical fruit and eggs, of which we filled our boat of what we needed; but we left what we thought to pay for them, such as handkerchiefs and the like, and went again to the ship, and before we got to the ship the natives came back and made good use of what we left behind and we made good use of what we took with us, such as eggs, oranges, bananas and pineapple. The boat was taken up, but the next day we went again, took with us some more things, this time some braid, combs, hairbrushes, and some soap, and such things as the siwashes would use, but they ran away again, but took everything with them that we left for them, and piled up lots of stuff for us, twice as much as we needed, but we could not get near them yet. But we kept this up for several days and at last they let us come to them. We gave them a looking glass and some pocket knives. It made lots of fun. They were a fine looking people, good size, and appeared to be all alike, somewhat dark, but not black, smooth faces, straight hair, and stark naked, most of them. The older men had bark clothes on, the women nothing, only what we gave them and showed them how to wear. I believe they were sorry to see us go.

We also caught lots of fish here, lovely large mackerel. But after three days we again got a good breeze and were soon on the coast of New Zealand. Here we lost a man. He had been sick with the consumption all the time and hoped to recover by going to Australia. He was thrown overboard on the coast. We were then going about 18 knots an hour. We went up through Bassett's straits into Port Phillip. We got into port on Saturday evening, or it would be Saturday with us, but Sunday with them, and no one could go ashore until Monday morning, and no one wanted to go very bad. We were all at home on the Ferdinand. There was never a quarrel or disturbance in all the sixty-seven days we were on board that ship, and I came near staying with her and going on to Liverpool.

But we went on shore on Monday afternoon into Port Phillip. It was only a landing place at that time. It was eight miles from there to Melbourne by rail, boat, or cab. Melbourne is a beautiful city, well lit up with good gas lights, the streets very wide and very clean. The buildings were all rock or brick and the rock was all brought from Sidney, five hundred miles away, in steamboats. The city was well represented with schools, churches and theaters. We fell in love with the city. We stayed there two weeks, boarded at the Prince George Hotel on Big Birch street, rode around the city daytimes, and went to the theater nights. There were then four of us, J. Holester, H. Pideler, myself, and William Kirkman, the man that ran the Pioneer Butcher Shop in Walla Walla, Wash., a long time afterwards.

There were five or six big brass bands in that city which made it a business to go around the city and play at the hotels and public places, about twice at one hotel each day. So we got lots of music while there.

But the time came when we bought our tickets on the stage for a mining camp, Mekiver, fifteen miles away, a new camp and a good one, too. We left in a six-horse coach, six beautiful horses, and on a beautiful road, straight as a lane, all macadamised with rock. We went the first fifteen miles and changed and so on all the way with nothing in the country all the time but the stopping places, until we came to Mekiver. It is a little town on a little dry creek or dry a good deal of the time. Here we saw some very rich diggings, some of them were taking out as much as ten thousand dollars in one day, and then one thousand, and the strike was all in private property belonging to an old lady, and she would have fifteen pounds a square yard before you could sink a hole in it, so we did not buy any of it. It was about twelve feet to the bed rock. The strike was very narrow and crooked, so it was not every one that bought ground that found the streak of gold, but all who found it were made rich, if they saved their money, but they did not. Some of them threw it away as fast as they could.

We started out on the prospect about twelve miles away to what was called Wild Duck river. We wanted to go somewhere where there was water. But when we got there we traveled up and down but found no water. At last we found one man and one woman and a little water, just enough for them to drink. But we searched for water and found it, and found some gold, but not on the creek about three miles away, but no water. We got some dirt there and washed it and found gold in it, but we were too far from water. If we had had water at the place we could have made twenty or thirty dollars per day to the hand.

We stayed away until our grub was gone, then started out for Mekiver

-64-

again without road or trail and we came there without road or trail, but on the way back we got lost without anything to eat. We well knew that we had gone far enough and had come to trees or brush, and we well knew there were none at Mekiver, so we did not know whether to go here or there, east or west. We had to look north for the sun in day time. We rested a while and talked the matter over and all disagreed about where to go. At last I struck off alone, left the other three sitting on the ground still. Then I waited awhile to see what they were going to do, and while waiting I heard a dog bark. I called to them and they would not believe me at first. But after a while I got them to come with me and we went about two miles, and then found two goats and a dog all alone, but we felt greatly encouraged and still went on and came to one lone tent and a woman in it. She seemed to be badly scared at first, but after a while calmed down. I asked her for some water. She said there was none in the place, but said we could get some goats' milk. I told her that was good and we got plenty of it, for which we gave her half a crown each, fifty cent in U.S. money. Her man had gone after water and grub five miles away. We stayed there that night and in the night the man came more drunk than anything else. He had some water and some liquor, and they soon got into a quarrel, from which we found out that they were Tages, which means outlaws.

In the morning they were free with us and told us where to find Mekiver. He was digging gold there, finding lumps in the dust, throwing the dust up in the wind to let the dust blow away, then pick it over; so he got lots of money, or all they needed. They were no better than the natives of that country, and as dirty as Indians. The water he brought with him was two five-gallon kegs on a Jack, for the Jack, two goats, a dog and themselves.

We bade them good-bye and soon found Mekiver. My partners bought into some property there, and I struck out along for Beachworth, about fifteen miles away, and I had seventy-five miles to go before I should reach the road from Melbourn to Beachworth. So one morning I struck out with swag on my back and club in hand, and traveled seventy-five miles through a lonely country with no water, only in holes that were all green and had to be strained before it could be used.

In two days I came out on the stage road at Honeysuckle. Here there was a small stream of water, and was one of the prettiest places I ever saw in all my life. There were only two hotels, two stores, and five or six houses. What they lived on I did not know.

Here I was tired, needed rest and refreshment, which I went to the hotel to get, and the landlord told me to go to the backdoor. I said, "No, sir, I am no begger, but am able to pay." Then he said, "Wait till supper time." But I would not. I needed something then and got it too. But when he saw I wanted a ticket to go on the stage when it came along, he treated me as another man.

So at four the next morning I was wakened up to go on the stage with clothes brushed and boots blacked. It is only the upper class that go in the coaches in that country. And again I found myself on the coach going on the jump through a level plain, the road as straight as straight could be, always straight ahead until we came about twenty-five miles from Beachworth. Then it turned into timber country, which they called white gum. The bark of the trees was white and smooth and the leaves are very thick and green. But the wood is brittle and worthless for anything but to burn. I got to Beachworth and found a large and thrifty town of about 75,000 people. Here I saw the first Chinese temple and the largest I ever saw. It was grand. I wish I could explain it.

Here was good water and lots of it, and good diggings also. I was offered work at six dollars per day, but I wanted to work on my own hook and prospect around a little. So I did and found nothing any good. Then I went to Yapandanda, fifteen miles from here, and found another creek of good water, and found also lots of white-washed Yankees and blue-bellied Yankees, as they call them.

Here I bought a claim and went to work for good on Corbey's Flat, on Yackandanda creek. I bought in with a man from California and one from London and one from the west of England. I payed $150 for one fourth interest. Here I worked very hard, as we did in California, and made about ten dollars per day, but as in other camps the boys spent it every night. Corbey kept a boarding house and dance house with fourteen girls in it on purpose to dance with the boys every night, and they danced until twelve o'clock every night. But this boy did not do it. I kept what I made until we worked the claim out.

Now it was here the manna fell. It came down in clouds, as white as snow and as large as popcorn after it is popped, and as sweet as honey. While it is on the ground everyone lives on it, but it loses its taste after the sun strikes it. I bought a bottle of it out of the country with me and it always looks good and sweet, better than anything I ever smelt of. It is only found in that part of the country where the white gum tree grows. These trees are evergreen. This place was about fifty miles from the Murray river on the Victoria side. It was very healthy and no cold weather, no consumption in the country and fever and ague never known.

From here I again went out on the prospect and found some good gold but no water as usual. But it made a good camp after I left the country when it rained, but it did me no good. I then went to Mount Harryratt gold field. It was no mountain, only high ground. There was no water, only what was brought from about twenty miles away. It sold for from fifty to seventy-five cents per gallon. The gold was found in spots all over the country, all coarse gold, all dry wash. There was an immense tent there guarded by mounted troopers that took charge of all the gold that was brought into the tent and every man had his name and the amount of ounces on a paper on his pail of gold. There were hundreds of pails all marked on the ground in the tent and when you wanted your money, you took it and paid the gold and also the royalty of fifty cents on twenty dollars worth.

Here I did not make much and did not get on a good spot, but I saw more gold than I ever saw before in all my life or ever expect to see again. There are millions of pounds of gold in that country and always will be, because there is no water to take out of the dust.

So I left with hundreds of others, came back to Yackandanda again and soon got ready to leave the country. By this time the gold was found up in British Columbia, and it was reported so big down there that it made me crazy to get away.

But before I leave I must tell of a horse race I went to while at this place. It was a great place for sports of all sorts. This horse race was for the whole district from Beachworth to the Millshead. There were hundreds of horses there. Some ran six miles and some ran one mile. There were thousands of dollars spent on each side and before night came there was not a sober man in the place but myself and the policeman. So the policeman swore me in to help him keep order. This was at Osborn's place. Osborn was the first man in that country. He got a grant from the British government which gave him seventy-five square miles of land, in which all these gold fields were found. But he let anyone mine who would by paying him the royalty of fifty cents on twenty dollars, as the government did. So it made Osborn a very rich man and the race track is at his place or it is his race track; so on that day I saved them thousands of dollars. They had one son and one daughter only and it appeared that they fell in love with me that day. When they knew I was going to leave the country they all tried hard to keep me there and the young lady wrote me a letter inviting me to come and see them and not leave the colony; and I have often wished I had stayed there with them and called her Berryman instead of Osborn. But I had to go and go I did. I went to Beachworth and got on the stage for Melbourne. I was alone when I left Beachworth at 4 o'clock in the morning and about 6 o'clock there was a young lady came aboard the stage with me. For a long time she was no company, would not talk nor sit in the same seat with me, but after a while other passengers came in the coach. Then she came in the back seat with me and began to make friends and by the next morning we were very warm friends. When we got into Melbourne she wanted to go with me, but I could not see it that way. I went to the Prince George hotel as before, but took her to the _____ and at night I went and took her to the theater, and around the city the next day, and found out that she was going to Vancouver, instead of England, where she first said she was going to go. So we went to see the ship that was going to Vancouver. We did not like her very well, but she was all there was to go, so we both bought tickets in the second cabin and picked out our staterooms right side by side. This lady gave her name as Miss Smith.

But the ship did not go as soon as was expected by two weeks, and then she found another young lady that wanted to go, by the name of Healit. I was made acquainted with her and asked to get a companion for her or someone to pay her passage, which I had no trouble to do, for I had already learned of a man who wanted something of that sort of a job. So the very next day I met Master Willson and made them acquainted and the job was soon fixed up, and they two went and bought passage along with us in the second cabin. By this time there were twelve in the cabin and eighty in the steerage. The cabin was full now and everything was all O.K. apparently, and as the ship was about to pull out the harbor master came aboard and said, No, the ship was not seaworthy. So that kept us there two weeks longer having a fine time. Some of them stayed on board and others went on shore to spend money. As usual I went back to the same hotel and was right at home. This time I did not care whether I went or not. Miss Smith and I were chums at this time. But in the mean time Miss Healit had come to me and told me her plans; that she had allowed Willson to pay her way to Vancouver, and she was going to marry him if she liked him; if not she would pay him back his money some time; and she wanted me to be a friend to her in case she needed one. She did not believe she could like him. And I was to be her brother. I said, "Mary, that will not work. Your name is already Mary Healit and mine J.E. Berryman." "Well, then," she said, "we can be half brother and sister" — and I had to promise her to help her in time of need. She stayed with me all that day and told me all the troubles of her life, which I shall never tell nor write. I found she was a married woman running away from her husband. I tried to get her to go back to him, but she would not go back. She was bound to go to Vancouver if the ship went.

Again the ship was allowed to set sail, with all on board. We went out with a good, fair wind until we got out of the straits, then we got head winds and the old bark could not stand against it. So we went to the north instead of the south for a long time until they all got to be afraid. We were now in a cold country and things began to look serious for us. At last the wind changed. A stiff breeze of fair wind rose. We had already been out ten days going away from home in very rough weather. Mary Healit had been very sick and Willson of course was very attentive to her. One morning, while giving her some hot coffee in bed, she threw it at him and told him to keep out of her state room, and if she wanted anything that her brother would bring it to her. That made Willson very mad of course.

Now there is too much of this to write about to tell one half of it, so I shall pass on. We got fair wind for a long time, until we reached _____ or the _____ islands. We went ashore for fresh water and some other things we were out of. Here again we had to pitch out old bark all over. She was leaking very badly.

There was a French counsul and his family at this place. They were very glad to see our ship come to port, and also were the natives. They were very free, too, with us, and wanted us to stay with them very bad.

We were here eight days and lived on the fruit of the island all the time. The natives would try, it seemed to me, to see which of them could give us the best attention. The women would come and hold an umbrella over your head when you sat down to keep the sun away.

But before this we stopped at New Guinea a little while and there we saw some good looking people. They appeared to be all alike, all about the same size, straight and beautiful, and also very free with us. No white people here that we saw could get what was wanted, and we did not stay long.

Now our ship was all tarred over and pronounced seaworthy again, and we went. The old bark rolled out on the water like an old washtub.

But Mrs. Mary Healit and G. Willson had not get married yet, but were very cross to each other. Miss Smith and I got on all O.K. We had a good living and nothing to do. But Willson got very cross with me at times, because I had to take my sister's part, and she would call on me for every little thing, which made him feel pretty bad.

There were four other ladies on board the ship. All claimed to be married to the men they were with, but they did not stay with them. Mrs. Stanley left her man and went with Mr. Chase, the first mate, and another woman left her husband and went with one of the other men, and the stewardess married the second mate, and the skipper was found whipping his wife and was taken away from doing it and said she was great with the supercargo of the ship, but no one would believe him, because he was a bad man to his wife and also to his men.

I shall not take time to tell one tenth of what happened on this voyage. By this time we had crossed the line again. The fresh water began to be scarce, and the steerage passengers were put on half allowance. Also was the meat very scarce, and the old ship was leaking very bad, so the seamen had to pump all the time, and the passengers also helped to pump. The passengers wanted to put into the Sandwich Islands, but the skipper said no.

One day a young Irishman brought up his dinner and showed it to Captain Stott, saying it was not fit for a dog to eat. The skipper said, "It is good enough for you or anyone like you." At the same time he gave the man a kick and told him to go below and mind his business. Instead of going away, as quick as a flash the man let fly and knocked the skipper down on the deck and gave him a kick after he was down. Now the skipper was a large man, weighed 220 pounds, was always a bully and this came very unexpected to him. So he got to his feet and ordered out the shooting irons. So the big chest of guns was soon put on the deck and the man ordered to be arrested. By this time the steerage passengers all had their pistols in their hands. Also the skipper gave orders to take this man and put him in irons, but the sailors failed to obey the order. But the young fellow says, "Take me yourself, you coward. Here I am, take me. I dare you to take me." But no taking was done. Then the skipper told one watch of the crew to arrest the other watch because they did not obey him, but they did not obey either. Then the skipper made for the Sandwich Islands. As soon as he got there he went ashore to the American consul, made complaint, and had all the crew arrested. A big boat load of marines came aboard and took them ashore. That set the cabin passengers to work with the supercargo. They got up a petition, took it on shore in the city of Honolulu and gave it to the consul.

He said, "I have nothing to do in the matter. It is a British bark and I turn it over to the British consul."

So we took the paper, with one he gave us, to the British consul, and he let the men out at once, put them on board, and took Captain Stott away from the ship and put another man in charge of the ship. He had her overhauled again.

Honolulu was then a very small place. We stayed there three weeks, and went over on the other island where the volcano is. I greatly enjoyed the trip.

Although I had been on board of this old bark Harginger for eighty-one days, I now concluded to leave her and go on a little clipper which was then going to San Francisco. So when I told my partners about it I tell you it was hard. One of them wanted to go very bad, but I was honest with her and was too young to get married, which was her desire. I left them on the same day I told them about it, but I would come to them in one year from the time I left them in tears, and so was I in tears.

I will say here Miss Healit was a very impulsive woman and had her own way almost in everything, and I was too young to trust even myself, much less her, but it was hard to part.

I did not want to go to Vancouver that time of the year, for it was now January 1859. So I went on the other little ship and got to 'Frisco in ten or twelve days. I did not stay in 'Frisco long. I was nearly out of cash and I made straight for Frenchtown, but everything was worked out and those I knew were all gone.

Then I went to Hangtown again and there I found one of my old chums whom I went to Melbourne with and whom I left at Mekiver, Jim Alderson, and many other friends. So Jim told me to come along with him to White Rock canon; I could get work there. So I went to work for them at White Rock for six dollars per day in a drift, and stayed until May. Then I found a little prospect and sold it. I do not know whether it ever made anything or not. Then I came down the river to Brockle's bridge and found some gold there and sold that claim too. I believe it would turn out some money if worked right.

I then heard I had a brother in the Guadeloupe mines and I went to see him, a younger brother who came there while I was in Australia. So I got there in four days and found him in a cabin on Sunday all alone while the rest of the partners were out on the tear, as they called it. But Henry did not know me. I talked with him quite a while before he caught on. Then he said, "I believe this must be Jim." "I said, "You bet it is." Of course he did not know whether I was dead or alive.

I stayed there about a week. I might have gone to work, but I did not like quicksilver mines. But a very beautiful country was that, everything lovely and lots of money to spend, and they spent it very freely. There were lots of young Spanish girls there waiting to take it from them and help them to enjoy it, too. But Henry was very quiet and still, saved his money and stayed at home.

But I was on the prospect again. I did not know as yet which way to go. But I went back again to San Francisco. There I found one of our passengers from Australia who came with me in the cabin. I was glad to see him and he was also glad to see me. He told me all about what happened after I left them. They all went to Vancouver and Miss Smith got married to one of the passengers on the ship, and a very fine young fellow. They stayed in Victoria, but Miss Healit was then in San Francisco with her husband, who came after her from Australia, found her in Victoria, brought her back to 'Frisco, and went to keep a boarding house on _____ street. So I soon went to the place and rung the bell. She herself came to answer. When she saw me she jumped on me as if to eat me up, took me to her husband, and told him I was the best friend she had ever met. He made me very welcome and said, "Make this your home while in 'Frisco."

I stayed there about one week, took out the wife to the theater every evening and he appeared to be glad to see it. She was a lovely looking lady and everyone seemed to think lots of her. Her man thought too much of her and she nothing of him.

But the time came when I wanted to go. She wanted to go too, but I told her I had no home and did not know where to go to get a living for a woman. But she did not care for that. But I did care and finally struck out without saying a word about it.

I went to the Klamath river, but worked a little while first on Humbug creek in a drift at six dollars per day. This was in Siskiyou county. Humbug is about twenty miles from the Klamath river. The Klamath at that place had no mining on it, but I saw it one day from the top of old Mount Scraggy. It looked so lovely that I made up my mind to go there to hunt gold.

It was in the fall of '59 about the time I and two other men got down on the Klamath river. We packed our grub from Humbug all on our backs. We began to sink holes on the river banks, but found it very hard to get to the bed rock on account of water. We found a little gold, but not enough to pay. We went back to Humbug after more grub and things to build a pump with. We went to work again, got bedrock, but no gold. My two partners then left, went back to Humbug, but I stayed longer. I went further down the river near a ranch. I found two men there, Joe and Handy, raising stock and milking cows.

After hunting around for a while I found some good paying gravel on top of the ground on the river bar. So I went to work and built me a good cabin and made ready to stay there that winter. I got a keg of syrup, some bacon and flour. That was all my living that summer. but then I got butter, milk, eggs and meat of them, or anything I needed. But I lived and worked along all the time. I had to build a wheel to lift water to wash my dirt with, and did pretty well.

About January two men came along and wanted to work for me, saying they were broke and tired, and were glad to work for their grub for a while. So I told them they could stay one week to rest up a little, and they went to work hard. At the end of the week I gave them three dollars per day and told them to go, but they did not want to go. They said that was good enough for them. So they stayed with me until March, when one of them got some whisky brought to him by the express and got drunk and crazy. Then I made them go and worked alone again.

I worked out all my surface ground, then went and ran a drift under the bar to find a channel back under the large flat. I knew there must be a channel there and I ran the tunnel three hundred and fifty feet and got into a deep channel but not gold enough to pay, and came near giving it up. But at last I found the streak of pay, and pay it did. I made about $3300 there in about two months.

In the mean time I was found out by two men from Scott river. They made me stake out my claim, then took one on each end of me, and caused a stampede from Scott river, and they took up the whole country up and down the river for three or four miles. About three hundred men got there in two days. There was lots of money taken out of those bars that summer and winter, but I got poisoned there with sulphur water in my drift. There was also a soda spring and salt spring on the same ground. The soda water would make some of the best bread in the world. But I got sick and had to go to 'Frisco again.

I was away about two months and came back all O.K. But I did not go to see Miss Healit this time. I thought I had better stay away while I was away.

When I came back I found my claim nearly all worked out. I had left two men in it, given them three dollars per day and one half of what they made over the three dollars. They said they did not make anything but the three dollars. Everyone knew better than that, but I let it go and went to work again like a little man and made thirty dollars per day until I was washed out in December. Then I went to work, hired men, got out logs, and sawed out lumber and put in dams to turn the river and got to work the second time and did about one and a half days' work on pay dirt and in the night the river began to rise again and about thirty of us fought the river all night, but it got the better of us, washed away all the lumber, logs, tools, wheels, sluice-boxes, and everything I and the other claims had.

Then I made up my mind to leave the Klamath river. So I stayed around there until summer and lots of the boys wanted me to stay there and try it again. Those men that had the ranch offered me all the grub I would need for the summer if I would stay there and prospect that summer. So at last I got a good man by the name of Wellman to come with me. He was one of the best men to travel with I ever met. He and I had some very rough times together and hard ones too.

About the first of April we began to climb the Siskiyou mountains towards Oregon, and found too much snow. Then we stopped and went to work in a big creek we called Hungry Hollow, and found some gold, about four or five dollars per day. There was lots of good soda water there, but that would not do. As soon as the snow got hard enough to hold up our horses, we struck out on it in the night and got over the worst of it in one night. Then we got on the waters of Rogue river. We were all right now and found gold at or in several places as we went on where _____ is now and at Jacksonville. It was a busy little town and we could make good wages there, but we were bound for Washington to hunt a new gold field. So I printed a card of big letters and sewed it to my back which read, "Salmon river or bust."

So we came to Portland, which was then one mud hole and nothing better. Everything was then very cheap in Webfoot. We could get a large steer for five dollars or anything at our own price.

From Portland we struck out on the old emigrant road. While going up the big Sandy I got washed down the river a long ways on my mule. The rivers were all very high and we had to swim most of them. My partner began to think I was gone for good. He was running down the other side on the bank throwing a rope at me in the hope that I could catch it, and at last I did. Both mule and I got out on the right side, and I did not lose one thing I had with me but my hat. That was not worth anything and I went for a while without any. We camped there that night, got dry, and the next day went on again. At night we overtook three other men going the same road for the same purpose. They were stopping because they could not get over the Cascade mountains for snow. So we all camped together that night. The next day we all struck out together, killed a bear and lots of other game, came to the snow, and there stayed a little while and dryed some meat to eat on the road. We struck out again in the night and got up to the corduroy road. There was no snow there. We stopped a little while and tried to get on the summit of Mt. Hood, but did not. The snow was hard and the sun would shine on it and take away our eyesight. Then we made for the Barlowgate on the east side and when we got there we got into a band of Indians. We saw they would not make friends with us. We did not know what to do, go or stay, as we knew we were in their hands either way. At last we asked them to take our cuitans and put them with theirs that night. That made them believe we were King George men and in the morning our horses were brought to us all O.K. We stayed with the siwashes all night, paid them for taking care of our stock, and went on our way rejoicing.

Here there was lots of good grass and lots of game. But we never shot one thing that we did not need. We got to the DesChutes and in trouble again to cross it, and we got into another band of siwashes. But we did as before, called ourselves King George men and stayed with them that night. The next day they showed us where to cross the river and they helped us across.

We then began to think and talk about Walla Walla, or the outlaws' camp, as it was sometimes called. But it was a long time before we came to it and when we did we did not find much but a lot of good grass, and good water, but no flour nor beef, nor a good horse, but plenty of whisky and siwash and ponies. There were no wagons, buggies, nor wagon roads, only three or four little trading posts in town. We went to the fort and could not get any flour there, but got some bread and some salt and some syrup and sugar and one of our crowd traded a gun for a sack of flour to some one. They had no flour until then for a good while. I had fifty pounds yet that I had not opened till I got a long way above here. Two of the boys bought two horses here and they were claimed away from them at once, and it made us believe it was a bad place, or outlaws' camp.

I will say right here, I expect there are some men in Walla Walla today that were in it then, but I believe they are better man today then they were then, and there might have been some all O.K. then, but very few, if any. We felt much safer with the Nez Perce Indians than we did with the whites of this valley then. The Indians were good to us.

We hunted for gold in Mill creek, but found none. The boys got other horses, and we took the Indian trail straight across the country for Salmon river. We went where Dayton is today and where Lewiston is today. Here we found some good Indians doing good work. They had gardens all down the Alpowa, and were growing apples, and when we got to where Chief Timothy lived we bought apples, beef and potatoes. There were lots of melons growing, but not ripe. This was the first time we felt safe since we left Webfoot.

We found gold on the Clearwater and on the Snake river, but not enough to do any good. There was not a white man in the country about Lewiston, or where it is now, at that time. But the missionaries were up above on the Lapwai, and it was they that taught the siwashes to work and they or the Hudson's Bay Company that planted the trees.

From there we did not know which way to go. Captain E.D. Pierce had been up the Clearwater and found good gold. So we made up our minds to go on the middle fork of the Clearwater. So we took the old Indian trail again and soon got to Craig mountain, where one of our men insulted a squaw and got into trouble and came near getting us all into trouble. I will say right here that most of the trouble is made with the Indians by dirty white men and whisky. But we got away with our scalps on, and I thought we were lucky.

But we went on and got away in Camus prairie, where we were met by a small band of Snake Indians and told to go back, which we did not do, but they would not let us go on, would ride in front of us every time, but did not show fight, and about evening another band of Nez Perces came along and then the Snakes rode away and went on with the Nez Perce Indians. They were going on a buffalo hunt.

It was not long till we got into the mountains on one of the worst trails I had ever seen up to that time, going over logs, rocks and mud. Those little ponies would climb logs as big as themselves with the squaws on their backs.

Then we began to look for gold again. The country was full of quartz

-74-

rock and wash gravel, the hills full of game and the creeks full of fish. We came to Newcome creek and found gold, good, healthy looking gold, and the creek was full of elk. It was a lonely looking park in the mountains. We all camped there one night. While the boys got supper I sunk a hole and got some gold, but not much.

The next morning I pinned a huge elk-horn to a tree and another man made a spot on it and wrote "City" with a burnt stick. Therefore it became Elk city to this day.

But we did not go far, about one and a half or two miles across the hill, over logs and through thick timber. We could hardly get our pack horses along. We came to another creek, where there was lots of water, grass, and wood. While crossing the creek I saw wash gravel on the bank on the other side. I jumped off and said, "Boys, lets do some prospecting here. This looks good."

They waited, but we did not unpack, any of us; but in a short time I found gold in the ground on the bank, and we sank a hole in the creek bar and found a good prospect in it. So then we unpacked and went to work for good, some chopping logs to hew out boards to build sluice boxes with, and another sank more holes to see where the best pay was. We went up and down the creek a good ways we began to work; so after a little we found we had good wages, though nothing big, about eight or ten dollars to the hand per day.

Here was lots of game of all kinds and salmon without number, and fool hens, which we could knock out of the trees with a stick, and little brown and black bears and elk and deer. We would dry deer meat for bread to save our flour, take their fat to make gravy with, and when it was cold we would use it instead of bread.

In the meantime while we were at work here, which we called American river, I went still further on the Indian trail till I came to another river, which is now called Red river. Here I went to work and found lots of gold on the top gravel. I did not get to bed-rock; that I had no need to do, it was sure to be good.

By this time there were other prospectors in the hills, and we had fairly opened up to work, making good money. But when I showed the boys the gold I brought back and told them how I got it, everyone said, "Lets sell out and go. There is a party right here that will buy us out, will give us fifty dollars each. Shall we sell?"

"Yes," I said, "but no tools."

The next morning they gave us the money asked, and we all started off to Red river, every one loaded down with all he could pack. After a long and weary travel I showed them the place. They soon went to work and found it; so we were all terribly excited. We soon dammed the river and went to work. We did well on the top gravel, but no money on the bed rock. We found we were sold, but worked out all we put the dam into, and then went to another place and tryed it with the same result. We could get big money on top, but never in the bottom. We were not satisfied and still went on to prospect further on other streams and hills. We found a little gold almost everywhere, but not enough to please.

By this time there were others on Red river too. As we went down the river we found a party of Germans, who had just begun on the same sort of a prospect as we had above.

We then went across the mountain and came to another fork of the river, which we called Crooked river. Here we also did some very hard work, but no pay; yet we found some very coarse gold on the river bed. Then we went down the river to the junction of the other stream. Here we went to work again and still found gold, but not enough to do us. On the morning of the third day, as we were about to leave, three men came to camp looking very ragged, dirty and hungry, and red as the siwash. Inasmuch as I spoke of it and of them, William, my partner, said, "You are just as bad, or worse." So we only then realized how dirty and bad we were looking. These men told us they were hunting flour or bacon, and asked us how far they were from Pierce city. We said, about seventy or eighty miles or more.

They got breakfast with us. We had fried mush that morning, which is one cup of flour put in about two gallons of water, then boiled until it gets thick then allowed to get cold and then cut in slices and fried in grease. We then told the men they could get plenty of grub by now about twenty or thirty miles from here at a new camp called Elk city, by going up the stream until they came to a creek which had dirty water in it, then go up it and they would find men to tell them where to go. They then told us that they had found good diggings and were going back as soon as they could get something to live on, and stay there during the winter. They also told us the landmarks to travel by and the distance as near as they could. Those were three of the discoverers of Florence city diggings, as it was called afterwards. They called themselves Eape Bastick, Burksher, and Weller.

We stayed together until dinner and we fried lots of fool hens for dinner and had dried venison for bread, and by this time we had found that two more of their company had gone around by Camas prairie to look for something to eat. So after dinner we parted, we to the south and they to the north.

It was then getting very cold and very short days, and that day it snowed on us about two inches and made it very bad for horsefeed, but we went ahead as fast as we could, but it was hard to go anything like straight. But after three days we got to the sugarloaf butte, or umbrella butte, as it looks like sometimes. From there we could see the location they told us about twelve miles away yet. We camped at the sugarloaf that night.

The next morning we set our course and set out through a thick cluster of timber. It took us about two days to make the twelve miles: We got into the opening of dead timber, but could not find their diggings, but found some of our own in a very short time on what is now known as Summit flat. We got in there about the first of October, 1861. It was cold and snow on the ground, but we found lots of gold, as much as twenty dollars to the pan, and sometimes more. The first three days I built me a cabin to keep out the snow.

In about ten days the stampede began to come in by the hundreds. A man by the name of Cap Beadslow brought in some beef and I bought three for three hundred dollars for myself and two other men; and I covered my cabin with the hides of the steers.

I had made about eight hundred dollars with the pan and rocker by the time our friends got back, and one of our men, Tolley, had made near to a thousand dollars, and others had made all the way from eight hundred to two thousand dollars. So the hills became full of people, and the town was layed out and named Florence by Dr. Furbar in honor of his daughter, who was to come to Florence in the next March; but she never got in there. The Doctor got there about the last of October with lots of patent medicine. He sold pills at twelve dollars per box and cough medicine at twelve dollars per bottle. One ounce of gold was called only twelve dollars, but it was worth $15.50 in the mint, and that is poor gold; most gold is worth eighteen dollars, some twenty dollars per ounce.

There was one man there, Monroe, who took out one hundred and forty pounds in two weeks, then left the country with the money, went to Portland, bought goods and packed up to Florence, and in one night the mules all froze to death. Then he had all his goods packed into _____ 62 miles on men's backs or hauled in handsleds.

There was no work done at this time but building houses, and men got ten dollars per day for that. It got too cold to wash dirt about the last of October. Some did work later, but had to heat water to rock with. The last day's work we did that winter, two of us rocked out 1240 dollars out of 140 buckets of gravel.

At last we got tired loafing around camp, so we got on our snowshoes, took a little salt and flour, and an ax, pick, pan and shovel, three of us, and went out over the mountains to see what sort of a country there was east of us. We traveled about from twelve to twenty miles per day. Our horses were all sent out long ago to winter on the Salmon river.

At last we found a low basin where it was not so cold and the snow was not so deep. Here we stayed for thirty days. Around here it was very cold; we did not know how cold it was. When night came we dug a hole in the snow about six or eight feet deep, cut green boughs and put on the snow, then our robes on it, then logs to make a fire with which would burn all night.

It snowed in Florence that Winter twenty-two feet. All you could see of the town were the holes where the smoke came from. We all kept well and got lots of game while outside, such as rabbits and fool hens and grouse. The big game had gone down on the lowlands or river beds.

About the last of December we turned back to Florence again. We got back to the sugarloaf butte and camped in the hole in the ground at night and on the first day of January, 1862, we climbed to the top of the butte and put the date with the initials of our names on an old scrubby tree that was growing there, and I have seen it ten years afterwards.

From the butte we had a straight shot down the hill towards town, and we could go about twenty or thirty miles an hour, but the cold was so sharp it would take away our breath to go fast, and so we had to take our time.

When we got back they told us the mercury had been frozen up ever since we were out. Some of them thought we were lost in crossing some river and some thought we had found good diggings, but it was neither. We had found some gold but no pay.

Some went to work and got up a big dinner of fresh beef, good bread and some cheese, almost made us sick, but we soon got used to it. But we could not get used to a hot cabin. My cabin was about ten feet under the snow and it was very warm. No air came in except through the doorway, and when I went out I was sure to take cold.

There were about three hundred men in camp then. Many of them had next to nothing to eat. They dug up the heads of the beeves that were butchered in the fall and lived on them and on flour sacks that had been thrown away and which were all hunted up and boiled to make gruel of. When it was found out that we had grub gave them some and sent lots of them down on the river where they could get plenty of game. Flour had got to be about fifty dollars a sack and salt about a dollar a pound.

About the middle of February we had new snow shoes and went out again another way. It was very hard traveling and a rough country. We went up toward the Bitterroot valley and the Deerlodge, but we did not know what to call it at that time.

We were away forty days and the snow had begun to get soft in places before we got back, and some of the claims had begun to shovel snow to go to work; but they could not work because water was all over the ground.

The three of us camped out in the snow that winter eighty-one nights.

At last summer came. The country was swimming with water until June. In May I went out to the Slate creek house on Salmon river. There I found one of my brothers and lots of other men waiting to come in to camp. I told them to come in, leave their horses and grub there and strike out on foot and come with me and take what they could pack on their backs.

So in the morning we all started with fifty pounds each. We had twelve miles to go up the mountain. When we got there it was night. The boys were sick and tired, too tired to eat supper. I laughed at them for being such babies.

We then had about twelve miles more to go to get to town, but we could ride lots of the way on a hard trail in the snow — sit on a shovel or pan and let it slide down the mountain.

By four o'clock we were in to town. I went and bought out a share of my own for my brother, or in other words, sold him half of my interest. Then I went to work and made the money back in two weeks, and worked there until August. Then I sold out to go to Wisconsin, and left my brother Henry there.

I got to San Francisco just after the Golden Gate went down. I found one man from Florence that was on board and had lost all he had in the water. We gave him passage money to go to the mountains again; so Dan went off rejoicing.

Instead of taking passage on the boat for New York I bought a ticket on the stage line across the plains by Salt Lake City. It was one of the best rides I ever had in my life. We rode day and night all the way. There were only five of us on the coach and I rode outside with the driver day and night. The other men were Ben Holiday, the owner of the stage line, Dr. Rabey, U.S. Marshall, Mr. Gould, and a Mr. Weller, a gay crowd, you bet.

We got to Salt Lake in ten days, stayed with Brigham Young one day and were shown all around the city. Harden was then governor, or tried to be. This was the first time I ever was in Salt Lake, but many times since. It was then a quiet place.

We got on the next day and in nineteen days we found ourselves in Fort Atchison where there was much trouble and hard work to go through an account of the war — towns on fire and bridges burned down. But we soon got into St. Louis, and then we were safe.

My father lived in Wisconsin and I went to that place. I had been away now over eight years and was altered in appearance a great deal. I got a man to drive me home from Hazelgreen in a buggy, and found father and mother alone out of the house. I asked father for work. He said he did not need any help. I told him I would work for him very cheap, but he would not have me at any price; he had no use for a man, for he was gone out of farming. He thought I was taking another census for another draft, but his boys were all gone from home. He had eight boys grown to be men, but they were all gone now. I asked him where was James now? He said, "I do not know for sure, but I believe he is out in Washington or a new place they call Idaho." I told him I did not believe that James was in Idaho. "Where do you think he is," he asked. "I answered, "He is right here; this is James," at the same time taking hold of my father. Mother ran away, saying, "It is not James; do not touch him." "I ran after her and said, "It is me, Christon." That was her name; she was my stepmother. As soon as I said that she knew me, saying, "I know you now, God bless you. They gave you up long ago, never thought to see you again." It was a joyful meeting for me that day.

I stayed with them and around there until the first of January, 1863, and had a glorious good time.

Then I went to Philadelphia to sell my gold and it came to $14.40 per ounce. It was found out soon with the brokers that I had gold and I was offered $3.30 each for every dollar I had with me.

There is where I missed it. I should have taken it and then put the paper money in land, and made three dollars on one again inside of one year. But I did not do it. I kept the gold and stayed in the East quite a while, in New

York, Washington, Baltimore, Boston, Portland, Maine, and many other cities.

About the tenth of Feb. I got on board the steamship, City of Washington, and sailed for Liverpool from Portland, with some boys from Canada who were going to Italy, and I made up my mind to go too, and around through Palestine and get back to Australia again.

We had a good voyage to Liverpool, got there in eight days and eight hours. We stayed in Liverpool eight days, saw all the best of the city and stayed in one of the fine hotels where all the big bugs stay. I wanted to see what they look and talk like. I found them very free and sociable.

I then went to London, the top of all towns. I stayed here two weeks and could not tell what I saw in that time. It is more than all other towns put together. The Crystal Palace alone is a world of itself and it beats all other places of amusement. I rode through the streets of that city for thirty miles.

From here I went to _____ and Glasco, then down to Bristol, which is one of the gayest and oldest cities of England, and one of the richest, too, for its size.

I then went to see the place where I was born and was shown it. I then felt glad that I had not made my condition any worse. No one from there knew me, but knew of my parents. It was a pretty place and one of the richest places in the west, right in the tin mines.

Here I got married in about one month's acquaintance when I never intended to get married at all, the very last thing I ever intended to do. Then in three or four days after we both started for Liverpool again and there stayed about two weeks more with my young wife, nineteen years of age.

Then we took passage on board the City of Glasgow for New York city. We had a lovely voyage and a good living. My wife was sick always in rough weather. There were other young ladies along going to their husbands in this country, who gave me a little trouble to get them through the Castle Gardens. But we got through all O.K. and into New York again. We stayed there about three days, then went straight for Chicago and then to Hazelgreen, Wisconsin, to the place where I left my father; but he had sold out and moved to Dodgesville, Wis.

I stayed there until the next March mining after lead; and I did well, but there was too much war and war talk for me. About in March, '64, I, with two other brothers, struck out for Montana, to the new gold mines of Alder creek. We went to Atchison and got on the stage for Salt Lake City. On the road we got snowed in at Laramie. We had to stay there six days and had nothing to eat but corn. We would roast it, fill our pockets, and walk up and down the long stable eating it. When the storm broke there were seventy-four of us waiting to go, and then we had to go on foot and break the road about six miles before the mules could travel through the snow. But we made it at last and got west of the range; then we were all right. But it was desperate traveling. For three days we had to get out and shovel snow and beat down a road for the mules. But as soon as we got on Bitter creek the snow was all gone, and when we got to Salt Lake City it was like summer, gardens were green and everything was lovely.

Then we bought a team of two horses and a light wagon and started for Alder creek. We put our bedding and grub in the wagon and all walked but one, except down hill, then rode. In about fourteen days we arrived in Alder creek, where everyone was busy and men wanted very bad to work.

This was the first of May and some of the boys went to work before they got up to the town, which was Virginia city. Wages on top were six dollars per day, and under ground were from ten to fourteen dollars per day. There were eight of us that went in that time, and they all went to work the first day but me. I did not want to. I wanted to look around a while and prospect, which I did for six days and was not satisfied. But I was asked to go to work one day and I did.

The drift was of very loose gravel, ready to roll in at any time. It was about thirty feet under ground. This was the first drift in Pinegrove district.

I worked here for eleven weeks at fifteen dollars per day. Then I quit to go to prospecting again. But before I got away from the creek the same boys came after me again and made me go back with them for a while to get through a piece of bad ground, which I did for two weeks more, then they gave me sixteen dollars per day.

But I got ready to cross the mountains and go to Bessy Basin and prospect on the road. My brothers were very much against my going off alone. I knew it was dangerous work, but I struck out all alone across the mountains a distance of about two hundred miles with no road and no guide, and worked hard sometimes on the way, but could not find one dollar of gold. At last I got to the lava beds. Then I knew I was somewhere, and then I found Boise city, or the place where it is to-day. There was not much there then. After looking around I found that I had gone about sixty miles out of my way, and I was then about one day's travel from the diggings. But I soon got there and found a good, lively camp, but nothing very rich like old Florence or Alder creek.

I went to work for a while on the creek to run a drift in under the city, at ten dollars per day. I only worked six days more. They would not pay ten dollars per day and I would not work for less.

So then I went off to Placerville, then to Granite creek, where I found one of my old Florence partners at work on a very rich claim. They were making about three hundred dollars per day clear. Tolley gave me a good chance to work with him or for him, but I did neither. I struck off up the creek to look for something for myself. Then I found another man, Tom Chandler, whom I knew in Florence in '61 and '62. I went with him still further up the creek and found some good gold in the bank, or on the forks of the creek, and we followed it in a quartz lead. It is now Old Granite, and has always been a good-paying mine. Tom always stayed with it and it made him rich, but I only stayed one month and then thought it was time to go home and see my wife and baby, whom I had not seen yet and only heard from once.

I had two brothers in Beasely at that time, Henry and Charles. I went to see them, and then got ready to travel back to Wisconsin. I got two good little mules, put a saddle on one and a pack of grub and bed on the other, and started. I got back to Boise, and found two other men to go with me on horseback. So we rode about forty miles per day. We got to Salt Lake, and there they had to get more horses, or trade them off. They were given out; my mules were as good as ever. There got three good horses and started afresh. We got to Ham's fork and one horse gave out again. Then we overtook two men going to Wisconsin, too, on horseback. They were from Silver city and had three good horses between them. Very fine men they were too.

The Indians were very bad on the road that fall, so we were glad to get to be five, and when we got on to _____ we overtook a train going back from Alder creek, in which I found one of my brothers, George, one of them that I left there in the summer. I soon tried around and got him on horseback, and then there were six of us, and we called ourselves good for sixty siwashes, in case we had to be.

We got to Polecreek, and there we found that the Indians had done lots of dirty work — left lots of dead bodies of immigrants on the road, and some not dead, but dying in their wagons with their grub and horses gone, and they crying and praying for help, and we could not help them, only with a little cold water, and bury those dead out of their sight, and leave them to the mercy of the wild savage. We saw the crowd that did it. I should think there were about seven hundred Indians only a short distance off, but they never came to us; neither did we go very near to them. We then gave our horses water and took a little with us and rode on until dark. Then we made a dry camp and never made a fire nor any sound of any sort when in danger.

The next morning about ten we got on the road again and met another band of about a hundred siwashes. They wanted everything we had, and we also wanted everything they had. But there was no trade and no fight. But we rode away very fast.

Then we went on until we found water and made camp in a pretty place with lots of grass. After supper, as was my custom, I went out to look around and saw about thirty siwashes all lying down behind some rocks with no ponies with them. I did not let on to see them; but I made signs to the boys in camp, and by the time I got to camp our horses were ready to travel again. When they saw us going to leave they gave the yell and ran towards us with all their might, but we did not allow them to get very close, but gave them all we had, about thirty shots in no time, which stopped them coming to us at once.

We rode on until dark again. I did not know what became of the siwashes, but we felt sure that they would never lie in wait for us any more.

That night we had a very poor camp, very little grass and no water; so at daylight we were up and off again looking for grass and water, and found none for a long time.

At last we saw a large body of horsemen or siwashes, we did not know which for a long time. At last they all got off and unpacked. Then we knew it was Boston, and we lost no time in getting to them. Here we found water and grass and about three hundred volunteers from Colorado after the siwashes. They were swearing revenge on them and gave quarter to none of them. They were as glad to see us as we were to see them. They took our trail and we took theirs.

The Indians had set fire to Joulesburg and murdered all in it. These men were now after them and I hope they got them, you bet.

We soon got to Joulesburg and found it in ashes and about fifty soldiers there, but they came too late.

We were now on the Platte river where we thought we were safe, but we were not, as the next day we got to House station and found it on fire and one driver and horse lying dead in the road. It was just at dark and they met us square in the road and did not appear to notice us, and we rode out in the brush a little ways and stayed there all night.

In the morning we found some men that came up from Fort Carney, and they told us that Uncle Sam had just made a treaty with these Indians and given them lots of blankets and grub. They also told us that they had burned the station at Pole river and stolen the stage horses not more than ten or twelve miles west of Carney. The next day we got there and found it was so, and also met the soldiers after the Indians. We got to Carney and found it was too true. This is the last of siwash for this trip.

We soon got into white settlement then and had to put my mules up in stables nights. But they began to get poor, so I had to quit it, let them out somewhere in a yard or field and throw them the feed, and that was all O.K.

When we got to Omaha three of the boys left us and stayed there, while the other four of us went straight to Wisconsin. My brother went to his farm and I to hunt up my wife and baby. I left her at Hazelgreen and found her at Dodgeville. She had gone to live near my father and family. They had begun to believe the Indians had got me for sure. I found all O.K. and was happy once more.

I was only forty-five days from Boise city, Idaho, to Hazelgreen, Wisconsin, and never lost a mule. But I lost lots of rest and lived very hard. We did not take much with us, but would buy what we needed at the stations on the road. All we had was fried slapjacks and bacon gravy or bread baked in the fry-pan, or sometimes it was baked before the fire in the fry-pan and kneaded out on a canvas or duck we carried under the flour sack.

They were glad to see me and made sure that I got a good wash and a clean suit of clothes before I went to bed that night. And I was very glad to do it and felt much the better for it, and in a week I was like myself again and ready to go to work at anything. So I went to work at digging lead.

I got my mules broke in to work in a sled and had lots of fun that winter sleigh-riding with my wife and other girls. The winter was very cold and I was about ready to go back to Montana again with wife and baby. My father and all the rest tried to keep me with them, saying the cruel war was about over and we could feel happy and soon get rich. But I got a little, light hack, or wagon, put our bed in it, and the first of April, 1865, I bade my father and stepmother adieu for the last time, and I felt it, and I feel it now, as I am writing it down, as though it were only a little while ago instead of thirty-nine years ago.

But we left in good spirits with two little mules and one poney tied behind the wagon. The roads were full of mud and snow. In four days we got into the highway. It was no better, but we kept on and after while got to Council Bluffs, and there found more company going the same road. But we were a long time getting here, going only about fifteen or twenty miles per day and stopping at a house every night; and our mules were good yet.

Here we crossed the river and struck off up the Platte river. Here the feed was poor and the roads very bad and we could not buy any hay, so we camped at _____ about one week and got a good many wagons together. It dried up nicely that week and grass grew good in places. so we went on pretty well, about ten wagons of us, and got to Fort Carney, where some wanted to stop a while and some did not. I stayed two days and drove on again, three wagons instead of ten, and got up to Fort Laramie. There we were held up until we got more force. Those at the fort said the Indians would kill us before we were gone two days. So we stayed at Laramie about three days and then there came up about eighty men from _____ with one woman and ten wagons, and my crowd and wife made eighty-seven men, two ladies and one child. Then we did not care for all the siwashes in the country. But the colonel at the fort said not to be too sure about that.

Most of these men were discharged soldiers and all well armed. So we went on to Fort Wayne, on Powder river. Some of the soldiers got whisky from one of the wagons and wanted more, which came near getting us into trouble, but did not. Then we went on to the Bighorn, or _____ river. The river was very large and high and swift and we had to swim it in our wagon-beds made into boats. There were but two wagon-beds that would do for boats, and it took us a long time to get across. There was a large band of Indians on the other side of the river, but they told us they were friendly and wanted to trade for flour, and it was so. After we all got over there were only two men picked out to trade with them for the whole train. We gave them nothing but flour, sugar, bacon, coffee and tobacco; and we got robes in return. There was one white woman with them and a pretty she was once, with very blue eyes and almost red hair. but she could not or would not talk with any one, either English, French, Spanish, or Dutch.

I lost my wagon in this river and part of our bed and stove. But I tried around and did well; got another very light one and left mine all behind but the tongue, which I put in the one horse buggy I bought of a man in the train.

The next bad place was Green river, where there was a rope across and about on the river it broke and drowned two men, father and son, and two horses, and we could not find any of them.

From there we had no bad luck and soon got into Last Chance gulch, or Helena city, or where it now is. They had then begun to build the town in the lower end of Grizzly gulch, and they were then at work mining out the town, and it was a good pay. I found they were making from fifty to eighty dollars per day to the company, and the ground was all taken up for about fifteen miles up and down the gulch. But I got a place for wife to stop and I struck out over the mountains to prospect. I was gone about two weeks and came back with nothing. Then I went to work for wages one week at six dollars per day, then bought a claim on Last Chance gulch, worked it all that summer and did pretty well. In the winter it all froze up and we could not work our diggings. It was very cold in Helena, about 25 or 30 below zero.

But some men whom I worked for on Alder creek heard of me and came thirty miles after me to work for them that winter. They had got another good claim, so I and wife and baby went to Diamond city. This drift was about thirty or forty feet from the surface and it was not cold down there, but very wet and ice water. I had to wear a gum suit all the time. They ran three shifts, eight hours each, and gave each drifter ten dollars per day. They also payed our way back and forth. It was a bad job. Before I could get from the shaft to the house my clothes would always be all ice. It was a very cold place and the hills were so high that you could not see the sun at noon-day.

But at last we got to bedrock and struck it rich. We took out as much as two thousand dollars per day lots of times. Very coarse gold it was; I could often see it washing down after the dirt in the drift. It was a very rich claim for a short time.

In the spring we went back to Last Chance again, but could not do anything until about the fifteenth of May, there was so much ice in the water and the ground.

At last we got to work and did well all summer. But all the whites were selling out to the Chinamen down at that end of the gulch, and wife got afraid to live down there with them. So I had to sell out, too, and it was a very bad sell for me and a good one for John. It was good ground and to-day the N.P.R.R. depot is on the ground that we sold. My brother Charley was with me when we sold out.

I then went to town and bought into another claim. It was good drifting diggings, and I worked all winter but made nothing any good, and worked out the claim. But since then that ground has also sold for a hundred dollars per running foot for building purposes.

When summer came I got me a team and wagon and went out with wife and babies to prospect, and with three other men in another wagon. Of course we could not take the wagons everywhere, but would leave them with one to stay with them. We went a long ways and worked hard, but found nothing for that summer.

We drove around the mountains and over them, first in Montana, then in Idaho, then in Utah and in Nevada. We went to Whitepine. Whitepine was a hard place, no water, no feed, no grub, no money. Then we came back and went to Elko, a new town on the N.P.R.R. From there we went to a new town called Cornacopia, and there I went to work with my team and made a little money pulling logs to build houses with. We did not think much of it and it began to get very cold, so I pulled out for Silver city, without a road and without a guide, I and wife and three babies by this time. On the second night the horses got away from me. I did not know whether they were stolen by Indians or strayed back. But I had to leave the wagon and family and go alone after the team. That was hard to do. When I left them I was afraid I should never see them again. I left with tears in my eyes, but I did not let my wife see it; and she, too, was weeping bitterly, and the babies were asleep in the wagon.

I believe I traveled ten or twelve miles an hour. I went straight across the lava-bed towards Battlecreek, the first watering place, and I found two men on horseback. I asked them to go to where my wife was and stay there over night. They said they would, but that they had no grub with them. I said neither had we anything but a pan of beans... But they went there and unpacked, but did not go near the woman nor say one word to her. About three o'clock she thought that she would take courage and go to see them, and as she got in speaking distance one of them called to her and said, "Your husband is comin with the horses." They saw me about three miles away. Then she sat down and did not go any nearer to them, but stayed there until I came.

I found them in the lava-beds. They had broken their hobbles, and the chain of one horse had hitched in a crevice of the rocks and he could go no farther, and the other would not go without him.

I went and asked the men to come and have some beans with us, but no thank you. I guess the poor men had not seen a white woman in five years and they were ashamed to see one.

It was thirty-five miles from here to Silver city, and the reason we had so little to eat was that flour was forty dollars per sack at Cope and other things just as bad or worse, and at Silver we could get flour for twelve dollars a sack.

Our friends went faster than I could over the rough country with wagon and no road, not even a sign of one. About two o'clock we got into some timber, and about eighty rods up in a gulch we saw a covered wagon and we knew it to be the Rogers boys' wagon, three men that had been with us almost all summer, but had left about one month before. It was then snowing very fast and there was about four inches on the ground. But we went for the wagon and found flour bacon and other things, and Mary was so glad she went to work to get supper. Soon the boys came and were over-joyed to see us, saying, "We have all we need here for all of us;" and they said to Mary, "We will build you a cabin in three days, then one for ourselves."

We got good diggings all around us. The next day I went out with them and panned out some gold. I told the boys the gold was only worth about eight dollars per ounce and would not weigh anything. I soon proved it to them. It discouraged the boys very much. The gold was wire gold, sometimes as long as a pin, but it was more silver than gold.

But we stayed there until the snow went off, and went to prospect every day. We found a large lead on top of the mountain, where all the gold came from, and it became a good quartz mining camp after that, and is to-day called the Red Mountain mines. It is good yet, but no good for us; we did not stick to it.

I went to Silver and went to work for the New York company for six dollars per day; but the boys stayed there until they washed out their dirt as the snow went off, but it did not pay them. Then they came to Silver city, too, but did not stay there but three or four days, then came down to Amilia city, East Oregon.

I worked on until I found I could not get my pay, and then had to leave without it, and came to Walla Walla, Wash. for the second time. But before we got there we got into storms and snow. We stayed at Boise city. It was then a very small place and poor and nothing to do. In Grand Round we came near being blown away, and on the Blue Mountains we had a big snow storm. When we came to Meachum we could not get into the hotel and they did not want me to put my team in the stable, but I did, and wagon too; and wife and babies slept in it all night.

The next morning we started. It did not snow but about six inches on the ground. It was very bad coming down the mountain. Sometimes the horses were ahead of the wagon and other times the wagon was ahead of the horses; but, thank God, we got down all O.K. to the Umatilla river, on the Thomas and Ruckles road, where there was sunshine, good grass, and everything lovely. What a change in about ten miles. It was like the paradise of Eden to us.

We then came to Walla Walla city. It was then yet very small and poor, but there was no snow or cold, although it was the 20 of December, 1869. I could not find a house in town to live in. Then I took my wife and babies out to the fort until I could do better for them. Smith was then taking care of the fort. He sent word and told me to get out, I should not stay there. I told him I should stay until I could do better, and he did not dare to put me out.

There were no soldiers there then; everything was empty, and I went in to one of the houses. The next day again he sent me word to leave the fort. I told him I would not leave until I could do better, and if he caused any trouble with my family while I was away he should suffer for it. At last I found a house on what is now east Main street above Colville. I hired it from O.P. Lacy for ten dollars per month rent. We moved into it to live about the 27 of December, 1869, and wife had a baby on the first day of January, 1870, but it came all O.K. Of course I hurried around and got a lady to come and assist her for eight or ten days, and I began to get a few things to live on. Everything then was very high or dear. I gave five dollars for the first five gallons of kerosene I got. I bought it of the Rame Bros. who were then keeping a store where the First National Bank is now; and three dollars for a little lamp I could now get for twenty-five cents. But flour and anything that was raised here was not worth anything. Furniture I went to work and made and have some of them yet and always shall have some of them.

But I could not find anything to do to make money at; so I took my team and went up Mill creek and bought some wood of John Fall at one dollar per load, which I thought was very cheap. I thought I could get two or three dollars for it in town. But I could not get any money for it, nothing but goods. I then hauled wood enough to Mr. Lacy for one month's rent. So I found it was cheaper for me to turn out my team and do nothing, so I did. But before I turned it out I went down on Hudson Bay or Whitman and bought some wood for myself of Mr. Heale, a very good old man who was then living there. I got enough wood for four dollars to last all winter. I believe Mr. Heale is alive yet somewhere. But the winter was very fine, no cold or snow until the first of March, then it snowed good for about twelve hours, then cleared off fine again.

When the snow came I was out at _____ station going up to the Baker city country to look for more gold again. So I had to come back and stay two weeks longer in Walla Walla. I got snow blind and could not see anything for one week. My wife would not go with me any more. She would not not leave Walla Walla and I did not want her to at that time.

There was another miner with me by the name of Sam Merrett. So we both came back tired and sick. I then made arrangements for wife to stay for the summer and we both went off again. We got to _____ and went to work for wages in hydraulic diggings at six dollars per day. We stayed there while the water was plenty, then went to Morman Basin and worked there while the water lasted, and did well also. What I did there I did with the rocker; there was no water for anything else. Then I went on Powder river and worked a while, but did not find anything to pay; then came back to Walla Walla and stayed about a week with my family.

While there I heard of Cedar creek. Then I struck out for Cedar creek and got there in time to help cut the trail to take up the first grub. We stayed in Cedar creek only five days, but worked hard every day. It was rain or snow all the time, but we got a good shelter in a cedar tree. There were hundreds of them burned out in the middle large enough for eight or ten men to live in and yet the tree was still alive and growing. There were lots of men went crazy there that summer and lots more went hungry.

But we went over another range and found a little gold, and good gold, too. But we could not find enough to pay. We called the place Sunrise. I believe it is working yet. Then we came down to the Missoula river and then struck across the mountains to where Butte city is to-day. We stayed there about one week and found some good looking rock and some very poor placer. There was not one house in Butte then. It was getting cold and stormy then, but we struck out again towards the south and west, but the traveling was horrible. The mountains and canyons we crossed were fearful. At last we got into the Coeur d'Alene range and found some men there at work, but we did not like it and the rock they were taking out did not look good to us. But it turned out good after while. But we found some placer diggings that would pay to the west of it a little way. But we did not stay with it. I wanted to come back to Florence and the other boys wanted to go to Morrages. Then we went for the Coeur d'Alene mission down the St. Joseph gorge. We found the mission in a very lovely country. The church and town were in the center of a very beautiful valley. We stayed there only one night and when the bell rang at six in the morning every Indian dropped to the ground to say his prayers. I thought that was better than we did. They were very kind to us and appeared to be busy at work, all of them, farming and making shingles, clapboards and rails.

This was the first trail we had found since we left the _____ river, about two hundred miles through the mountain range. From here we got a good trail to Lewiston, and then to Florence. Here I wanted to stop, but the other two boys had about seventy-five miles to go yet to get to Meranges, but they went right on. It was now gettin late, short days and cold nights.

But I did not know Florence. I left here in '62. It was now '70. Eight years before the ground was all turned bottom side up for ten or twelve miles around, but I thought I made money here once and I could again. And before I got to the town I ran across a man who wanted to trade me some ground for one of my horses. I went to see the land and went to prospect on it. It had been worked some. As soon as I found it was all O.K. I made the trade and went to work there, and then with pan and rocker. There was no water for anything else and very little for that. But Dr. Walker went out rejoicing on the horse and I was also well pleased with the trade.

I had left this place about eight years before. There were then five thousand men there, and it was one of the best camps in the world and had the most money taken out of it in the shortest time; but now there were only about fifty men in the camp, and they were burning up houses for firewood that it took five thousand dollars to build, and some of them more than that. The ground I now bought was some of the first found. It was the Discovery claim and went by the name of the Pioneer gulch.

I went to work and dug out the bedrock and wheeled it to the water and rocked out about three hundred dollars in about three weeks. I used all the water there was and it began to freeze very hard. So I layed over my claims and came again to Walla Walla, where I called my home, and it was really the first home I ever had.

I came down and bought some lots of Mr. Baker and built us a little house and did some work about town, helped Charley Shobat to put up ice, and planted lots of grape vines, and in the spring I worked on gardens and built fences and began to get acquainted with the people. The lots I bought were due west of Baker school house, where Mrs. William Kirkman lives now.

In May I went back to Florence again on the same ground and went to work on Wildcat with my partner, Ch. Palmer, on ground sluice and did well all summer, and left lots of ground for another summer.

We came to Walla Walla again to spend the winter. This time I could get all the work I could do. I planted all those trees which are now around the Baker school. Mr. Ceech, Mr. Cook, Dr. Day Williams were the directors. There were trees then put all around, but when the new house was built more than half of them were taken up to make a play ground for the boys. When the old house was sold to Mr. Webber I cut it in two and moved it away for Mr. Webber, and he made dwelling houses out of it. Then they began to build the brick house.

But I went to the gold mines some of every summer for the first five summers and then worked around town the balance of the time. In '76 and '77 I did not go away. In '79 the siwashes got on the war-path and lots of the boys from town went after them. I did not go.

In the mean time the upper country had begun to settle up around Colfax and Four Lakes and Spokane. M.G. Havermale and M.E. Halder had gone to Spokane Falls and taken up a homestead, and Dr. Burch, his daughter, and three babies went up to see them, and a fine looking lady was with them, who became the wife of Sheriff Jim Thompson afterwards, and is yet in Walla Walla city, now keeping a first-class boarding house.

While they were up there the Indians broke out and all outside had to fly for safety. Dr. Burch did not know how to get his family home, and did not have courage enough to go after them himself. He sent one man and team once and he went as far as Colfax and then came back and told Burch that no one could go to Spokane. One morning I met Burch in the street almost crying. I asked him the trouble. He says, "My wife and babies. I am afraid the Indians got my wife and family. I cannot send for them nor hear from them."

I said, "Dock, go get them yourself."

"I cannot," he said; "I have not the courage and if I did go I know I should never come back."

I said, "Dock, what will you give me to go?"

"Anything you ask," he said, "or all I've got you can have to get me my family."

"Well, Dock, " I said, "get me a good team and I will get your wife and family in six days."

The doctor brightened up and went to Mr. Small's stable and asked for a team to go to Spokane Falls, "and the best team you have." Mr. Small said, "It is risky business; but give me five hundred dollars for surety and you can have one; but who will drive it?"

Burch said, "This man here,"—looking at me.

Mr. Small said, "Well, Berryman, if you risk yourself you can get the best team in this town. When do you want it?"

"Right now," I said; "I will go home and get some grub and bedding and camp on Snake river to-night."

I went home and told my wife. She got very cross and said I should not go and should have no bed nor grub. But I got ready and Burch came with the team and a light hack. By this time she felt pretty bad and was crying. But I jumped in the hack, saying to Burch, "If I do not come back with your wife and family you must take mine." She said, "You will leave me for Mr. Burch, will you?" I sang out goodbye and away I went.

I got to Texas ferry by night and stayed there all night. I took the team away from the ferry to get grass. There was no feed there, only what I brought with me.

In the morning a white man and his squaw came in from the Rock creek country saying the whites all had to leave. They had some hogs with them and had been traveling all night. They told me I had better go back, and so did the ferryman. I was well acquainted with him. But I told them I did not believe the siwashes would hurt me, and so went on by Rock creek. There was a man killed in his cabin the night before and the Indians had got his horse. All the settlers had gone into a little log fort and got their grub with them. But I went on to Rebel Flat. There I found a barn and house and lots of feed and grub all deserted. I unhitched and stayed all night and took some feed with me for the team when I left.

I got to Hangman creek and met lots of siwashes on the road. I called to them and asked what the trouble was. "All Boston six no kumtux, pale face no good." But I called again and they said they were going to help Joseph. So I went on rejoicing.

About four o'clock I got in sight of Spokane and found about three or four hundred Indians on the ground having a big pow-wow with the agent, Gary, Moses and two or three others. I told them what I wanted and Old Moses said, "You can take away all you please, but bring none back." So I did not stay long.

Going toward the river I could see someone coming from the island in a boat, get on the land and run towards the hack and was ready to jump in the hack and give me a royal welcome. This was once in my life when a woman was glad to meet me. She did not know who it was, but knew it was someone after her and she had dreampt the night before that it was me coming after her, and she made sure it was so. Her father, mother and Mr. Glover, and another whose name I do not now remember, but I believe he is there yet, were all glad to see someone from the outside. Mrs. Burch wanted to start back that night, but I said, "No, the team must rest to-night and get something to eat." She said, "There is not a thing in this place a horse can eat, for you see the Indian horses have eaten up every living thing." But I stayed and got supper and then took the team away up the river about three miles till I found some grass. Of course I told them what I was going to do, saying I would be back at daylight. They said they were afraid they would never see me again. But I had good luck and found good feed and lots of it. I did not sleep much.

I hitched up in the morning and on going to camp or to where they were, two or three Indians ran out against me and wanted whisky, taking hold of the team. I told them I had none. They said I must get some for them or I should not go on. They said then that they would give me twenty dollars for two bottles, but I would not. I told them to get in the hack and I would drive them up to the Mission, but no. They then said they would give me the woman for one bottle of whisky and wanted me to take her, and she began to beg me to take and get the whisky by and by, but all was no use. I had to drive off at a gallop and left them hanging to the team.

But I got to the camp and all were waiting and more than glad to see me. We got a good breakfast and were soon loaded up and away. We took the two ladies and three children and Glover and the rest of them stayed there. They felt much better after I talked to them a while. I made them think it was all right and no danger.

We had no trouble through the day, but the ladies were very fearful. We camped for dinner at Oxes and at night again at a farm house on Rock creek. They were all gone for fear of the Indians. The two ladies slept in the barn on the hay and I slept near the door.

At daylight we got breakfast and started off. We came to Snake river at Texas ferry very late, but Weller, the ferryman, got up and made us welcome, you bet and told them that he never expected to see me nor the team again. I had brought some feed with me this time from Pine creek and Weller had got a little hay from somewhere, so we all did well.

At daylight again we were getting ready, and as soon as we got on the south side of the river my friends began to feel happy and safe, and not until then. They were joyful all that day, and we got to Walla Walla about five o'clock that evening. That made Dr. Burch happy once more, and I was glad to see them meet; it did me good, too. Mrs. Burch always called me her savior after that and she said she did not think she could have lived another day if someone had not come for her. But since then she went there to live again and is there yet and has good property in that city, and her father, Mr. Havermale, got rich there and died about one month ago. Such is life in the far west. That was one good man. He used to preach for us in Walla Walla before he went to Spokane Falls. He was a grand man also.

In '78 I was made street commissioner of Walla Walla city, the first that ever was, and I suppose had more trouble than all that came after me, because I had to break the hard crust. I put the first cross walks in town and straightened out Main street and graded down Second street.

Jim McAuliff was then Lord Mayor of the city and John Justice, Marshall, F. Stine, W.P. Winans, Geo. Stuett and M. Coaloff were the city counselmen, and Mr. Reynolds the banker, and he was a good one, too. T.H. Brents was then city attorney and before then.

I did well in Walla Walla city, but my family had very poor health and I then began to think about moving and finally concluded to dig for water and found it, and loaded out here on the old Colville road twelve miles north of Walla Walla on what is now known as Berryman. After a while we got a railroad, then a grain station, then a Post Office, then a telephone. It was a very pretty place to live and a good climate, and we had the best of health, although we had the sad misfortune to bury three sons grown to manhood, one with stomach trouble and two with typhoid fever, and had one married daughter die in Plaines, Montana, Mrs. Hartman, leaving four children.

Now during this time I did not give up nor stay away altogether from the gold fields. After the boys grew up I began to go again and hunt for some more new country and new gold fields. I have found no new placer mines but I did find the Buffalo Hump, a very rich group of quartz; but it did me no good. Being too generous and believing everyone to be truthful, I was swindled out of the whole thing. I found there was very little prospecting done since '61 and '62. I can find our blazes and our marks all through the mountains of Idaho, and I think I shall try it again, if I live, in a short time. Last summer I was out with my youngest son up about the Hump and found some good rock which came from some rich lead not far from where we found it.

I have been back east twice on the train since living on the farm. We were the first to settle in those bunch-grass hills and the first to find the old government surveys and the corner stakes. It was pretty hard to do. We made many new roads around those hills which were then covered with bunch-grass. But before we settled here I rode all over the upper country, from here to the Columbia Bend, and from there to Spokane Falls, and in Paradise valley and in St. Mary's and St. Joseph. I found lovely country, but very cold and frosty nights in summer and longer winters and more mud than we get here.

Al R. Hawk

*The Hawk family traveled over the
Oregon Trail in 1852, part of the way with some Mormons
emigrating to Salt Lake from Nauvoo, Illinois.
An unusual feature of this overland trip was an
unsuccessful attempt at floating down the Snake River
in a boat constructed from the wagon
box of their prairie schooner.*

On the first day of March, 1852, the Hawk family, consisting of father, mother and six boys, of which the writer was the eldest, then not 13 years of age, and Melvin F., the baby, less than two years, started from DeKalb County, Indiana, in company with Samuel Russell and family for Oregon. We were also accompanied by Elliot Cline, a kind friend, who shared with us the hardships of that tedious trip. Mr. Cline settled at Dungeness in 1853 and died a few years since.

Our wagons were well constructed for a hard journey. Our teams were oxen, three to four teams to each wagon. We frequently used cows under the yoke also. Our journey through Indiana and Illinois was not pleasant, the weather being cold and the snow plentiful. When we reached the Mississippi we laid over about three weeks in order to rest our teams, as corn was plentiful and cheap. We wished to cross the river at this point but it was impossible on account of so much ice. To continue the journey we had to follow down the river until we could find a suitable place to cross.

The ground was thawing out very fast, and the back water from many places in the river made our progress very slow. We finally succeeded in making a crossing at Fort Madison, and after leaving that place we headed for Cainsville on the Missouri River. The trip across Iowa was just as bad as it could be. It was hard wheeling on account of the mud, and very tiresome walking. We fell in with a large train of Mormons from Nauvoo on their way to Jordan-Salt Lake. The Mormons were very poor hands with oxen. When they would get in a bad place the men and women would get on each side of the train and scare them out of it if possible. My father often helped them out of difficult places.

We arrived at the Missouri River the latter part of April and found about two thousand emigrants waiting their turn to cross the river. It was a terrible rush, and many a squabble took place with the ferrymen, as all wanted to get across first. A little incident occurred while we were waiting our turn to cross, this is still fresh in my memory. A drunken Indian came into our camp and seeing one of my brothers sitting on a chair, holding the baby, dumped them out of the chair and attempted to occupy the vacant seat, but his head came in contact with an iron fire-shovel in the hands of my father that almost would upset his dissipated career.

The river at this place was dangerous, being full of snags and driftwood, which made it very difficult and dangerous to cross with those poorly constructed flatboats. I saw two or three boats strike a snag and go bottom up, men and cattle struggling together in the swift current. One fellow got on a snag, but the thing kept flopping up and down so that it was a hard thing to hang on to, but as it was the only thing within his reach, except muddy water, he managed to stay by it until his friends got a rope to him and he was soon landed safe on shore. Before we got across another incident occurred that might have caused the death of a good many people. It seems the Indians on the opposite side of the river were trying to communicate with their friends on our side.

We could see the people plainly passing back and forth by the campfire on the opposite side of the river and the people on our side came to a hasty conclusion that the Indians were killing and scalping all the pilgrims on the other side. In order to deter the Indians from that unpleasant amusement, the excited mob on our side commenced shooting across the river. I don't suppose there was as much powder burned in as short a time at the battle of Bull Run as there was on the banks of the Missouri on that dark night. It was a terror. Everyone who had a shooting iron was doing his level best. It was a perilous undertaking to attempt to cross the river after dark but a company of twenty-five or thirty made the attempt, and our Mr. Cline was one of the first to volunteer his services. They succeeded in getting across but it was quite a difficult task to get the men on our side to stop shooting in order to give the brave boys in the boat a chance to make a landing. They soon discovered the mistake and returned. No one was hurt. Mr. Cline said afterwards that when he got across the river that night he felt like cleaning out all the Indians on the plains. We crossed the river on the fifth day of May. A great many families that knew of the difficulty that father had with the Indian on the Missouri side were afraid to travel with us unless organized in a large train for better protection against the Indians, as an Indian never forgets an injury and they would try to get all our scalps. We organized a company of eighty wagons. James Allen was elected captain and the train was named the Washington Union. Mr. Allen died in Olympia some years ago. We soon discovered that it was not very pleasant to travel in such a large body and our family and Russels and two others pulled out to one side and let the large train move on ahead. We found it much more pleasant and got along nicely. The only inconvenience we were troubled with was the Indians following and boarding with us, besides stealing anything they could hide under their blankets. It was astonishing how many big chiefs there were among the Indian tribes in those days. A big, painted buck and his squaw would travel for days with a train for what they could get to eat. I saw one big chief come to grief very suddenly one day. The chief's appetite was splendid, and Mr. Pilgrim's provisions were getting low, and in order to get rid of his painted friend, he said he would give him something that would stick to his ribs. He got his Pike County revolver (ox whip) and the way he laid the lash on the salmon-colored hide of that dusky warrior was fun for the audience. After that when an Indian came into camp and demanded food, you would soon see the terror of the plains climbing sage brush on the tip end of an ox whip. It was a cheap diet, and it worked like a charm. I remember an Indian coming into camp very early one morning, and was very anxious to let us know how he had come out second best in a little difficulty he had had with a bad white man and an Allen's pepper box. He must have been a wonderful medicine man to carry off so much lead alive. The pilgrim must have been painfully near his Indian, as his yellow hide showed plainly the marks of every shot.

When we arrived at Shell Creek the Indians had an emigrant train in confusion. They were determined to have a fat cow as toll for the whites crossing their territory. When they had found that they could not get the cow they showed a disposition to fight. One Indian drew his bow on Mr. Cline, but that did not work to the satisfaction of the Indian, as Mr. Cline in short notice had Mr. Indian covered with his trusty rifle and was ready for business. He saw at once that to precipitate a fight would bring death to many of them, as it had to some of their tribe the year before.

I counted a great many skulls lying around on the old camp ground. The trouble was soon settled with the Indians by giving them a few presents. The Indians left and the train went its way.

As the summer advanced water and grass began to get very scarce, and long drives between watering places were the result.

One stretch of about forty miles over a sandy desert, I remember, was a tiresome drive, men, women and children tramping along the hot sand. The poor, sore-footed cattle seemed ready to drop under the yoke. It was pitiful, indeed, and when we reached the water it was a sickening sight to see the number of dead cattle that lay in the stream, but it answered very well to wash the alkali dust out of our throats. Many places the grass had been burnt for miles along the route by mean white traders, in order to get the starved cattle cheap. And many times we were compelled to make long drives from the main road in order to get sufficient food for the stock. It was always necessary to keep a strict watch over the stock during the night to keep them from straying away, or being stolen by the Indians, and it was also necessary to keep one's weather eye peeled for trouble during the day. A sudden fright will sometimes stampede a train in a moment. I saw an Indian one day rise up out of the sage brush and wave a red blanket, and in short order that train was rushing across the country like a tornado. It is astonishing what a lively motion a tired out old work ox can get up in an emergency, after traveling hundreds of miles.

Buffalo in droves often caused trouble of that kind. We never encountered any on the entire trip through the buffalo country, although we could hear great herds of them crossing the road ahead and behind us. We were always in hopes that we might see some of the great American bison, but the desire was never gratified. Antelope was the only game that was plentiful. They were to be seen at all times. Mr. Cline went out one morning to secure an antelope when he was surprised by some Indians, and they relieved him of all the valuables he had with him except his scalp. It was not safe to get too far from the train, as a person didn't know just what moment he was liable to get into difficulty. Many objects along the route appeared to be near, and yet they were many miles away. I have seen parties leave the train in the morning to visit some object that seemed nearby. They would travel for hours and then have to give it up. They seemed to be no nearer the object than when they first started out, and perhaps they would not overtake the train until the following day.

Our course lay along the north side of the Platte River, while many others crossed the river and went up the south side. Many places along the Platte there was no wood, and it made it very inconvenient to cook. As a substitute we used buffalo chips, but they are not as good as oak, or hickory chips.

We experienced one severe rain and wind storm on the Platte. We had just gone into camp, and only had time to stake the wagons down with chains when the storm swept over us. It was first-class in every particular. In a few minutes the country was covered with water. We had to stand on the ox yokes in the tents to keep out the water. But the most disastrous storm that swept through the Platte Valley in 1852 was the cholera. It went through the trains like prairie fires, and left its victims on the plains, in unmarked graves, by the hundreds. I have counted from twenty-five to fifty new graves per day. Our family was indeed fortunate. I was the only one that had an attack of cholera, but, thanks to a kind mother and plenty of cholera medicine, I was pulled through. It was a common thing to see covered wagons standing by the roadside deserted, and many others burned. Ox yokes, chains, bedding, cooking utensils and tons of miscellaneous articles lay scattered along that desolate route. Of the many large families that the cholera attacked that summer, but a few of them reached the promised land of the west entire. I have talked with a great many emigrants that came to this country as early as 1845 and as late as 1860, but can't find any account of such a fearful death rate as there was on the plains in the summer of 1852.

The only redeeming feature of the Platte Valley that I can remember was Chimney Rock. It could be seen plainly for one hundred miles. As near as I can recollect, we were some weeks in sight of that wonderful rock. Independence Rock I call the "bulletin board of the Sweet Water Valley." Thousands of names were to be seen on that rock. It seemed that every emigrant that had a tar bucket left his name and date there.

There were many beautiful sights to be seen on the route through the Black Hills, as well as over the Rockies, for a person that was comfortably provided and traveling for pleasure. It was different with the emigrant as he tramped alongside of his teams day after day nearly choked with dust. His object was to get to the end of the road as soon as possible. The long, tedious trip had soured his disposition so much that the least provocation would cause trouble. Friends that had left the states together, through the slightest cause would separate, perhaps never to meet again. I think it was when we were camped on Snake River that Lou Russell and myself got into a little scratching match and the consequence was that the Russells pulled out and left us and we did not see them again until we met in Portland.

We followed down on the south side of Snake River, but a great many crossed the river and proceeded down on the north side. It was the most treacherous river I ever saw. I have seen the emigrants swimming their horses and cattle across to islands in the stream in order to get better feed, and some of the stock would sink, apparently without a struggle, and a great many men were lost the same way. The under current was fatal in many places and it required a man with nerve to undertake it. We never attemped to cross the river in order to better our condition. As we had been on the trip a long time, our stock of provisions was getting low, and buying anything on the route was simply out of the question. Those that had a quantity of provisions would not sell for fear they would run short themselves. There was nothing to be had at Fort Hall, and that was the only place on the route that we could reach without crossing Snake River. Fort Boise was also on the wrong side of the river for us. At any rate, we never had an opportunity to get any supplies until we reached the John Day's River in Oregon.

Nothing of any importance transpired after leaving Fort Hall until we arrived at Salmon Falls. We camped at the American Falls and saw the Indians spearing salmon by torch light, but at Salmon Falls the Indians caught the salmon with nets.

From this point I would like to be able to give the reader a correct account, in detail, of what we endured in the next four weeks of that perilous trip on Snake River, but it will be impossible, and all that I can do is to write from the imperfect recollection I have of the trip, aided by information that I got from Mrs. Willis Boatman of Puyallup, as told to her by my mother after we arrived in Portland.

There were two miserable white scrubs located at Salmon Falls for the purpose of swindling the emigrants out of their stock. They would induce the pilgrims to sell them their cattle and horses, and convert their wagon beds into boats and float down Snake River to The Dalles, telling them it was a pleasant trip and without danger, and could be made to The Dalles in a short time. What a great relief it was to the tired emigrants to quit the dusty road and take to the water. What a glorious change it would be, and the idea was hailed with delight. We bit like fish.

We converted our wagon bed into a boat, and in order to make it watertight we took the hides from dead cattle, which were plenty, and covered the bottom of the bed. They were stretched on tight, which gave more strength to the bed and kept it perfectly dry inside. Father would not dispose of his team, for he thought if anything should happen to us we would have something left to help us out of our difficulty. So Mr. Cline took the team and running gear of the wagon and hit the trail for The Dalles, where he expected to find us waiting for him. But the fond hopes and pleasure that we expected to enjoy on that boating trip were never realized. How many families had preceded us I can't say. One I do remember—a violinist and his wife. We found, where their life journey had ended: two new graves on the bank of the river, where they had been buried by the Indians. We left Salmon Falls with a full crew. Besides our family of eight, we had Jim Riley and Bob Wallace. We drifted and paddled along where the current seemed the strongest, and were getting along very nicely as Riley remarked, on a four-mile current. All seemed to be perfectly satisfied with the boat in preference to the wagon until we got into quick water, when the river seemed to stand pretty nearly on end for about half a mile. It was impossible to make the shore. The boat and all hands were at the mercy of the angry waters. But we shot through those waters so quick that it didn't give us time to realize the danger we were in. From then on the boat hugged the shore pretty closely. We now began to discover the disadvantages of river travel. The river was a continuation of rapids for miles, and it required the greatest care to keep the boat from swamping. And then again for miles it would be without a ripple and but little current. At times we would be near the road and could see along the emigrant trail. What a blessing it would have been to us if we had stopped when relief was near, but we kept on, drifting nearer trouble every minute.

The river seemed to narrow down to half its width, and the current became very swift and terminated in some very dangerous rapids. Mother and children were put ashore to get along the best we could, while the men, with ropes, let the boat down over the rapids, and from then on we had only one day of pleasant boating. It was along a low, flat country, and the footing on the banks was good. One day a brother and I were enjoying a walk along the bank which was a great pleasure after being cramped up in the boat so much, and we were, boy-like, fooling along gathering shells and other curiosities. In the meantime the boat had got quite a start of us, and in looking back up the river, to our great surprise, we saw three Indians in hot pursuit of us. Prickly spears and brush didn't deter us from making the best kind of time until we reached the boat. On relating the circumstances of the pursuit, the men got their guns in readiness in case the Indians showed a disposition to be hostile, but they never put in an appearance. I think they took in the situation from some friendly bush on the river bank and gave up the chase. The river soon made a change for the worse. Going into camp that night at the head of a very swift rapid father killed a large salmon with the axe and I think it was the fattest fish of any kind I ever saw. They must have been land-locked salmon, for no salmon that ever left the sea could climb the Shoshone Falls. The following morning in making a hasty examination of the river below, it was found to be very bad. However, the men started with the boat and mother and children clambered along the steep hillside and among the rocks the best we could.

The banks became so steep in places that it was impossible to manage the boat from the shore, so the men had to take to the water and in many places it was from knee to neck deep. The men were compelled to manage the boat that way for days, and over many difficult places we had to take everything out of the boat and let it down empty. Quite often we had to take the boat out and carry it around dangerous places.

An old Indian and his two boys were our only companions. They became very attached to us. In about ten days, as near as I can remember, our hearts were made glad by the appearance of Mr. Cline and the team. It was the work of a short time to get the water-soaked bed on the wagon again and rolling over the prairie, and we were as happy as a picnic party.

We had lost much valuable time, and, as it was getting late in the season, it stood us in good hand to make the best time possible. To add further to our over-stock of misfortunes, father was taken down with rheumatism, brought on by being so much in the water in Snake River. He was not able to help himself until we arrived at The Dalles, where he could get some medical assistance. Starvation now began to stare us in the face. The provisions were about gone and no possible chance for us to ride, as the team was about played out, and it was with difficulty that they could haul the wagon, father and the baby, and what few traps we had left. Mother walked, day after day, with us, and made no complaints. In order to get some relief we would all get behind the wagon and hold on; the wagon cover would give us some protection from the hot sun.

From the time our provisions gave out it was three weeks before we reached the John Day's River. There we met the relief train sent out with supplies for the starving emigrants, but all that we could get from the train was ten pounds of flour, for which we paid $10. Without any further trouble, in due time, we reached The Dalles, where the cattle and wagon were sold, and in the course of a week father was able to be on his feet again. In the meantime mother was baking pies and cakes for the hungry pilgrims at which she did a rushing business.

We were conveyed on a large batteaux down to the Cascade Falls. The portage we crossed on a car hauled by a mule. At the lower landing we took passage on the steamer Multnomah for Portland. It was about the tenth of November when we reached Portland, having been almost nine months on the trip.

During the entire trip, after crossing the Missouri River, my mother seemed to stand the many hardships we had to endure better than any of us, but soon after we arrived in Portland her health gave way completely. She always complained of her head. The fall she got on Snake River was no doubt the cause of her trouble. She died the 12th of January, 1853.

After mother was quietly laid to rest there must be homes provided for us children. Father succeeded in securing us comfortable places to live. He came to the Sound in the summer of 1853 and remained until the spring of 1854, when he went to Astoria, where he married his second wife. He returned to Olympia in August, I think, and located on a claim about six miles east of that city, where he resided until his death, which occurred on the 19th of March, 1883, surrounded by a large family of children.

James M. Cornwell

Born in Indiana in 1834,
Cornwells' family moved to Illinois in 1839.
His mother died in 1843 and James and his seven
brothers were parceled out to separate homes. In 1852
James with his brother, nineteen year old Francis,
worked their passage across the plains to Oregon.
Their wagon train paused at Ft. Boise short of
provisions and the boys went on alone
almost meeting starvation before
reaching the Dalles.

They started on foot from their Iowa—(we were about to write "home," but they had none) with five dollars between them, for crossing the plains to either California or Oregon. They cared little to which of those regions they wandered, for it was the country where the sun set that they were seeking. Upon their arrival at a town on the Mississippi river, James obtained a situation as teamster for an emigrant, who proposed to furnish him food for his work until they reached St. Joseph, Missouri. In addition, the brother was permitted to put his little bundle of clothing in the wagon; and what was left of the five dollars went for crackers for that brother to eat along the road. At St. Joseph both brothers obtained positions as teamsters with a train that was bound for Oregon. They were to receive their food on the route as pay for their work, but, they were to continue service one month after reaching the Coast, to pay for the privilege of driving team the six months that it took to reach that place. There was a great deal of sickness that season among the emigrants, and the new graves along the overland road became thicker as the Cascade range was approached. Young James was taken with the mountain fever after crossing the Platte river, and a month passed during which he narrowly escaped adding one to the numerous unknown graves scattered along the route. The party with whom these lads were employed, were professional men, coming with their families, and they arrived late in the season at Fort Boise short of provisions. Short, because they had delayed along the way, and had disposed of provisions that had been provided in the start. The owners of the trains became frightened, fearing starvation on the way, and proposed to the teamsters to leave them, go on ahead, and look out for themselves, eight of them consenting to do this, the two lads being of the number. They left Fort Boise on foot with three days rations, to reach civilization on the Coast, and the nearest certain point to obtain food, was the Dalles, over 300 miles away. Chance opportunities for procuring something to eat was their only reliance for getting through, and unless obtained on the way, death from starvation was a certainty. It was a forlorn hope, moving, that October in 1852, with short intervals for rest, night and day while along the old emigrant road, struggling in the face of famine, in a wilderness, weary, footsore, heart sick and desolate; their only hope of rescue lay in the accumulated store of vitality in their systems, nourished by the least possible amount of food that would prevent its utter exhaustion. Days passed, nights came and went, while their store of food was used up, and as they came down the west slope of the Blue mountains, nearly famished, to Meacham's creek, they came upon an emigrant camped near the water. He was another that misfortune and sorrow had claimed as their own. Along the road between him and the States his family were scattered, one here, another there, buried by the wayside. His poor worn out cattle could go no further, and his rations were exhausted. This famine-wrecked emigrant, aided by the forlorn hope, killed one of those "leankine" that had traveled over the plains, and they feasted upon the dried up sinews of that poor ox, as the gods might have feasted upon ambrosia. Again the journey was resumed, and the eight moved on. One-half of the distance lay still beyond them, while the chance for passing over it grew less and less. Why follow them step by step? Can not one imagine what it must have been for those two boys, who struggled on through the days with hunger gnawing at their vitals, with weariness laying hold of their bodies with a strength that made every fiber ache with pain? At length, in the night, Alkali flat was reached, east of the John Day river, and they all started to cross it. Finally one lay down exhausted, and the balance moved on and left him, then another and another yielding, dropped out of the ranks of the forlorn hope, until but the two young Cornwells, of them all, were left. These two, hand in hand, aiding each other, staggered and struggled on until Jasper spring was reached.

After quenching their thirst, the two lay down to sleep on the ground, without a blanket to protect them from the night chill of October. In the morning they pushed forward to the river, where an Indian was met, who had a fish that would weigh about one pound. For this, James gave the native his shirt, and thought himself fortunate to have one with which to buy a further lease of life. They remained during the balance of the day at the John Day ford, after crossing it; but night found them struggling, half dead, along the road that led over hills swept by a cold fierce wind that chilled them to the heart. Like that terrible night on the alkali plains, they held each other by the hands, and struggled on till the flickering lamp of hope went out. The feeling came over them at last, that life was scarce worth purchasing with such a struggle. The elder advised that both lie down and yield the contest, and had they done so, a few short hours would have been enough to enable those penetrating winds to end it. There seemed no use in further resistance, for possibly, yes probably, there was no one to help them within fifty miles; still they pushed forward, staggering before the blast and reeling along, first to one side of the road, and then the other, like persons drunk. Suddenly James, in casting a hopeless longing look ahead, thought he caught the glimmer of a light, but his brother could see nothing, and they concluded that it was a delusion of the bewildered brain. Still it was a transient stimulus that caused them to hold out a little longer. They finally gave up; there seemed no use in attempting to go further, and they stopped there in the road. The wind wailed around them, the darkness shut them out from the world, despair enveloped them like a great wave, and the two lads believed they had found the grave where their hopes in the world ended, when suddenly that light flashed again, clear and distinct, and then disappeared. Both saw it this time; it was certainly no delusion, and hope was again revived, for human beings were near at hand. They managed to reach the locality of the light, and found an emigrant, with the surviving members of his family, encamped in a nook sheltered somewhat from the wind. They were stopping for the night in a little tent, and had been for a number of days living on gruel made from corn meal, of which they had so little that none could be spared the two starving boys. The mother of the little family gave them a bed quilt to sleep in, and they lay down on some boxes in the wagon, and passed the remaining hours before day, gnawed by the pangs of hunger, and chilled to the marrow with cold. During the latter part of the night, James became partially delirious from the long continued sufferings, but the warmth of the coming morning, with its bright sun, brought back the wandering mind to realities. Through that day they pushed on, then came another cheerless night, but with the morning an Indian came to camp with a rotten fish that he had found on the bank of the Columbia, and James gave him a knife for it, when the two lads made a breakfast of this last resort from starvation. At the crossing of the DesChutes river, the boys gave an old pistol for being ferried across, and to their great joy and surprise, were overtaken at this place by the six comrades supposed to be lying dead on the alkali flat, where they had given out. Among the whole party there was not sufficient means to pay for ferrying the new comers; and the boatman finding such to be the case, demanded a shirt, and, as none were willing to go naked for the sake of paying his demand, he threatened to turn the Indians loose and have them all massacred, but the threat failed to increase the number of Shylock's shirts. The Dalles were at length reached, where the party, again numbering eight, set out in search for something to eat. They found that want of money was likely to leave them still starving, when it was decided that James Cornwell should go to the commissioners, stationed there by the people of Oregon for the purpose of relieving destitute emigrants, and beg provisions for all of them. He went to the cabin where the coveted food was stored, and learned that a scant supply only was on hand. He was told that because of this, it was impossible for them to deal out rations except to orphans and widows who had lost their parents or husbands on the way overland. This was a discouraging state of things but hunger made young Cornwell desperate, and, looking the man in the face, he said, "If there is an orphan between the two oceans it's me;" and the commissioner taking a long look at his gaunt, youthful, emaciated, shadowy appearance, replied, "I guess that's so." This lucky hit procured him *two pounds* of flour, that, being made into bread by a kind emigrant woman, was divided among the eight.

Chapter

Indian Wars

"We only did our duty and no more."
A.G. Lloyd

*L*and was generally the most valuable possession of a settler. A fundamental difference existed between the Indians and whites in their perception of the land and its ownership. Unlike the settlers, who wanted individual ownership, the natives considered the land to be communal, a natural resource to be used by all when needed. Each tribe roamed throughout their territory living where the food and water was plentiful and the climate the most moderate. As the influx of emigrants continued to arrive in the Pacific Northwest and they began to scatter out from the Willamette valley, it was inevitable that the two antagonists would eventually come to conflict.

In 1853, Washington Territory was created from the old Oregon Territory and Isaacs Stevens was appointed its governor. On his way West to accept his position, Stevens, who had also been appointed the Territory's Indian Superintendent, polled the Indians on the east side of the Cascades as to whether they would be willing to sell their lands. Receiving what he considered an affirmative answer, Stevens invited the Indians to a council to draw up treaties. Chief Kamiakin, of the Yakimas, selected an old Indian council grounds, located in the Walla Walla valley, as the site for the talks to be held in May of 1855.

At the treaty council after much oration and heated talk, all of the Chiefs, excepting Kamiakin, were persuaded to sign the agreements which turned over ownership of the Inland Northwest to the whites. A.B. Roberts, a volunteer soldier in the wars that followed the treaty signing, states that another council was held after Governor Stevens had left the area, and all the Chiefs from the Inland Empire were present. Kamiakin tried to persuade the others to join the Yakima tribe in war against the invaders. Peo-Peo-Mox-Mox, the head Chief of the Walla Walla was willing to join him, but the Umatillas and Nez Perce would not break the treaty. How did Roberts come to know about this secret council? Well, he claimed that the Indians told him . . . Let's join the old Indian fighter as he remembers an incident that happened near The Dalles at the start of the Yakima War in 1855.

A.B. Roberts

*Roberts, a veteran of the 1855-56
Yakima Indian Wars, tells about
his experiences as a volunteer soldier.*

This story is not intended to be a history of the Indian wars of the Northwest Country, but only a statement of the facts, the causes and the results of the most serious conflicts which had occurred between the races during the settlement of this interesting country by the white men. It is a fact to be noted, that there were more wars and conflicts between the races during the settlement of Oregon than in any other portion of the United States during the settlement of the Far West.

Beginning with this Cayuse war in 1847 we find the two Rogue river wars, the great Yakima war that covered all of Oregon and Washington, the Modock war, the Joseph war (Nez Perce) and the Bannock war.

The greatest of all these wars was the Yakima war of 1855-56.

Previous to this time the Oregon and Washington settlements were confined to the West side of the great range, the Cascades, but in the winter of 1854 the administration took up the idea of opening the Inland Empire or the intermountain country for settlement and accordingly called all the Indians east of the Cascades and north of the Blue Mountains and as far east and to include the Nez Perces to meet in council in Walla Walla in June for the purpose of making treaties for the purchase of their lands. To this council the Government sent commissioners consisting of Governor I.I. Stevens of Washington; General Palmer, Superintendent of Indian Affairs of Oregon, and Colonel Cummins of the army.

The council was fully attended, the meeting place being exactly where the city of Walla Walla now stands. To be more particular, it began on the north side of Mill Creek about where the N.P. depot stands and after a few days was moved to the south side to about the grounds occupied by the Y.M.C.A. building and the Christian church, where the treaties were completed and fully signed, excepting one only of all of the great chiefs. To this one name "hangs a tale" worthy of being told at another time.

Now, to continue this story we must explain the facts that lead up to the ignoring of the great treaties of Walla Walla in June, 1855.

Soon after treaties were signed settlers began to locate in the fine valleys and the Indians began to realize that the greatest portion of their domain was now in the hands of the white man.

Years ago the West side from California to British Columbia had been relinquished and now the intermountain country was gone.

The first payment was to be made in cash the following September, and for 20 years other annuities were to be paid in cash. At once steps were taken by the Indians to ignore those treaties, but the other party—the white man—was not called to their councils. But the Chiefs of all the tribes of the Coast country and all the East side were finally assembled on the Umatilla in the early part of September and at that grand council representing all of that country in which settlement had begun it was agreed that once more a united effort would be made to drive out the white settlers and a refusal of the payments and the ignoring of all treaties would be made. Only the great War Chief Lawyer and his sub-Chief Lapi of the Nez Perces and Winumsnoots and Timothy of the Umatillas held out, and through their great influence over their people prevented those two tribes from joining in the greatest of hostilities known as the Yakima war of 1855. It is awful to think, that if those two, the most powerful of the Inland tribes had joined with the great combine of hostile Indians, what the result might have been.

How did I come into possession of these "state secrets"? I chanced to spend many years of my life in the most intimate and friendly terms with the two leading Chiefs referred to, both of them being Christian gentlemen, educated by the lamented Dr. Whitman, and it may be here remarked that the works of that martyr subsequently saved not only Oregon to the United States, but saved the unprotected settlements of that period from total annihilation by the combined tribes.

But to take up the ignoring of the treaties of 1855.

The intentions and results of that council of Chiefs on the Umatilla were not published and the first that our people or Uncle Sam knew of them was when the Government agent, Mr. A. J. Bolan, who was sent in September to the Yakima country to pay to Kamiakin and his sub-chiefs of that tribe their cash annuity which was due at that time as per treaty stipulation, when he was foully murdered and his money taken, and about the same time Colonel Nathan Olney, agent for the Cayuses, Walla Wallas and others, went to those tribes for the same purpose and he was told in plain language that the treaties were ignored and that they would not kill him but to take back the money and immediately remove all of those settlers who had taken claims in the Walla Walla Valley, which he did at once.

Now the commanding officer of the U.S. troops at Fort Columbia (The Dalles) sent Major Haller with the majority of the troops under his command over to the Yakima country to bring in the murderers of Agent Bolan and he was met by Kamiakin, and his troops completely routed and their horses and outfits captured and on foot and destitute they reached The Dalles and the Indians at their heels firing across the Columbia into the villages, when the Oregon volunteers came to their relief.

Yes, the ball was opened and the greatest Indian war of the Pacific Coast had its first battle and the enemy was victorious.

Now the Governor of Oregon Territory was called upon for volunteers and at once within twenty-four hours after the call was posted in Portland 95 young men left their homes and employment and were at The Dalles to drive back old Kamiakin and his victorious warriors.

It is no part of this narrative, but I just stop long enough to say that we have never received the pay offered by our Governor and that we are now asking Congress to place us on the pension roll on the same footing with those who served in other Indian wars of the Rebellion or Civil War.

The object of this story is to tell the awful experience and miraculous escape of an old friend of mine by the name of Ferguson (Old Shake) who with a Mr. Ives, was bringing on some beef cattle for the use of Major Haller's command. Mr. Ferguson or "Old Shake" as he was usually called, was one of those characters frequently found in the Far West frontier. He was a man of fine education and much ability, one of those who had seen better days. But the "call of the west" induced him to join the pioneers who made the trails and subdued the hard conditions that confronted those who volunteered to develop the farthest and fairest of Uncle Sam's great domain. We find him in 1855 at The Dalles, Oregon, a place where no man had the right to a home under any government land laws; at The Dalles they were merely knocking at the door of the great Inland Empire and helping to open it and doing the dangerous work to prepare for a more timid generation. And so in line with his duties it was necessary for him to attempt the hazardous work of bringing up supplies to a command of government troops who had gone to the savages to capture the murderers of a government agent.

So those two men pushed on with their small herd not having any idea of the fate that had befallen Major Haller's command. They were met by a band of hostile Indians who swooped down upon them and only the speed of their mounts made it possible for them to save their scalps from the bloody knife of superior numbers. They fled across to a level open plain bordered on one side by a deep canyon with heavy pine timber and small brush up to the edge of the level plain. On they flew; the Indians not stopping for the beef cattle but only intent on securing a couple of scalps. "Old Shake" was riding a fine mule but it was not as speedy as Ives' extra fine saddle horse. Shots were being fired after the fleeing whites and gradually the Indians were overtaking "Old Shake" who had given up all hope of escaping. As bullets were flying in his vicinity he yelled to his companion who was some distance in advance 'that's a good shot' and at the same time he threw himself from his mule. The Redskins hotly pursuing Ives and thinking "Old Shake" was good and dead paid no more attention to him.

Finding himself in a bushy canyon "Old Shake" easily rolled into cover where he was safe for a time as the Indians after their fruitless chase for Ives had no means of locating him. I say fruitless chase; they followed him until their horses gave out; Ives' horse was too fast for them.

Mr. Ives reached The Dalles in safety after a ride of two days and two nights and reported the death of "Old Shake" and the circumstances accompanying it. "The Indians attacked us," he said, " and captured the cattle; they overtook "Old Shake" on his mule; that as he fell from his mule he hollered 'I am shot.' Thinking 'Old Shake' was done for the Indians turned their attention to me but owing to my fine mount I got away from them."

About the same time came the report of Major Haller's defeat and that he was returning with his demoralized troops. An Indian war was on and Governor Currie of Oregon territory was called on for a regiment of mounted volunteers, and, in less than three days from the call, Company A, of which I was a member was at The Dalles where we found Major Haller. He was on the north side of the Columbia not having as yet been able to cross over to the post. The hostile Indians were at his heels; they made their presence known by firing occasional shots across into the village.

We located a camp near the village and acted as a guard until other companies of volunteers could be raised and pushed to the front. In five or six days the news came that "Old Shake" had made his appearance at Major Haller's camp. Glad to learn of my friend's escape I secured a canoe and crossed the river to see him. I found him comfortable on a cot in the guard tent where he had crawled on hands and knees the previous night about 2 o'clock; and when he was hailed by the picket on guard who called "who comes there," he answered: "Old Shake." The picket ran like wild to the guard tent and screamed into the sergeant's ears that "Old Shake's" ghost had appeared to him. The sergeant returned with the picket and found Ferguson crawling on the ground as he had been for over a week. I sat by his bedside and listened to the story of his miraculous escape. He told me that as the Indians, some 15 or 20 in war paint, swooped down upon them, they made an attempt at escape by flight; that Ives on a fine horse was gradually gaining on him and the Indians on their ponies were also gaining on the speed of his mule; shots were now being fired at them and some coming dangerously near him he saw that his only chance was to fall from him mount and feign dead. He did so and the enemy rushed on after his partner as he had expected. As soon as they has passed out of sight he rolled into the nearby canyon and hid in the brush. At the creek at the bottom of the canyon he found a trail which he knew would lead to The Dalles and Simcoe trail. He was afraid to follow this trail less his shoe tracks would give him away so he pulled off his shoes and threw them away in the brush. Throwing his shoes away was a mistake as his tender feet became sore and he was unable to walk. But he struggled on for days or mostly nights living on roots and berries and most of the time crawling on his knees--his trousers being "foxed" with buckskin as was the almost universal custom in those days. He came over the little mountain range some 10 miles north of The Dalles and really in sight of that village, and yet he crawled for several days before he reached Major Haller's camp.

From the foregoing story those of the present day can have a glimpse of the work of those real old pioneers who opened up this beautiful Inland Empire.

George Washington Miller

*Mr. Miller relates his story
of the largest battle of the 1855-56
Yakima Indian War which took place in
the Walla Walla Valley in December of 1855.*

I, G.W. Miller, was born in Crawfordsville, Ind., on the 6th day of April, 1830. At the age of 6 years I moved with my parents to Mercer county, Illinois, where I lived at home until I was 21, and learned the trade to plow and hoe corn.

On the 9th of April, 1851, being 20 years of age, I started across the plains with my parents and landed in Linn county, Oregon, twelve miles south of Albany, on the 1st day of September, the same year, being four months and twenty-three days on the road.

In the spring of 1852 I went to the Jacksonville mines and worked that summer, getting home that fall with just about as much as I started with. In the fall of 1852 I located and settled on a donation claim two miles west of where Shedd's station (10 miles south of Albany, Oregon) now stands, and commenced improving and cultivating the same. On the 8th day of October, 1855, I enlisted (as a private) in a company of volunteers, organized at Albany, who elected their officers as follows: Davis Layton, captain; A. Hanan, first lieutenant; John Burrows, second lieutenant; W.G. Haley, orderly sergeant. On the 13th of October we took up our line of march, and were mustered into service in Portland on the 17th day of October, 1855, as Company H, (Linn County, 1st Reg.) Oregon mounted volunteers, second battalion, under command of Major Mark A. Chinn. On our way from Portland to The Dalles we marched by land to the Columbia River, at the mouth of Sandy. There we went aboard the hull of an old steamer, drawn by two tugs, to be taken to the Lower Cascades, but, on account of a dense fog and the inability of the tugs to make much headway, we were landed on an island quite a distance below the Cascades. The part of the river on the Washington side was said to be fordable, but some of the boys in attempting to ford the stream got into swimming water and lost their guns and equipments, but swam to the other shore and secured a small boat to cross the balance of the command and aid in swimming the horses.

From there we marched by land to The Dalles, pitching our tent on Three Mile creek, where we lay awaiting reinforcements.

On the 12th of November, Companies B, H and I, under the command of Major Chinn, took up their line of march for Fort Walla Walla. Pushing forward they reached Wells' Springs (14 miles south of Boardman, Oregon) on the 17th. That night Johnny McBean came into camp as a courier from Narcisse Raymond with a report that Peu-Peu-Mox-Mox had sent a large force of his warriors to watch the movements of the volunteers, and that Fort Walla Walla was already in possession of the Indians, about 1000 strong, and that all the adjacent positions around the fort were in their possession. This information determined Major Chinn to abandon the attempt of reaching that place until reinforcements could be obtained from The Dalles, for which he sent a courier. Next day he pushed forward to the Umatilla river and fortified, picketing in with large split timbers, a stockade 100 feet square, and erected two bastions of round logs on two of the angles, and from rails found there built two corrals for the horses and cattle. This place he named Fort Henrietta, in honor of Major Haller's wife. On the 21st of November, from this point, Major Chinn sent another courier to The Dalles asking for two more companies and artillery to assist him in moving upon Fort Walla Walla.

On the 27th of November Captain Cornoyer, with Company K, arrived at Fort Henrietta to reinforce Major Chinn. On the 29th of November Captains Wilson and Bennett, with Companies A and F, arrived at Fort Henrietta (north side of Umatilla River, across from Echo, Ore.) with Lieutenant Colonel James K. Kelly who took command of the forces at the front. Colonel Kelly, soon after arrival, learned that the Indians were in possession of Fort Walla Walla and its immediate vicinity, with all their available forces. He at once commenced active operation, and on the evening of December 2nd his command moved out from Fort Henrietta, hoping to surprise the enemy at daybreak next morning, but incidental delays of the night's march, caused by a heavy rain until late next morning, prevented their reaching Fort Walla Walla until late in the forenoon, finding the fort pillaged, defaced, deserted and everything of value carried off. The forces remained there to reconnoiter and forage until next morning, when Colonel Kelly, with 200 men, without baggage or rations, marched to the Touchet river, thence up the Touchet to the canyon, to find out, if possible, the location of the Indians. Major Chinn, with the balance of the forces, about 150 men and the baggage, were ordered to the mouth of the Touchet river, there to await orders from the main army.

Colonel Kelly, after reaching the foot of the canyon, sent scouts in advance to look out for prowling bands of Indians. After reaching a point where the hills on either side of a deep canyon shut out the surrounding view the advance guard in approaching the summit espied a party of six Indians in their immediate front, advancing toward them. In an instant they were covered by the guns of the guard and ordered to halt, and one of the party, carrying a flag of truce, proved to be Peu Peu Mox Mox (Yellow Bird). A parley ensued, but it was soon discovered that a large body of Indians were coming from the direction from which the chief had come. A signal was given and the advancing party halted, every one of whom dismounted and stood by his horse.

Then the old chief asked if Nathan Olney, the Indian agent, was with them. Being told he was, he expressed a desire to see him. A messenger was sent back to report what had transpired at the front. The volunteers were halted on the hillside in plain view of the flag of truce, while Colonel Kelly and Agent Olney, with John McBain (John McBean) interpreter, went forward to meet the great Walla Walla chief. When they met, Peu Peu Mox Mox, in an insolent manner, demanded why an armed force had come to invade his country.

Colonel Kelly, answering, said he had come to chastise him and his people for wrongs they had committed. The chief talked about peace negotiations, saying he had committed no wrongs, and that he desired to live in peace with the whites. But Colonel Kelly told him of the pillaging and destroying Fort Walla Walla, the seizing of government property there, the carrying away of the Hudson Bay Company's goods, the burning of the storehouse of Brooks, Noble & Bunford, and appropriating the goods to their own use.

When confronted with these criminal acts he denied having done any of these things, but finally admitted they were the acts of his young men whom he could not restrain. When informed that Howlis Wampum, a Cayuse chief, had testified to seeing him distribute the goods to his people with his own hands, and lay out a great pile of blankets, as an inducement for the Cayuses to join with him in war against the whites, he made no reply, but finally offered to make his people restore the goods as far as they were able, and make payment for the balance.

Colonel Kelly explained to him that this would not be sufficient remuneration, but that his men must come in and give up their arms and ammunition. To this the old chief gave his assent, promising to come in the next day and deliver up their arms and ammunition.

But Colonel Kelly believed from his deportment, that he only desired time in which to make ready for battle, therefore he instructed his interpreter to explain to him distinctly that he could take his flag of truce, and go back to his village and get ready for battle, but by so doing an attack would be made on his village immediately, while, on the other hand, if he and his associates chose to remain with the army until the terms of his proposed treaty were fulfilled, his people would not be molested.

Thus hard pressed the haughty old chief consented to remain as a hostage for the fulfillment of his words, assuring Colonel Kelly that none of his people would remove from their camp during the night, and that he would have his people cook plenty of food for the soldiers to eat next morning.

Colonel Kelly, after marching his force a short distance with Peu Peu Mox Mox, saw he was being led into the canyon. Calling a halt, and holding a short consultation with his officers, he moved back a short distance and camped for the night, without wood, without water and without food, for the reason that he thought it necessary to be cautious when all the surrounding circumstances went to show there was a probability of his having all his forces stationed at different positions in the canyon to cut off retreat.

That evening the old chief asked permission to send one of his men that was taken prisoner with him, to his village to apprise his people of the terms of the proposed treaty, and instruct them to fulfill it. Colonel Kelly granted the request, little thinking he would ever come back, and sure enough he did not. The young Nez Perce that was taken prisoner with him understood their language pretty well, and afterwards related that when that wily old serpent instructed his messenger he told him to tell his women to pack up in haste and go to the mountains.

That night the elements spread their fleecy mantle of white over the thin blankets of the volunteers. During the night the Indians kept shouting messages from the hill tops to the prisoners in camp in a language but little used at that time, and not understood by the interpreter. Next morning another Indian was captured which took the place of the messenger who failed to return the evening before, and the son of Peu Peu Mox Mox was permitted to come into camp and talk with his father. When the two met, the old chief said he wanted his people to come in and make a treaty of peace, but his son said they were waiting for Five Crows to come back before deciding what to do. This proves another fact related by the young Nez Perce prisoner in his narrative to Colonel Kelly after the battle, when he said Peu Peu Mox Mox had sent all his available force of warriors, under command of Five Crows, 60 miles distant to accomplish a feat of prowess over Major Chinn's command at Fort Henrietta. No doubt but the most absorbing thoughts of his mind were that Five Crows would obliterate the little band of volunteers and the soil of Umatilla drink up their blood as it would a shower of rain.

When the volunteers were ready to start to the Indian camp, his whole purpose was delay, he knew that every moment he could delay Colonel Kelly's movements, brought Five Crows that much nearer his relief. He was anxious to delay, saying his people needed time to prepare and cook food for so many soldiers, and he wanted it ready for them to eat, on their arrival at his village. Thus he delayed our movements until nearly noon, when the volunteers made a forward march toward the Indian camp, with a vague hope of having a sumptuous feast on their arrival there; but note their consternation at finding the camp deserted, and only a few Indians to be seen on the surrounding hills, to watch the movements of the volunteers.

This was an exact violation of the treaty of peace, concluded between him and Colonel Kelly on the preceding day, and you will note that every act of his from the time he signed the treaty with Isaac I. Stevens, governor of the Territory of Washington, until the day he fell by the hands of his vigilant guard, showed treachery on his part, and had he been dealt with according to the laws of nations his life would have paid the forfeit.

The command being overcome with hunger, and knowing they could not get a bite to eat until they reached Major Chinn's camp at the mouth of the Touchet River, were soon on the march to that place, arriving there soon after the dusky hues of night had settled down around them. That night one of the prisoners, a large Indian by the name of Wolf Skin, who was very talkative, tried to make his escape by running, but his guard at that time being the fleetest runner in the command, overhauled his prisoner in 100 yards distance and brought him back to camp. After this the prisoners were all tied until morning.

Early dawn revealed the fact that half of Five Crow's army was on the hills surrounding camp, which substantiates without a doubt the narrative related by the young Nez Perce prisoner.

On the morning of the 7th of December, 1855, commenced the battle of Walla Walla. Companies B and H crossed the Touchet and formed in line on the plain; companies I and K soon fell into line, companies A and F being ordered to take charge of the baggage train and prisoners. The Indians had been gathering in considerable numbers on our left and front, and before any movements were made the report of a gun was heard on our left. This seemed to be the signal to charge, as the companies formed in line and dashed forth, opening a heavy fire on the enemy as they ran. A running fight ensued across the hills eastward to the Walla Walla river, the volunteers pursuing the Indians at the top of their speed, shooting whenever an opportunity presented itself. Those having the fastest horses sped away, leaving others behind, until they became widely scattered. The horse I rode was a small, heavy-set cayuse, which seemed, when jumping over the sagebrush, to be going up one side and down the other. The consequences were, I didn't get along as fast as some, but I soon found I was nearing the front from the sound of musketry and the deafening yells of the Indians. The forces of the enemy kept increasing in numbers from the time the skirmish commenced until we reached the La Roche (LaRoque) cabin, on the Walla Walla river, while the forces of the volunteers were growing less. Here the enemy became more stubborn and slow to move along. This gave the volunteers who had been left behind an opportunity to come to the front. The Indians were driven almost at the point of the bayonet only a short distance above the La Roche cabin, two miles below Whitman's station, and eight miles from the place where the fight commenced.

By this time their whole force became engaged in the battle, and estimates were made by different ones, ranging from 600 up to 2000. My own estimate, put down in my diary at the time, was 1000. Colonel Kelly, in his official report, estimated the number of warriors engaged in the fight at 600.

From Governor Stevens' report (1000 to 1200 warriors) my estimate is low; but, be this as it may, their numbers became so overwhelmingly in excess of ours that our forces were checked. The hills were on our left and the Walla Walla river on our right. Here they formed a line across the plain, from the foothills to the river, it being partially covered with brush, while the hills were covered with mounted hostiles, who played an active part, commanded by leaders of matchless skill and daring. Their purpose was to leave no foes to rise behind them; their policy was the policy of extermination; their flags were the scalps of our people, murdered in cold blood, whose gray locks floated from poles raised on every prominent point on the hills to our left, with a squad of those bloody fiends dancing the war dance around them. From the brush on the plain and the timber on the river they poured a murderous fire on the volunteers, who were compelled to fall back. This was the hottest place anywhere during the engagement. Here Henry Crow and S.S. Van Hagerman fell mortally wounded and several others were wounded. At this critical moment Lieutenant J.M. Burrows with a small detachment was ordered to cross the fence that surrounded the La Roche field and charge upon the Indians in the brush, the writer being one of the number who crossed, and when only a few steps beyond the fence the brave Burrows fell dead and Captain Munson and several others were wounded. A dispatch having been sent to Captain Wilson of Company A to come forward, he and his company came at full speed, dismounted, and with fixed bayonets pushed their way through the brush, driving the enemy before them. In a short time Captain Bennett with Company F was on hand, and with these reinforcements the Indians were driven about one mile farther up the Walla Walla river, where they took possession of a house with a close built fence around it. In attempting to dislodge them Captain Bennett of Company F, and Private Kelso of Company A, were killed.

Soon after this a howitzer, found at Fort Walla Walla, was brought to bear upon them by Captain Wilson, but having nothing but a sandhill to lay the piece on, when firing the fourth round it burst, wounding Captain Wilson, but dispersing the enemy from their stronghold. This was immediately followed up by the volunteers, and the bodies of Bennett and Kelso were recovered. The baggage train and flag of truce prisoners had already arrived at the La Roche cabin, which was used as a hospital. Peu Peu Mox Mox, with his stentorian voice, began to cheer up his warriors and encourage them to be brave, receiving responses from them at short intervals. Colonel Kelly had just rode from the front back to the hospital, when Frank Crabtree came in with his shoulder shattered and his arm dangling by his side, and reported Captain Layton wounded, and surrounded with five or six others on the hills at the front. Just at this critical moment the question was asked, "What shall be done with the prisoners?" Colonel Kelly took in the situation at once and said, "My men are all needed at the front. Tie or kill them, I don't care a d--n which," and rode back to the front. Ropes were procured to tie the prisoners, but they refused, except one, a young Nez Perce, who crossed his hands and said he wanted to be tied. One very large Indian, known by the name of Wolf-Skin, who was very talkative and who tried to escape from the guard the night before, drew a large knife concealed in his legging, uttering a demon-like yell, and began to cut his way through the guard, wounding Sergeant-Major Isaac Miller severely in the arm. The others, except the Nez Perce, who had been tied, were trying to make their way through the guards and escape to the hills, but their efforts were futile. It was only the work of a moment, brought on by their own remorseless hands, when they fell to the ground weltering in their gore. If the body of Peu Peu Mox Mox was mutilated, the act was brought on by a relentless foe, whose mode of warfare always was insensible to the feelings of others. At this time and place those brave volunteers had their feelings wrought up to the highest pitch, and their excitement ran wild as they saw the scalp, perhaps of a brother, a sister, or some relative, flapping from the top of some pole planted on a prominent point on the hills to our left. A fair and candid mind could hardly look on the scene before him without exonerating the boys in all that was done.

The contest lasted till after sundown, when the Indians withdrew and the volunteers returned to the La Roche cabin tired and hungry, having had nothing to eat since early morning. Camp fires were built, and camp kettles and coffee pots were hung over the blaze to prepare a scanty meal for the boys who had fought so nobly for us during the day. A guard of twenty, the writer being one, were on their way up the hillside to be stationed on duty. When about 300 yards from camp a ball from the enemy's gun came whizzing by; the wind from it was forcibly felt. Over went the camp kettles and coffee pots to extinguish the fires, and all hands were on guard till morning, the enemy firing a few shots into camp during the night.

Early on the morning of the 8th a hasty meal was prepared and partly eaten when the Indians came with increased forces, retaking all the positions they were driven from the day before. Lieutenant Pillow with Company A, and Lieutenant Hanan with Company H, were ordered to charge upon and drive them from the brush on the plain and the timber skirting the river, and hold these positions if possible. Lieutenant Fellows with Company F, Lieutenant Jeffreys with Company B, Lieutenant Hand with Company I, and Captain Cornoyer with Company K, were ordered to take possession of the most available points on the hills, and assail the enemy at other places if practicable. The Indians fought for their positions with all the skill and bravery of the previous day, especially in the brush, where they fought like demons. Three of Company H and one of Company A were wounded, but they were driven from their stronghold, where they shot with the skill and precision of a marksman. I saw Lieutenant Hanan while in a low place pull off his coat, hang it on the end of a pole, then place his hat on top and raise it above the brush; in an instant the brush was mowed around the object by bullets from the enemies' guns. But few shots were exchanged after darkness came on, and the warwhoop ceased as the Indians withdrew from the field. That night a courier was sent with a dispatch to Fort Henrietta for companies D and E to come in haste to the battlefield. On the morning of the 9th they were at their work again, but not so early as on the preceding morning. The volunteers being fatigued and nearly worn out, Colonel Kelly chose to act on the defensive and hold the position, the same as before, until Companies D and E from Fort Henrietta came to reinforce us. During the day attacks were made on Companies A and H in the brush, and B on the hills, which resulted in great loss to the enemy. The other companies on the hills did good service in repelling the attacks made on them during the day.

Early on the morning of the 10th it was discovered that the enemy had possession of every available position that was held by us the previous days. As soon as breakfast had been eaten Lieutenant McAuliff, with Company B charged on the Indians who had taken possession of the breastworks thrown up by them the day before, on the point of a hill, to protect them from the flying bullets from our guns. They had not taken such a deep hold in the brush as usual, on account of the severe loss they sustained the day before. Companies A and H soon recovered the brush, and drove them from the pits on the sand knoll. The companies from the hills made preparations for a charge, and as many as had horses suitable for the occasion were mounted, and gallantly charged the enemy in the face of a heavy fire, scattering them in all directions, to return to the battlefield no more.

Thus ended the long contested struggle between contending foes. Colonel Kelly in his official report says: "I cannot say too much in praise of the conduct of the officers of the several companies, and the soldiers under their command. They did their duty bravely and well during those four days of trying battle."

The loss Company H sustained, killed and wounded during the engagement, nearly equaled that of all the other companies, as will be seen from the list of killed and wounded: Captain Charles Bennett, Company F, killed; Lieutenant J.M. Burrows, Company H, killed; privates Andrew Kelso, Company A, killed; S.S. VanHagerman, Company I, killed; Jasper Flemming, Company A, mortally wounded; Joseph Sturdevant, Company B, mortally wounded; Henry Crow, Company H, mortally wounded; Sergeant Major Isaac Miller, Company H, wounded; Captain A.V. Wilson, Company A, wounded; Captain L.B. Munson, Company I, wounded; Captain Davis Layton, Company H, wounded; privates Casper Snook, Company H, wounded; T.J. Payne, Company H, wounded; Frank Crabtree, Company H, wounded; Nathan Fry, Company H, wounded; John Smith, Company H, wounded; A.M. Addington, Company H, wounded; Isaac Miller, Company H, wounded; Frank Duval, Company A, wounded; G.W. Smith, Company B, wounded; J.B. Gervais, Company K, wounded.

It's a difficult matter to get the exact number of Indians killed in time of battle. The bodies of 39 were counted on the battle field after it was all over, and it is estimated that at least 30 were carried off in time of battle and that many more were dragged away at night by putting ropes around their necks and pulling them with a horse. It was plain to see the trails where they were dragged away. At that time no one put their loss in the field at less than 100. The ratio of wounded to the number killed is generally estimated at two and a half to one. At this ration the killed and wounded during the battle would be 350. This would be at a close estimate one-third of all their warriors engaged in battle.

On the 1st of June 1858, the volunteers were discharged by proclamation, and on the 8th of June I arrived at my place of residence in Linn County.

Narcis Provo

*Narcis Provo tells of
the Indian fights that took place
in Eastern Oregon in 1856
during the Yakima Indian War.*

"I was stationed at the old emigrant crossing at Umatilla with Company K, of the volunteers, in command of Captain Goff, First Lieutenant Hunter and Second Lieutenant Jesse Drumheller. We occupied that place in June (1856), and the same year were ordered into the Camas Prairie country to pursue the Umatillas and the Cayuse Indians, who were on the war path, killing and pillaging. Our force numbered 126 men, the Indians greatly in excess of that number, but we followed them through the Camas Prairie country, along the John Day to the headwaters of Burnt River, where they were overtaken.

An engagement followed, in which two of the volunteers, Daniel Smith, and John Esters, were killed, and another, Jim Cherry, severely wounded. After the skirmish the Indians decided they could make no headway against the volunteers and withdrew. The family of the injured soldier lived in the East, and it was necessary for us to improvise a litter, which was attached to a horse, and the invalid brought to this Valley, from where he was sent by Governor Stevens to The Dalles, and thence to his home in Illinois.

After leaving the headwaters of Burnt River, and while proceeding through the Grande Ronde Valley, we again met the Indians, killing fifteen of them without the loss of a volunteer. We then proceeded to the Walla Walla Valley, and camped on Mill Creek, a short distance above where the city is now located, as near as I can estimate. Some of the Indian chiefs at that time sent messages to the Governor, asking him to make treaties, and the reply was returned that treaties would be made under certain conditions. Accordingly word was dispatched to all of the chiefs that a council would be held here on a certain date, and giving them seventeen days in which to assemble. They came from far and near, one and all, I suppose about 3,000 or 4,000 in all, and the work of the council was taken up.

With but four exceptions, the chiefs present consented to the terms of the treaties proposed, leaving the number of hostile warriors at about 1,500 roughly estimating. The time of volunteer service had expired a few days after the company had reached the Valley, and in response to a call from Governor Stevens, sixty-five volunteered to reenlist until the council had closed. The Indians realized the weakness of the company, and during the last two days of the council, the 1,500 hostile warriors became aggressive, arrogant and annoying.

A strong guard was placed about the council ground by the Governor, and after the terms of the treaty had been finally agreed to, one of the chiefs not in the combine walked up to Governor Stevens, patted him on the head and indicated in Indian language that the executive would be scalped before he left the Valley. That was either Chief Moses or Chief Joe--I'm not certain which.

It was our intention, following the close of the council and the formal declaration of peace, to proceed to The Dalles, where we could be mustered out of service. We had proceeded about a mile and a half to the southwest, when we were surrounded by the hostile tribes, and kept there from 1 o'clock in the afternoon until the next morning, when we were liberated by a company of regulars summoned from the Walla Walla River by the Governor. One of the volunteers, Lige Hill, was killed and his body is now buried on an island somewhere in Mill Creek, a short distance above the city. Hill was from Linn County, Oregon, and I am told his parents still live in Benton County, Oregon.

During the time we were surrounded, about all we could do was to maintain guard about the camp, protecting what stock we owned, and what we had captured from the Indians. We could do little toward repulsing the attacking party, and were in a predicament indeed, until, after the third call by the Governor, the regular troops arrived on the scene. After night the Indians fell back, and the next afternoon, after burying our dead comrade, Hill, we started for The Dalles. The Indians did not bother any more after the treaty had been signed up, as the regulars drove the hostile braves up Mill Creek after our experience with them.

Lewis McMorris

Lew McMorris reminisces
about Christmas day spent at a
lonely army post in the wilderness in 1856.

Christmas meant so little to us who were here in 1856 that there is really little I remember about that day, the first Christmas day ever spent by white men in Walla Walla. We had little thoughts of Christmas, little that marked the day. We were located here as a post of army men, and we thought little, that day, what the word meant to the millions who were celebrating the birth of Christ throughout the world.

Shut out as we were, from the rest of the world, our communications with the outside civilization severed for the winter, the cold oppressing us those brief days and almost interminable nights, we had nothing to bring to our thoughts the meaning of the word Christmas.

Men there were among us, and many of them I have no doubt, thought of the Christmas they used to spend at home, in the East, by the fireside in comfortable homes. Some there were who could no doubt remember luxuries of earlier holiday time, when the world, cold then as upon that day in 1856, was clad with the pure white mantle of snow. But the meaning of the snow in boyhood days, when it meant fun and pleasure, was far different from the meaning it had for us beleaguered men in our lonely fort, more like a prison, in that hard winter.

There were about 200 of us, if I remember right, stationed here that winter. We were under the command of the gallant officer, Colonel Steptoe. Four companies of soldiers and about eight or ten of us quartermaster men, composed the garrison. There was no communication, in or out, during that long, hard winter.

It was one of the coldest winters I remember in this part of the country. For six weeks the snow and bitter, damp chill which accompanied it, was unbroken. Feed was scarce for the horses, and amusement for the men was almost entirely lacking. With nothing but the snow, stretching on one side as far as the eye could reach over the rolling prairie, and ending on the other at the top of the not distant mountains, it seemed we were but sailors, tossed on the white billows of the rolling prairies. As far as the eye could see, stretched the white, white, nothing but that plain white. Our camp was a ship, but we made no progress. The waves of the great white ocean never changed.

Of Indians we had little fear. They were not apt to be troublesome in the winter. Indeed, the cold we dreaded was our safeguard and as long as it lasted we were in little danger of attack from that quarter. Our danger was more likely to result from sickness. But we had very little sickness that winter.

Homesickness? Well, we were not the kind that got homesick. We never thought about home, if we had we would have made poor pioneers. Home seemed to us a word, nothing more. If it had any meaning it was only a suggestion of something we had once known, something long past, almost forgotten. Home meant little to us hardy fellows and if any of us was homesick, he dared not mention it.

Christmas mail? No, the Christmas mail of those days in Walla Walla was easily handled. In fact, I think the last mail we had that year was early in December just after the last government train had left The Dalles, our nearest point of succor, had anything happened. No letters were brought us to read around a campfire on the night of Christmas eve. We didn't open any packages containing presents from loved ones. We had no Christmas dinner to remind us of times long since past. Christmas, like home, was a word.

Christmas day that year dawned late. The clouds hung low and the wind blew chill up the Valley. Housed in our log huts, roofed with sod and dirt, we shivered about our fires as daylight crept over the mountains and announced to us that another year had passed, another Christmas had come.

Nor had we any Christmas of the year before to look back to. That year we were stationed at The Dalles and the winter there was cold, and it was lonesome. We had no more celebration in that bigger post than we did in Walla Walla in 1856. We had no time, no reason, if you will, to think of Christmas.

Our breakfast was the breakfast of a hundred other days. We thought of nothing different, we got nothing different and our dinner was the same. It was a day of the week, of the month, of the year. It was nothing more. We had our routine duties, and when we had performed them, we were through, we had no Christmas.

Christmas turkey we had not. Whether we had any extra prairie chicken that day--the only wild bird we could shoot--I do not remember. But this I know, had there been anything out of the ordinary, I am sure I would have remembered it.

The day was spent by most of the boys in herding the horses through the tall rye grass that used to grow as high as your head on the banks of Mill Creek. This was all the feed we could get them. Everything else was covered with snow. The horses were herded down the creek in the daytime, and were returned to the corral at night, where they huddled in the cold of the long winter darkness. But it was the only way we could protect them from being stolen from us by the Indians. While it was too cold for the Indians to fight, I hardly think it ever got too cold for them to steal horses, had they been given the opportunity. And even then, of course, we occasionally lost an animal. This was the occupation that busied the men on Christmas day of 1856. They could not sit around and tell stories, listen to any music or happy laughter of little relatives, the horses must be fed. And we had no thought of Christmas.

You think perhaps, that it would have to be indeed a strange condition that would make you forget Christmas and the thoughts of homecomings at other times. The conditions were strange, to you. To us they were a matter of fact. We were there. We were doing our duty, we were carrying out the orders we had. And our orders did not mention Christmas. You cannot understand, probably you will never be placed in that position, but Christmas that first year was anything but the Christmas of present days.

There were no buildings in Walla Walla then. We were camped on the east bank of Mill Creek, on Main street, as the town is now laid out. Thoughts of brick buildings, brilliantly lighted streets, paved and swept, never occurred to us. Why should they. Where the biggest stores now stand, where most of the Christmas presents and good things to eat are now purchased, was that year snow, white snow. No we never thought street cars would run down past what was then our camp. We never realized that the shade of big buildings would some day fall across the ground where we were camped. We never gave it a thought whether even there would be a city, or a town here. And least of all were our thoughts of Christmas.

Oh, I don't mean to say there were none of us who thought of Christmas that day. I don't mean to intimate that there were none of us who did not think of home and wonder what loved ones were doing as we ate our plain fare. I do not mean to say there were not many who had a thought of mother in a distant eastern home, or a sweetheart waiting for him when this land of promise should open up and give forth its bounty. There were many of us, no doubt, who thought all these things. But they were too good soldiers to think of them long, or to talk of them at all.

We were not the kind, I have said, to get homesick. And during that long winter there was not a complaint, not a whimper, from one of those hardy sons who were there that the country might some day be open to you. In silence the hardships were endured, or if they were mentioned, it was only to pass them off as a joke, to make light of the things that were bringing premature old age upon that little band of men. They laughed at the dangers from their dark skinned foes. They joked away any suggestion of possibility. And when things, sometimes, grew so dark that jokes were out of place, silence succeeded.

There were no men in the army that having put their hand to the plow, wanted to turn back. Hardy sons of the western frontier, they were there to open the country, to make possible the settlement of this greatest valley of the Northwest and of the world. They were doing a great work, doing a work that no one else could do, and they were doing it well.

Small wonder, is it then, that they had no thought of Christmas. If the day was mentioned I do not remember it. It was simply one of those days of our long, cold stay. Simply another space from dawn to darkness, simply a part of the week, routine of life that had to be endured. That was all. Christmas as you mean it now was not related by even ever so slight a thread, to the Christmas of 1856. Little romance, little of interest, just a day of the 365, just a part of the year, just another notch in the stick by which we kept time. That was Christmas day of 1856.

Michael Kenney

The 1858 expedition of Colonel Steptoe
and his subsequent defeat by the Indians
took place near present-day Rosalia, Washington,
as recounted by Mr. Kenney.

Michael Kenney was born at Castlecomer, Ireland, September 21, 1831. He arrived in New York, July, 1853, having made the journey on a sailing vessel which required seven weeks. At that time he remembers that there was but one trans-Atlantic steamer.

New York, the metropolis of America, was a small place then. On Forty-second street there were only two small houses.

America made a favorable impression on the new-comer, except the New York summer, which was altogether too warm. On one occasion he got up at two o'clock in the morning and took a plunge in the Hudson for comfort. Although he felt the heat severely, he went to work in the Fall at carpentry and received $3.00 a week for his services.

February, 1854, he enlisted at Governor's island, in the United States army. Uncle Sam's fighting force was in its infancy then. It consisted of two regiments of Dragoons and one regiment of mounted riflemen. The latter was organized to fight Indians in Texas.

Mr. Kenney with others who had enlisted were taken to Jefferson barracks, Missouri, and later to Fort Leavenworth, where their numbers were increased by more recruits. From this place, under the command of Col. Steptoe, the force started westward with Salt Lake City its destination, where it arrived in September and spent the winter. The city was surrounded by a wall eight or nine feet high and about two and one-half miles long by one and one-half miles wide.

"We had our first experience with Indians in Utah," remarked Mr. Kenney.

"In 1853 an eminent entomologist, under military escort, Captain Gunnison in command, went on a searching expedition into Southern Utah to collect bugs for the cabinets of some Eastern institution. The entire party, with the exception of three soldiers, were killed by Indians. Colonel Steptoe went out to chastise the Indians for these murders. Near Sand Pete the chiefs gave up three Indians; these were tried at Salt Lake City by a Mormon jury, which brought in a verdict of manslaughter.

"In May our forces were divided. Fifty of our men, under Lieutenant Maurey, went to San Antonio, New Mexico, headquarters for the First Dragoons, Colonel Steptoe, with two companies of artillery, went to San Francisco, and fifty dragoons, of which I was one, came to Fort Lane, Oregon. We arrived there in July, 1855. We experienced some real Indian warfare here with the Rogue River Indians. We met the red men twice in battle, at Cow Creek on October 31, and at the Big Bend in May or June, both desperately fought battles.

"Three chiefs had a conference with Col. Buchanan, about five miles distant from Big Bend. Two acceded to the Colonel's wish to go upon a reservation he had selected, but the third openly refused. The consenting chiefs asked that Troop C would meet them about three miles from the command, that they might have a conference with Captain A.J. Smith. The request was granted and the troops moved to the appointed place for the council and camped. A friendly Indian notified the captain soon after dark that the Indians intended making a night attack on the camp.

"Lieutenant Switzler selected a place to make a stand for a battle on a height, and we traveled all night, carrying our camp paraphernalia on our backs, to the place, which we reached early in the morning.

"The Indians came to our new stand and wanted to mingle with the troopers, but Captain gave orders to keep all Indians out of the camp.

"Indians were gathering from every direction. About seven o'clock they opened fire on us, which did not cease, except in the darkness of night, until we were reinforced by Troop G from Colonel Buchanan's command.

"The Indians climbed up in the great oak trees near us and fired, while the Indians on the ground loaded and passed the guns to the men up in the trees.

"One man passed the enemy's cordon by crawling on hand and knees through the thick underbrush at night and reached the command. Company G was sent to our relief. At its coming the Indians retreated and ceased hostilities.

"We had been surrounded by Indians and cut off from water for forty-eight hours. The Indians had evidently been severely punished, too, for they came in next day and surrendered. They were marched to Port Orford, where a coast steamer waited to take the Rogue River Indians and some tribes that lived on the immediate coast, to Fort Yamhill. The Rogue River Indians could not be induced to go aboard the steamer; they were afraid of the water. They willingly marched along the beach, a distance of 100 miles, to the Grand Ronde reservation, set apart for them, where, for nearly fifty years they have maintained the most friendly relations with their white neighbors."

At Fort Yamhill, Mr. Kenney states, Phil Sheridan was quartermaster and Dr. Gleeson, after whom one of the principal streets in Portland was named, the physician. Later Fort Yamhill was named Sheridan in honor of the distinction won by General Sheridan. The winter of 1856-7 was spent at this place. Mr. Kenney and Mr. McEvoy arrived on the present site of Walla Walla in 1857. It was occupied then by the Cantonment, consisting of a few log huts on the present site of East Main street, west of Palouse, those on the south were the homes of the officers and the ones on the north, barracks for the soldiers. These huts were built the fall of 1856 by the soldiers. As there was no feed obtainable for the horses here at that time, they were sent to Vancouver, then occupied by officers of the Hudson Bay Company, for the winter and Mr. Kenney was one of the number sent on this errand. In this valley noted far and near for its many productive fields of grain and hay, then it was necessary to wait until the grass grew in the spring to bring the horses back, on account of the lack of forage. At this time the Americans and British were surveying the boundary line between Washington territory and British America. May 6, 1858, an expedition to Colville started, composed of 152 men in command of Col. Steptoe, who had been ordered to this place by the department commander to settle some trouble between the miners there and the Indians, and to locate a camp for the surveying parties for the winter.

Peace had been established here at the Indian council, held in 1855 and Col. Steptoe had no anticipation of meeting hostile Indians. Chief Timothy and Sub-Chief Levi, both Nez Perce Indians accompanied the expedition as guides; rendered most valuable aid. Orders were given that all sabers be left at home; guns were taken as all soldiers are supposed to carry a gun. Two howitzers were taken, Mr. Kenney thinks probably more for show than use.

There were no ferries nor bridges then and crossing Snake river was a problem that confronted the troops. At this critical point Timothy mastered the difficulty. The crossing was to be made from the home of Timothy's tribe. The squaws took the soldiers, saddles, blankets, food, etc., into canoes, and rowed them across the river, which is estimated to be a quarter of a mile wide at this point. The Indian men on their cayuses compelled the horses to swim across. The crossing was accomplished in a single day.

"In the forenoon of Sunday, May 16, (at Rock Creek) the Indians first showed themselves. The command stopped, and Colonel Steptoe talked with the chiefs. They did not want the troops to go into their country and positively refused to take the command across the Spokane River, and made a most warlike demonstration during the holding of the conference.

"Naked Indians, in war paint, on horses having a coat of paint, circled around the troops, giving the war whoop. One had the audacity to spit in Captain Taylor's face.

"As it was impossible to reach the intended destination without the canoes to cross the Spokane River, Colonel Steptoe started on a retreat homeward Monday. A priest from Coeur d'Alene Mission overtook the command shortly after it started, and told the Colonel that the Indians intended to attack him; that he could control the Coeur d'Alenes, but the others he had no influence over.

"Indians appeared soon after we started. About eight o'clock, as we struck Pine Creek (five miles from present-day Rosalia), the Indians in the timber attacked us in the front, on the right and on the left. Lieutenant Gaston, at the head, gave the command to charge up the hill. The whole command followed, covering the pack train. The howitzers were taken off the mules and turned upon the Indians with such a leaden hail, with aid of a charge from the troops, that the hostiles retreated. The howitzers were again packed up and the retreat resumed."

When asked if he could give an estimate of the warriors engaged, Kenney replied, "I could not. The hills were full of them. There were the Palouse, Colville, Spokane, Yakima and other tribes.

"As the troop moved down into Cash Creek, Lieutenant Gaston, Company E, commanded the left wing; Captain Taylor, Company C, the right wing and rear; Col. Steptoe, with Lieutenant Gregg, Company H, were in front with the pack train. The Indians tried to circle in between us and the pack train. It was a running fight for two hours. At the end of this time Lieutenant Gaston was killed. News was brought to Col. Steptoe five minutes later that Captain Taylor was killed. Captain Taylor's body was brought in, but two men were killed and three wounded in doing it.

"The men with Lieutenant Gaston were unable to get his body. Their revolvers were empty, their rifles were strapped on their backs and they had no sabers.

"A camp was made on a hill commanding Cash Creek. Captain Taylor was buried here, amid the flying bullets of the Indians. One man was wounded who was assisting in the burial.

"About noon the Indians made camp, probably to get dinner, but returned in a few hours and continued the battle, trying several times to charge the camp, but were repulsed.

"About 2:00 o'clock the ammunition gave out with some of the men on the outer post. A messenger was sent to the camp for more, when it was discovered that the three cases ordered to be brought had been left at Walla Walla. When this discovery was made, Lieutenant Wheeler, who succeeded Captain Taylor, sent out among the troops and gathered up all the ammunition among the men, and found that there were three bullets to each man and six over. I was sent to distribute the six to the men at the front.

"A council of war was called about 2:30 o'clock by Colonel Steptoe. No sabers and no ammunition meant annihilation or retreat. Retreat was the alternative.

"The Indians drew off about dusk. The howitzers were buried where the trampling horses destroyed all trace of the work. Five or six mules were loaded each with one sack of flour. One man was detailed to lead a mule and another to drive the animal. Men were ordered to leave blankets, all clothing except what they wore and everything else that could lighten the burden of the horses.

"Nine men, of whom I was one, kept watch on the Indians while the command made ready for the retreat, which began at moonrise, about 9:00 o'clock. When the escape had been safely effected, a messenger was sent to us to leave our post and follow. We went to the camp, saddled our horses and joined the retreating column.

"The Indians wanted the pack train more than they wanted us, and I consider that Colonel Steptoe's judgment in leaving it behind was all that saved us. Besides its value to them, they did not watch our movements as long as they could see the animals at the camp.

"It was pitch dark some of the time that night, and had it not been for the guidance of the Nez Perce chiefs we would not have reached safety. This was not the only service our Nez Perce friends did for us. We reached Snake River Tuesday night and slept that night. Wednesday morning the Indians rowed us across the river in their canoes, spending the entire day in this work. They also swam our horses across, by their superior knowledge of horseflesh and possibilities. We could not compel, coax or persuade a horse to take the water, but our Nez Perces had little difficulty in accomplishing the feat. The horses were tired and hungry, and a swim of nearly a mile was a task they rebelled against."

"Were the Indians ever recompensed for this work?"

"No. They never received a dollar for this hard work.

"At a camp on Alpowa Creek Wednesday, we had our first meal since Monday morning. Each of us was given a quart of flour. On pieces of canvas and flat stones we mixed some water with this and baked it on stones around the camp fire; some twisted the dough around dry twigs and cooked it before the fire. It had no salt or baking powder, but it tasted as good to me as any bread I ever ate.

"Captain Dent met us the next day with a six-mule team and provisions. We made a camp at the present site of Pomeroy and we had a good meal.

"What do you think of some of the criticisms reflecting on the bravery of Colonel Steptoe?"

"I consider them unjust and most unreasonable. His retreat was not cowardly, but was the only thing he could do and he did it well. I have the first one yet to hear say that Steptoe was a coward, of all the men who fought under him; none others are capable of judging.

"Critics who have reached our land, once a savage wild, by way of the palace car, and fight Indian battles in the comfortable chairs of the modern parlor, don't have very hard fighting. If these latter day heroes and heroines were fighting as we were, without ammunition, 100 miles from everywhere, in a strange country, surrounded by the Lord knows how many Indians, then they would have some experience."

J.J. Rohn

Colonel Wright's expedition to punish
the hostile Indians of the Inland Empire
for the attack on Steptoe's troops earlier that year
is the subject of J.J. Rohn's account.

"Our forces consisted of 150 dragoons and our attack on the Indians, who numbered close to 500, was a success in every particular. There was simply nothing to the skirmish for as we rode into the redmen, we rushed, routed and scattered them in all directions before one could say Jack Robinson. Best of all we didn't lose a man during the engagement. In addition to their home made implements of war many of the Indians were armed with Hudson Bay rifles and why they didn't put up a stiffer fight is something that will always remain a mystery to me. When the fight started the Indians were rigged out in all kind of fancy trappings; the head-dresses of many presented a novel sight, in fact, the Indian warriors we met in this particular engagement, looked altogether as if they were equipped for a Fourth of July parade. After the skirmish was over and the majority of Indians had made their escape the battle ground was littered with feathers and Indian fancy trinkets of almost every description. Accompanying our troop was a number of friendly Cayuse Indians who were not slow in picking up the trappings left behind by the routed foe. Incidentally these friendly Cayuses also did a little scalping. Every dead Indian they ran across was scalped by them. Especially did one Indian, well known throughout the country at that time as 'Cut Mouth John', do much effective work in the scalping line among the dead of our enemies. The Indians made much ado about the scalps that fell to them so easily and that evening they celebrated on a big scale by holding a 'scalp' dance."

The troopers saw a dust a few days later, up in the mountains near Liberty lake. It was caused by the Indians driving a band of horses. The troopers were sent after them. The Indians fled leaving all the loose horses. These were driven down to a corral where the Indians shut them up when they desired. There were more than a thousand of these horses. The Nez Perce Indians were given 130 of these and some of the officers took some of them the rest 986 were shot to death in the corral. It took two days to accomplish this slaughter of the innocents.

This was not all of the lesson. Seven Indian storehouses fitted with wheat were burned. It was a terrible lesson but it settled the peace question and the Indians have been friends of the white man ever since.

On the return trip Mr. Rohn with a detachment of 25 men was sent to the Steptoe battlefield and secured the remains of the slain and conveyed them to this place and they were buried in the military cemetery just west of Ft. Walla Walla. Captain Taylor was the only one of the slain that was buried on the battlefield.

Later the remains of Captain Taylor and Lieutenant Gaston were removed to the military cemetery at West Point.

Two howitzers buried by the troopers before the retreat, were dug up and brought here by Mr. Rohn and men. It is not known what became of them although it is claimed that one is in Spokane.

Dr. John Tempany

*Dr. Tempany, an army veterinarian,
joined the Dragoons in 1858. When he retired in 1911
he held the record of the most years of service
in the army at that time.*

"Walla Walla suits me and I expect to spend the remainder of my days here," is the decision of Dr. John Tempany, who has made his home in many states of the Union and journeyed through many more.

Dr. Tempany is one of the earliest pioneers of this valley as he arrived here with company C, 1st Dragoons, November 16, 1858. The date was an important one as it was the day that Col. Wright returned with his troops from his successful campaign against the Indian tribes of the northern part of the territory.

When asked if there was celebration of the coming of the victorious troops, the reply was: "Only a big drunk. Every one drank then."

Dr. Tempany was born in New York City, December 29, 1838, and was deprived of a mother's care at the age of eleven. His early experiences, no doubt, were valuable in developing the character that has marked his success in life, but were anything but pleasant. After the death of his mother, he went to live with an uncle in Susquehanna County, Pennsylvania. This uncle had a house full of children and did not care to have this addition. Soon after the coming of the unwelcome boy, his uncle bound him out to a nearby farmer. His wages $3.00 a month, board and clothes. He received the clothes and board and they were good but his uncle always collected the $3.00 and kept it. Why?

"It was his pay for looking after his poor relative," Dr. Tempany says.

After three years of this apprenticeship he left and secured employment driving a team on the construction work of a canal running parallel with the Susquehanna river. Following the canal work he entered the service of a man who owned a race course and horses, in Lucerne County. His experience with horses was a great aid to him here, where he was a successful jockey until his employer informed him one day that his legs were too long for a race rider, and he was transferred to the stables. This change decided his life work, for it was here that he got the idea of being a veterinary surgeon. His employer treated all the horses of the course. He assisted the owner in the treatments and thereby received the most valuable experience and knowledge then obtainable, which has been a great factor in the success of his profession.

Dr. Tempany states that at that time there were no circular race courses, only the straight away tracks.

The next occupation was driving a canal boat on the Erie canal, where he began with a salary of $15.00 per month. The salary was increased to $16.00. Later he returned to his first home, New York City and enlisted in the United States army for a five year term, and became a member of company C, 1st Dragoons. The Dragoons corresponded then to the cavalry of today and there were mounts to be cared for, and Mr. Tempany was put in charge of the stables on account of his knowledge of horses. His entire school attendance consisted of three winter sessions while he lived in Pennsylvania, but he had ambition, a factor that seldom fails to reach success.

The army afforded the best possible opportunities for education in his chosen profession; there was much leisure time, a state of affairs unknown to him in the past; plenty of horses and a salary although small, one that would continue for five years. He treated the horses and secured books on "The Horse" from all authorities obtainable which he studied in his leisure hours.

The army regulations required the services of a veterinary surgeon. Mr. Tempany, although not yet 21, was selected for the place. A unique situation was presented which demonstrates the advance made since that time in this important department of army regulations of the present time.

The appointee must pass an examination to receive the official appointment. The board of examiners chosen for this duty, seemingly had a duty that baffled them as to mode of procedure. They made various suggestions as to what such an examination ought to be, to all of which the candidate, who was consulted failed to agree with.

"Then examine yourself," he was told. "How?" he asked. "Cure an imaginary case," was the answer.

Then in the presence of the board, Mr. Tempany proceeded to examine himself. He imagined a horse suffering from colic. He proceeded with his treatment, and the imaginary horse was restored to health. The board agreed that the treatment was fine, and unanimously endorsed Mr. Tempany for the appointment of veterinary surgeon and the appointment was confirmed.

In coming to the Walla Walla Valley, Mr. Tempany came by the way of Panama in company with 300 recruits. Some were left at Benecia Barracks, some at Vancouver and the rest came to Walla Walla. When he arrivd here, he wondered how the first man ever succeeded in getting across the mountains and valleys and wound his way here.

In 1861 Mr. Tempany was ordered to Washington, D.C., with other troops of Ft. Walla Walla, in command of Captain A.J. Smith stationed here at that time, to join the Pacific coast contingent, went by way of Panama. He was assigned to company C, 1st Cavalry, on arrival at his destination and this company was selected as body guard to Gen. McClellan. Many of the members of this company were couriers. The most important battle in which this company took part was that of Fredericsburg. He remembers the cordial feelings that existed between the rebel and union soldiers at rest times.

Mr. Tempany's enlistment expired in 1863, and he went to New York City, where he secured work in the machine shop of Burbeck and Hodges and has the distinction of being one of the builders of the Monitor. In 1867 Mr. Tempany was married to Miss Elizabeth Sperry, whom he met in Boston. The couple later went to make their home on a small farm in Minnesota which cost $40 per acre.

One day Mr. Tempany's mail contained an official document from Washington, it contained his appointment as veterinary surgeon of the 9th Cavalry. It was a perfect surprise and came wholly unsolicited by him.

"It was gladly accepted," Mr. Tempany remarked, "as I was broke. I have never been successful in land deals or management. I left for my post and Mrs. Tempany remained behind, and sold the farm for just half what it cost, then joined me."

He learned later the appointment came through the efforts of Gen. Edward Hatch, whom he had met at Louisville, Ky., when the scourge of epizootic afflicted the horses throughout the United States and a convention of the eminent veterinary surgeons met here to discuss remedies and plans for cure of this disease.

Mr. and Mrs. Tempany are the parents of four sons: Arthur, of Omaha, Neb.; Harry, Clarence and Frank, all of this city and one daughter, Mrs. Douglass of Idaho. They also have two grandsons and one granddaughter.

Dr. Tempany was retired in 1911. He is nearing the eightieth milestone and has a remarkable record in one respect, that is in regard to health. If he ever had a day's sickness it was in his earliest infancy, as his memory records not a single illness.

He is well preserved for his age; is one of the most active workers in G.A.R. affairs and takes a deep interest in the issues of the day.

Louis Scholl

Architect for Fort Dalles,
Walla Walla, Simcoe and Colville
tells about his army life in the Northwest.

In Carlsruhe, Grandduchy of Baden, I was born in 1829. Our family dates back to 1207 and a family tree in my possession contains every member of each generation as far back as 1437, when a Scholl was Burgonmaster of Nuremberg.

Carl Friedrich Scholl, my father was President of the Staats Amortisations bank. He founded the Staats Savings bank and the First Orphanage for boys in Durbach, also one for girls in Donanachingen, then the residence of Furst von Fuestenberg, one of the most liberal and kindly of reigning princes, and only by his help could my father carry out his Christian desires. In consequences of the revolution of 1848 that banished, not only my oldest brothers, Carl and Emil, but many other patriots, like Senator Hecker, Carl Schurz, and Franz Siegel to the United States, brought myself and three other brothers also. (We were a family of ten.) My oldest brother took refuge in Zurich, Switzerland, another came with me to New York.

In 1852 I journeyed by ox-team to the New Eldorado, California, to seek my fortune, and 1853 found me in Oregon. Returning east by overland trail in 1853, in the spring, when encamped in Thousand Spring Valley, near Goose Creek, at the head of Humboldt River, some of my animals were stolen. Butterfield's express rider carried my letter to Utah's Representative in Salt Lake City, and the thieves were captured and one "Williams" sent to the penitentiary.

Returning to California I again renewed my venture for 1854. In the Sacramento "Union" of Feb. 21, I learned of the capture of the thieves and on arriving in Salt Lake City, with cattle, I endeavored to recover my stolen property. There I had interesting interviews with Chief Justice Smith, editor of the "Deseret News" and Governor Brigham Young. Pontius sent me to Pilatus and vice versa--I saw the mayor of the city, riding one of my stolen horses but never recovered anything. The proceeds of this sale had been appropriated for the perpetual "emigration fund." Then I appealed to the newly appointed Chief Justice Kinney and Attorney General Holman (who had traveled under Colonel Steptoe's protection from their eastern home as the first appointees of the United States for Utah Territory) but they took no steps for the recovery of my rights.

It was in September 1854 that Colonel Steptoe's command reached Salt Lake City, and was, on my arrival, camped on the public square. Part of the Cavalry was moved some 28 miles Southwest of the city, also all quartermaster stores and equipment, but after the trial of the murderers of Capt. Gunnison and party was ended, and Indians hung, most of the troops were encamped within 8 miles of the southwestern shore of Salt Lake; most of the officers, however, were domiciled in the city. Col. Steptoe occupied a plainly furnished room near the public square. Chief Justice Kinney and family occupied with the Suttler's store the first story of a two-story adobe building. Attorney General Holman roomed with clerks in the upstairs big hall and there was mirth and song every night. A melodeon at which I presided was the musical instrument. Often the officers had dances when some of the Mormon ladies were surreptitiously taken to the gatherings without the knowledge of parents. Some good performances were given at the beautiful theater and there the sisters Guggenheim were the stars.

The expedition ostensibly destined for Fort Lane, Oregon, with 125 fine bay horses to remount Capt. A.J. Smith's command (whose mounts had been mostly killed in the Rogue River Indian war) was also incidentally intended to show the strength of the government to the roving bands of Indians, who still inhabited the country.

Until January 1855 I held the position of Clerk of Chief Justice Kinney and had the promise from Colonel Steptoe, newly appointed governor, to be his private secretary, should he accept the position offered him by President Franklin Pierce. After 24 hours deliberation he declined the honor, not desiring to give up his military career and mix with politics. The envelope which contained his appointment as governor, only saw the eyes of Justice Kinney and myself and it never was known to anyone else beside the colonel. January 1855, I accepted a position as commissary clerk under Captain Rufus Ingalls--the quartermaster of Col. Steptoe's expedition at the same time making a map of country from Salt Lake Valley to California and Fort Lane, Oregon, giving distances from watercourses to next camp. Among the artillery officers was Lieut. Tyler, a nephew of one of our presidents, who was wit and life, and musical light of many pleasant evenings.

Seven years later I was near him on Rappahanock Heights during the bombardment of Frederick City. It was Lieut. Kip, adjutant to General Burnside who brought the order and General Tyler with his 12 large siege guns opened the cannonade with "solid shot" when the signal gun at one o'clock was heard.

In April, the artillery detachment, under Lieut. Maury, (afterwards Governor of Arizona) started, via Las Vegas, New Mexico, for San Diego, California.

Somewhat later Col. Steptoe, with the infantry and cavalry division, started down the Humboldt river. The coal had given out and I volunteered to burn a coal pit near the head of Salt Lake, being absent from the command with ten cavalrymen and five employees for six days. We loaded a large flatboat (on wheels) during a heavy snowstorm and started slowly home. Between two small streams, while laying asleep on the coal pile, I smelt fire; we finally extinguished the smouldering, charcoal with buckets full of snow.

At Humboldt Meadows Capt. Ingalls with Lieut. Ashton's cavalry turned due west and with the two strings of fine horses we reached Fort Lane on a bright day--the day before, our provisions running rather short, and the talk of mulesteaks being revived, some of the officers with spyglasses ascended a nearby hill and brought the glorious news, that they had seen the reapers in the wheatfields of the Rogue River.

Colonel Steptoe continued his march down to the sink of Humboldt, crossed the Carson desert and the Sierra, through snow and down through the Sacramento Valley to Benicia with the infantry. Lieut. Ashton, who had commanded the cavalry forces across the plains, here resigned his lieutenancy. He was the son of the Governor of South Carolina, and had a fine conveyance, with coal black horses and a negro coachman, all the way from the Missouri River.

From Fort Lane in the autumn of 1855 I guided the employees from this expedition to Benicia, past Camp Jones, Captain Floyd Jones commanding, and I prepared the official map of the expedition from Salt Lake for Colonel Steptoe and Captain and Quartermaster Ingalls. In December I returned to Oregon, accompanying Capt. Thomas Jordan by steamer to Fort Vancouver. During a storm on the voyage we threw overboard 120 barrels of lime, the waves having set the casks on fire. One day later the cry of fire again startled the steamship. Capt. Dall placed Major Morris, Third Artillery, and myself to guard one lifeboat, Major Vaughn of Vancouver and Lieut. Walker, Third Artillery were placed over the opposite swinging lifeboat. Close to Port Orford the course of the steamer was changed and Port Orford was reached and the fire extinguished after about half of the 20 tons of powder had been thrown overboard. Amongst the lady passengers was the wife of Capt. Dent, Ninth Infantry, the sister of our General Grant of future years. I see yet Capt. Jordan toiling up the steps with a 100 pound barrel of powder on his shoulder. I rolled them overboard, continuing my vigil over the lifeboat. The few ladies aboard had been placed in the cabin on after deck. Blankets and provisions and kegs of water littered the floor. At one o'clock with a full moon brightly shining, the steamer left that safe harbor, the fire under control. On January 20, 1856 we reached Fort The Dalles and no more winter weather visited us. I was employed by Capt. Thomas Jordan as clerk and draftsman and for three years following acted as supervising architect of the government, making all the plans for Fort Dalles, also for Fort Walla Walla, Fort Simcoe and Colville.

All doors, windowshashes, mantels, bookcases, etc., for these far posts, were transported, some by packmule, but mostly by large 6-mule wagon trains. Chas. Russel's, the wagonmaster's 24 mule teams were for two years constantly employed towards Walla Walla and a pack train of nearly 50 mules, moved between Fort Dalles and Simcoe.

I prepared all working plans for the 49 carpenters and masons. Fort Simcoe was commanded by Major Garnett, Fort Walla Walla by Col. Steptoe and Major Lugenbeel occupied Fort Colville, and during the absence of Col. George Wright with all the available troops, Capt. Jordan was the protector at Fort Dalles of the families of the Ninth; the family of Major Haller, Fourth Infantry, also occupied part of the old loghouse erected by the Rifle Regiment in 1849.

During this Yakima Indian war, all eyes at Fort Dalles, with powerful spyglasses were frequently directed towards the hills--8 miles distant from the Columbia river--to see if our express rider, Pearson, was safe. The savages having intercepted him on several occasions and delayed his arrival from the seat of war. One night, after a theatrical performance in the post's newly erected building of slabs, when the officers' ladies served supper, our express man, Pearson, who had arrived after dusk with joyful dispatches, was found asleep, standing behind an open door, after his 65 mile ride from Fort Simcoe.

April 1859 found me employed, during summer months by General Harney, through Capt. Ingalls, as scout and guide of the expedition to find a new overland route, avoiding the Snake River from Raft to the Owyhee River. Capt. Wallen, Fourth Infantry commanded the expedition which I guided through Harney Lake Valley partly over Stephen Meek's old trail of 1845 near the Malheur River. I had previously traveled with three Indian prisoners, a Warmspring, a Cayuse and a Snake, over part of this route. At the mouth of the Owyhee River, a tributary of the Snake River, Captain Wallen decided to follow the overland route up Snake River "to protect the incoming imigrants," and with 10 cavalrymen and packers and cook, I started up the Owyhee River to find the new route over into Jordan Valley, which I named after Capt. Jordan; and it bears the name yet. (Captain Jordan, after resigning in 1860 joined the confederacy and occupied the position of Chief of Staff to General Beauregard. Major Garnett followed suit and was killed, leading some confederate forces at Cherry Creek in Virginia.)

We encountered many hostile bands, but thanks to interpreters, particularly the Snake Indian, I safely reached Raft River, having mapped a new and better route. I met there Capt. Wallen, also Col. Lander, who had completed cutting a new route through the Port Neuf wilderness, a heavily timbered region, that gave a shorter and better route for imigrants (Lander was afterwards a general in the U.S. army and was killed in action.) From Raft River camp I carried Capt. Wallen's dispatches to Camp Lyons, traveling solely by compass to the ford of Bear River, avoiding roads and trails and with but one cavalryman and George Rundel as companions. Camp Lyons was occupied by U.S. troops and is situated 20 miles due south from Salt Lake City, near the Jordan river. My itinerary of that summer's campaign is found in Secretary of War Jeff Davis' report to congress, of '59 to '60 in Buchanan's administration.

April 29, 1860, I started again from Fort Dalles to guide Capt. A.J. Smith's command through Harney Valley. Attacked in the Owyhee country by Shoshone Indians Capt. Smith retraced his steps to the meadows of Harney Lake Valley for safety and to await the arrival of Major Steen, who was then exploring a new route across the Cascade Mountains near the head of Des Chutes River. I volunteered to go to Vancouver for reinforcements and Captain Smith offered me choice of horses in his command. I chose the First Sergeant's fine sorrel and started with Geo. Rundel, called "Cayuse George" all over the Northwest. George had a good farm in the Tyhe Valley, but loved the sport of roaming. The Indians had followed and paralleled the command's trail all the way and were then on the west side of Silvey River. Leaving the command at 6 p.m. we both approached the crossing of Silvey River with cocked pistols, but found our trail open. Three nights and two days we traveled the 380 miles to Vancouver the last 90 miles by water, reaching Fort Vancouver on the third day at noon. We had passed Major Steen at the mouth of the Ochoco (near Prineville) who retraced his steps to Harney Lake and hurried on to The Dalles which we reached the third night in time for the steamer.

Arriving at Fort Vancouver I delivered dispatches to Capt. Ingalls just as he was about sitting down to dinner. "Come Louis, dine with us," said the captain, and ushering me into the dining room, just as I was in my campaign garb, I met Gen. Harney, Col. Geo. Wright (who had that morning assumed the command of the Department of Oregon, General Harney retiring) and Colonel E.D. Baker, (called then the "silver tongued orator," just elected by the Oregon Legislature to the U.S. Senate.)

I sat opposite Col. Baker at the table and my recollection of his personality is not a pleasant one.

Major Andrews, 3rd Artillery was ordered to join Major Steen, (who by reason of seniority had assumed command of the troops in the field,) and the second morning we started for the front, where three troops of cavalry and the partly mounted artillery began a lengthy campaign against various Indian camps.

One day, crossing a snow-capped mountain range called now Steen mountain, we saw from the summit by our field glasses, a party of Indians on ponies, in the valley a thousand or more feet below.

The doctor of our expedition (I believe it was Surgeon Hansom,) doubted the ability of the command to follow down the steep declivity; but we camped that night at the foot of the snowy mountain.

The first hostile was captured the very next morning by the Warm Spring Indian scouts. This captive declined to answer Major Steen's questions save by grunts; these questions having passed from the Major's lips to those of the Warm Spring scout, who translated to the Cayuse, who in turn interpreted to the Snake Indian, the latter captured by the Warm Springs Indian, in the spring campaign and of whom I have previously spoken.

The prisoner still refusing to answer, the Major turned him over to the scouts to be dealt with as they saw fit. They led him up a nearby hill, where a Cayuse Indian shot him in the back; next with fiendish yells, they scalped him in plain sight of the camp, and carried the bleeding scalp around with much tom-tomming of their drums. The body was left to the ravens and coyotes.

At evening the camps of various hostiles were revealed to us by their signal fires. (These smoke signs were an alphabet in constant use by the Indians, with possibly as elaborate a manual as in our army "wig-wagging.")

The next day Capt. Johnston (afterwards general in the Confederate army) captured and brought in to camp another party of Indians, mostly women and children, the men having been killed in the battle. These also were turned over to the Indian scouts, who gambled for their possession. Some of the boys, six or eight years of age, were later sold at The Dalles, for a few dollars each. (One of these was purchased by John F. Noble for $2.50.)

One morning, while we were at breakfast the Indian boy appeared at the table holding up his mutilated right hand. He had accidentally cut off a joint of his index finger in a straw cutter, yet stood stoically under our gaze without a tear or murmur. He died within six months, not being able to stand civilization, domiciled in a comfortable log house.)

Major Steen's command roamed over mountains and through pine forests east of Harney and about the then supposed head of the South Fork of the John Day River, for many weeks, but never again met an Indian. They had vanished entirely from that region.

At the close of the campaign I returned to Fort Dalles and prepared the official map of the expedition.

For a description of the surroundings of Fort Dalles at this time I have referred to a brochure entitled "Reminiscences of Eastern Oregon," by Mrs. E. Lord, published in 1903. This was compiled with great care and published at her own expense for private distribution. Mrs. Lords' father, Judge Laughlin was one of the first settlers east of the Cascades, taking up a land claim, adjoining the eastern line of Fort Dalles in 1853, after the boundary of its five mile square tract had been reduced to one mile.

The Catholic Mission claim, also a mile square adjoined the post to the west, and there I first saw alfalfa growing. Father Mesplie, the priest called it "lucerne" and brought the seed from Belgium. Capt. Jordan sowed the parade ground and surrounding best spots of land, mixing with it a little white clover.

My readers will pardon the digression if I now relate some of the experiences upon the plains occuring just previous to the summer spent in exploring new lands of which I have just been speaking.

(That the capital I's would so often occur I had not foreseen, but do not call me egotistic: how can that upright, stiff character be avoided in an autobiography? Be generous and regard me as a friend telling his adventures, not as an author writing a feigned history.)

Upon that memorable journey with ox-team in 1852 I remember most vividly sketching some of the important objects along the route. Chimney and Court House Rocks, the Platte bluffs and valley covered in places with thousands of buffalo; parts of Forts Kearney and Laramie, (where our good Uncle Sam sold to the passing emigrant, who feared a shortage, provisions at eastern prices; flour, bacon and even luxuries.) Then there was Independence Rock with its hundreds of names painted upon its smooth surface; Humboldt Mountains and river, etc, etc. Twelve of the sketches made at this time earned me my first money in the new Eldorado, being published in the Christmas number of the Sacramento "Union," and bringing me a check for forty-eight dollars.

Among the prairie incidents I recall that of my first buffalo hunt. A few of our party started one day for the hills, from which we could plainly see for 20 miles up and down the Platte, and all along this way there crawled the lines of canvas covered wagons drawn by patient oxen. Following a narrow buffalo trail worn deep into the ground, and lined with a thick matting of hair, which they shed in the spring, we came upon our quarry a few hundred yards below us. Some 70 of the brutes were in line like a company of soldiers, all busily grazing the succulent buffalo grass, excepting two enormous bulls, who stood guard, one at either end of the herd, constantly turning his head from right to left, watching for intruders.

We charged down the hill and the buffalo ran wildly toward a ravine. Firing, I distinctly heard the thud of the rifle bullet on his shoulder blade; not a solitary one did we take to camp. But others were more successful, and from that day we counted many graves along the road, victims of the change from bacon diet.

The crossing of the Platte proved a serious matter for some of our fellow travelers. Some who did not heed the warning of quick-sand, too impatient to wait their turn at the proper crossing, were rescued with difficulty, minus all their household goods.

While camped at Ash Hollow, during the evening meal a roving Indian party appeared and the chief offered our captain twenty ponies in exchange for his young wife. The poor woman ran screaming to her tent, much to the surprise of the Indian.

At La Boute river a sad thing occurred. A young man was condemned to death, after a jury trial. The men ran two wagons together with tongues high in the air and from this improvised gibbet the young fellow expiated his rash act. They buried him there placing his name upon the head board, with the words, "Hung for killing his fellow-man."

The summer of 1861 I spent at Fort Walla Walla, the guest of Major Steen, then commander of the Post. My good friend, the Major's portrait, I see upon the wall when I lift my eyes from my writing. His was a tall soldierly figure, with noble open countenance, and clear, loyal eyes. He died years since. Major Steen joined the Catholic Church at the earnest solicitation of his young wife, then at their home in St. Louis. Father Mesplie performed the rite of baptism, Gen. James McAuliff and I being the invited witnesses, in that little first church built by the Catholics in Walla Walla. It is the building since removed to the corner of Seventh and Poplar streets, and now occupied as a dwelling by the Paulist fathers. On a subsequent Christmas night I remember singing there the "Adele fidestes" at the close of the services.

In the autumn of 1861, an expedition was ordered fitted out by the War Department, to be sent by way of Mazatlan, Mexico, to the relief of Fort Worth, Texas; six hundred mules, and all available army-wagons from Simcoe to Colville were assembled at Fort Walla Walla for the journey. These were sent to Fort Vancouver and from there to Benicia Barracks, California.

This part of the expedition was in two sections; the first in charge of George Wright, eldest son of Col. Wright, left Fort Walla Walla, as I have said, in the early autumn of 1861, and I followed, with the second section.

Arrived at Vancouver we were given choice of land or sea route, the order coming from Capt. Kirkham, chief quartermaster in San Francisco, by the first telegraph line then just completed, across the Columbia River.

Wright chose the sea route and embarking his mules and wagons (that were charged for by the number of cubic yards of space they occupied) reached Benicia after a stormy voyage with the animals unfit for service and at an expense to the government of $20,000.

I chose the land route and after three weeks travel reached Benicia Barracks with all animals in fine condition, and at a cost of only about $3,500.

Meanwhile that order for the relief of Fort Worth had been countermanded. The Mexican government had objected to an armed U.S. force marching through her territory, and Fort Worth had surrendered all the immense war material to the confederacy. These munitions of war had been piled up, (so it is said) by Jefferson Davis, then Secretary of War, with a view to the coming conflict.

I sailed from San Francisco in December for New York, and New Years' day 1862 found me in Washington, D.C., domiciled with Senator Nesmith, who occupied the lower floor of No. 221 Pennsylvania Avenue, just opposite the well-known Willard Hotel, whilst Lieut. Col. Ingalls, afterwards chief quartermaster of McClellan's command, had the upper floor.

During January and February I acted as private secretary to Senator Nesmith, preparing chiefly the transfer of Indian war bonds to their owners in Oregon.

I cannot forbear to speak here of the Senator. From him I imbibed some valuable lessons in politics. An upright democrat, and a staunch union man when the conflict came. I well remember listening to one of his passionate appeals to his hearers, when "stumping" Oregon in the campaign for U.S. Senator. A stern, doctrinaire, bold and outspoken; a politician at the moment so fierce in invective, and so withering, with a combativeness quite implacable when roused, was James Willis Nesmith, Senator from Oregon.

Before leaving Pacific Coast events for a time, I would say a few words about two prominent men whom I knew and greatly admired, whose services were of the utmost value to the Inland Empire.

Gov. Isaac I. Stevens, whose treaty of 1855 with various Indian tribes assembled at Walla Walla, secured the basis of a permanent understanding between the whites and the Indians, passed through The Dalles in 1856. Nobody would have suspected him to be a United States Engineer and Territorial Governor and an accomplished military officer. He appeared in a faded old coat, dilapidated hat, and enormous boots, apparently several sizes too large for his feet--a figure most unlike the then popular idea of a civil and military hero, but in spite of appearances the little man inspired only feelings of respect and admiration.

The other was Col. George Wright of the Ninth Infantry, who broke the backbone of the Indian power. Forethought, benevolence and carefulness spoke from his eyes. He looked and was a type of the real soldier. Kind and thoughtful of his men, but severe in discipline and a most just man in treating with the Indians.

The battle of Spokane Plains, Sept. 5, 1858, ended our fighting with the Spokanes, Coeur d'Alenes, Palouses and Pend 'Oreilles and his order to kill their 900 ponies captured on the 8th of September, closed the drama east of the Columbia River. His answer to Chief Garry, "I did not come to ask you to make a treaty of peace; I came to fight," was so like him. That was the very day before the appearance in the sky of the comet, that frightened the Indians into utter submission.

If any of the men prominent during those years in "Old Oregon" deserves a monument let the people be just to Col. Wright and Gov. Stevens.

It was Feb. 28, 1862 that Lieut. Col. Ingalls informed me of the coming of troops to Annapolis and offered me a clerkship in his department, where my chief work would be superintending transportation. Often I accompanied the Colonel to Arlington Heights, where he at that time had his office, and amongst his thirty-five clerks I found my friend Donald McIntosh as chief. McIntosh had been chief clerk to Governor Stevens in 1854-5, during the earlier Indian war and afterwards for four years occupied the same position at Fort Dalles. His father was a Factor of the Hudson Bay Company and in 1830, Donald, then a babe in swaddling clothes, had been carried in a basket over the mountains and valleys on horseback and by batteaux all the way from Winnipeg to Fort Vancouver by one of the company's voyageurs," Crate by name. "Crate's Point" on the Columbia, three miles below The Dalles is named for this man. McIntosh subsequently held the chief clerkship under Gen. Rucker, chief Quartermaster of the Defenses of Washington City, and received a Lieutenant's commission from President Lincoln in 1864. As a captain of the 5th Cavalry under Custer he was murdered with the entire command by the fiendish Sioux. His honored name is engraved with those of the others of the 5th on the column erected by the Government on the bloody battle field on the Rosebud.

McIntosh once told me--it was in 1860--speaking of Captain Jordan's regime as quartermaster of Fort Dalles, and the expense of construction in those days, that a trifle over $240,000.00 had passed through his hands. This sum had been expended not alone for building officers' and soldiers' quarters, but for innumerable purposes. There were besides material and labor, wagon and pack trains to be outfitted, sawmill machinery, blacksmith and wagonshop expenses. The single item of ferryage of troops and trains, across the Columbia, Des Chutes and John Day rivers, was constant and enormous. Then the pay of express riders, Indian scouts, exploring parties--up Mill creek looking for water supply--and coal and ores; exploring of the ranges toward the Yakima Valley where wagon roads had to be cut through heavy pine forests; the purchase of lumber from Mosiers Mills and hauling same (for not a foot of lumber was brought from San Francisco or around Cape Horn for this work); the purchase of hay and grain added much to the expenditures. One winter large quantities of potatoes were purchased in Portland, oats and barley being unobtainable, and these were fed to the animals, after being boiled and mixed with bunch grass that had been laboriously cut by the Indian squaws, and delivered each morning, even in the snowstorms. Thus the quartermaster's many horses and mules were kept from starving; the grain and timothy hay being reserved for the cavalry horses.

The building of the blockhouse and corral with high stockade 28 miles north on Klickitat creek was another large item of expense, that showed the foresight of Capt. Jordan, for it proved a harbor of refuge on many occasions for soldiers and pack-trains and later for the wagon trains on this road that was completed by Lieut. Allen of the Ninth Infantry who just as he had completed his work was murdered by an Indian near Toppenish River.

(That wagon road has been witness to many a tragedy. I remember well when Capt. Bowman left Fort Simcoe on leave to visit his family at Fort Dalles. Impatient at the slowness of the wagon train, he hurried on, on foot, one moonlight night some twenty miles from the river, and was never seen again alive. The search parties sent out followed his trail for several days before they discovered his body, partly devoured by wolves. The supposition was that losing his way he had wandered until overcome by hunger and exhaustion. Capt. Bowman's widow and daughter took the body to their eastern home where the Citizen Soldiers of Wilkesbarre, Pennsylvania gave him military burial.)

A stone warehouse with tower for defense near the present Celilo, was also built under Capt. Jordan's direction, from material close at hand. It collapsed in 1862 being undermined by the great flood of that year. It was known as Captain Kingsbury's hermitage, as this government officer lived a solitary life there for many years, in charge of batteaux and transportation.

Our townsmen, Jesse Drumheller and Sam Johnson, were the contractors for hauling the government supplies for Forts Walla Walla and Colville, from Fort Dalles to this point, near the mouth of the Des Chutes River, where until the 60's much of the freight was loaded on batteaux and brought up the Columbia to Wallula as in the earlier McLaughlin days. The contracts for delivery of government stores to the vessels for Wallula landing were held by R.R. Thompson, and proved the stepping stone to his becoming one of the original stockholders with Capt. Ainsworth in the O.S.N. Co., the forerunner of the O.R.& N. Co.

The cost of everything was so great that the wonder is not that army maintenance expenses were so large, but that they were not larger, especially after that terribly hard winter of 1861-2 when the thermometer went to 36 degrees below zero--hay was $75.00 per ton and little to be had and firewood was $50.00 a cord. The snow was 24 inches deep, with its surface frozen nearly all winter, making it impossible for the cattle to reach the bunch grass underneath. In May, 1862, Col. James Fulton, formerly of Yamhill county (who was the first to bring large herds across the Cascades to graze the "bunch-grass" of the Inland Empire) passed through Walla Walla on his way to Oro Fino mines, and there refused the government offer of 22 cents per pound for the best of his herd.

Chapter

Settlers
and Frozen
Dreams

"Mother made the
most delicious scones,
dropping the dough in a frying pan
which she placed in front of the fire."
Cora Clark

*C*olonel Wright's punishing victory over the Indians in 1858 made it safe to open the Inland Northwest to settlers. There was, however, little inducement for settlers to venture to the newly opened country, except for the possibilities of raising stock. One of the most appealing areas to the stockmen, who came from California and the Willamette Valley, was the Walla Walla Valley. At the foot of the Blue Mountains this fertile valley covered with knee deep rye grass and criss-crossed with small streams, was located one hundred fifty miles east of The Dalles, Oregon. An added incentive to locate in the valley was the presence of Fort Walla Walla, which provided both protection and a market for their beef and grain.

In 1857, a rude village had begun to form near Fort Walla Walla. The merchants and saloon keepers who were catering to the military, located their tents and buildings on the Nez Perce Indian trail, a couple of miles distant from the fort and near where the trail crossed a large creek where the packers watered their mules. The tradesmen probably figured that the soldiers would walk the extra mile to town for that ration the military didn't provide, and the extra business from the packers was certainly welcome.

As the valley floor filled and good grazing land became hard to get, the stockmen started spreading out to settle on the Touchet River and other streams in the area. In the latter part of 1860, gold was discovered in Idaho and because the Walla Walla country was the closest supply area to the mines, more cattle and goods were brought into the country.

Then came the winter of 1861-62, the worst ever known on the Pacific Coast. The deep snow crusted with ice and made it impossible for the cattle to feed, with the result that very few animals made it through the winter. The dreams that seemed so promising were frozen and the settlers were practically wiped out.

A few of the volunteer soldiers who had so recently battled the Indians for this land had noticed the possibilities of the valley and were among the first settlers. Charles Actor, who joined Governor Stevens' party in Montana at the Blackfoot Indian Treaty in 1855 and stayed in the Governor's bodyguard until 1858, was one of these early settlers. Let's join him now as he relates his story about life around Fort Benton when he worked for the American Fur Company in the early '50's.

Charles Actor

A lad of eighteen,
prompted by the spirit of adventure,
finds himself working at Fort Benton
on the Missouri River in 1853.

Charles Actor formerly owned the present site of Dixie, Washington, and made his home in that vicinity.

Mr. Actor settled on the farm in 1858 and lived there until the early eighties when it was sold and platted into town lots.

The American Fur Company in the early fifties would send a representative to St. Louis in the early summer of each year to sell the winter's harvest of furs and on the return trip take back supplies of provisions and clothing. Prompted by the spirit of adventure, Mr. Actor succeeded in getting a position with the company on the return trip and left St. Louis, which was but a small town then, June 3, 1853, for Ft. Benton on the Missouri river in Montana. The journey by boat was long, tedious and hard. When the supply of wood was consumed the steamer was tied up on the bank, the crew went ashore, chopped down trees, cut them into convenient lengths and carried them aboard.

The steamer arrived at Fort Union on the Missouri river, July 4, and this was the extent of the steamer's route. At this place the supplies were transferred to a canal boat.

Supplies at Fort Union were much higher than at the present high price of living. Flour was then two pints for $1.00; teacupful of coffee, $1.00; teacupful of sugar, $1.00; but wild game was abundant, buffalo, elk, deer, antelope, bear and other game. One was never out of sight of buffalo at Fort Union.

The journey from this point was exceedingly hard. A crew of eighteen men walked on the bank and pulled the boat up the river, a distance of several hundred miles. When there was a bend in the river it was necessary for the crew to cross the river as the water was too shallow for the boat.

Fort Benton was reached late in the fall, where the company went into winter quarters. The Fort consisted of two officer's quarters and quarter for the men. The buildings were of adobe. The Fort was surrounded by a high wall 200 feet by 300 feet with a bastion on two of the corners. This wall was built for a protection against the Indians. The whole number in the fort at this time was about twenty.

The company's store was on the inside and this was where the Indians bought their supplies or traded furs for blankets, red paint, guns, shirts, tobacco and other things kept in stock. The Indians at that time were not safe neighbors, especially when they had an advantage. For some reason they killed the oxen belonging to the chief factor of the company. Being at the mercy of the Indians, in a way and so far from help, the chief factor of the Fur Company felt that he must teach them a lesson that would not be forgotten and in this he seemed to outclass, even the Indian in treachery.

He invited the Indians to a feast. The Indian's favorite dish made by the white then was a soup made of water and flour and sweetened with sugar. When the party arrived and were within the wall, he turned a howitzer on them and killed nine out of fourteen.

He was a stern commanding person that was good to his help as long as they did faithful service. When a man was disobedient he would discipline him by taking him into a room where pistols and bowie knives lay temptingly convenient on a table, and if he could not persuade the disobedient one to terms he frightened him into terms. The principal work for the winter was cutting and hauling wood and cutting and sawing logs for making boats.

When the goods came the Indians would bring in hides of buffalo, deer, elk, antelope and beavers and receive a few loads of ammunition for their cargo. They would give a horse for a gun that would be worth about $1.50 at the present time.

A messenger was sent by Governor Stevens, Washington's first governor, to Fort Benton to be sent to Col. Cummings of the U.S. army. Mr. Actor took the message, going alone 360 miles. The journey was made on an Indian pony.

In 1855 Mr. Actor left Ft. Benton with a company of which Governor Stevens was one, coming to The Dalles. Some of the Indians were hostile at this time, and the company encountered some of this type, but they had a force of 40 Nez Perce Indians as guides.

The Indians saw a lone Indian in the distance. Governor Stevens ordered him to be brought into camp. He proved to be the son of a chief of one of the hostile tribes. Governor Stevens sent this Indian back to his tribe with the command that his father and his followers give themselves up to him. His command was obeyed. The father met the governor at the present site of Pomeroy and accompanied him and the company to The Dalles.

On the way the governor and company stopped about four miles southwest of the present site of Walla Walla for about two weeks to rest the animals after the hard trip through the mountains. The company subsisted almost entirely on beef while in this camp, which was procured from the Indians.

On Wild Horse Creek good horses were found that belonged to the hostile Indians. Men of the company were ordered to drive a good number into an Indian corral and enough horses needed to supply the company were taken. Mr. Actor remained with Governor Steven's guards until 1858. Soon after severing his connection with the guards he returned to this vicinity and was one of the early settlers of the Walla Walla Valley.

Charles W. Clark

*A recent widow, soon to be a mother again,
leaves civilization to settle in the wilderness.
This account, "Recollections of the First Boy in Walla Walla",
was written by her son, Charles W. Clark.*

I was born on August 29, 1846, in Oregon, on my father's claim near LaFayette, Yamhill County, from which the family was taken to Oregon City and thence to Portland.

Needless to say, Portland was then a raw, crude town on the edge of the Willamette River, with no business places except on the Front and First streets.

In 1855 my father, Ransom Clark, left home for Colville mines. On his way home to Portland he selected the place on the Yellowhawk, since known from his name, ran out the lines with a pocket compass, for there was no Government survey. The place was nearly in a square and extended from about where the road just east of Harry Reynolds' house now is to the present Whitney Road.

My father was on the place in 1855 when the Indian war broke out, and he, like all the other settlers--few in number, of course--was ordered by the United States commandant to leave the country.

That war prevented my father's making proof on the claim, but the Government ruled that since the settlers had been obliged to leave on account of war, they should not lose their time, but could resume possession and continue to prepare for making final proof.

We lived in Portland until 1859, when announcement was made that Indian disturbances were at an end. In the fall of 1858 father had returned to the claim. With the coming of winter he went back to Portland, but on March 1, 1859, he went back again to Walla Walla, taking me with him. I was then twelve years old, a strong, active boy, and accustomed to all sorts of work and capable of being of much assistance to my father in starting the place.

We came from Portland with a team and wagon, putting them on the steamer at Portland and going as far as The Dalles; thence driving to Walla Walla. Moher was left alone in Portland with my brother Will, then two years old.

We had quite a lot of apple and peach trees which we obtained at the Tibbetts and Luelling nurseries, near Oregon City. I can tell you the Walla Walla Valley looked beautiful in those early spring days. It was just a waving sea of new grass, green all over without a fence or anything to obstruct riding anywhere that we might wish.

We reached our claim on March 18th. So far as I remember there was not another white boy in the whole valley, except at the fort, or whose parents were employed at the fort. Some of the army officers had children, but I hardly ever saw them. I had no playmates except the Indian children, and they were very friendly. There were no women, that is, no white women outside the fort, unless two or three transients. There were several Indian women married to white men, former Hudson's Bay men, down the valley at Frenchtown and elsewhere.

When we reached the claim we discovered that "Curly" Drumheller and Samuel Johnson had done some plowing on the south edge of our place, from the spring branch to Russell Creek. We sowed it with oats and there was a good crop, which we threshed out with flails in the fall. We set out some of our fruit trees on the flat just southeast of where Harry Reynolds' house now is. Those were, I am sure, the first trees ever brought to Walla Walla, that is, after those that had been raised from seed by Doctor Whitman at Waiilatpu. John Foster bought the trees which were set on his place from our lot. The bill for those trees from Seth Luelling is still in possession of my brother Will.

After remaining six weeks my father returned to Portland to get my mother and brother. I was left to keep the place, in company with Robert Horton. We had nothing but a tent for a house, but we managed to get along very comfortably. My main work was to cook. I helped plow on John Foster's place to help pay for the logs which Foster had gotten out that spring or summer for making our cabin. On Sundays and sometimes on other days I would go to "town," which was just a mongrel collection of shacks and tents, with a confused mass of settlers, Indians and soldiers straying through. The chief amusement was horse racing and gambling. There was a straight-away track where the cemetery now is and another just about through where the chief part of town now lies. The first circular track was laid out by George Porter about three miles down the valley, running around the peculiar hill on the Sam Smith place, afterward the Tom Lyons place.

The saloon business was very active then and every species of vice flourished. There was a man named Ed Leach who had come with father and me from The Dalles, who had afterwards drifted around town.

One day I was near the saloon owned by W.A. Ball, and I saw that there had just been something going on, for there was a bunch of men standing around talking excitedly.

Ed Leach was there, and seeing me he pulled me over to a place where I saw blood on the ground, and he said, pointing out the puddle of blood, "There, Charlie, is where I got him." He had just killed a man.

Nothing was done about it, so far as I know.

W.A. Ball was an uncle of my wife, and one of the first business men in Walla Walla. He was the one especially who insisted on giving the name of Walla Walla to the town. Some wanted to call it Waiilatpu, while some favored Steptoeville.

One day while in town a man called to me saying that he had heard it rumored that my father was dead. I paid no attention to this, for I had heard from him a few days before, that he had safely reached home, was getting ready to return, and that everything was well. There were no mails at that time and the only way to get messages was through the army or by stray travelers. It would take a week or two to hear anything from Portland.

But though I paid no attention to the rumor it proved a sad reality. That very day after I had returned to the tent which I called home, my mother's brother, Uncle Billy Millican, who is still living in Walla Walla, appeared and told me that it was only too true, that my father had been taken suddenly sick and had died a number of days before, and that my mother was even then on her way to Walla Walla.

The next day she came, having come on the Steamer Colonel Wright, of which Lew White was captain, on her second or third trip from The Dalles to Wallula. From that place she came with Capt. F.F. Dent in an army ambulance to Walla Walla. That Captain Dent, by the way, was a brother-in-law of General Grant.

As you can imagine it was a sad, hard journey for a woman who had just been made a widow, and who was soon to be again a mother.

It shows somehting of the nerve and heroism of pioneer women that they could go through such experiences. My mother had been strongly advised to give up her claim. A man had offered her $300.00 for it, and Judge Shattuck, one of the leading lawyers of Portland, urged her to take it, assuring her that it would be the most that she could ever get out of it. But father had been greatly impressed with the prospective value of the place and the prospects of the town, and my mother had been so much impressed with his views that she determined to hold the claim.

Accordingly, after spending two weeks with me she returned to Portland. I spent that summer, sometimes a very lonesome one, in the tent, or hoeing the garden which he had put out, and in September Robert Horton and Uncle Billy Millican put up a cabin from the logs.

The cabin was put on the present location of Harry Reynolds' house. It was moved from there a few feet many years ago, and put on a good foundation, so that it is now just about as sound as ever. It is undoubtedly the oldest house now existing in the Inland Empire, in which a white woman lived. My mother was about the first white woman in this region, after the missionary period.

My mother came back to Walla Walla in October of that same year, 1859, with her newly born child, then six weeks old, to live the remainder of her life in Walla Walla.

During those early years the valley seemed to be filled with Indians, but they were very kindly and well disposed, and we had no trouble with them, even though a good part of the time we were alone, mother and the baby and the little boy and myself as the nearest a man about the place. We had

-149-

plenty of horses and cattle and chickens and garden and had an abundance of necessities, though no elegancies.

There were two principal Indian chiefs, and they, with their squaws and children were often around the house. They were fine Indians. Yellowhawk was one of them, and his location was on the creek named after him, on what is now the Billy Russell place near the Braden schoolhouse. The other was Tintimitsy. His location was on what became the J.H. Abbott place.

As I remember the old town in 1860, there were several shack stores. One was that of Neil McClinchy, on what would now be between Third and Fourth streets.

Baldwin Brothers were about between Second and Third. Frank Worden was located just about where the Third National Bank now is. Guichard and Kohlhauff had a store on the same corner where the White House Clothing Store now is. John F. Abbott had a stable right in what is now Second Street, just about what would be between the Jaycox Store and the Jones Building. There was no order or system to the streets for many years, and, as we know, they are very irregular now, having followed convenient trails or breakings though the cottonwoods and birches which grew on the creek.

The creek at that time ran right on the top of the ground and in high water ran out in many places. Quite a stream at high water ran through just about where Senator Ankeny's house is over through the presnt high school grounds and thence joining Garrison Creek.

During the long, cold nights of winter in 1860-61 we lived alone in our cabin. Mother and I would grind our flour in the big coffee-mill. One regular job we had, and often we were up till midnight working at it, and that was to make sacks for the flour-mill which A.H. Reynolds, in partnership with J.A. Sims and Capt. F.F. Dent, put up in 1859 on what is now the Whitney place.

But my mother was anxious that I should have some schooling, and having become married to Mr. Reynolds, she sent me to Portland Academy for two years, and two years more to LaFayette where I lived with my grandparents.

When I returned in 1865 I was a man. Walla Walla was growing. That was right in the midst of the mining times and the Vigilantes, when they had "a man for breakfast" nearly every morning. It was a wild, exciting time, but through it all Walla Walla has grown to be the beautiful city of which we are now so proud.

A.B. Roberts

The killing of Citizen McGarry
in 1859 by soldiers from Fort Walla Walla
was an incident that almost caused a riot.

Civil government was established for Walla Walla County, Washington, and for Wascopon County, Oregon, the following winter (1858), and the U.S. troops were located on a section of land where a garrison had been built, and, as the war was over, it was supposed that military rule was to be limited to that section.

The military authorities were slow to give up their wide range of sway, which resulted in a final conflict with the civil authorities and a grand battle on the streets of the village of Walla Walla early in June, 1859, following the killing of Citizen McGarry, the circumstances of which were as follows:

Mr. McGarry had purchased a mule from a discharged soldier by the name of McCool.

The Government herder came to town and claimed the mule, which McGarry refused to give up, and reported the matter to the quartermaster at the garrison. A corporal's guard was sent to town with the herder, accompanied by Wm. A. Mix, the quartermaster's agent and the wagonmaster, George Russell. The mule was tied to my fence, just in the rear of James Galbraith's saloon on Main Street. I chanced to be passing on horseback as the herder and the others came up, and my curiosity caused me to stop and see how the Government did business off its reservation.

The herder took possession of the mule and led him away. McGarry, with Mix and the soldiers followed along, Mr. McGarry declaring that he had bought the animal, that there was no Government brand on it and giving other reasons for his claim. Mr. Mix said to the corporal, "take this man to the guard house." The soldiers surrounded McGarry, who walked with them to the lines of the street, where he made a stop and the soldiers all leveled down on him and put four bullets through his body and he fell dead at their feet.

The newly appointed sheriff, Mr. Ball, was in the crowd of bystanders and immediately leveled his six-shooter on the corporal and called them all "his prisoners," and they seemed to believe he meant "business."

Mr. Mix then called to Mr. Russell, "Go down to the garrison and send up a good, strong guard," and he went a-flying.

The prisoners were taken to the office of John A. Simms, the new justice of the peace, where a preliminary hearing began at once.

As I had seen the trying-out of this application of law in my new country I went on about my business, which was to have my horses shod at the garrison, as there was then no blacksmith in the town. I had gone but a short quarter of the distance until I met a company of dragoons.

In a short time I met another and another company of dragoons and I was told by a trooper that the commanding officer (Major Rains) had given orders "to bring back those soldiers or burn the town and kill every man in it." So I returned with them, as I thought there would be possibly something more to be seen, as everybody was on the rush. Just ahead of the troopers I met Dr. Gove, a dentist, who, as he met Lieutenant Johnson of that company of troops, whirled about, and, as he came by his side, said to the officer, "You are going up after those soldiers; now I am going to ride by your side and if you order your men to fire I will put a bullet through your head and you will find every officer now there guarded by dozens of determined men ready to kill the first and every one who gives the order to fire." And so it was; as we rushed in to town we found about 300 troopers mixed in with about 200 men of the country or town, and every one of the latter was armed with guns, pick handles or crowbars, standing among the troops and from five to ten determined men surrounding each officer, and the trial continued at justice court, Simms' officers with Sheriff Ball and a number of deputies standing about. Thus main Street from about where the Dacres Hotel now stands, up to the First Street bridge, was a seething mass of angry men, who were determined that military rule in the Walla Walla Valley should be confined to the limits of the reservation and that the civil authorities should control. And so they moved and mingled, like troubled waters, from 10 o'clock until 3 p.m., when the troops began to retire and the prisoners were held for the higher court and sent to jail and later were tried for the murder of McGarry. And by this great struggle came the transition from the military to the civil rule, or the last change.

Margaret Gilbreath

Mrs. Gilbreath tells how she and her husband,
a veteran of the 1855-56 Indian wars,
came to the newly opened Inland Empire in 1859
to settle near present day Dayton, Washington.

S. L. Gilbreath and I were married at Albany, Oregon in March, 1859, and started at once for Washington Territory with a band of cattle, one wagon and team, and three herders.

At the Cascade Mountains two other men, John Wells and Tom Davis, with a wagon and cattle, joined us. We soon found it impossible to hurry on with the wagons, so they were left behind until the road was opened, the rest coming on with the stock. Pack horses carried the camp equipment. It was hard work opening up the trail on account of fallen trees and deep snow. We camped on Butter Creek and sent two men on to find suitable grazing land for our cattle. They returned in a few days reporting that good land with plenty of bunch grass could be homesteaded on the Touchet River. Having succeeded in bringing up our wagons under much difficulty, we continued on our way to Walla Walla.

Captain Dent, commander of Fort Walla Walla, stopped us and insisted that we settle near Walla Walla. We could not do this as the horses of the garrison had eaten all the grass from the range and we were looking for good pasture.

We inquired of the captain if we would be safe from the Indians if we went to the Touchet Valley. He assured us that the Indians were peaceable, which Mr. Gilbreath believed as he had served as volunteer through the Indian wars of 1855 and 1856, and knew of the Nez Perces fighting and scouting for the whites through the war. We found them always friendly, unless they had been drinking.

Leaving Walla Walla we proceeded on our way to The Crossing, which is now Dayton, reaching there August 27, 1859.

Mr. Stubbs, whose real name was Theodore Schnebley, lived here in a log house with his squaw wife. He sold whiskey to the Indians, thereby causing the whites much trouble. In coming into the Valley of the Touchet we left the Indian trail and came down a ravine, in some places having to shovel out places in the ravine to keep the wagons from turning over. These wagons were the first brought into the Touchet Valley.

The next day, after our arrival at The Crossing, we started to build a corral for the cattle, but discovered a den of rattlesnakes. After killing ten we decided to move down the valley to a fine location near a big spring of pure water. This land we homesteaded.

The Indian chiefs were frequent visitors at our cabin, calling soon after we came. Timothy and Lawyer and their friends sometimes sent messengers on ahead to tell us they were coming to dine with us. We would hasten to get ready a good meal for we thought it best to keep them friendly.

Many times we expected trouble from them. Once they rode up the trail shouting and firing off their guns. That night they burned the house of Mr. Stubbs. Sometimes they would imitate wolves howling and slip up near the house to see if there was a man there to know whether to scare the white woman or not.

Once they came and demanded food and money and continued to frighten me until I grabbed a rifle and started toward them. Then they threw up their hands and laughed and said I was afraid.

Several times they would run a beef into the woods and kill it, carrying home the meat. One night when the Indians had been drinking and were giving us a great scare, two men hunting cattle and Reverend Berry, who preached at our cabin once a month, happened to be there. We were certainly glad to have company.

One day Mr. Gilbreath was plowing rye grass with oxen when Reverend Berry came riding up. He stopped his work and waited for Mr. Berry to come up to him, then said, looking at his clothes and general appearance, "A Methodist preacher, I suppose." "Yes, I am," was the reply. "Well, go on to the house. My wife is a Methodist and will be glad to see you." Reverend Berry preached in our cabin all that fall and winter of 1859 and 1860. His congregation consisted of Mr. and Mrs. Herren, Mr. Stubbs and his dusky wife, Mr. Gilbreath and I, and men who happened to be in the neighborhood. Mr. Berry afterward made his home in Walla Walla for some years.

Whiskey Creek was so named because a band of outlaws made this region their rendezvous, selling whiskey and stealing cattle. Their names were Bill Bunting, John Cooper, Bill Skinner, George Ives and several others who were later hanged in Montana for crimes. The authorities there evidently knew their business, for these were the men who caused the Vigilantes to organize against them. Many prominent men took part in ridding the new country of these undesirables, among them Anderson Cox and J.W. McGhee. It was said that in dealing with the thieves Mr. McGhee said to George Ives who was up for trial: "George, we want you to leave, and we want it to be a long time before you come back." Mr. McGhee's deliberate way of speaking evidently carried weight, for George left.

The first crop of wheat in the Touchet Valley was raised on the land of Israel Davis on Whiskey Creek. He was leaving for the Willamette to buy sheep and Mr. Gilbreath harvested the wheat by cradling, and threshed it out by horses tramping on it. One night a wind came up and Mr. Gilbreath and hired men got up out of bed and began the work of cleaning the wheat by pouring pails full of it from a scaffold to the ground. In this manner over a thousand bushels were cleaned. This was intended for seed for the coming year, but the hard winter of 1861 and 1862 followed when food for man and beast became so scarce that most of it was sold to the needy for food, and to keep the teams from starving. Some of the settlers ground the wheat in coffee mills and used it as porridge. We sold our wheat for $2 a bushel. We could have sold at any price but Mr. Gilbreath would not take advantage of their great need.

This was the most terrible winter ever experienced in the valley. The snow drifted so deep that many of the cattle were frozen standing up. Out of 300 of ours two cows and a calf, which we fed, were left. The timber wolves killed a good many cattle that winter. One day a wolf attacked a calf and the mother heard the cry of distress coming from some distance. When she reached it, the wolf was starting to devour the body. The cow fought it from the calf for a day or two, making the most piteous cries. Other cattle smelled the blood and came bawling for miles around. The sound of hundreds of frenzied cattle bawling will not soon be forgotten.

We were fortunate in having plenty of supplies that winter, as we had prepared to send a small pack train to the mines at Elk City. The deep snow made it impossible to get supplies, so the neighbors called on us, and our stores were opened to feed them. Our stock of food was divided among thirteen families. The snow was so deep that only a narrow trail could be kept open to Walla Walla by miners coming to and from the Idaho mines. The snow lay on the ground until March, and in shady places until June. We had to go to Walla Walla in the spring and buy barley for seed.

Miller and Mossman who ran a pony express to the mines, stopped at our cabin for meals, and for exchange of horses. Their saddle-bags were often loaded with gold dust. Joaquin Miller, who is now known as one of our best western poets, was then a rough frontiersman, dressed in buckskin.

Having moved to a new log house, school was held in our cabin in the spring of 1862. Five or six children attended. Mr. Harlin, an Englishman, was the teacher, and he stayed with us.

Another school was taught in 1863 in the Forrest brothers' cabin. These men were brothers-in-law of Jesse N. Day, who later founded Dayton. Frank Harmon was the teacher and A.W. Sweeney of Walla Walla was the first county superintendent.

Reverend Sweeney organized a Cumberland Presbyterian Church at Waitsburg. Among others, Mr. and Mrs. Long and daughter and Mr. Gilbreath and I were charter members.

Our first child who died in infancy was the first white child born in the territory now included in Columbia, Garfield and Asotin counties. The oldest living person born in this territory is Mrs. John Steen, daughter of George Miller.

I was the only white woman in this territory for two months, until Lambert Herren and family came and settled near. Mrs. Robt. Rowley, who was two months old at that time, is the only living one of the Herren family of eight children.

Mrs. Herren was a typical pioneer woman, fearless and kindhearted, nursing me and others in times of sickness, in the absence of a physician. When the Indians threatened me, I sent for her and she came with shotgun and indignation, and rescued me.

Great changes have taken place since those early days, and many incidents of vital interest to us then have been forgotten, but the kindness and simple living of the early settlers are not easily forgotten.

John Kelso

*John Kelso, who ran a blacksmith shop
at Fairfield, Washington, for many years,
tells about his life in pre-Civil War Kansas,
the goldfields of Colorado in 1859,
and his journey to Oregon in 1862.*

September 1, 1853, I, with Benjamin Lewis and Lucinda, his wife, and son, ten months old, left Clinton County, Ind. with three horses and a wagon, two horses to the wagon and one riding horse. Without any very bad luck landed in Buchanan County, Iowa, in about 15 days, as near as I can remember. At this time we settled in a small cabin with a Mr. John Rodgers, who had been out there in the early spring and bought the place, so the cabin was ready for us. Mr. Rodgers accompanied us from Indiana, so Mr. Lewis and family wintered with Mr. Rodgers. I went over to Vinton, the County Seat of Benton County, and went to work for Mr. Edward Downing, who had the job of building the Court House, I worked there until September, 1854. During the summer I got hold of a team and wagon for my wages; and a yoke of oxen added to the wages. During the season the County Commissioners broke into the Court House building and took all the old man had. They concluded to move up to Lafayette, M---County, 75 miles west of Vinton. Mr. Downing got me to move them. When we got all up, which was three or four loads, I concluded to stay there. From that on I was engaged in hauling wood for the town folks, and flour from Cedar Rapids; also store goods from Davenport and Muskatine and Iowa City until the spring of 1857, when, with four others, I went to Anderson County, Kansas. The other three went back to Iowa. I stayed there. During the summer I worked at different jobs, such as driving, breaking, teaming, helping build houses, digging wells, and so forth.

In December eighteen of the settlers took a 50-mile walk down in Linn County to liberate some Free Statesmen who had resisted some of Fort Scott officers. They had taken several 6-mile teams and went out 12 miles where the farmers had plenty of corn. These Fort Scotters wanted the farmers to pay taxes that the farmers had no right to pay. Consequently, the farmers, teamsters, and officers had sort of a fight. They arrested the farmers, about four of them, put them in Fort Scott jail. Word was sent all over the country and old John Brown gathered up 100 sharprifle men and Captain Montgomery with as many more, Jim Lane had enough more of such as our 15 was, to make an army of between 450 and 500. Well, our little company started at three or four o'clock p.m., walked 50 miles without stopping only long enough to eat a little. We came to Lane's company a few minutes after the men at camp turned out. Got our breakfast, after which we were all on the drill ground except John Brown's 100. Those were not seen by our men, but we had good evidence that they were there. Well, we had to find boarding places, so the farmers in the county took two and three and four of us, according to the financial abilities of the farmer. Soon after drilling, Lane dispatched twelve of his mounted men to Fort Scott and demanded the farmers released. They came back with the word that this would not be done, so Tuesday morning the same performance with the same result. Wednesday morning the same order was sent with an additional demand that if the men were not out on Thursday morning, for the families to get out of the town by noon or take the consequences; so when the guard came back Thursday morning the prisoners were out and we were disbanded, and went home. Got home on Christmas morning.

Next day I started on foot and alone for Iowa. In eleven and half days was at Lafayette, about 500 miles; two days after got a ride to Berling, Hardin County, where Father and the rest of the family were then living. I was there a few days; went back down to Lafayette to make ox yokes for some boys that were going with brother James and me to Kansas. The first of March, 1858, six of us with seven yoke of cattle and two horses appeared as if the bottom had dropped out. I had 600 on a low-wheeled wagon, and for the next 35 miles those axles were dragging half the time on the mud. We began to trade the flour for corn, but flour was worth nothing, as well as corn at that time. We got rid of some of it by hunting for some poor widows in town where the deep mud was so bad we had to unload some of it and throw it away.

On account of the loss of our diary I cannot at present give the number of days we were on this trip. We finally wallowed through until we passed through St. Joe., Mo. Camped four miles out that night; had a fine camp. The cattle being very tired, we fed them plenty of corn; did not tie them, but we had seen no grass until this camp, did not think the cattle would leave the wagon. About midnight there came up an awful thunderstorm and so dark that we could not see an ox, and they scattered, we know not where. When morning came we all but one started in as many directions as there were men and hunted all day, and not a single ox found that day. Next morning the same, only we took a lunch along so we could get farther away. One of the hunters came across a pair of cattle that day so we had enough to move the wagons to a corral where we hauled them so we could all leave camp. Next day we held a council and concluded to start the horse team with all of the boys, but two. Four of them about the sixth day pulled for Anderson County. I and one of the boys that owned the cattle stayed and put in several days of hard work running over the Missouri bottom; the underbrush so thick we could not see an ox 50 yards unless it was in a road, and as we were almost petered out one day after hunting all day and seven miles from camp, we came across some of the cattle and made our way home with them. On the way we found the others. Next morning we were on the way to Kansas, 25 miles from Leavenworth.

Well, it was as muddy as ever. In six or seven days we came to Fort Leavenworth, then we hardly got the wheels wet. This was Kansas. We made as many miles in one day as in four in Missouri. We finally arrived where we were going to make our home and where I and one of the boys that owned two yoke of the cattle that I had to the low-wheeled wagon, joined together and went to Breaking Prairie, which we followed until it was too dry. Then we hauled sawlogs, there being a sawmill on my claim. After this hauling was done, my partner and I cut and hauled hay for a man by the name of Cavenis. Along in between the log hauling and hay cutting there was some shaking with the ague. Everyone of our settlement had the chills. First one man had it and was cured with cold water. Doctor cured him and he ate a good big watermelon, took a relapse and died. He was off clearing lumber at the sawmill. It was very hot, with no roof over the mill; he should not have eaten the melon. Three days after we buried him. At the same time we all were shaking and chilling. Four of us buried him while some of us had the chill coming on. Brother James, Isaac, Dean, John, Wycoff and I. Well, we were all cured by this same water cure. Dr., we all called him Dr. He was one of our band, as we called it (I will bring him in this history later on). Most of us got well, but some of us took the second dose, that is of the shaking, not the water. Would not faze me the next time, so I was shaking until it began to rain and snow, and then Wycoff was going to move to Westport, Mo. Wanted me to go with them, so during the chilling and the sitting around, Howard, John, Eaton and myself took the notion to go to the Pikes Peak Gold Diggings, so I went down to Westport to get some kind of a job to get my outfit with. I went and I worked and shook every third day and never missed a chill all winter. I shaved 595 ox yokes for seven cents a yoke.

As I said sometime previous, on the account of the loss of diary I am defficient as to dates, but in April, 1859, I got home and went to getting ready to cross the plains to the Gold Digging. So by the first of May we were pulling over the old Santa Fe Trail, three of us with two yoke of oxen. We stopped in Lawrence a few days to finish our outfit. One of the men in the company took the notion to take his wife and little girl along, but one of the company would not have it, so the two of us left home without the third man. We were to wait at Lawrence for him. In a day or two he came on with his family, then we drove out four miles to grass and wood and water, until Eaton found some way for the wife to go. We were in camp four or five days. Every day Howard would go to town to see Eaton, so we would know when he was ready.

One day Howard and a Mr. Robinson, who joined us at Lawrence, came back to camp and said Eaton had made arrangements to travel with the wagon that took the wife, and as the grass was not very good where we were camped, we were to go slowly until they came up. Well, I was having chills and fever every third day and did not go to town, and thought everything was right and did not once think that Howard or Robinson would tell me what was not on the square. So we kept on going slow, of course, as we had to give the cattle time, all the time wondering what was keeping Eaton back. It was that way the whole way. I never thought we were trying to get away from Eaton at all, but such was Howard's idea all the time, and he came very near doing it. We were in the mountains a month before Eaton came. I sent him word where to find us. He came in and old Howard would not do a thing towards settling until Eaton and I got twelve miners to settle it for us; then they had to threaten to put a rope around his neck. I would not let them do that, and paid the judgment all myself rather than see the old scamp hung. Then the scoundrel, with Robinson, left me in the mountains with those everlasting chills. They went out; said they would send the mail-carrier in with his pack horse and help me out. They took good care to not let him see them, for in a few days he was in, as his wife was with us, that is, her father and brother were camped there. He took his wife out, but not the camp things, so they had to carry their trumpery up a Mt. about two and a half miles long; so that is the way I got my things out.

I will now go back for the incident on the way we had good grass and splendid roads, not many cattle for the first 80 miles after leaving Lawrence. I think we were the first team on that 80 miles of road. At Council Grove, we came up with a team that traveled up from Fort Smith, Arkansas. They had stopped a day or so, so we came up with another team of three yoke of oxen and three men. The grass grew better and better every day. As I have said before, owing to loss of diary, the dates and miles are out of the question. We have three wagons, nine yoke of cattle, ten men for the ten days, and splendid weather; everything lovely except my chills and wondering why Eaton did not come. In the next two or three days another team caught up with us. They had four yoke and three men. Here we thought of organizing and electing a captain. Camped at Lost Springs while talking about the matter. There was another team of six yoke and four men so we elected the camp captain Kyle from Ohio. Here we began to see Indians, the only beggars who wanted mostly tobacco and fire water. We gave them tobacco, but whiskey was not in it.

We had good luck until we came to the Santa Fe crossing of Arkansas River. It rained and flooded our camp so everything was wet. We were in a bottom; it rained nearly all night as hard as I ever saw it. We were about three-fourths of a mile from the highland; could not get to that. Every bed in the camp was in the water so then we were awhile at this camp. About fifty wagons came up, nearly all from Cape Gerdo, Mo. Some few from Arkansas. Those from Missouri all turned back. Those Missourians must have buried 100 each of picks and shovels and other miner's tools. Everybody had all they wanted; they could not sell, but a few articles. The passengers we had with us bought a shovel for twenty-five cents. Here at this camp more wagons came up. They came thick and fast from this on, besides those that turned back there were nearly a hundred wagons started from this camp. Here also was the first incident happened with the Indians. There came to camp some hand-carts and one pony-cart; two men with this pony, one of these said if an Indian came in his camp he would kick the Indians out. So sure enough, one went in and was kicked out. All that heard the threat advised not to execute this threat, but he paid no attention. The Indians waited until this big camp pulled out. The eastern bound on their way home, the western part of the campers on the way. Then the teams were scattered all along, five and ten in a bunch. Then the Indians put in their work; took everything that the man had but the pony and cart, did not have a single thing of his camp kit. You might wonder why the Indians waited until the crowd separated; they waited until the Cape Gerdo train was fifteen or twenty miles on the way down the Arkansas River so the man would have to get his outfit from those that were going West, as they could not spare much. The cart-man went 75 or 80 miles, traded his cart for enough to take him to Denver, which was 100 miles from Fountain City where he left his cart.

Well, after this, one of my oxen began to weaken. We had to slow up some, but always came in to camp at night. One day about this time, we were moving just before hooking on, as the freighters say, the Wade Comanche Tribe came by--our horses, men, women, dogs, children all on the move down the Arkansas River. I believe they were one hour and a half passing our camp horses and dogs with tent poles, with camp fixtures, dogs with a missle of some description or other. An old squaw rode up to our wagon and took the ox from the hind end while one of our men was in the front eating his lunch. The Indians and horses and poles were so thick that one could not follow it, the ox, I mean. Well, that was the worst of our troubles up to this time, but now the ox began to give out, so we had to stop a day and make a half yoke. Old Dick put him in the lead of the little half buffalo we started from home with. After this I had to bind gunny-sack on that ox's feet and walk and drive that ox for 150 miles. He was so slow that I was out of sight of the wagon half the time, but we were out of Indians entirely. We had passed through them all at once. We saw no more until we got to Denver City, which contained about a dozen cabins and about the same number of tents.

Everything all right except the ox. Him and me were still poking along, good roads, grass and water here. Old Dick wanted some water; he took the buffalos, wagon and all down into Cherry Creek where he came very near upsetting the whole business. Here also I had the first disagreement with old Howard. He took up a rock about four inches in diameter, was about to knock old Dick in the head. I picked up one some smaller, saying, "You hit that ox with that, I will hit you with this." We got out of this difficulty without anyone getting hurt, only the man's feelings. He let me drive the team the rest of the way to town. He was sulky for a week after that, but I had all the other men with me so I did not care. Drove about a mile in to Denver; at last we were there. Camped at the crossing of Clear Creek. We were at this camp two days when the partners packed a lot of stuff on old Dick, left me with the wagon and cattle until the men went up to the mines --Gregory Diggins--they hunted around six days. Howard got in with some other fellows; they staked off 700 feet for three of us and four for the other four men, one an old mountaineer and prospector. This fellow was to follow up the excitements, stake off as many claims as there were men in the company in all the many camps he visited. We grub-staked him, he had his own horses.

Well, Howard came back to the Golden City camp. We went to work, tore the wagon to pieces, sawed the bed in two, made a cart, loaded our things in it, pulled out with the buffaloes for Gregory, were on the road two days, the only twenty-five miles. We were hemmed in by fires for three or four hours; didn't know but it would be our last as it was all around us, but there came some teams from the way we were going. They said if we were in a hurry we could get through. We had taken the cattle off the wagons, found a prospect hole in which to put the powder in case we had to get out with ourselves alone. We hooked up as quickly as the teams would allow and drove as far as the cattle could travel and just made it by a scratch, as luck would have it. Went about four miles and camped, and of all the sights that night! Was the grandest I ever have seen in all my life. The timber was very thick pitch-pine and fir needles were four or five inches deep all over the ground that made fire enough to burn a man to death in a few minutes, so when it got to one of those pines or firs the blaze would shoot clear to the top in a minute--75 or 80 feet-- and catch in the tops of others and keep going on and on as long as there was trees to catch. When the fire would come to a gulch such as we were in it would check it. We were camped one-fourth of a mile from the timber and one could see to read a newspaper handy enough. We did not sleep any that night, it was too grand a sight. There was in that crowd twenty teams, forty or fifty men, some one yoke, some three yoke of cattle to the wagon.

We drove six miles the next day, camped on the claims, went to work, got a water right, made a sluice box, or a Long Toms, as they were called-- sixteen feet long, bottom sixteen inches wide, sides ten inches deep, nailed sides and bottom, one end with head in it for the upper end of the Tom. Made a box two feet long same width of Tom, bottom of box is made of sheet iron, perforated, sets on top of the Tom; dirt and gravel shoveled in this box and what water can run through about eight one-inch auger holes over this box of dirt. The man shovels the dirt in and when it is perfectly clean he shovels the gravel out and so on.

Well, we are now ready for work. Howard made a bargain with a man that we had traveled most all the way from Council Grove with. He had four yoke of cattle, two boys and a wagon, he being an old California miner. Neither of us had ever seen the washing done. We put our four claims against himself, four yoke of oxen, his two boys and wagon and was to run the dirt through the Tom and take one-eighth of the clean gold. Our cattle could be taken out to the Valley. Well, we had to haul the first dirt, had to haul it one-half mile to the tom. We had the water right also, and the Tom, and the boys were to do the herding and drive the cattle. We had to do the digging, load it in the wagon. We hauled eleven cartloads, as much as the little buffaloes could haul. It was all down hill so all they had to do was hold up the tongue. The miner ran the eleven cartloads through, cleaned up that night and had 180 cents. Three of us with the oxen and cart worked a half day with all our mights. Next morning the California miner was gone to California; our company busted, scattered, skedaddled, and I never saw hair nor hide of the four other men afterwards, not one of them stayed in those diggings.

Well, Howard and Robinson looked for some work. I fell in with two of my Kansas friends, went to what was called Deadwood Camp, hunted several days and found nothing. I and one of the men took his oxen and cart and went down to the valley six miles below Golden City, prospected several days, only made a scant living. This was now September 1, 1859.

The third man joined with us two and the cart. We quit prospecting and started out hunting. We hunted eight or nine days--caught nothing in that part of the country on Bowlder Creek. Went back to Arapaho where we were camped, replenished our grub box and started south to where the Platt River comes out of the mountains, hunted several days. The Indians were there and had the antelopes all so wild that we could not get within sharp rifle shot of them, which was calculated to carry a half-mile and hit an antelope. Two of us were not No. 1 hunters, but the third man was a splendid hunter and sure shot. We got one deer here and hunted one more day, went home to camp, packed our camp kit in the cart and went back to the Russell Diggings. Here we joined in with eight others, bought in a claim No. 11, below the discovery of Green Russell, the discoverer of the gulch. We were to work the claim as the owner directed, give half as it was taken out. If we only got 100 he would get 50, and soon we were to use a Georgia Rocker, which was a pine log about two feet in diameter, nine feet long, hollowed out until it was about two inches thick. On three feet of one end was a hopper, or box, with perforated sheet iron as the Long Tom. This was set on timbers so that it would rock, but not move endways. In these diggings it took ten men to run a Georgia Rocker, as the stripping was from seven to eight feet deep; it required six to eight men to dig the dirt and throw it up to the rocker. One man fed it, one stood up and rocked and had to work as steady as machinery would, as the gravel had to be shoveled out without interfering with rocker or shovel.

Well, all was ready, cabin built, stripping began the 1st of October. Stripped a pit twenty feet square down to pay dirt, or where it had ought to have been. We rocked all of the pay dirt there was in that twenty foot pit in one day. We worked eleven hours that day. This man, the owner of the claim, was to watch our men that did the panning. He took care of the cleaning out of the rocker next morning. Vance, the owner, watched the final clean-up and we had one ounce of gold. Well, Vance said we had mined the pay streak; we thought so too, so he showed us where to strip another pit the same size. We all had worked at this, so all ten of us pitched in; in about two days more we had another pit twenty feet square stripped down to bedrock. In this pit there was no pay streak at all. We were right on the pitch of a considerable fall in bedrock--all the gold and gravel had sloped off and lodged on the next claim below. Our bedrock was so steep and smooth that nothing could stick to it, so there we were, most of October gone. Had grubbed ourselves out of the digging.

We went to work on another pit the same size. This Vance had so much confidence in the claim that he advanced us $100.to keep us at it. We pegged away until it began to freeze, so most of the miners were leaving the mines. Among them was our landlord. We owed him ten dollars apiece. We had until the Fourth of July to work the claim out, but we gave it up and loaded ourselves in some wagons and went back down to Arapaho. I hunted around for a job. Found where I could get to work for my board--went to work for some fellows that were burning lime. There were seven or eight men in this work; we worked about a week. They busted up, we scattered everywhere. This lime kiln was at a small town at the foot of the mountains where they started a toll road called Mount Vernon and Torriall Road. Well, I went back to Arapaho and went to work for our old friend of the mining claim on another toll road called Golden City and Torriall Road. This takes me through November.

There were in this road thirty men in the same straights as myself. In the first few days of January, the company hired us for ten dollars per month to go on another toll road about twenty miles from Arapaho, called Bradford and Tarriall Road. We loaded ourselves up with our blankets and ration of bread and meat for two meals, as we were going in the foothills. Thought there perhaps was some snow, and sure enough, we had about six miles of snow twenty inches deep. It was after night when we got to camp--worn out foot sore. I was with those everlasting chills. We worried along over a month, got the road graded up an awful mountain--thirty-one diggers when we got to the top of the mountain. When we got done with grading, the company discharged half of us. We had to hunt for another job. We gathered up our blankets this time without any ration, went sixteen miles without a house. About four miles of this tramp was through two feet of snow and thick timber, over hills and down gulches, over rocks and logs. The four miles was worse than the twelve miles of the rest of the way to Mount Vernon, where we put up with friends. There were four houses; we divided up among the citizens and got supper and breakfast.

The next morning I pulled out for the Gregory camp, as the friend with whom I stayed all night told me that a man that we were acquainted with had the care of a quartz mine with the privilege of panning out enough to keep him and his wife until the owner came from the states in the spring, so I thought I might find a chance with him by paying the owner part of what we panned out. It snowed that night and the roads were very slippery. The snow about an inch deep which the sun soon melted, made it awful walking. I went seven miles and was very near give out, as all the foot covering I had was moccasins made out of old bootlegs, some kind of old cloth for socks. Well, that was only one-fourth of the way. Here came another friend whem I knew at the Lime kiln. He asked me where I was going. I said "Gregory diggings." Well, he said I could not go any farther, that I had used up more than a half-day coming seven miles and twenty-one to go yet, so I stopped there for the night. He and another man were making shingles and said if I could put up with such as they were putting up with I might stay with them, so I went no farther then.

I stayed on that ranch until September, 1861. We made shingles, got out of everything of the eating line and was where we could get nothing. Several families within four miles in the same condition, so we could not borrow. We had a wagon load of shingles ready to send off to Denver. A man by the name of Davis lived four miles from us said if we would have the shingles ready by Sunday morning he would take them to Denver for us. We were twenty-five miles from Denver, all down hill. We put on all the wagon would stand up under, had to pack the shingles. Sunday morning we had them ready and the last mouthful of grub eaten. The man was to try to get back on Tuesday and did not get back until Wednesday in the night. Do you think a fellow would be hungry in that time? Well, we were, for we had been on short allowance for a whole week before this Sunday morning meal. We went to baking and eating--not much at a time, but a little at a time. When we got the flour our shingles brought, it was Mexican flour, worth $28 per 100. It bloated us so we had an awful time. We lived that way a day or so, I think, until Sunday. On Monday morning two of us walked twelve miles to where they started to work on a toll road. We got a job on this for a month at one dollar per day and board and we did not have to work Sunday.

This was in March and April. One man took care of the ranch, as we had concluded to establish a ranch, it being on this same toll road we were working on. When this work was done we went back to the ranch. The man that stayed on the ranch had worked most all the time in the town six miles from the ranch, so we had nearly a hundred dollars when we all got back to the ranch.

Now we bought three yoke of cattle, got an old log wagon, and went cutting and hauling saw logs to a sawmill about three-fourths of a mile from our cabin. They sawed the logs on halves. We hauled about one hundred and fifty logs. As soon as the logs were all in we went to hauling the lumber to the miners. One camp was 25 miles, another 30 miles off; also we took cattle and mules to the ranch through the summer. I would have said horses too, but there were none in the mountain at that time--that is, if there were any horses, they were used in prospecting, so there were none at the ranch. I knew of four ranches within twelve miles of us with from 75 to 100 head of stock and not a horse on one of them. We hauled lumber and brought out stock. We had 75 head. I took one man's whole time with the stock, then just as we got ready to haul lumber, two of us bought the other man out. There were but two in the ranch, and cattle and mines. We felt first rate about then. Got quite a lot of household trumpery and began to feed travelers, but everybody that came along said we should have a woman to make anything, so I took a load of lumber up to Gregory. After unloading it I started home; was driving past where a Mr. Eaton, whose name appears in an earlier part of these writings, stopped me and said he wanted me to haul him and his household goods out on the Tarriall Road, 25 miles from our ranch. This is the same road on which we were living. While we were talking he all at once thought of some teams that came from Lawrence, Kansas. He says, "O, I have just thought" Mrs. Bruer just got in yesterday and wants a place to work." We got acquainted with her in Lawrence while finishing our preparations for crossing the plains the year before, so I went and saw her. My pard and I had never said anything about getting any woman to keep house, but as I was hauling all the time, I said I would take her to the ranch and if Williams was not satisfied I would haul her back to the digging or wherever she wanted to go if within 30 miles of our ranch.

When I got home, we made arrangements for her to do the cooking, we furnish the provisions, she have half of what the eating department brought in. We had pretty good success until about the first of October, when Williams took a load of lumber to Idaho City, sold the lumber, gambled the money off and the oxen ran off. Hunted three or four days before he found them and sent a young man he knew in Kansas to tell me to hurry in to Missouri flatts and get some cattle which he wanted taken to a different part of the mines from where he had sold the lumber. I did not know what to think or do. I had never seen the man and all I had to go by was to take the man's word. I studied awhile; he was to take care of the stock while I was gone, so I started. About fourteen miles from home I met Williams coming home--he had found the cattle. I asked him why he did not let the young man bring the stock out without my having to walk 25 miles after them, when he could have had them to the junction where the two roads met, or the man could have taken them to the ranch as he was riding horseback. His excuse was the owners would not trust the man. At the same time the owner was acquainted with me, he being one of the men that came across the plains with our outfit. I went and took the cattle out. Williams got home the day I met him and when he got there the man he sent had let the stock get scattered. They had an awful time getting them as they were not used to them and did not know when they were all found until I got home.

Mrs. Bruer said she never heard such swearing as Williams did when he got home. He gave me fits for leaving the ranch, at the same time had sent for me, but he went on just as tho I had volunteered to leave it. It was all right when I met him tho. Well, as good luck was in my favor that time, they had found all the stock. The woman had a little son who was always with me after the stock. He was seven years old, but as smart as could be. He was pretty well satisfied that they had all of the stock. He told his Mother that he knew it was all in, but they let on as if there was one or two head out. It worried the two men awfully until I got home and looked over the corral.

Well, that almost broke up the company and after we finally did settle I came to the conclusion that this man and Williams had planned the thing on purpose to dissolve the partnership. We were in a close place, as some of the mules we had were valued at two or three hundred dollars per head, so I sent the owners word to come and get their mules. We were getting five dollars per man for two of the mules, but should we lose them we would have been in for $500. I did not want to take any more chances after that scare. We divided up and Williams and his man skedaddled for the states. Williams had a wife in Kansas and pretended he was going home, but he did not, as I got acquainted with his father-in-law here in Dayton, Columbia County, Washington. He said that Williams never went home. This man's name was Hobbs. How I found out was this way: a Dr. Markham had doctored this Hobb's eyes and had a bill for the same. The Dr. lived in Umatilla. I was going up to Dayton so he had me go and see Hobbs. I went and found out where he was from. I knew where Williams' wife was, so I asked the man if he knew Williams. "Yes," he said. "The rogue married my daughter." I told the old man all about our troubles and he said it was nothing new for Williams to do so. He never went to his wife while Hobbs was there. That was nine years years after Williams left me.

He had not got quite enough off of me, so he goes from the ranch to Golden City and goes to the store where we were doing our trading, altho we never ran in debt at the store, and gets $16 worth of stuff, as that is what I call it--mostly whiskey--charged to Williams and Kelso. We had never bought a drop of whiskey in the town, but the store keepers knew that we kept an eating house so they thought it was all right. In about a month the store firm sent the collector up with the $16 bill for me to pay. Well, I said I would pay no such a bill. They said they would sue me and I said go ahead, they would get nothing out of me on that bill. They went away and tried to find out whether I had anything they could get hold of. They went to a man that we had bought the cattle off in the spring (this was in the fall) and found out that we had bought three yoke of cattle of them and that Williams had only taken one yoke away with him, so back they came thinking there were two yoke of cattle on the ranch yet. They found out that the man who informed them that we had bought three yoke of cattle of Owens, the informer, and that Owens had borrowed one yoke of them to haul a load of lime to Denver and that he had sold the oxen to a butcher, and when we tried to find them they were eaten. I had sold the others to Mr. Lock who was on the ranch with me, having come along and married the woman that was cooking for us. The store firm tried to scare me, but they saw that they could not, so they went away and left me. They would see me every once in awhile for a year after that, and always say something about it, but I said to them that they had no business to let Williams go in debt, as we had never owed them a cent ten minutes in the two years we were there.

I had the good luck to get all of the ranch stock away but one ox. We kept him a long time in the winter and no one came after him, so that was once I had some luck of the right kind. As one of the oxen I had gotten in settling up with Williams died we did not need a team much. We could carry our wood, as there was plenty within reach of the house; we did not have to go to town, as there was peddlers on the road all the time and we could buy as cheap of them as in Golden City, seven miles away, where Williams got his whiskey.

We built a big house--18 by 30, story and half high--after Williams left. This man Lock that married our cook had a little money. We put what little we had gathered off of stock ranch, fixed up in some style, and went to keeping travelers. Lock wanted to keep whiskey, but I did not want to. Finally he got some and I need not have anything to do with it if I did not want to. Well, we lived along through the winter of '60 and '61. We wintered a man for what meat he could kill; he got some deer and a great big old bull elk that weighed about 400 pounds, as he was guessed. We had no way of weighing.

In the spring the hunter and I went in the mines. We went to what was called Jackson Diggings--worked for $1.25 per day and boarded ourselves. We worked ten or twelve days, that job gave out, went to work in another claim. The water was cold and the miners who worked in that kind of digging were taking the Mountain fever all round us, so we gave that up and went and leased a tunnel that was in the hill 90 feet, and a lot 100 feet above the water. We wheeled and washed until the owner came from the states. He had to leave it with someone, so we had a pretty good thing, that is, it would have been a good thing if we had not went through the pay streak, which is always my luck in mining. Well, we wheeled and rocked there a couple of weeks and made a living, that was all. Lived very economically. We had no beefsteak nor butter, nor sugar in our coffee. We used mostly tea at this camp.

Along in the summer we started over to Tarriall Digging, got 40 miles on the road and met some parties coming out of those diggings who said there was no one in there but owners of claims, and they would not hire anyone as they had all the help that they wanted. They tried to get work, but could not, so we went back to Clear Creek, about four miles from the Ranch, and went in with some boys in a hill claim, dug along ditch, set a Tom, and sluiced there two weeks. Made expenses, got acquainted with about a dozen miners that were working there. Some of them were doing well, some not very well. They had not had a square meal for over a year, as we had a woman cook, every Sunday they would come over to the ranch and get a square meal. Lock had some whiskey, too. It was only four miles up the longest hill in the country. It was so long and steep that we gave our sluice horses away rather than take them out. All we made at this camp was some friends and what we made off of the Sunday dinners.

Time flies, and there is some more camps in the country, so we go again, find everything full of men. We go prospecting, find ourselves a load, but it is a long mile from water and on top of a mountain too steep for a man to climb, let alone a horse, so we would no spare $1.50 to move the thing. We go back to the ranch and stay there until the week in August when we sold the ranch, or swapped it, for a house and lot in St. Joe, Missouri, and started for Omaha with two old plugs of horses and a middling good wagon. I now think we started from Denver about the 1st of September. We were in Denver a few days waiting for the deed. The man we traded with was looking for his wife, who was on the road from St. Joe. While we were waiting we camped out of town a little ways, the tongue pointing Eastward. There came a man along who wanted to go to St. Joe. We told him it was dangerous to go there as they were fighting all over Mo., so we wanted to go to Omaha. This fellow had just come from St. Joe with a freight train. We got to talking about St. Joe and the war; he said it was not safe to go to St. Joe. We said that we had traded a ranch in the mountains for a house and lot in St. Joe, named the man with whom we had traded, then he said his sister was living in the same house, that there was a mortgage on the house, but he did not know how much. We did not know what to do. I wanted to get back to the states, so after waiting a day or so longer for the woman to come to Denver with the deed, and she did not come at all, we started for home. We were all the Eastward team that was on that road down the Platt River that we ever saw the whole way to Omaha. Camped every night by our lone selves--four people, two horses, one dog with one foot shot off. He was a splendid shepherd dog, we though so much of him we were hauling him most of the time. One day we were on a cut-off nearly one-half day without water and when we came to the river and let the dog out, he did not wait for us to get to the river, but went straight to the water. We had to go quite a ways further down so we could get the horses to the water, so we watered and ate our lunch, hitched up and the dog did not come. We went back to where he had gone down the bank, but could see nothing of him and we never set our eyes on that dog again. What became of him has always been a mystery, as there was not a living thing in sight except ourselves. It was seven or eight miles back to a ranch, there was no one at it as we passed it, the same stock were around the premises. We went on without the poor dog. If it had not been too far back and the horses had not been so tired, we would have gone back to the ranch and looked for him, tho he was in the wagon when we passed. He had seen it and perhaps made up his dog's mind to go back there and go to Omaha. Well, we had good roads, good grass and splendid weather all the way down.

After going 5 or 6 days from Denver, the horses began to weaken, as they were not used to working to the wagon, having been ridden all summer. Were not in a very good fix when we started, so came to a station where we swapped the two horses for a yoke of cattle and $10. The oxen could travel faster than the horses and we got along better, for we had to picket the horses and the cattle could go where they pleases; they fattened where the horses fell off. We kept moving on down the beautiful Platt, stopping for nothing but to eat and sleep, still alone, on and on, until we came to Carney City, about a mile from Ft. Carney. Here we were prevailed to stop and cut hay for the Government, the woman to cook for the haymakers. We got one dollar and fifty cents a day, cook one dollar and her boy's board. We worked two weeks. I came very near staying here all winter, but I had an interest in the team and could not get it out without giving too much away and I had bought too much already, so I had to go on, so I went.

We pulled out of this camp, still good road, water and grass, nothing to bother one way or another. We went on and on; we got to Lincoln, Nebraska, where we traded the oxen for horses again, with the same ten dollars to boot. So we had a span of horses when we got to Omaha. We found a small house and went in it until we could hear from St. Joe. The war was going on hot and heavy all along the Missouri River. We could not go by land as the Bushwhackers were taking all the horses they could find, so I went to chopping wood, Lock to hauling. We cut and hauled six or seven loads, just made grub and horse feed. We had to go five miles after the wood. It had been culled, so it was tough and knotty. After walking four miles, cutting all day, I could not get a cord. Lock had to travel a mile farther than I as the path I went was straight through, where a wagon could not go. He made two loads per day. He could not haul a cord on account of the hills, so we gave this up.

Then I went to work for a man that did a little of everything. He had men carpentering and repairing wagons, some papering--everything one could think of. After I had worked at several jobs he put me at something that he nor I knew nothing about. There was a good workman working at the collar block by the side of me at the same bench. I was asking him how he would do the job I was at. He said how he would if he was doing it. The Boss was away off somewhere with some carpenters and when he came back it did not suit him at all. He began to curse, and swear, call me names, and I don't know what all he did say. I threw the tools down and told him to go to Texas, I would not work another minute for him for double what he was giving me, which was four dollars per day. The other man was getting $4.50, as he was a splendid mechanic. I went to the house where I was boarding with my partner. It was in the middle of the afternoon. This other man boarded with us--he was one of the miners that took the Sunday dinners with us in the mountains. Well, I said to the family that I was out of a job again, so we held a council and concluded to send me down to St. Joe and see what the prospect was there, so I went down to the boat landing to see what it cost to go by boat. They said four dollars, and me board myself and they would be in St. Joe Tuesday night. This was Monday night--they would start at seven o'clock on that evening. We had supper and filled a good sized pail with substantial food. When the carpenter came to supper he said he had quit the man also just because he had abused me so. He said he would not work for such a man, altho work was scarce and he was getting good pay.

At the appointed time I was on board. The old west wind blowing a big eddy. About midnight the old tub ran on a sawyer, as they are called--a big tree in the river teetering up and down. This one was stretched out just right for the boat to slide on it, and hang up. They puffed and snorted there for a half hour or more, finally got off, went to the shore and tied up until day light. Next morning on we went, ran on a sand bar, was at this perhaps one-fourth of a day, pulling and hauling. They got off of this after awhile. We went on until night, tied up till morning. This is the night they were to be in St. Joe and we were not half way. My dinner pail empty. In the morning I had nothing to eat until about ten o'clock when the mate came to me and asked me if I had anything that morning. I said no. The roustabouts had such a job in the early morning that they had not had their breakfast, so when they had their soup and bread and beef, the mate gave me some. This is Wednesday morning. We floated on until night, tied up until morning, had supper with the deck hands, also breakfast Thursday morning. Floated on until we could see the steeples of the city churches, got on a sand bar about ten o'clock a.m. Was on that until nearly sundown. I just got to the house that was ours, in your minds eye, at sundown.

Well, was I hungry? Oh, no, it was someone else. The boathands worked all the time, three-fourths of that day and never ate a thing, consequently, I got nothing. Maybe you wonder why I did not get something in the cabin. For the very good reason that I had paid the last cent I had to get to ride in that boat. I had ten cents in my pocket when I landed in St. Joe. The folks who lived in the house said I could stay there until I could find something to do, so next morning I went to the man that had the mortgage on the house to see what we had to do. He said all we could do was to pay $400 and we could have it. That was impossible. All we had was those old horses and wagon, the whole thing was not worth $100. I wrote up to Lock how everything was and for him not to come down if he could get anything at all to do, as I could not find a single thing to do in the town. I hunted two days for work.

On Sunday morning Mr. Albett, the man I was staying with, came to me and said there was a Mr. McKorkle who wanted ten men to drive a bull team from Ft. Leavenworth to Ft. Logan, about 500 miles, gave a dollar per day. This was the best thing I could do. We had to start at twelve o'clock that day, so I wrote a letter to Lock that I was going to start with the train Monday morning from Ft. Leavenworth to Ft. Lyon, and would perhaps be gone all winter.

Monday morning would be the tenth of November 1861. I told Lock that they had better stay in Omaha until I came back from that trip. We got on the trail at the appointed time. In due time we were at the Fort, twenty-five miles from St. Joe. The train was already, the cattle about a mile from the wagon. Four of us after supper went out and slept with the cattle. That next day we drove them to camp, and yoked up. Here was a job--to go in a corral with 300 head of cattle and pick out six yoke of oxen that you had never seen until that morning, and only an hour left before the yokes were all piled up at the front wheel of each wagon. After the cattle were in the corral, the wagon-master says, "Boys, mount your front wheel and select your wheelers and when I say jump, every fellow break the ox off you have selected, yoke them and put them on the tongue. All wait until the wheelers are on the tongue, then all start at the same time for the leaders, yoke them, chain them to the front wheel the same as the other." So every one had the same chance. After the first day we went at it as tho we had been following it for a living. I made a good selection and got a good team. You ought to have seen those 27 wagons that day. We were in a lane in Salt Creek Valley. The road had been thrown up in the middle, great ditches on each side deep enough almost to upset the old schooner. The four extra men had all they could do to steer some of worst through that lane which was five miles long. After that lane was passed we had all open country, no lanes for a long time. We herded the cattle fifteen miles that day, camped there two nights.

The company was to bring out our outfit--boots, blankets, tobacco and whatever we wanted here. The company wanted us to buy a gun and ammunition for use on the wagons, but the wagon-master informed us before the goods came what they wanted us to do and said for not one of us to take a gun, that if they wanted their freight guarded with guns they should furnish them, so we had not a gun of theirs. One of the extras had a gun and revolver, as he intended to stay with the cattle until it was time to start back with them, which was as early as the feed would permit. So went that whole trip, without shooting iron to guard their freight. After all, the whole trip, if we had had guns they would have been in our way, for when we needed them at all there were more Indians than we could handle. When they bothered us at all there were ten of them to one of us, so we had to do as they wanted us to. We got our outfit started the day after it was completed.

We had good road for several days. As for distances, we were as ignorant of them as there was no such thing as miles, but as we drove night and day almost, we made the time, mile or miles for several days. We had good weather. I got our teams gentled somewhat after some days. We were somewhere in the vicinity of Topeka, Kansas, when it rained on us while driving along. We wanted to get to the creek to camp that night and the roads became slippery so much that we had to double up some hills and it delayed us, so we were after dark getting to the creek. The road ran along the sidehill and was very slippery. One wagon, about two wagons behind me, upset, the driver being in with the ague and an extra was driving. He was not used to the team. The bed stayed in the standard, wheels on top as if it had been put there on purpose. The man was under that load of shelled corn; it never phazed him. How it kept from mashing him is more than any of us could tell. His name was Philip Black. Teams that were handy stopped and rolled the wagon off. Some one yelled, "Philip, are you hurt?" He says, "No." The corn in some way saved him. There were three tiers of sack under him, while in the wagon, but he was not hurt a particle. He said, "I thought I vas kilt already." He was a Dutchman.

When we all got to camp, the cattle turned out, it was about ten o'clock and pouring down rain. We had an awful time getting anything to eat. Maybe there wasn't anybody tired that night! We got the man out and let the load stay there until we had our grub-pile, as that was what it was call-ed. We had no more trouble for a long time, unless you would call driving after night, and we were driving every night it seemed. We did not drive in the rain any after the upset. In fact, there was not much more rain on the whole trip, the farther we went, the dryer it got. We were getting in the In-dian and Buffalo country, and traveling most every night. The whole coun-try was as level as a barn floor. We could see nothing but level plains as far as the eye could reach. We rolled along, as tho the country's safety depend-ed on our getting there, without any trouble for several days. One day we lost half a day in repairing one of the wagons, but the cattle needed the rest, for after that it was driving day and night almost.

It was getting along in through December and if we had any bad weather it would come soon. Just the night before we came to the Arkansas River, the worst sand storm I every saw or felt came on. It was too bad the herders had to bring the cattle to corral and stand at the open ends with whips to keep them in. Sometimes we thought the wagons would be blown over; it was almost a hurricane--no rain or snow, just wind and sand. We were about seven miles from the river. We hooked on as soon as we could see. We were not long in going the seven miles. We had driven a half day and part of the night, made a dry camp, so we were in need of a rest. So soon as we were in camp on the bank of the beautiful river we gathered wood for a whole day and night's rest. A short time after breakfast there came a big old Buffalo Bull close to the camp. One of the men shot him from the wagons. He was so old and poor and tough that we could not eat it, he was what they call a solitary. The young bulls drive the old ones out of the band so they wander about until the wolves get them. As soon as we were away from the sight the wolves had a feast.

Well, with a good rest and good roads, we went on and on for several days without any incident worthy of note until two days before we got to Fort Larned. We were in among the buffaloes until you could not rest. Our man behind the gun killed two calves just at camping time. That is, if there was such a time with us, but we halted and got supper, watered the cattle and about sundown started on a cut-off, left the river about seven miles to our left. This saved ten or twelve miles for the poor oxen. We traveled about eight hours, made a dry camp early. The next morning when day began to break I never saw such a sight in my life. As soon as I could see I started to round up the cattle to go. We could not tell where our herd ended and the buffalo began, they were that close together. We could have had a wagon load of buffalo meat if we had wanted it, but having killed the calves the evening before, we did not want it. We corralled the cattle, got breakfast, and just began to yoke up when the first thing we knew a Kiowa Chief rode right in the corral and demanded of the wagon-master sugar or any thing eatable that we had. The boss gave the Indian a cake that had been left from breakfast. The old Indian threw the bread down and took hold of the boss' coat collar and ripped it off of the coat (the boss weighed over two hundred). The Indian was on his horse, he tried to raise him out of his boots. The Boss hallooed, "Boys, drop your yokes and come here with your bows." We all gathered around the boss and Indian. Our interpreter came and took the old scalawag away and got the crowd some breakfast and gave them every scrap of the buffalo meat. We had some hard bread at that time, also a little sugar, but little tho it was, divided it out. They let us yoke up and move on.

We were about a day's drive from that camp and getting to the river again and had a pretty big hill to go down to get from the highland to river bottom. The hill was just about as long as our train. Just as the lead team got on the level and stopped to unlock the wagon, both hind wheels being dead locked, the Arapaho Indians barred all further progress. There we were hanging on that hill for an hour and a half, so steep that with both hind wheels locked, the wagons kept crowding on the cattle so much that by the time the Indians let us go the wagons were all locked with one another, the cattle along side of the wagons. We gave the Indians some more of our hard bread and green coffee and flour. They left us alone for a few days.

Soon we came to Fort Larned, had our load inspected, gave an account of what had been given to the Indians and what tribes they were. We rolled along for several days without any trouble and not seeing any Indians until we were about 100 miles from Fort Lyons, our destination. We came to a sand creek; dry sand it was, about as wide as the half of our train, which was thirteen wagons with cattle. Here the right wing took five yoke of the cattle and hooked on the left wing to double through this sand. Just as the leaders got on solid ground about 100 Comanche Indians rode right up to the heads of the cattle and would not let us move a wheel until they went through every wagon hunting sugar. The whole 27 wagons were looked over, even raised up the top tier of corn sacks before they would be satisfied. After that they made us go off of the road about one-half mile and camp and cook that whole band some dinner. Gave them bread and bacon and coffee, then a barrel or two of hard bread. Our load was hard, shelled corn and bacon and coffee. At this place a week before these same Indians had robbed a Mexican trader from Santa Fe, New Mexico; he had twenty-eight mule teams and had been to Kansas City after groceries. He had an ambulance with two mules, also had his wife with him, and their feather bed. The Indians took nearly all of the store goods he had and ripped the feather bed open and scattered those feathers. Some of the magazines they had gotten at Kansas City to read they took too. The prairie was covered with feathers and papers.

While we were here the Santa Fe mail wagon came along, drove out where we were and told us about the robbery. We were getting close to the Fort so after this they let us alone. That was the third time they had corralled us. We had no more trouble unless you would call driving nearly all night trouble. So still that you could not hear the driver next to you, in front, or behind. On the night before reaching the Fort the hindmost team got off of the road and was three miles away from the train, but it was as dark as Egypt and those old tar-poled wagons never made a particle of noise, not a chain rattled, not a boy spoke to his team. The four extra men were either in the wagons asleep or riding along with the lead teams. So no one saw the team, neither did the driver know that he was away from the rest very far, as the country was smooth and level. We were about a mile from the river and could see the lights of the Indian's fires and hear the tom-toms. This was within ten or twelve miles of the Fort. We had traveled until after midnight, got out of hearing of the tom-toms and camped. Quite awhile before we camped the lost wagon was found and was all right. Not until we were on the way home did any one know that the team had been three miles from the road. One of the men followed his track and said at one time the wagon had been that far away from the road.

We were two days at the Fort, then on the way home again. Left all the wagons and cattle except two wagons and ten yoke of cattle. The wagon-master wanted two drivers to drive back. He said all we had to do was to take the whip in the morning after the team was hitched up and drop it as soon as we drove in camp at night. Everything was done by the other men so I volunteered to drive home. On the way out we drove a great part of the way after night. We rushed the cattle, so on New Year's day was half way home. Here we met a train bound for the same Fort as we had left. This was Fort Larned. Here, too, we heard that one of our men had set the prairie afire. The fire had run about two miles from the road, got to creek bottom where the grass was about as high as a horses back, burned up a man's farm, barn and hay, did $1000 worth of damage. The wagon-master we met here did not want to go any farther and our master did not want to go home, as he had to make his presence scarce on the Missouri border, so we swapped bosses. We were told that the authorities at Council Grove wanted the driver that set the grass on fire. It happened only two miles from Council Grove. There were but two boys in the train that saw the fellow set the fire out, so when Mack, as we called the Boss, was not going home with us, he told me and the assistant wagon-master in our train who the man was and for us to keep on the look-out for him as we got close to Council Grove. It was kept so still that the man did not have the least idea that the officers were looking for him, so when we got there they came to our camp and got his note for quite an amount, I never heard what it was, also his wages--a dollar a day from the time he left Leavenworth until he returned, which was

70 days.

Well, here at Council Grove we left the cattle. The snow and ice was so bad the cattle could not travel. We got some four-horse teams to take us home and it was awfully cold. We froze our feet and fingers and suffered awful. We were four days going 100 miles with horses. We stopped at a small town one morning to get our breakfasts; the only hotel in the town had no wood nor meat in the house. The man had a big crib of corn and we had plenty of bacon. We soon had their old stoves full of corn and bacon. The hotel had some bread stuff. It wasn't long till that old house was full of warmth and happiness, for we were going to stay there all day and eat and get warm. This was Sunday.

Monday we rolled out; it was cold as Greenland, and in two days after we were home and payed off. We scattered out around the Fort and City in a day or so. Six of us banded together, went down twelve miles below Leavenworth City in the Missouri Bottom to cut cord wood for the City Gas Co. When we got there we found the wood had been culled out so much that the best choppers could not cut and split a cord in a day. We payed a man six dollars to haul us down, chopped enough wood to pay for our grub and hauling us back to the City and gave up that job. Went up to the Fort, hired to the Government to drive bull teams to Fort Scott, 100 miles below Leavenworth. We went to camp, eighteen bullwhackers, went to work, while the wagon-master was repairing the wagons, to loading twenty-two six-mule teams with stone to build a commissary warehouse at the Fort. We had to load and unload eleven in the forenoon and eleven in the afternoon. We worked a week at this work, then we had to clean out some old warehouses that had all of the camp tools, tents and harness that was brought back from the Mexican war. There was enough of that trumpery to keep eighteen of us carrying out for two days as hard as we could work. There were camp fixtures for a regiment of soldiers and harness for the same. We thought there was harness enough for 1,000 wagons, six mules to a team. After we got that done we got to work loading the train for Fort Scott. Loaded twenty-six wagons, hauled them out on the parade ground. The cattle had to be brought in from the country, twelve or fifteen miles out. As soon as we let the General wagon-master know the train was ready and loaded, he says to our wagon-master, whose name was Anderson (he always called him Bill) "Bill, there is a train of boys camped here. Some of the boys got in some mischief and I want you to let that outfit have that train you have ready." Bill said, "What do you say, boys?" We said all right. Then we went to work and loaded another train. When that was done the General wagon-master says, "Bill, there is some more boys that want to get rid of. Can you let them have that train you have ready?" "All right," Bill said. So we loaded three different trains and never went to Fort Scott at all.

We worked there around the Fort fifty days. The first of the month was pay-day. We went to the paymaster and got our pay. I and two others wanted a change, so we quit that job and went up to St. Joe, the first of

April, 1862. Two days, or three, after landing there I ran across the Dutchman who I spoke about in a former chapter, that was upset on our Fort Lyon trip. He was working for some men that were fitting out some mules to go to Oregon. Their name was Openhiemer. I went to work in the stable for a dollar and twenty-five cents a day and board, but the woman was most too fine for us, that my friend and I (my friend Philip Black--altho his sister was working at the same house) quit and I went to another place to board. I worked until about the first of May. At that time I wanted to go back to Colorado and see about our house and ranch trade, for as soon as I wrote from St. Joe to Lock at Omaha that I was going with a Bull train to Fort Lyon and would be away all winter, he sells the horses and wagon and comes down to St. Joe and finds out just what I had written him He was so disgusted that he sent his wife to Boston, Mass. He joined the army as a teamster, was in the fighting in and about Vixburgh or Island No. 10. I never heard anything more about him or wife after.

Well, while I was working in the stable I was looking out for a chance to work my way to Denver, but all such chances were scarce, as the Bushwhackers were taking everything they could get hold of, no matter what side they were one, so there was no one starting from St. Joe. I began to look for a way to cross the plains to Oregon. By this time the men I was working for had their teamsters hired, so when I took the notion to go to Oregon that chance was gone. One day just before the Openhiemers were to start for Omaha with their outfit, one of them came to me and said if I would help them with their mules and horses he would get me in the Emigrant Escort, which was then buying mules for him in St. Joe.

We started for Omaha. We had to be on out guard for the Bushwhackers, for they were all over the country. We were four days getting up to Omaha. I stayed with the Oregon outfit until they were ready to start--five or six days, I think it was. About this time Captain Crawford came to Omaha with part of his outfit. My friend Openhiemer was the Captain, who said he would give me a chance but did not want to hire anybody just then, but as soon as the wagons and some more mules came he would establish a camp, then I could come. In a few days the wagons and more mules came. We went and made the camp, about 83 men. When we got this done, it was getting along in May.

We were breaking mules and loading until the sixteenth of June. When all was ready on the above day, we started and went out twelve miles. We just settled to getting supper when we were startled by a pistol shot. One of the cavalry boys, while working with his revolver, accidentally shot himself in the foot, so this was the first day, first camp, first accident, on this long journey. We traveled and camped on and on for a long time without any excitement, at the rate of eighteen miles per day. About 100 miles from Omaha the herders let some mules get away. They went a day's journey back towards Omaha, which delayed us one day when we did not need to lay over, but we had to take a rest. We pulled out the next day, rolled on and on. We were traveling up the beautiful Platt country, Nebraska, also good roads, nice weather. I don't know whether anybody ever traveled over as much of Kansas, Colorado, and Nebraska roads as I did without some bad storms. It seemed to me that I missed all the storms that tore things up, I mean. I was in one rain in '59, but rain only. Some farther back of us the wind was so hard that it upset a big wagonload of whiskey and rolled the barrels all over the prairie, but did not damage them. In '61 I was in one wind that made it disagreeable for the herders. I slept the most of the time and did not know that it was so bad until morning.

Well, we rolled along for a long time without any accident. All smooth traveling. After while we reached Fort Kerney; the Platt River was so high that only two of our company went over as we were on the opposite side from the Fort. We got our first letters from home, as I had my friends to direct them to Kerney, in care of Captain Crawford, Emigrant Escort. So on we went without trouble until we were away past the junction of the two Platts. We were on the north side of the North Platt, winding our way between Kerney and Fort Laramy, still good roads and all is well. Some days after this we began to have use for the Captain. We came across a family with a team that was given out, so we had to haul and feed them fifteen or sixteen hundred miles. Not long after this we came to another family, busted up, and we had to take part of them in. One of this party was a gunsmith, and as our outfit had new guns they had to all be resighted, so that fellow payed for his hauling.

All went well for a long time. Next trouble was two men and three yoke of oxen from Denver loaded with whiskey. As near as the Captain could find out, one of the men had fitted up the team and loaded it with whiskey and the other stuff for a saloon with all the fixtures, and agreed to take the other man as a passenger for his work in helping him. They were with other teams on their way to some parts of the country. Well, this outfit got somewhat alone, but there was plenty of the train still not far away, so this passenger thought he had a good show to get away with half interest in the team and load. Not knowing that Captain Crawford was within a thousand miles of them, they commenced quarreling about the outfit. Finally they got so far along that they could not move the wagon. They were sitting on the wagon tongue when Captain came up. They got some of the Captain's company to ride on and overtake those that had traveled with the whiskey outfit. They were brought back, and a trial was held. Captain Crawford was judge and as near as he could find out the passenger did not own a thing in the wagon or its load, so he used the Mrs. Coxis notion on the barrels of whiskey and saloon fixtures and fed the fishes in the Platt with whiskey and left the men to go on their way, if not rejoicing, a chance to curse the Captain of the Escort. They went on ahead of us and we never saw them again.

This was near the Antelope Springs. No more trouble for a long time. Good roads and weather, tho getting warm as it was getting along towards the 4th of July. About this time our company began to show that wedded life was not all smooth sailing. The assistant wagonmaster had his wife along. He got jealous of the Lieutenant and threatened to shoot somebody. The orderly sargeant was called on to arrest him and disarm him. He was disarmed, that was all. Our orderly sargeant was the Hon. Joseph Dolph, of Portland, Oregon. That busted up one mess, as the parties messed together. The woman had been riding in the ambulance, so they had to make different arrangements, so we were at that two nights and one day. We had no more trouble for some time. The next trouble was one of the mules getting snake bit. They saved him, but he was worth nothing; swapped him off for another by paying the worth of the other to boot in money.

Well, now some of the mules began to peeter out. Came to Fort Laramy, traded six of our poor mules for the same number of good ones with the Government. This time I was luck in getting two of the good ones. All went well until we got to the Sweet Water; there was a company of soldiers camped here. The night before we got there the Indians killed their herder and ran the mules off. The Colonel wanted our Captain to stay and take care of the camp while the soldiers went after the Indians. He did not want to, but the Colonel telegraphed to Fort Laramy and the Commander telegraphed back for our Captain to stay, so we stayed there until the soldiers came back. They never saw an Indian or mule. We rolled away and had no more trouble to amount to anything until we got to Green River. There we had to block the beds aobut a foot above the bolsters, then some got wet. One of the cavalry boys lost his gun where his mule had to swim. All the little mules had to swim; the driver had to get up on the saddle on his knees and hang to the manes. The assistant wagon-master led the leaders over. He rode a tall horse. The leaders swam. The wheelers had to haul the wagon. We camped and dried what got wet, they went on and on. No more trouble with ourselves or emigrants. We had lots of good times as soon as we came to the Rocky Mountains.

About this time we had very near one hundred wagons in the train. The emigrant's boys wanted to camp somewhere close. Our Captain said if they corralled close they would have to submit to the regulations, put the stock in the same herd and stand their share of guard duty. When we came to a good place where wood was plenty we all joined and built a big log heap and made a light that could be seen several miles away. If the ground was suitable the dancing part of the crowd would dance till the chickens began to crow in the morning, and then those that not dance would sing. We had plenty of these along. We made the mountains ring. We were progressing on and on. Somewhere here we met a Mormon train of twelve wagons going to the Missouri River after some Mormon emigrants. We met them in a rough place and they would not turn their cattle out of the road. We could hardly turn out on our side, when they had good road on their side. Came near running their oxen right on the mules, so near that we had to stop and let them pass. Just at this moment one of our boys shot at a jack rabbit. The old Mormons got their guns in a hurry, but the Captain halloed, "All right, no harm done." It looked mighty exciting for a few minutes. I was second team and was right at the Mormon's lead team. He looked daggers at me. We got out of that place without getting hurt.

Nothing happened for a long time. Then the next one was an Indian scare. We had camped quite awhile before night as the mules were getting pretty well fagged out, had to let them have a longer time to feed. About sundown, while the cooks were putting the mess kit away for the night, some-one yelled "Indians!" with all his might, but when everybody got there, no one could see any sign of Indians. We had been in camp an hour and a half and were all over the ground, scattered everywhere. The Indian must have been hidden right in the camp, for the fellow said he jumped right through the camp. We made it up that some one of our men had done it to create an excitement, for out of a hundred people not one saw an Indian or sight of one. At any rate there was some excitement. The camp was double guarded that night anyway. All went well for a long time. Coming close to Snake River now and also in the month of September.

We happened to camp on the ground where some emigrants had been at-tacked just a month to the day before us, I think the tenth of August. They killed a woman in the fighting — the date and age and name and how killed was on the headboard. While we were there an old Mormon came to our camp. He had a ferry boat on Snake River and wanted our Captain to cross and go down on the north side of the Snake. That would have caused us to have crossed again at Boise, but the Captain had crossed the plains three times before, so he was not taking any Mormon's advice on this trip. Also while at this place a Captain of an emigrant train came back, a whole day's ride all alone, hunting for some of their horses that strayed from them two days before. He had nothing but his horse and gun with him, right in the neighborhood of the Indian raid. The Captain persuaded him to let the horses go and go back to his train, so he stayed with us one night and went back. The train had waited for him; when we came along they had gone on.

Some time after this we came up with two men with a light wagon and four mules. They had started from Omaha with three men, two brothers owned the outfit. One of the brothers was sick and was not able to do much in camp. They were several miles behind the main train, so one day they stopped at noon and one was watching the mules feed, the other cooking. The sick one went down the creek to see if he could catch some fish. They got the dinner ready and waited awhile for the sick man to come to his din-ner and he did not come, so the brother went down where he had been fishing and found his tracks in the sand and followed them some distance in the willows. Finally he lost the boot track and found a moccasin track. They hunted all the afternoon and found no more trace of the brother. The next morning they overtook the train they had been traveling with. They were now nearing Salmon Falls where there was a company of Oregon soldiers camped. The brother stopped there and got the soldiers to go and look for the lost man, so when we came up all but a few of camp were out hunting.

We stopped a day or so, overhauled our loads some and prepared for an all night drive. When we started the soldiers had all gotten back from the hunt, never saw an Indian in all directions in two days travel as hard as their horses could go. Horses all most worn out, for they could not let them rest but little, day or night, so they had to give him up. When we started on again the lone brother went along with us to Auburn, Oregon.

Well, we started on this long, day and night drive just as the sun went down. There was no moon that night and the sage brush on each side of the road was as high as the wagons and as big as an eight-year old apple tree. We traveled until midnight, stopped right in the road and gave the mules a little water and some flour. Each wagon had a ten-gallon keg of water swinging on his hind axle, and that was twelve wagons, one ambulance, which made 130 gallons of water. We rested about an hour and a half here; started on again, traveled until sun up, gave the mules a little water and some flour, and ate a little ourselves, of course. We had prepared for that while resting at the soldiers' camp where we had plenty salmon to eat. We had had beef all along until coming to the soldiers camp; their butchers had killed a beef two days before they came to this camp and butcher was poisoned. The Dr. that belonged to the company said the cattle had eaten something that had killed some of this cattle on the road, so we had no more beef after that. We started from Omaha with sixteen head of steers, had three at this time.

On this dry drive the emigrants had taken their stock about six miles off of the road down one of the worst hills on the Snake River. The hill was three miles long. They got their stock down to the water all right, but when they got back to their wagons the cattle were worse off than if they had pulled the wagons the balance of the way to the other end of the desert, which took our teams from sundown until next day noon, with three hours rest. When we got to camp the Captain had our boys load several mules with water for the emigrants that were still on the road about half way across the desert. When they got them some, they had several head of oxen and one man lost. He could not move his wagon, the others that were with him had to divide up their teams to get him to where we were camped. They kept coming all day. We stayed the two nights. After the emigrants were all in camp the Captain had us over-haul every wagon in the camp, not excepting our own, and of all the loads some of them had, it beat the world! Log chains, hub bands of wagons, braces off of harness, great big sugar kettles. We called them that, they held ten gallons. Big pots holding four gallons, big dutch ovens weighing ten or twelve pounds. I cannot think of what all there was that was of no use when their cattle were so nearly given out. We went through the wagons and threw everything, that the Captain thought they could get along without, in Snake River. Where we had thrown a big oven away, we gave them a small skillet, as we had quite a lot of them for this very purpose. Where we had gotten away with a big pot we gave them camp kettle sheet iron, and so on. I think we must have lightened the emigrants wagons 200 lbs. apiece. Then the Captain let those that lost their cattle have our beef steers, as we were not going to eat any more of them, besides we hauled some of the people and lightened them as much as we could. Our mules were getting poor and tired.

We rolled along slowly. A short time after this we were taking rest at noon when two of the men (teamsters) got to playing cards for money. They got to quarrelling and one of them took a shot at the other. The bullet went between the man's legs and through our fire where we were cooking dinner and scattered the coals and ashes all over the victuals. The orderly took his pistol away from him. While I think of it, there is something I had forgotten that happened on the Sweetwater: This same man that did the shooting here stuck his knife in the shoulder of another man about the same business — playing cards. We had to take his fighting tools from him then. About all the trouble from this on was getting the mules along for they were getting powerfully weak, if there is any such a thing as being powerfully weak. Now we were wearing September out, as well as the mules. Getting on towards Burnt River Mountains, that beautiful range whose top is decked with cedars and its sides with pine grass. Well, this was the most tedious part of the road. We had to cross this river eleven times in a day and a half with considerable of a hill to pull up that was trying on the poor mules. We kept at it tho and after a while landed on the ground where Baker City now stands. Took a long rest here. Eighteen of us concluded to stop and go in to Auburn where they were mining, so we were honorably discharged and paid off. I and a man by the name of Hubbaal took the job of cutting and stacking about one mile below our camp, which was the same ground we camped on while with the escort. Three of us put in and bought of the Captain some cooking tools for a camp of three or four men. My partner and I got some flour and coffee of the Captain. We went and got some scythes of a man that traveled with us from the Sweetwater. He had been living there two or three years and when we came along he came and brought the haying tools with him; saved us the trouble of buying them. We cut and stacked the hay, was up to Auburn and bought a horse. The three of us together loaded 150 pounds of him and with about 100 other men and packs, went into what was Grimes Creek. It had been struck in August and a few of the men had come out to Auburn after supplies. They tried to slip off so no one would see them, but they were closely watched and when they were ready there was about 100 men after them, full tilt, I with them.

We got to the diggings as soon as they for we kept in sight of them all the way, but when we got in there everything was claimed that had the least sign of anything having gold on it. We ran around several days and got disgusted. About 75 or 80 of the crowd went out, I with them. We went back to where we crossed the Snake River, met a man by the name of Smith who was trying to get up a company to go to the Lost River where some emigrants had found some rich prospects. He soon got twenty-one men, with himself and I, and we went somewhere near one hundred miles. We were nearly out of grub; and divided it with half of the crowd. They went on, we went back to Auburn. This was now in December. The mines began to freeze; those that had no claims went to hunting winter quarters. My pard and I struck out for Walla Walla. We crossed Grand Rond Valley on Christmas Day, had some snow, the first eight miles out of Auburn. There was no snow in Powder River Valley nor Grand Rond Valley, but when we reached the Blue Mountains, then we caught it. We were from Christmas to New Year's Day getting 125 miles; had two horses. All we had that number of days was grub and a good roll of blankets. We had to foot it some part of the way. The road was teetotally snowed under all the way. We could tell where to go by some blazes on the trees. We wallowed thru after so long a time. After getting in the Walla Walla Valley no more snow — so New Year's day, 1865, we were in Walla Walla City.

That night we camped on the Yellow Hawk, about half way between Walla Walla and the McGuire place. One of our comrades camped on the McGuire place, by the name of Urriah Storms. We stayed a month; while there we helped the McGuires raise a stable, that is all we found to do there, so we packed up the two horses and pulled out for Grand Rond Valley by the Krause Mission, Umatilla Reservation. No snow yet. The first day on the mount, not much, but the next day it paid us up for all the valley traveling we had. We wallowed through one day that was awful, but in the evening a pack train of fifteen mules passed us, so we followed them--one day quite handy, but they got the start of us about an hour and it snowed so fast it covered up their tracks. We had never been over the road and there was two roads. We took the wrong one. All the same we came to a house and stayed all night. Here we had to wade Grand Rond River, as the horses had all they could get along with flour and such. Two days after this wading the river we were at Captain Pyle's ranch in Pyles Canyon. Stayed there until the fourth day of March. Six of us together started with a pack horse apiece for the Idaho Basin Gold Fields. We had snow in Powder R. Valley. Eighteen miles after then no snow at all. When we struck the road from Auburn it was full of miners on their way to the same place as we were making for. The further we went, the more people there was. This is the same road I was on the fall before and to the same camp. We plodded along until we came to Payette River. We did not have to cross it, but traveled up along its bank, a good day's walk for us. Ere this I should have said we had to wade Burnt River eleven times and it used me up entirely; was laid up so I could not travel, the rest went on into the mines, left me some grub and wood and in a cabin. I was by myself through the day, but always some one there at night. I was there about a week then along came a Doctor that had been with us on the trip upon the Lost River hunt. He gave me something that started me on the mend in a few days and I was able to go out of the cabin and walk around. While here the owner of the cabin came and what do you think his name was? John B. Kelso, from Colorado, the same identical man that took all of my letters out of Golden City Post Office. Well, I stayed there until a team came along that I was acquainted with. The man hauled me to the foot of the Mountains at a camp where they always stopped and unloaded the wagons and packed the goods on animals. I stayed there a week. One day a packer came along with an extra horse and took me to where my partner was. I hunted around a few days, but the miners had all the hands they could use.

After finding nothing at this camp, some of my friends were going over on what they called Black Warrior, 25 miles from this Idaho City. We hunted several days, found nothing to stay with so went back to the Idaho City; found a job at night for six dollars per day. Worked a week, the water gave out on us, had to give that job up. Went to work for another man from Walla Walla, his name has slipped my mind. Worked for him for six dollars per day, worked three days. The water peetered out here. By this time August was coming on. I was loafing again. There came a man hunting a hand, I heard him asking for someone to work after night and said I was out of a job just then. Well, he says come to such a place at six o'clock in the evening. He stopped and said, "Say, I suppose you know that today they knocked the price down to five dollars a day?" I said, "I did not know it; in that case I will not work this evening." I would not work in the water after night for five dollars.

Next morning I was down at a store where they were unloading a packtrain. The Boss Packer came along and says, "Hello, John, what are you doing here?" I said I was looking for a job mostly these days. Told him about the water giving out on my last two jobs. He says, "Come and go with us to Umatilla and ride the Bell mare and cook for two of us. We will board you; it will take about a month." I said all right, so we started the first day of August from Idaho City and made short drives in order to let the horses get in good order for another load. So nothing happened worth mentioning, but the third of September I landed in Umatilla City and stayed with my friend Bill Rose, the Packer. He was one of our comrades in the escort and one of my best friends on the plains, and he and I did the cooking in our mess all the way across. The other part of mess got the wood and water. The teamsters were twenty-four in number, divided in three messes. That put eight in a mess. Out mess never had but one little misunderstanding. Two of the boys had a disagreement and a little fight, did not hurt one another much, made it up.

Well, I went to hunting for a job as soon as the pack-train loaded up and got away. There was a blacksmith had a shop at the lower end of the town. There had been a wagonmaker working in connection with him during summer, but had gone to Portland to winter. He had left his tools and some timber. I went to him and wanted to work for him on shares, but he wanted to sell the tools and timber. I could not do that so kept hunting. Finally I found a man doing all kinds of work. He wanted a man, so I went to work for him at four dollars per day. I had to pay nine dollars per week for board. I worked until I earned eighty dollars. I had landed in Umatilla with eighty in a chest, so I bought $120 worth of tools and timber. About this time there was a man by the name of Franklin building a hotel twelve miles out from the landing; also there were two men starting a blacksmith shop there. They wanted me to come out there with the wagon shop, as it was where the freighters always stopped with their teams until they engaged their loads. I paid a man twenty dollars to haul my outfit out there. This twelve miles was nothing but sand; it took four horses three-fourths of a day to get out there. Well, I was out there three weeks and all the wagon work I did was to put one axle-tree in, but I got some work on the hotel, or I would have been in debt. As it was, I just came out even.

Soon after this along came a man that I knew that wanted a lot of work done on his wagon. Said if I was in town he would have me do it, but he would not stop there. I was on the point of going back to the landing anyway, so I got him to load my stuff in his wagon and moved back. Rented a twelve by fourteen lean-to for seven dollars per month. Worked about a month in that; went in with a man by the name of Bird. We bought a shop twenty by twenty, moved it about three blocks on a leased lot. We were living in this while moving it. The sand got frozen solid, so we could roll the thing without planks under the rollers. Not much snow that winter. Just cold and dry. We had about work enough to keep us through the winter. When spring came we sold the shop, as the lot was right where we could not use it for a wagon shop. As soon as we sold that a man who had a sawmill on the Klickatat got us to build a blacksmith shop, 100 by 24, and cut off sixteen feet for a wagon shop. I worked in that from May, '64 until November '69--paid $25 per month until the last six months when I had it free. I should have said we did not pay rent from the first of December to the first day of May as the freighters did not run in the months of December to May, 5 months. For all that, we made money.

Well, when the most of the freighters pulled off of the Umatilla road and went on the Kelton road, I sold out of the shop and went over on the Yakima with another man and bought twenty-one hundred dollars worth of cattle, paying forty dollars per head for forty head of cows; thirty dollars for two-year olds, twenty-one for yearlings. This was in March, '70. We drove them cattle to Umatilla and summered them where Pendleton now is. We milked the cows until the first of August and then I took a load of vegetables up to Auburn in Baker County, Oregon, with 200 pounds of butter. We did very well on one load of vegetables, but one load glutted the market. So the next load we took two loads of watermelons, did tolerably well with them. Came back to Walla Walla and took a load of fruit--peaches and early apples--we did middling with that, only we let a man have a part of it on time, he paying the next load. We kept on hauling, he kept paying part, but finally he owed us a hundred and eight dollars and skipped the country. My partner in the cattle went up to Walla Walla and I had to stay with the cattle. We had a man to peddle the fruit. He was not particular enough and let the settlers fool him and got away with all our profits.

While this was going on the cattle partner had bought two thirds of a crop of corn and it was on a farm five miles from Walla Walla, I think, about 300 acres. Part of this was good, but the other part of about ten acres was not a half crop, but paid as much for the poor as for the good. Here we were, soaked again. Then the owner of the farm came down on us after one-third of the poor part. Then, again Gifft, which was the partner's name, had bought a big straw-stake which the renter had no right to sell. We had a powerful time getting things settled. Well, we kept the cattle on that ranch two winters. Gifft took up a claim near Waitsburgh, but we could not keep the cattle over there as the land was all fenced up so I was with the cattle most of the time. This is through the winter.

In the spring of 1871 we concluded to see what was on the north side of Snake River. I, with a man by the name of Roads, fitted out two wagons and four horses, came over to the Palouse and found nothing that suited us, took our things back on the south side of the Snake, put in some wheat and oats. Only about one-third of the wheat amounted to anything, so we gave that up. I got an old reaper, cut about two-hundred acres, sold the machine for what I was to pay for it, and got out of that scrape without losing anything for a wonder, for everything I undertook was a losing game, after buying the cattle. Well, I worked and worried until August '72, kept losing cattle all the time. By and by a man came along and bought what I had left, got me to help him take them about 100 miles from Walla Walla. We got them down there--I left him and went to The Dalles and worked awhile there. While I was there a man that I had repaired wagons for while at Umatilla wanted me to come up to Baker City and work up there, so up I goes. Worked there from November '72 until May '74. Came back to Walla Walla in May.

I looked around a few days, could not find work there, so I went to Umatilla. Went to Folsom's shop to get work, but he wanted me to buy his tools, and what timber he had and make the best of it, but I would not buy it. I went out 14 miles on the Umatilla River. Was out there from May until the first of September. Went back to Walla Walla and the the fall of '75 I sent for sister Adeline and brother J. Kelso. Met them at Kelton about the twentieth of September. On the way from Kelton we had some bad weather, but got to Walla Walla on the third of December with no very bad luck, except being delayed at Baker City four or five days on account of cold and snow. Well, I traded my mares for a barn and lot; made a house out of the barn lumber. Lived in the house two summers and one winter. Moved up to Hangman Creek in October 1877, Section 12, T. 21, R. 44, where I have worked at various times.

Frances Ellen Page

The daughter of Joseph Gale,
fur trader and prominent early settler of
California and Oregon, tells about her early life
attending school in Oregon, commuting by horseback
from San Jose, California to Forest Grove, Oregon.

Frances Ellen Gale, the daughter of Mr. and Mrs. Joseph Gough Gale, was born at San Jose, California, in 1837.

Mr. Gale was a prominent man in the early affairs and development of both California and Oregon. He was born at Baltimore, Md., and was a graduate of one of the best colleges of the time and a man of great force of character. He built the first flour mill, also the first saw mill in Oregon, both near the present site of Forest Grove. Probably few if any of the pioneers of his time made the effort to provide educational facilities for his children as did Mr. Gale.

His early residence in California was during the Spanish possession, and he did not like conditions as they existed among those people so moved to Oregon in 1834. Later, however, becoming dissatisfied, he returned to California.

Near the present site of Forest Grove, the Rev. Harvey Clark established a school, the first or one of the first in the territory. He built a log cabin about 10x12 feet for his home and this was also utilized for two years as the school room. Seven children were in attendance at this school. Activities of the day in this small room at times consisted of studying, reciting and cooking of the noon meal.

After two years of this crowded condition, a log cabin of larger dimensions was built not far from the Clark home.

This building was used exclusively for school purposes. At this time "God Almighty" Smith kept a boarding house at which all the pupils lived. Mrs. Page considers Mr. Smith's first name a misnomer.

The name Forest Grove was given by Mrs. Crosby, who accompanied her husband, Captain Crosby, on a voyage to Portland, and they visited the school during their stay. Forest Grove was the name of Mrs. Crosby's old home in Vermont.

Mrs. Page made the first trip from California to attend this school at about the age of seven. The entire journey from San Jose was made on horseback. The horses had to swim all the rivers. The travelers had to get Indian canoes to cross in, leading the swimming horses during the journey across the rivers. Mrs. Page graduated from the school at the age of sixteen, and as she spent the vacation in California, many journeys were made and all but the last few, which were made by boat, were on horseback.

Among here schoolmates at this school were Harvey Scott, the famous editor; William Green, Catling brothers, Ed Ross and L. Crosby.

After finishing this school Notre Dame convent was attended, principally for the purpose of learning the arts of sewing and embroidery. Later she was a government employee, a court interpreter for the Spanish.

January 11, 1857, at Los Angeles, California, Frances Ellen Gale became the wife of Thomas Perciful Page. Mrs. Page well remembers this day for other reasons than that it was the day of her marriage as on this day the most terriffic earthquake ever recorded in that part of California occurred.

Mr. Gale was engaged in raising cattle. He had an immense tract of land for this purpose for which he paid 30 cents per acre. Mr. Page was a government employee, but resigned and had also invested in land and cattle. Many cattle were killed by the earthquake.

Mrs. Page's brother was riding on the range when the quake began. His steed, a mule, seemed to have a premonition of the danger, for it stopped and could not be persuaded nor forced to go farther. Soon immense pieces of stone from the mountain began tumbling down onto the prairie killing many of the cattle owned by Mr. Gale and Mr. Page. Water from Tulare lake was thrown three-quarters of a mile from the lake and rows of fish like waves of the ocean were left on the land, producing an odor that was carried many miles from the lake.

Mrs. Page lived at San Jose when the "vigilante committee' was in power in San Francisco and vicinity. Many examples of the "vigilante" methods of meting out justice were in evidence. In passing through an oak grove on a trip from San Jose to Monterey, she saw the bodies of four men suspended from limbs of the trees.

Among pleasant reminiscences of her early life, is a journey on a sailing vessel to Costa Rica, Central America, with her father, who was captain of the vessel. The trip was made for the purpose of getting a cargo of coffee.

James Marshal, the discoverer of gold in California, lived at one time at the home of the Gales.

Peter H. Burnett, the first American governor of California, lived at one time just across the street from the Gales.

Mr. and Mrs. Page moved to the Walla Walla valley the early part of the winter of 1859, and settled on Mill Creek five miles east of the city, where Mr. Page engaged in stock raising. Later he was postmaster of Walla Walla.

Martin Campbell

*An account of life at sea,
and how Mr. Campbell saved the Captain's daughter
after she had accidently walked the ship's plank.
He also relates his adventures in the gold fields
of California including his inadvertent membership
of the "committee" in San Francisco.*

M r. Campbell was born in New Jersey, February 13, 1833, and spent his earliest life there on a farm. His father was both a farmer and a miller. At that time milling was never a separate business in that part of the world.

"When twelve years old, I just walked away, because I had a roving disposition," as he states and went to New Hope, Pennsylvania, fifteen miles distant, where he secured work on a canal. Here he drove horses on the canal and received in addition to board and lodging $6.00 per month.

In the winter a storm caused such a flow of water that the canal was broken in places, thus putting him out of employment.

Instead of returning home, however, he went to New York, "bummed" rides when he could and paid when he couldn't. Here he became a common sailor on a sailing vessel (there were no steam ships then) and sailed for San Francisco. He has sailed around Cape Horn five times. Later went to Boston and was seaman on a coast vessel for awhile, then returned to New York and made a trip to Pernambuco, Brazil, and one voyage continued to the Sandwich Islands, now territory of Hawaii. One trip included Liverpool, England. Again shipping from Boston, went to San Francisco.

On this voyage the ship carpenter was making a portion of a mast to replace a like piece that had become impaired, and for the reason that the captain did not want to wait in port for the work to be done, a log was taken on the ship so that the work could be done at sea without loss of time. One day when Mr. Campbell was at the wheel and the ship was sailing slowly along, near the equator and the sea was without a billow, the captain's little six year old daughter was picking up the shavings made by the carpenter and carrying them out to the gangway to see them float on the ocean. In throwing an armful she fell overboard. Mr. Campbell shouted from the helm, "Girl overboard," ran to a rope which he threw over and slid down to the water. He was an expert swimmer. "At that time I could almost swim standing," he said. He succeeded in reaching the little girl, as the water is very buoyant there. The captain was a very good swimmer but very large; he was overboard soon after Mr. Campbell, but gave out with the effort of swimming and the boat lowered to take in the little girl and her rescuer was the means of saving the captain's life as he could not have endured the strain but a short time longer. For this act of bravery, Mr. Campbell was promoted to second mate.

"A man that will jump into the Atlantic ocean to save a life is a noble person," said the captain's wife. "The fact that this good woman had faith in me made me think that I was somebody and I tried harder than ever to do good work, and my whole life was influenced for good by that incident."

When this voyage ended at San Francisco, hearing of the rich strikes in the gold mines Mr. Campbell was attacked with the "gold fever." He left the ship and started for the mines. He had no idea of the country or in what direction the mines were located, but left San Francisco and went to Oakland, then a small village surrounded by rich farming land, and started to walk to the mines. On his tramp he came to French Camp about six miles from Stockton.

Here he entered into a contract with the owner of a 160-acre farm to dig a ditch three feet deep around the entire acreage. This occupation entailed the duty of cooking, as Mr. Campbell had to board himself and this new responsibility was not one that gave any pleasure to the wanderer, as it was his first experience in the art of cookery. Nevertheless the camp became a kind of wayside inn, as there was at times many quitters returning from the mines, who wanted meals, but "they were always all broke." He hired them to work at the same wages he was receiving, 50 cents per rod. Sometimes there would be eight or nine. None of them wanted to work long. After a short time at work, they would offer to make a big discount to get cash, and others came to take their places so, this boy of 18 finished his contract, without doing much of the work, and made money on the short time workers.

Faring so well on this contract he took another in the San Joaquin valley at big wages. This was clearing willows from the land. "I got the willows, and the mosquitoes got my blood. I have never seen so many mosquitoes in all my travels." Leaving the scenes of his last work he went to Stockton, which was a small village then. Hearing of good prospects for work at Bernicia, he boarded a steamer asking the watchman to call him in time to land at this town. When he awoke, he saw ships with tall masts and many buildings and realized that he was landing in San Francisco, instead of Bernicia. The watchman did not call or the tired boy was sleeping so soundly he did not hear.

While in San Francisco trouble commenced between the law-abiding citizens and the "roughs." The trouble was started by a man named Casey, of the lawless element, who killed Senator Williams, editor of the San Francisco Bulletin, who published a statement that Casey had been an inmate of the Blackwell's Island prison. Great consternation was caused by this act. As a means of safety, Casey's friends took him to jail. A meeting was called by the friends of Senator Williams. At this gathering, the streets were so crowded that pedestrians in that vicinity were unable to get out of the crowd. Mr. Campbell was one who was carried along with this tremendous crowd, which was marched to a place that proved to be a government arsenal. All the guns at the arsenal were taken out and 4,000 people armed.

Through the accident of this crowd he unintentionally became one of a "Vigilance committee," but he did not have any idea what that meant. The crowd was addressed by some of the leaders, who explained why this action was taken and what was to be done. All members of this newly appointed committee were to be at a certain place on Sacramento street at a certain hour next morning and to be "ready for action."

This committee was formed into large companies and marched to the court house. Mr. Campbell distinctively remembers that ahead of him were two cannons set, ready to be fired at any minute. A demand was made for Casey. Corey, the sheriff refused to give him up. He was informed the building would be blown up in fifteen minutes unless Casey was delivered to this committee. The jail was unlocked in less than fifteen minutes. Corey escorted Casey to the place on Sacramento street, where Casey was tried by a jury of 40 men and was convicted. A gallows was ready and the extreme penalty of the will of the better class was the fate of Casey. The whole proceeding took place in daylight. A general clean-up followed. Many undesirables were deported and San Francisco began a new era of law and order.

Mr. Campbell left San Francisco. He embarked on a bumper vessel for the Puget Sound in 1856, and landed at Port Gamble. Later he went to Seattle which was a very small village.

From Washington he crossed the line in to British Columbia. While there a report of the discovery of gold on Frazier river was reported. Mr. Campbell heard of it and determined to be the first on the ground. He purchased fifteen pounds of rice and six of sugar and walked the entire distance of 200 miles which included crossing the Cascade mountains. The discovery of gold was almost a myth.

After this long journey and disappointment in not finding a mine of gold, he started south, passing through the Indian belt and had adventures with these people that caused him some thrills, not of pleasure, either, but fortunately, he was able to continue his journey and arrived in the Walla Walla Valley in 1860, barefooted, with $1.85 in his pocket.

Armanda Smith

*Mrs. Sergeant Smith
relates her journey to Oregon
in the year 1859.*

Mrs. Seargeant Smith was born October 1849 in the vicinity of Chicago. Her father, John Sheets, homesteaded 160 acres which is now a part of State street. He later sold it for $900 and moved to Fremont, Iowa, where he made his home until 1859, when in May, he joined an emigration train of one hundred wagons on its way to the Walla Walla valley and arrived the first of September. This was the second train to start for the west that year. Nearly all members of the first train were murdered by the Indians. For the protection of the second train two companies of soldiers were sent out from Ft. Laramie as an escort through the country of the hostile Indians.

Mrs. Smith remembers the great herds of buffalo that roamed the prairies then. These herds had leaders, who were at the head of any cross-country movement. There were also strategic points on rivers where crossings were made and trails from the entire buffalo region led to these crossings. When the herds were coming or going and their paths crossed the emigrants' road the buffalo procession held the right of way. The train was compelled to halt until the passing of the herds which often numbered in the thousands. This sometimes necessitated a camp in the middle of the afternoon.

Mr. Sheets was accompanied by his brother who had made the trip across the plains previously and by his advice ample provisions were made for the trip. Mr. Sheets had five wagons, four of them mostly loaded with provisions. Several cows were brought with the train and Mrs. Sheets had a unique method of supplying the family with butter. Fresh milk was put into the churn each morning, the lid was fastened securely and at night there was always nice fresh butter in the churn. Others in the train had cows and milked them but Mrs. Sheets was the only one who possessed the automatic churn. Another interesting memory of the journey was the use of the Dutch oven. Mrs. Smith well remembers the fruit turnovers her mother used to bake in the evening and how appetizing they were.

Mr. Sheets and brother considered taking homesteads on the Walla Walla river but after seeing Dry Creek they like the location much better. Mr. Sheets took a homestead there and his brother took one beyond. This land was in their possession and the log houses they built were homes for many years.

Mrs. Smith was Miss Armanda Sheets. She was married to J.C. Smith, February, 1865. Mr. Smith had been a sergeant in the Oregon volunteers and was always called Sergeant Smith. Many of his intimate friends never knew his real name.

Mrs. Smith was one of a family of seven girls. At the time of her coming there was a great scarcity of young women, and girls at a very tender age participated in the pioneer festivities, especially dancing parties. It was a time when there never were wall flowers at dancing parties.

The Sheet's home was the scene of many festivities and there never was a lack of callers.

Mrs. Smith is the mother of ten children, eight of whom are living. She is well preserved considering the many hardships and trials of her pioneer life and is surrounded by a large circle of friends.

Philip Cox

Philip Cox and companions
leave the Willamette Valley in 1859
for a "life of ease" in the Walla Walla country.

Mr. Philip Cox remembers Walla Walla as a village consisting of four houses and the cantonment, the latter, rude huts constructed by Col. Steptoe, from the trees along the banks of Mill Creek to house the officers and soldiers of his command the winter of 1856. These buildings of which the officer's huts were on the south side and the soldier's barracks on the north side of East Main street, were between Palouse and Spokane streets and were the first buildings on the present site of the city. The buildings of the village were a blacksmith shop, a store and two saloons on the road leading to Fort Walla Walla which was then occupied by troops. Lumber was very scarce then and the store was constructed entirely of slabs. It was owned by William Stevens and Mr. McCullock, the former a well known character of pioneer times.

Mr. Cox a mere youth then was one of a company of four, all of whom were of Albany, Oregon. Other members were James Houston, Oliver Price and Morgan Paine, all persons prominent in the early development of the Inland Empire. Houston and Price were among the volunteers who fought in the battle of Walla Walla, December 7-10, 1855, and on their return, talked much about the Touchet Valley; the excellent opportunities it afforded for a stock range with its limitless expanse of hill land, covered with the nutritious bunch grass, and the mild winters, all constituting an ideal locality for raising stock of any kind.

The result was the coming of the four young men to the "Promised land" as it seemed to them. Each brought from 200 to 250 head of stock. They had no intention of cultivating the soil or doing any kind of hard work. They looked forward to a life of ease, anticipating a good living and a yearly addition to their capital, by the annual increase in their herds.

The only crop they saw on their way to the Touchet valley was on the land of a squatter. There were opportunities to work. The government offered them $85 per month for driving ox-teams in bringing supplies from The Dalles to Ft. Walla Walla; an offer of 10 cents a pound for all the oats they could raise, was made. They declined both offers as they did not intend to do hard work.

The first settlers in the Touchet Valley were Henry Bateman who settled four miles up the Coppei and Mr. Patton who settled farther down the stream. Of the company of the four, Mr. Cox settled on the old Bruce place now a part of Waitsburg; later he took up land on the Coppei where he planted apple trees that were the nucleus of the oldest orchard in the Touchet Valley. He went to The Dalles and bought 80 trees, which in addition to his bed and cooking utensils he packed on a small pony. He walked all the way home, leading the pony.

Mr. Cox remembers that the first field of grain raised on hill land in that section was planted by Henry Bateman. For this innovation Mr. Bateman was frequently complimented by such expressions as "What is that crazy fool doing? He will lose all his seed."

The year of 1861, much stock was brought into the valley. However the young men made no provisions for winter, for they had the impression there was no winter in this region. When the memorable winter of 1861-2, beginning December 22 and continuing until April with the coldest weather and deepest snow ever known here was over, every one of the herd belonging to the four young men was dead, but one.

The "hard winter" changed the whole of this part of the country. The inhabitants who had dreams of easy life on the stock ranges had to resort to the cultivation of the soil, to make a living. Many of the would-be stockraisers who had friends in Oregon, went back there and got horses and a few cows and began plowing the lowlands where gardens, fields of grain and corn were planted, all bearing good results. The ones who discovered the fertility of the soil were the men with families. With them cultivation was a necessity in order to live.

Mr. Cox was born near Mt. Pleasant, Iowa, 1843, and crossed the plains in 1845. The journey required six months. Steven Meek was the pilot. He lost his way and the entire expedition had a narrow escape from death by starvation. The first winter in the west was spent in the vicinity of Albany where Mr. Cox's parents settled.

Mr. Cox was married June, 1864, to Miss Julia Kitchison. Mr. and Mrs. Cox moved to Whitman County in 1869, where Mr. Cox engaged in farming and stockraising. He now farms 8,000 acres in the vicinity of Colfax.

Mr. and Mrs. Cox were the parents of five children. They are, Arthur and Anderson, who live on the farm; Mrs. Minnie Hoback, Canada; Mrs. Alma Gilliam, Washtucna and Mrs. Carrie Lancaster, San Francisco. Mrs. Lancaster was the first white child born in Whitman County.

Among the reminiscences of the early pioneer days Mr. Cox gave a few that form a strong contrast with conditions of today.

Luke Hinshaw who lived a few miles west of Waitsburg, was the owner of a large coffee mill. This was utilized by many of the pioneers in grinding wheat and corn for bread. Mr. Cox remembers taking a small sack of corn to this mill, which he ground into meal for making bread.

When sugar and flour gave out, the young men selected a beef from the herd, drove it to Fort Walla Walla where it was sold to the government and supplies were bought with the money. That was an easy life, but the hard winter put an end to this desirable condition, at least for the four.

The amusements for that time were dancing. The puncheons were taken out of the middle of the cabin floor and dancing enjoyed to the music of a Jew's harp, till after midnight. "With all the hardships," Mr. Cox states, "the pioneer life was the best life of all and I would like to live it over again."

Charles Sweazea

Mr. Sweazea tells about
the party in 1860 given in his honor
for being the first white boy
born in Walla Walla.

"Yes, I am the first white boy born within the present corporate limits of Walla Walla," said Charles L. Sweazea. "My father, Thomas Jefferson Sweazea, came by ox team from Missouri in the fall of 1859. He bought several lots and built a log cabin on Main street, between First and Second streets. I was born on July 6, 1860, in that log cabin. Our log house stood not far from the site now occupied by the First National bank. We stayed in Walla Walla for two years, when we moved out on a farm, eight miles southwest of Walla Walla, on Cottonwood creek. I have lived on the old place ever since. A girl baby was born a few weeks before I was, and several babies were born at the fort, or on nearby farms, before 1860, but I guess I am the first white male child to be born in Walla Walla.

"Captain James McAuliff told me that when I was born pretty nearly everybody in Walla Walla who amounted to anything, got drunk to celebrate the occasion. Captain McAuliff had been in the army. He hunted up his fife and they serenaded me. They played as long as the whiskey lasted. From what the old timers tell me, I guess Walla Walla in the early '60's was a very lively place. The miners used to winter here and, with the soldiers, packers, bull whackers, mule skinners and gamblers, they used to paint the town a bright crimson on frequent occasions.

"There used to be lots of dances given during the winter. They would be advertised as "five gallon dances," or "10 gallon dances," and the festivities would be kept up until the five or 10 gallons of free whiskey was gone."

Frank M. Lowden

Mr. Lowden
finds that the price of beans
can vary on the frontier.

"Yes, I have been in this country quite a while," said Mr. Frank M. Lowden. "I was born in Boone county, Kentucky, on February 7, 1832. In 1844 my folks removed to Illinois. My father was a carpenter and he wanted to settle in the village of Chicago, as he thought it would grow to be a good-sized town, but the others thought it was too low and marshy, so they went on to Central Illinois. Kentuckians are pretty clannish, and my father stayed with his Kentucky friends.

"In 1849 when I was 17 years old, three other young fellows and myself started for the California gold mines. The oldest one of our party was 19. California in '49 was a young man's country. You rarely saw a gray-haired man. We traveled light and made good time across the plains. I mined for two years, and then started a pack train. I packed for the next 25 years. I packed all over California, Oregon, Idaho, Washington, Montana and Nevada.

"For 25 years I lived in the open, and was always on the go. I came to Walla Walla in 1862. I made Walla Walla my headquarters, and freighted to the Idaho mines. In 1868 I bought 5300 acres of good land, at what is now called Lowden station. No, I can't tell you much about my 25 years as the owner of a pack train. You will have to see some one that has the gift of gab. To tell the truth I don't see that there is much to tell. Of course, a few things have stuck in my mind about my trips.

"I remember when I was coming up with my pack train from the southern Oregon mines to Walla Walla, I passed through Silverton, Oregon. I was out of beans. I stopped at Sol Hirsch's store and bought about fifty pounds of beans, all he happened to have. I paid eight cents a pound, I went to the other store there, and I found they had plenty of beans, so I priced them. They were three cents a pound. I went back to Sol Hirsch and said, 'How does it come you charge eight cents a pound for beans and the other store only asks three cents a pound?' It never feased Sol. He said: 'I bought those beans several years ago, when they were higher than they are now, and then, too, I have to ask more to get interest on my money that has been tied up all this time in those beans.' For years after that, whenever I saw Sol I would ask what is the price of beans? He got so he would leave a crowd whenever he saw me coming. Oh, yes, we all were pretty hard joshers in those days. Sol Hirsch was a popular and wide-awake merchant, and I guess he made a good-sized fortune before he died."

Joseph Myers

In late 1860 a wagon train was met by a contingent of twenty-two dragoons near Ft. Hall to escort them through a dangerous section of the Oregon Trail. After six days however, the troopers, in a controversial decision, left the train. Two weeks later, the Indians attacked, killing many of the party. Mr. Myers relates in an interview at Oregon City in November of 1860 how he and his family survived the ordeal but were forced to resort to cannibalism.

Survivors of Snake River massacre arrived last week, 13 in number, Mr. and Mrs. Myers and 5 children, Mrs. Chase and child, Miss Trimble, Mr. Munson and Mr. Chaffy; Joseph and Jacob Reith came in some time ago to Umatilla Reservation, as did Schneider, first to arrive; of 44 immigrants in one train, on way to Oregon, only 15 are known to have survived; four children, 3 girls and 1 boy, are supposed to have been taken prisoners by the Indians; one girl 14 or 15 years old, one 12, and others younger; all others were either killed or died of starvation; Mr. Myers of Salem, Oregon went out to meet his brother and family, found them on Grand Ronde River; the Myers immigrants came down from Walla Walla, Washington Territory, on last trip of steamer, on way to Salem, Oregon, with brother; Mr. Myers said, "Train consisted of 8 wagons, all from Wisconsin except Chase family from Geneva, Illinois, and Teith brothers from Minnesota; 44 persons in train; left Missouri River June 5, 1860. Were not molested by Indians until time of massacre, some 90 miles east of Owyhee River, Southern Idaho Territory, about 350 miles from Walla Walla, Washington Territory, September 8, 1860; Indians first attempted to stampede stock, were unsuccessful; train corraled themselves for defense, in favorable position, but no water near; Indians repulsed in attack, threw down arms, made signs to be friendly; we received them; many were fed; they appeared to be satisfied, and made signs for us to go on to water, and that they were friendly; so we started toward river; after we had moved on out of our strong, protected position, they started another attack on the train. Two of our men were shot down before we were "corraled" again and cattle chained; attack started about 10:00 a.m., September 8 and lasted until night of the 9th. Two more of our men were killed, Kiechnell and Judson Gracey; weather was very warm and we were nearly famished; being hemmed up two days and one night made it necessary that we get to water; cattle getting uneasy, no feed or water; loose stock had been driven away, teams inside defense of wagon; killed 25 to 50 Indians. One boy, Charles Utter in last wagon, shot 5 Indians, as fast as he could load his rifle. His father was wounded, entirely disabled. We started for river about sundown with 4 men mounted on horses ahead, Murdock, Shamberg, Schneider and Chaffy, two Reigh boys were on foot; Indians came in on all sides. Forward guards fled and left those in wagons for fate and Indians; efforts to make peaceable deal with them had no effect. Mrs. Utter refused to leave her wounded husband; she, two daughters and small son probably killed outright; so many of our men were killed, we could not get teams along and fight Indians off too.

We decided to leave everything and steal away on foot; traveled all night and kept traveling nights and sleeping in day times; had no food but one loaf of bread Chase grabbed from wagon on leaving. Two dogs followed us. Both were cooked and eaten. We were well armed and Indians, who followed us for 4 days, were afraid to come near. Finally they quit us. In days following, we caught fish when we could, ate rosebuds, berries, snakes, frogs, lizzards, and mussels out of streams; sometimes shot ducks and geese. Got one stray cow. Thus for 8 or 9 days; and entirely worn out we reached Owyhee River. Here we stopped, built shelter of willows and grass; had no blankets and very little clothes. Had traveled about 90 miles by September 17th.

About October 25th, about 47 days after the Indian attack, Captain Dent and some of his men found us there. After we had been in our camp about 3 weeks, the Van Norman family, himself, wife and 5 children, Samuel Gleason, Charles Utter and Henry Utter concluded to leave and travel on as best they could. That was the last we saw of the Van Normans; Captain Dent found the bodies of all but 4 children, where they had been murdered by Indians on Burnt River; bodies were brutally beaten and cut with knives. After Van Normans left, we traded everything we had to Indians for something to eat; we traded needles, pins and even our clothes until practically naked; Mr. Chase ate too much salmon at one meal, contracted hiccoughs, which continued and he died; Indians kept coming and were determined to trade for our guns; all we had left.

I finally buried my pistol and ammunition and traded for such salmon as they would give us; they promised to bring more but never did; one of Trimble boys volunteered to go with Indians, make friends and get them to bring us food; they treated him kindly and fed him; in company with Indians, he came every few days with salmon for us; one day someone happened to mention "soldiers" in presence of Indians, although they did not speak or understand English, someone of them did immediately get this

-197-

word. "Soja." "Soja!" was exclaimed by one after the other; a curious, devil's look came upon their countenances. They went away and the boy followed along. We waited some days, but no Trimble boy nor any Indian ever came again. One day I saw down river, where something had been dragged across trail, I followed the trace, hoping to find part of a deer left by some wild animals that I could take home to eat; I found nothing except a lock of human hair which proved to be that of Trimble boy. On way home that day, I found carcass of horse, the wolves or coyotes had deserted. Not much meat left, but I took a shank home to camp. We used that whole carcass, we burned the bones, and ate them and roasted the skin and ate it. We ate every dead carcass we could find. We ate the weeds, grass and anything at all to stay hunger. Finally one of the children died; we cut it up and ate it, and so on until we had eaten 3 of them; the mother helped to eat her own children; Mrs. Chase lost all of her children but one. The Indians dug up Mr. Chase's body to steal the old ragged clothes from corpse. We decided to eat him; so we cut him up in pieces; a day's ration in each piece. But before roasting this, Captain Dent and party came along just in time to save us from that awful ordeal. The body had been buried over 10 days. We saved every one of our children; Mrs. Chase lost hers through selfishness and through starving them to feed herself; she argued that we were all bound to die right here and that it was better that the children die first than for us to die and leave children to mercy of wolves. But Mrs. Myers insisted that Providence would yet deliver us alive back to civilization, and that we would try to keep all alive as long as possible; Mr. Myers, of Salem, brother, says when he first saw them, survivors of these experiences, they were mere skin and bones; children were so weak they would tumble down if they attempted to run; fingers like bird claws, eyes sunken, cheeks hollow, and they seemed to be half out of their minds.   When these starved people saw Captain Dent coming, they ran out toward him, fell on ground and begged for something to eat. Those who were strong enough to ride were placed on mules, and the others were carried on litters suspended between mules. They reached Walla Walla on October 31, 1860.

A.B. Roberts

*Mr. Roberts goes out to meet
an incoming wagon train
that is traveling the same route
a year after the Van Norman massacre of 1860.*

For many years such articles as butter, pickled pork and even flour came to us around Cape Horn as did our mail and all news from home. And how glad we were when the Government extended to us mail facilities although our letters cost 25 cents each and were two months on the way; in some isolated districts it would cost $1.00 extra for some private expressman to bring your letter from the near Coast towns.

But the work of the old settler was just beginning; after he had whooped, boosted and blowed about the great country he had found and his friends with their families began making the long journey across the plains and mountains, many among these had teams that failed them on the last lap of their journey and of necessity they must have assistance sent out to them, such as fresh animals and provisions. Many months of time were spent in that helpful work and yet many of the emigrants perished unsuccored while many worried on through unaided on foot and carrying helpless children and still many perished in the mountains where they were caught before help could reach them.

But all of these matters were of little consequence compared to the days of terror which began in the early fifties when the Indians began to become hostile. Up to 1851-2 the Indians contented themselves with stealing horses and cattle and occasionally killing a man on guard with his herd some distance from camp. Later trains were openly attacked and many killed; sometimes the entire train; finally the many massacres of 1854 including the entire train known as the "Ward Train" consisting of over 50 persons were all but two slaughtered in Boise Valley about six miles from where the city of Caldwell now stands.

This was a finish. No more helpless emigrants attempted the Oregon road or trail until an overflow of the "Pike's Peak" excitement pushed on over the Rockies to seek homes somewhere in the far West. Of this crowd the Walla Walla Valley received her first settlers from the East by way of the 'plains across' or this wagon route.

This was the first year of the reopening to settlement of this beautiful Inland Empire and the Eastern emigrants joined with those settlers who had come from the West in one grand effort to tell all the world the kind of country they had found here. They must have done some "telling" for soon began a tide of emigration from the East and West; steamboats were put on the river and a stream of immigration every Summer came rolling over the old abandoned wagon road, and again the work of going or sending out help to meet and assist our friends on the last stages of the journey began, and horrors of horrors, the savages of Snake River began their bloody work with renewed determination to prevent all white people from passing through that awful country. Yes, passing through for nobody thought of stopping in that country although one could realize and see the beauty and richness of its valleys and many thought of the hidden treasures in the adjoining mountains; but few expected to live to see the savages ever removed. Yet, the Snake River country alluded to above was in the very centre of Old Oregon and every year some of its settlers were murdered. And so we were not only having the time of our lives here but many of our friends were being massacred by the savages almost at the door of our homes. It is well to note here that all Indian troubles began after the weary emigrants had crossed the great Rocky Mountains and were pushing their way over the sage brush deserts of the Snake River country in the very heart of Oregon.

I have seen and talked with many while they were camped at the garrison here in Walla Walla after being rescued and heard them describe the awful occurrence of their disaster and the weary nights that they struggled on carrying helpless children, before they were met by troops sent out to rescue them and how they screamed and wept for joy when they saw the soldiers coming. Remnants of those massacred trains are now among the old settlers of this bright and beautiful country. If I could see some of them today I could hand them some souvenirs that I picked up on the ground of the Van Norman massacre of 1860, ten months after it occurred; among them are many interesting papers and a lock of golden hair evidently torn from some poor woman's head as she made her deathly struggle against the savage fiends.

No, we didn't come in Pullmans or even chair cars when we came to develop this interesting country and to make it possible for greater interests to take up and continue the work.

Yet, the conditions that existed in this far off country when the American settler began were not very enticing but there was something about the times at that period that enchanted and entangled the lover of adventure and push that held one spellbound and impelled one on to greater efforts in helping to develop the unbounded and great natural resources of a wonderful country.

This story was started to tell of a trip the writer made out onto the plains into the very hottest of that hostile country in 1861 to meet friends who had crossed the mountains and deserts to come to us after many years of reading of my glowing accounts of this Inland country. These were a brother and sister with their families who were coming over the identical spots where the Van Normans and other emigrants were killed the season previous. 'The season previous;' you see, emigration came but once a year to this country in those days, and it was in the Summer season.

I was proposing to practically go alone; had only hired one man, James

Veasey, to go as pack helper; I had seven packs of provisions and 5 or 6 saddle horses. A young man from Goderich, Canada, by the name of Angus McKay, arrived from Portland. He had a letter of introduction to me from our mutual friend, G.C. Robbins. This young man had left his home in the East to see the great West. He was another of those adventurers who had just found this country. Learning of my trip onto the plains it struck him as in line with his work, his ventures, and offered to go with me. I told him horses, saddles and supplies were at his service and his company would be exceedingly pleasant as we both were members of the same fraternal order. T.P. Denny of Dry Creek, who had crossed the plains the year before, was anxious to send help out to meet his son, Frank, who was coming with his family; he sent his son Than and a hired man by the name of Henry Calkins. Now, there were to be five to go out hundreds and hundreds of miles from any civilization into the heart of the most desperate savages in the United States. Some of our more cautious friends assured us that we would not live more than 24 hours after crossing the Blue Mountains into the Grand Ronde Valley.

I had no fear of going out but it was coming back with trains loaded with things desirable to the savages and the valuable stock, helpless women and children and men of no experience in Indian strategy or tactics. Here was where the danger came in--the home trip.

My brother-in-law, Phillip L. Hawley, had come out by way of the Ithsmus the fall previous and was to remain at my home during my absence. We packed up seven loads of grub-flour, bacon, sugar, coffee, tea, and, in fact, nearly everything eatable, saddled our horses and in two days were at the agency on the Umatilla. Mr. Abbott, the Indian Agent, assured us that it was reckless and foolhardy for such a small party to attempt to go out among the hostile Indians who were yet redhanded with the blood of hundreds. I said, "Well, Mr. Abbott, if the Indians murdered hundreds last year it is time that some help or protection is rendered this year." He replied, "but you won't last 24 hours after you reach Grand Ronde," and, so with these cheerful assurances we left after stopping one day, and buying one big, gentle Cayuse horse from our friend Winumsnoots. Just before leaving the agency we were joined by two men from Linn County, Oregon, Henry Watson and his old father, who were going out to meet their friends. So now there was seven of us.

We started on our trip soon after the Fourth of July. The second day after leaving the agency we arrived in the Grand Ronde Valley and encamped for a few days where the city of La Grande is now located. My object in starting so early was to map out and prospect for gold as it was my idea that the placer gold existing in the north extended South of the Blue Mountain range.

The Grand Ronde Valley as we came in was a virgin meadow with no track of a domestic animal in it except the footprints of one lone horse. A Umatilla Indian who had committed murder some two months before had crossed the mountains while the road was wet and muddy and that track was always before us and served as a useful pointer; for by this sign we could tell that no other Indians were near ahead of us. And I will here remark that it is of such renegades as this that inhabited the larger portion of the lower Snake and Shoshone Indian country. We stopped here several days. Mr. McKay and I took the North end to where the Grand Ronde river goes through a canyon into the beautiful pine covered valley which we called "pine valley." One day we went around the south end and as we skirted the foot of the mountains we came to a great patch of willows which forced us up onto the mountain side; there we smelt a strong odor of sulphur and looking over the willows we saw a boiling sulphur lake which we at once named "Hot Sulphur Lake." It is now known as Hot Lake where is built a very fine sanitarium. For a few minutes we discussed the future development of this very interesting place and then we led our horses up the steep mountain side to the summit which we found covered with heavy pine timber through which we made our way down a gentle slope into the open Powder River Valley. Here we found numbers of antelope in every direction like range cattle on the grassy plains. We made many herds skidaddle and had some good shots.

Upon returning to our camp we found some 25 or 30 Indians from the Umatilla had ventured over. The next day we moved up into the Powder River Valley and the Indians went with us. We located well up to the foot of the Blue Mountains on Pine Creek under some splendid trees. Now, for the first time I took my gold pan, pick and shovel and started to prospect for the precious placer gold. I was successful in finding many "colors," sufficient to assure me that here was a rich mining country. Some 10 or 12 months later was discovered, on another tributary of Powder River the greatest placer gold camp ever found in the state of Oregon—a camp that offered up its millions in one year and that is still profitably worked. But this pan of dirt was very probably the first ever taken up in Eastern Oregon that showed the precious metal. On Burnt river a few days later I found very rich "prospects" and there predicted a golden future for this locality; and I have since seen for miles along this stream many thousands of acres made a desolate waste by the gold miner, and while much gold has been taken out there never will be enough to pay for the destruction of the land, for this is the most perfect grape and peach district in all Eastern Oregon.

As the evening of the second day here drew near, came a great scare. Some Indians returning from antelope hunts had seen "Snake tracks"—signs of the hostile Indians. They had evidently crossed each others' tracks as later developments showed. So the old chief sent Johnny McBean, a half breed, over to our camp to ask us to return to Grand Ronde with them where we would fight the Snakes together if attacked. But we declined and advised them to stay; for awhile they seemed satisfied, but later scare reports came in and after sundown the whole mob pulled out and rushed back to Grand Ronde and very soon went over the mountains home. And a few days later it was reported in Walla Walla that our entire party was murdered by the Snakes.

It was certainly the "time of their lives" for those Indians for they caught hundreds of fine salmon and killed much game. They just loaded up with their "catch" of salmon and antelope. You will remember that these two Valleys were disputed ground between the Umatillas and the Shoshone tribes and either party coming into Powder River or Grande Ronde Valley was expected to be on the fight; hence fish and game was severely let alone by both parties.

Well, we came over the mountains expecting to see "Snake tracks" so early the next morning we hit the trail again. Crossing the great valley in the direction of the Granite Buttes near the present city of Haines we struck the main Powder some miles above the emigrant ford and found a crossing and in a few hundred yards came again into the old road and here again was that Indian murderer's tracks in a muddy road travelling on to join his kind in the Snake River valley.

As we were now in a dangerous country we adopted more cautious modes of traveling. Two of us, generally McKay or Veasy and I in the lead and three with the train and two in the rear. It is a well known fact that Indians will not attack a party of well armed men well strung out, when they will not hesitate to do so where the same number is in a bunch. It is more uncertain to hit a single man than to kill one of a bunch and when one is successfully killed the whole crowd is more easily demoralized, captured and destroyed at leisure. So we adopted the policy that in dangerous places that one should lead and the others to follow at a safe distance. We made it a point to start early and make a drive of 20 to 30 miles and camp early and dig rifle pits in which one in sleepless watch would sit from dusk until daylight at which time our horses were untethered and taken to graze as they were nearly all picketed at dusk.

We of course looked upon the Shoshone or Snakes as red-handed murderers for the last one seen of them was in the act of attacking a train of Oregon citizens on the very ground we were now to travel, so it was determined that no murderer was to come near us without a white flag and then only one at a time. And then it became necessary for us to be aggressive and when we came in line with them to make them get out as though we would just eat them up. And thus one day we overtook a number of Indians on our trail; McKay and I being in our lead rushed for them and drove a dozen or so across the plains into the foothills of the Owyhee Mountain. But if a party of Indians had been camped ever so near our trail we would have gone on without noticing them or apparently caring. The only safe policy in an Indian country is to let them know that you are not afraid and that you are always on guard and believe them to be your enemy. It is a mighty good plan to never attempt friendship with hostile savages.

As I said we camped early, turned our horses on the grass, keeping one under saddle which the horse guard could mount when necessary, cooked dinner, which was usually our principal meal; some would go to nearby prominent points on the lookout for Indians and sometimes prospecting was done for placer mines, and always looking for the tracks of the renegade Indian who was still on the trail before us.

And every day we moved on and on through those desolate valleys, and, to pass the time away, we were generally discussing the future prospects of their resources.

One day as we were going down the Burnt river canyon we came to the big bend where the river makes a sharp turn to the west for over a mile and again to the East and coming back to within a quarter of a mile of the same place. I said to McKay, who was then with me "that sometime a railroad will be built through this canyon and right here a tunnel will pierce that narrow ridge." I have lived to pass through that tunnel on the cars dozens of times and to see the thousands of acres of hills and bars torn down by the miners to obtain the gold where we on that trip found the first "prospect" of the yellow metal.

Our first camp on Snake river was at the Big Bend where the great river leaves the vast lava bed plains and enters the Blue mountains to plunge through 180 miles of canyons to join the Columbia as it comes from its northern home.

We dug our rifle pit on the level plain near the river where we could see the approach of an enemy more than a gun shot away and if necessary we could take shelter behind the nearby river banks. Thus we were always safe, and while the Indians often had signal fires in many directions around us, they dared not make an attack and during our traveling hours we feared no one.

The next day 22 miles brought us to the Malheur where we stopped at noon and spent the balance of the day--spending much time in bathing in a fine pool and giving our horses also a great bath, taking them in separately and learning them and ourselves to swim together.

During the afternoon Henry Watson and I went upon the great butte across the river where we could see for many miles around. We could see a great camp of nearly 1,000 Indian wigwams down towards Snake river but no emigrants on the road to the East. But here I received the scare of my life; as we tramped through the sand and scattering sagebrush I heard that dreadful whir and rattling noise so well known as that of the deadly rattle snake. I made a sudden jump and turning around saw a monstrous rattler with his head raised some 18 inches, flashing his tongue and glaring with red eyes at me. But a shot from my revolver finished the snake.

At the Malheur we saw no more of the tracks of the Umatilla renegade. He had joined with his kind and was ready to take part in the massacre of the next emigrant train that come over the Oregon trail.

As before intimated those lower Snakes or Shoshones were made up mostly of renegades of all Indian tribes and even some whites who had found this country as a place where they were absolutely secure from any attempt to recapture. This I was told by Mr. James Cragie, the oldest trader and trapper of the Hudson Bay Company and who trapped in the Boise mountains during the time his company maintained Old Fort Boise on Snake river at the mouth of the Boise. I once wrote the Shoshone language which I learned from Mr. Cragie. He was probably the brightest and ablest of all those early trappers.

Leaving Malheur we made the drive to the Owyhee some 20 miles and as it was early we concluded to go on to the Snake river which was reached after traveling 10 miles. As we came over the plains from the Malheur we descended directly towards the mouth of the Boise and as we looked eastward we could see that beautiful valley with its line of great cottonwood timber winding through its grassy plains for 50 miles and in the background those beautiful Bosie mountains with their pine covered tops raising up in some instances into perpetual snow. Veasey and I were riding together and as we contemplated the beautiful scenery before us I said, "Veasey, five years from now you will see those mountains full of miners." In the early spring of 1863 I met Veasey in the Boise Basin where we had come with the great Boise excitement and he remarked that my "prediction came true earlier than I expected."

During the next three days we passed the fatal spot where the Van Norman train was massacred. While contemplating the conditions surrounding this affair my blood boiled to see the evidence of the awful result. Burned wagons, bones of dead horses, remnants of books and valuable papers, locks of human hair and the evidence of the very shallow burial of the dead, which was done by a company of cavalry.

Would it be interesting to hear of these matters? They have never been written or published and I have been on all of the surrounding country and I have had the whole story told to me by one of the women whose husband fell in that dreadful affair. First of all the selection of the place to "round up" was unfortunate. Now it must be remembered that the first attack was made on this train at Catherine Creek, 10 miles east, in the morning soon after leaving camp at that place, and one man was killed there. But the train moved up on a little dry valley among low hills driving the Indians back for 10 miles where they passed a narrow point and opened on to the plains again near Snake river. Descending a short distance a slight ravine was on each side of the road and the main trail continued on parallel to the river and a "camp road" turned down to the river a quarter of a mile away where there was a beautiful meadow of about 40 acres with the river running by and a perpendicular bluff many hundreds of feet high on the other side. This was an ideal place to camp, perfectly protected from assaults from all sides, with plenty of grass and water and where that emigrant train could have protected itself indefinitely. But instead of proceeding on to this safe place they rounded up their wagons in the road among the sagebrush with a ravine on each side in the road 50 yards away where the sagebrush grew as high as a man's head. The Indians, of course, took possession of those ravines; and also secure behind the sagebrush they could pick off anyone who came in sight or could kill the stock as they desired. Thus they were surrounded without water or grass all day and the following night when it was determined towards morning to try to make an escape. Some of the teams were hitched up; two young men were selected to act as a van guard and were to proceed to drive the Indian back. But as the train began to move the Indians made a final rush; the two young men skipped and the awful work was soon completed. But 13 of all that train escaped alive and they hid as best they could along the river in willows until those two young men reached Fort Walla Walla and a company of troops were sent out to their rescue and to bury the dead. Upon the arrival of the young men here I went at once to see them at their camp at the garrison and while talking with one of the women one of those two young men joined us. The woman would hardly speak to him, but sneeringly said: "Yes, you skipped out over the hill and left us." The young man took a walk.

After spending a few hours here at this awful spot we moved on. We camped one night at Sinker Creek; all of these creeks come from what is called the Owyhee mountains, and, believing this to be a mineral range I concluded to sink a "prospect" and was rewarded by finding what I thought was "paying diggings" and looking towards those mountains I said, "if it was so that we could go into those mountains safely I could make a fortune there."

We camped one night on the Bruneau river and yet no emigrants had made their appearance on the Oregon trail. Why are they so late? Had the many massacres on the trail the previous year scared the emigrants off or have they switched their route and gone on with the emigrants to California? Could it be that my folk at a late hour had given up the dangerous journey entirely? We had received no letters telling of their actual starting when I left Walla Walla. Well, this was not all of our troubles. The old Mr. Watson assured us that he was unable to go any farther with the uncertainty of meeting anyone who could help him to return to his home. We assured him that if we failed to meet any Oregon emigrants, that we could more easily reach Soda Springs and from thence to the Mormon settlements near Cash Valley, than to return. But he didn't want any Mormon settlement in his and declined to go farther. To let him and his son attempt to return alone would be like casting them out to certain death. So it was finally decided that the Watsons and Denny party with my man Veasey should stop at Bruneau while McKay and I would make a rush on to the Three Island Crossing of Snake river where it was possible that the emigration was crossing as it some times did to avoid the great bend and the deserts of the south side of Snake and its greater distance and also avoid what has always been considered the most hostile country. So the next day began for McKay and I a ride of 125 miles in a hostile country without sleep or stop; and yet no emigration in sight.

Returning to Bruneau after this strenuous and fruitless ride alone and in the center of hostilities, where 10 months previous the Indians had murdered about 50 Oregon settlers, we found our party waiting very patiently but not daring to attempt to make a move towards a return, for every mile of the first 75 was so recently marked by the blood of our friends. We were told that the Indians had been around them the previous night and we were shown moccasin tracks where the enemy had been within 100 yeards of the camp, and so they urged that we should pull out at dark on our retreat. But we said, no; if the Indians had any use for us they can just as well find us here as anywhere, and to attempt to move in the night would show that we were afraid of them which would encourage them to an attack. So we remained overnight and again had a false alarm by old man Watson and were shown "Snake tracks" by the young Mr. Watson. But no one believed the scare reports, so we leisurely packed up and started on our return to Walla Walla.

We found a large tin can which we cut up and on the bright sheets we wrote a very indelible letter which we left telling my friends of our efforts and where we had left "caches" of provisions. If I had been reasonably sure that there was any Oregon emigration on the Snake river trail, I would have remained at the Bruneau indefinitely. But it was now doubtful if any would venture down the south side, but might be crossing that river near old Fort Hall and across the Blackfoot and Camas Prairie country and recrossing at the mouth of the Boise River. So we returned at a leisurely pace, hoping that we might meet them there. This Blackfoot route is about 75 miles nearer than the south side.

No incident of importance occurred on our return until we reached the Owyhee. We had made a drive of 30 miles starting in the morning and with the understanding that we would camp at that place early and we would from there see if any emigrants were over on the Boise or at the Snake river crossing. McKay and I rode in the rear that day and at the bend of the Snake river we made a detour across the plains to the Owyhee, striking that stream several miles above the wagon road crossing; crossing over we came down the west side, just as our outfit reached our proposed camping place. Here we met a "big scare" again. Below us and near the Snake and Owyhee were what looked to be 1000 Indian wigwams. The Watsons refused to go into camp and proposed to push on 20 miles more to the Malheur in the night. I said no to this and proceeded to select a sure location and to unpack the tired animals. At near sundown the Watsons and Dennys pulled out for the Malheur.

We dug our rifle pit near the river on the edge of the smooth level plain; nearby us was a little bunch of willows, from our position we could see our enemy approaching for over a quarter of a mile.

By ten o'clock the Indians had "signal fires" all about us. Soon after 12 I called to McKay and called his attention to the Indian fires; he very cooly said: "Well, let them come." But they didn't come and at sunrise Veasey had a good breakfast ready and we packed up and started on our way over the plains to the Malheur expecting that we would meet Indians coming back from an attack and probable murder of the Watson-Denny party; but we had little fear of an attack upon us in daylight.

Well, we arrived safely and to our dismay we found that my "cache" of three pack loads of provisions had been dug up and was gone. Later I learned that the Watson party had met Capt. A.D. Pierce with a party of prospectors who was getting short and told him that they had a cache which they could not need and that he was welcome to the supplies.

So we pushed on and saw no human being until we reached the Umatilla where we found Zeph Bryant, an acquaintance of mine from the lower Columbia and his party of prospectors. We had driven from Lee's Encampment about 25 miles and my date was up to be at home and I was anxious to always fill my promises. I asked Bryant where he was going and he replied that he was just out looking at the Interior country. I proposed that he go to Walla Walla and he said he would. We left our respective parties at Umatilla to travel home at their leisure and our forty-five mile journey to Walla Walla was uneventful. We arrived home in the evening on time to find my wife, Mr. Hawley, and two of my Portland friends, U.S. Jacobus and Fred Harbaugh, sitting around a table with a 40 pound watermelon; they were waiting for me, my wife assuring them that I never failed to come as I promised.

Yes, home again after nearly two months of a strenuous journey. There is no record of any half dozen white men leaving all base of civilization and defying the most red-handed murderous savages and penetrating the very center of their wild and almost unknown country, and even recklessly challenging them on the very ground where a few short months before they had massacred over 50 men and women and carried off much valuable property. Yes, we saw the murderers flying in the breeze the scalps of those unfortunate beings scarce cold in their shallow graves. But the cowardly savages, they would fly from well armed, unencumbered men from the West.

But now we had no time to waste; my brother-in-law, Capt, Hawley, had letters from our folks telling him of their starting and being now out on the plains west of the Missouri and another effort must be made to help them. And so it was concluded that as soon as my outfit and Mr. Bryant's got in from Umatilla that Mr. Hawley with three packs should start again and Mr. Bryant volunteered to accompany him.

Soon they were on their way over the plains to the Umatilla, over the Blue mountains and across the beautiful Grande Ronde Valley, up into the magnificent Powder river plains and as they began the descent into the Burnt river canyon the first weary wagon train was met. This train reported almost continuous conflict with Indians after crossing the Rockies and all the way down the Snake river and assured Capt. Hawley that it was unsafe and useless to go on, as the body of the emigration was behind and under a government escort. But Mr. Hawley had grit and was fully determined to push on and meet his family as soon as possible. So they pushed on down the great canyon and over to the horrible Snake country and across the deserts to the Malheur meeting emigrants frequently all of whom assured them that their efforts were hazardous and useless.

On the plains between the Malheur and the Owyhee mountains they met Samuel King's train. Mr. King told him of having had a serious fight with the Indians at the Owyhee and that he must not go any further. So they returned with the King train to Burnt river where they attempted to await the enemy.

After stopping one day the Indians became too numerous and they moved back into the Grande Ronde where they found some emigrants had actually located homes. They awaited at this point until our friends came on. Our friends were with the escort and had been for several hundred miles, as Capt. Madorum Crawford of the escort had borrowed their light rig to send forward assistance and broken it, after which they were given a government wagon and were taken into the government train for the balance of the journey. It was said that after my letter written on the tin was found far up on Snake river and being thus evidence that friends were out making an effort to assist them, Capt. Crawford was very solicitous with his assistance. So possibly my efforts were of some account after all.

This "government escort" was taken up on account of the various massacres during the previous years and was continued for three seasons. It was not composed of U.S. soldiers, but was only in command of an army officer. It was made up by enlisting 100 young men who wanted to go to the Far West and who were willing to be discharged at the end of the trip. Many of these young men became useful and prominent citizens of the Walla Walla Valley while others went to adjacent mines and some to Oregon. Two of these escorts were disbanded at Fort Walla Walla and the third at Fort Boise, it being the policy of the government to disband the escort upon reaching the first military post.

James Stott Kershaw

Kershaw, an emigrant of 1861,
arrives just in time to experience
the worst winter ever known
on the Pacific Coast.

James Stott Kershaw was born in Yorkshire, England, July 5, 1835, and came to America when seven years old. His father was a member of the Kershaw Brothers who owned a spinning factory at that place.

An uncle came to America, and settled at Carbondale, Pennsylvania, where he discovered coal. He returned to England very enthusiastic over his discovery which meant wealth for all the family and succeeded in persuading his brother to come and join him.

Mr. Kershaw's father planned to come and began to dispose of his holdings and when the plans were completed, he was stricken with appoplexy and died.

Mrs. Kershaw decided to carry out her husband's plans and after the estate was settled, she and her four children sailed for America, the journey requiring more than five weeks as it was made in a sailing vessel and they had the experience of the ship running ashore. Ten days after arriving here the uncle at Carbondale died. Mrs. Kershaw settled near Poughkeepsie, New York, where there was a factory, so that her children could work as they had learned this kind of work in England. Here her only daughter, Hannah, aged eleven was drowned in a creek, while washing the cotton prints. At that time, calicoes and other prints were printed by hand, and the blocks washed by hand.

The family then moved to Fall River, Massachusetts, another manufacturing town, where Mr. Kershaw's brothers worked in the factory and he learned the carpenter trade.

July, 1856, a move was made to Belvidere, Illinois. This was an interesting journey as it was partly made by ocean, river and Erie canal. The family arrived at its destination in the early part of August. This move was made because the west was considered a better country for the poorman as there were more opportunities to get a start in the world as land could be more easily obtained. This move was not a disappointment. Mr. Kershaw secured work at his trade soon after his arrival and his two brothers got work on nearby farms and soon after were able to buy an acre of ground and build a little home on it in the late fall. It was well for them that the home was completed before winter as the winter was very severe.

Mr. Kershaw became acquainted with some men who made a business of driving horses to California for sale and these recommended the Pacific Coast very highly in regard to climate and opportunities for young men. The result was that the family decided to move farther west, and the home was sold, a team bought, provisions procured and a start for the unknown west made in the spring of 1861. What place in the west the family would select for a home was not fully decided upon but there was a preference for California.

Some one who had crossed the plains had given the Kershaws the advice to "Never camp twice in the same place," and when the train reached Ft. Laramie and made a halt of a few days, four families, the Kershaws among them pulled out and continued the onward march; this act decided their location.

Near Devil's Gate they fell in with W.H. Babcock and three other families. Soon after they were joined by four more and later caught up with a train of eight, in command of Col. Black. In the latter addition were Messrs. George, Andrew, Asa and Noah Evans, all residents of this city at the present time and Messrs. Joe and Phil Hoon, well known residents of the vicinity of Milton. This train was headed for Oregon.

Mr. Babcock was a resident of Walla Walla valley settling here in 1859 and was returning from the east, with his family. He gave such glowing accounts of this valley that the Kershaws decided to come here. Those intending to go to California wavered. It is told by one of the party that one who could not reach a decision decided to be guided by the falling of a stick. In the evening a stick was selected and a crowd gathered around to witness the falling which was to decide such a momentous question.

"Now ready," he announced. "If this stick falls south, I go to California. If it falls north I go to Washington." The stick fell south. He looked at it a while then said:

"I'll be hanged if I don't go to Washington anyhow." And he did. After arriving here, the Kershaws and others of the train were the guests of Mr. Babcock for several days. Mr. Kershaw was much impressed with Mr. Babcock's hospitality, and said perhaps he was never in a state of mind to appreciate hospitality to such a degree. It was a most happy ending of the long journey. Mr. Babcock killed two beeves and distributed them among the emigrants.

After a few days' rest a search for locations was begun and the Kershaws decided on a quarter section joining Charles Actor at the present site of Dixie and they made their home the first winter with Mr. Actor. He lived in a small cabin, but gladly opened his home to four more. He was glad to have this addition to his family and they were indeed fortunate to have such a comfortable home for the winter.

Mr. Kershaw remembers that there was no rain after August 31. The first moisture that fell was a deep snow on December 22, and winter began. The snow did not melt until April and in some places there were large drifts in May. How cold the weather was no one knows for there were no government thermometers then and few if any of any kind in the territory. But there was a crust on the two feet or more of snow, so thick that a heavy man could walk on it.

Mr. Kershaw remembers that there would be a moderation in the temperature and the older inhabitants here would tell him that a chinook was coming and all the snow would be gone by morning, but instead more snow came everytime and he did not have the pleasure of knowing what a chinook wind was until the next winter.

The winter was long but Mr. Kershaw says he was too busy to find the time dreary. First was the care of the herd which consisted of three oxen and two cows. Each morning some one of the boys went into the corral with a few ears of corn in his hand and performed a short marathon in which the cows and oxen joined. After the herd seemingly was warmed up, each member was rewarded with three or four ears. They also had to be watered and the creek was frozen for all these months and that meant that the ice crust must be taken off every time, nor was this all. There must be some coarse food, for cattle cannot live on corn alone. This was supplied by cutting the small limbs from the willow and other trees and was no small job as it had to be performed daily for over four months. Mr. Kershaw's herd all survived the winter, while nearly all the cattle in the valley died. He considers the reason of this to be due to the fact that his cattle came from a cold climate and were hardened to the cold weather while most of the cattle here were from California and Oregon which have mild climates.

The wood was a commodity that disappeared almost as if by magic. The lowness of the mercury required a high pile of wood all the time. The supply was furnished by the trees along the creek and as the months of intense cold continued the trees near at hand gave out and those farther away had to be brought to the cabin. The snow was drifted so deep in many places that they had to make a trail using the fence stakes along the field that had been fenced for the guides. The trees were cut down and if small enough were dragged to the cabin. If too large, cut in half and taken in two sections.

The menu that winter was small and had very little variety and required much labor to prepare but they were very thankful for it, such as it was. It consisted of beef and flapjacks. The latter part required the work. The wheat had much smut in it and each day someone took enough for one day's supply to the creek and washed the smut out of it. Then it was taken to the house and dried by the fireplace. The last process was grinding it on an old government coffee mill. For months this was the daily fare without any variation.

In the early winter a pack train bound for the Oro Fino mines reached Mr. Actor's place and learned that it would be impossible to reach the mines. The load which consisted mostly of flour was left with Mr. Actor.

In the early spring the slapjacks palled on the taste of members of the entire household and Mr. Kershaw took the liberty of appropriating one sack of flour to his own use. Flour at that time was worth $22 per sack. However the sacks were about twice as large as the present day sacks. When the packers arrived he allowed the sack of flour for the storage which was very satisfactory to the Kershaws and Mr. Actor.

The Kershaws leased Mr. Actor's land giving him a portion of the grain, and in the spring they plowed the land of the Actor farm then began improvements on their own land, among the first was a log house. After the land had been fenced and cultivated, a more pretentious home was built across the road from Dixie. This home as was the log house was ever noted for the great hospitality dispensed there.

The three brothers were musicians, Jack and William were violinists and all were fond of singing and one song they sang that was new at that time was "Dixie's Land." Whenever they sang and wherever, this number was always called for, so popular was this song that many people knew them by the singing of the song and they were known by the name of Dixie boys.

Many never knew what their real name was. When the founders of the town of Dixie were selecting a name for it, the many friends of the Kershaw boys requested that it be named Dixie in honor of them and it was.

Ambrose A. Owsley

Dick Owsley relates
his experiences during the
terrible winter of 1861-62.

I landed at Walla Walla on August 25, 1861. From there I went to Whetstone in what is now Columbia county and met Tom Whetstone, one of the earliest settlers of that region. He was living in a tent, and desiring to build a house. I contracted to construct it for him. We went from his place up to the mountains on what is known as the Eckler mountain. We wintered right where the Eckler mill was afterwards located for the purpose of getting out logs and timber. A little while before New Years we made a big sled and took a load of shingles to Walla Walla; myself, Bill McCormick and Jake Hybarger, who came across the plains with me. We made the shingles ourselves. We split them out with a frow from pine timber and shaved them with a drawing knife. We made ten thousand. The snow started to fall and we supposed it would be good sledding, so we put the shingles on the sled with five hundred pounds of dried deer hams, ten bushels of wheat and some feed corn, and started to Walla Walla with three yoke of cattle. The deer were thicker there than cattle ever have been since. You could kill all the deer you wanted--could go out any time and get one in an hour.

The first day out we went as far as Dayton to the crossing of the Touchet. The weather was bitter cold. We drove into the creek, and the pine sled, having no shoes, as soon as it struck the rocks it stayed right there. We got out in the water and unhitched the team and packed the shingles and hams to the other side. It took us all night. Next morning we hitched up and drove to the mouth of Whiskey creek, on the Coppei. McCormick froze his ears and Jake froze his feet. This was done in the daytime. I was lucky enough not to get frozen. We camped on the Coppei that night with Bill Bunton at the Bunton house. We put our cattle in his corral and packed corn fodder down to feed them. It snowed all night. Jake didn't know his feet were frozen until they began to thaw in the house. We took his shoes off and had him place his feet in a tub of ice water. After that he danced and hopped around all night. The next morning we struck on to Walla Walla. Jake was suffering terribly and could not wear his shoes. He tied gunny sacks on his feet and went with us. The snow was just up to the top of the sled then, about 2½ feet deep. We unloaded the shingles and went on to Walla Walla with the wheat and deer hams. The next night we camped on the flat between Dry creek and Walla Walla. We put the cattle in a large house, just built, the first house on that flat. The next day we went to the mill out south of Walla Walla. It was the first mill there, I think it was the Reynolds mill which is now owned and operated by J.H. Coyle.

We sold our deer hams in Walla Walla for 25 cents a pound, got our wheat ground at the mill, and the next day we started back. It had been snowing all the time and was still very cold. We got back as far as Dry creek and there we had to leave the sled and the load of provisions for the winter with a man by the name of Kimble. We took the cattle and started on that evening and got up in the hollow above Dutch Charley's, where Dixie is now located. There our cattle mired in the snow and couldn't get any further. I unyoked them, racked the yokes up and left them there. The outlook was gloomy and we had little hope of ever reaching home. We put the cattle up on the hillside where there were a few weeds sticking up out of the snow and went back down to Dutch Charley's and called there to get shelter in his cabin. By this time you could track Jake Hybarger by the blood from his feet that dripped through the gunny sacks, and McCormick was having quite a time with his ears. We made arrangements to stop at Dutch Charley's cabin that night. We cut wood out of the creek and packed it up to the house after dark.

The cattle followed us down to the house along the creek. The next morning I found them back down at Kimbles. I got some corn from Kimble to feed them and we stayed there for ten days. We found Dutch Charley a pretty nice man after we got acquainted with him. Every day we fed the cattle a sack of corn. There were some old straw stacks there and there were dead cattle around those stacks so thick that you couldn't walk through them. The corn I fed my cattle kept them all right.

The tenth day, father and the expressman from Florence, Idaho, came through on snow shoes. They supposed we had perished. If you had been close enough you could have seen a few tears as we met. The snow was then five feet deep all over the Walla Walla valley. The next morning after father came through we packed two of our steers with our camp outfit. One went ahead to break trail, following the high ridges. It was very hard work, but we managed to get over to Coppei that day and stopped with Sam Gilbreath who had a public house at Coppei. If ever I thought I was in heaven it was that night around the hot stove. Gilbreath gave us a good hot toddy and we had a good meal and a good rest. The next morning we struck on over to the Touchet and made it there. Our bill at Gilbreath for four of us and six steers was $20.00, and we had not a cent to pay with. We gave him a lien on the shingles over the hill from his house.

We found when we got back up to Stubb's ranch, where Dayton now stands that three or four pack trains were snowed in there, and the community would have suffered if those trains had not been there. They were loaded to go to Colville and they let everyone have provisions, to be paid for in the spring or when they could. We got provisions, flour, coffee, etc., and packed them up to where we were wintering and where our camp was.

When we got there we found the snow about twelve feet deep. Mother, Barney and Belle had stayed there all the time supposing that we were all lost, the old man and all the rest. They had plenty of meat to eat, but had nothing else for ten days. They could get neither in or out, the snow was so soft. We packed our provisions, walking on clumps, broad pieces of wood which we tied on our shoes. We went down to Stubbs' after another load of provisions and the wind blew a little, and when we got down on the ridges the snow wasn't quite so deep. All the side of my face was frozen and blistered by the wind. We packed about fifty pounds apiece, and got back home about midnight. All the rest gave out on the road. Ben Hurley gave out and father had to kick him around there to keep him from freezing. I sent Barney out with a pine torch to meet them. He went about a quarter of a mile and the old man hallooed when he saw the light, and Barney located them and brought them into camp. Barney was about seventeen years old then.

We managed to stay there in that cabin, packing our provisions in until about the 20th of March. The snow crusted then so mother and Belle could walk out. They went out on top of the snow and we took them down to For-sythe's, below Dayton. Hybarger had lost the front half of his feet, they came off all but the sinews, and I cut them off with a razor. He suffered intensely and begged me to shoot him; when I refused he begged me to give him the pistol so he could kill himself.

The last day of March we all went to Florence. The snow was gone on the Tucanon and the Pataha, but there was about four feet on the Alpowa ridge. It snowed there the day we crossed it and I never saw it snow harder. We left the Pataha and went up the hill right where the road leaves now. It went right up that back bone. The trail came down just above Long's place at the forks of the Alpowa creek. When we went down there a man by the name of King had commenced to build a house and when we came back in the fall he had a big log house. He sold it to one of Vine Favor's brothers.

When I came back in the fall Dutch George had settled right up here where the park now is; the Rigsby place was settled as we came up. There was some man there, but I have forgotten his name. I think he had a house there, built out of pine logs. When we came back in the fall the old Owsley place had been taken up and a blacksmith shop had been built; and Hybarger who was a blacksmith hired out there. I went on down home.

I had been to the great mining camp of Florence, where I saw $500.00 washed out of one shovel, and then didn't get rich. It was the richest place in the world. They were the richest placer mines anywhere. People thought that the mines covered the whole basin, but they only covered about two sections. I saw ten thousand men there.

It was during this winter that the three men were frozen to death on the

Deadman Gulch, and it is from this incident that the gulch takes its name. The bones of these men were buried on the place recently sold by Art Whitmore to E.L. Sanford. The bones were found the next spring by Cayuse George and John Turner. The names of these men were unknown, but they had left Florence with twenty or twenty-five pounds of gold dust, which has never been found. It was in rawhide purses and was probably scattered over the hills by the coyotes.

It began to snow that winter on New Year's eve, and continued without stop for forty days, day and night. Sometimes the fall was heavy, sometimes light, but it never stopped altogether and it was fearfully cold all the time.

This is my recollection of the winter of 1861-62.

Chapter 5

The New Eldorado

Sports, Vigilantes and Pony Express Riders

"It was a common thing for
a man to come in and sit down
with you to eat in the morning and say,
'Well, we have got somebody
for breakfast again.'
Everybody carried a pistol
and a knife, as a rule."
M.C. Seek

*G*old was discovered in Idaho in the fall of 1860 and another gold rush was triggered when word reached Portland. As the ice and snow melted in the spring of 1861, thousands of men headed up the Columbia River, passing through The Dalles and Walla Walla on their way to the mines. Until Lewiston was established on the Snake River, Walla Walla was the closest supply point to the mines and many of the miners wintered there.

Along with the miners came tradesmen, merchants, and other honorable people. Unfortunately, another class of citizen also appeared in the new eldorado. They were the gamblers, thieves, thugs and hold-up artists, or as they were called in those days, "sports and badmen". All kinds of violence and treachery was committed on the law-abiding citizens, but the civil authorities, who were sometimes themselves of questionable repute, refused or were unable to do anything about the criminals. Those who were caught either escaped or were found innocent by a jury of their "peers". Finally, conditions got so bad that vigilante committees formed and soon the problems were settled by the noose.

In the goldfields, new discoveries were continually being made as the prospectors explored the mountains of the Northwest. Gold was discovered in Oregon's John Day country, the Boise Basin in Idaho, and finally in Montana. Pony express riders carried the mail from places like Canyon City to The Dalles and from the Idaho goldfields to Lewiston and Walla Walla, while mule trains loaded with supplies criss-crossed the rugged terrain.

As was mentioned earlier, conditions were sometimes dangerous in the mining districts of the 1860's, as all sorts of outlaws and desperados preyed on the unwary. Just how bad it was stood out prominently in the pioneers' memories, and a lot of them recounted their misadventures in the goldfields. Let's join an oldtimer now, (who preferred to remain anonymous for some reason), as he tells us about the character of the Inland Empire.

Old Timer

Written by an anonymous pioneer
that all might know "the none too pleasant conditions"
that existed in the Inland Empire in the 1860's.

About the worst period of the early settlement of the Coast country was the early sixties soon after the beginning of the civil war. It was the beginning of the discovery of placer gold in the intermountain country. Gold had been discovered near Fort Colville and Capt. A.D. Pierce followed it south to Pierce City in 1860 and in 1861 rich discoveries were made at Florence and Elk City on the Clearwater and the same year the old Auburn mines on Powder River in Baker County, Oregon, were discovered and George Grimes found the richest placers in the United States in the Boise, Idaho country which caused a great rush to that country in 1863.

Now it so happened that Walla Walla was the great center where many hundreds of miners came to spend the winter, and of course a great many gamblers congregated here to fleece and rob the miners out of their summer's clean-up. Thus it was that Walla Walla became a center for the worse class of bad men that ever congregated in any one place on the Pacific Coast.

Following the discovery of mines in Montana many of the worst element of Walla Walla went out there and a vigilant committee there hung by the neck eleven of what they called "Walla Walla Horse Thieves." Among them was one Bill Buntin.

During the flush mining period of 1863 to 1865, when more than a million of gold per day was carried by stage and other conveyance out of the Boise Basin and adjoining camps, Rocky Bar and Silver City, that country was infested, or the roads leading from it were lined with the most persistent set of road agents and stage robbers ever found in any country.

And what a wonderful field they had to operate in.

In its time the richest mining district in the United States and in extent the largest unsettled country, being from Walla Walla to Salt Lake in width and from The Dalles, Oregon to Nebraska in length, with only two organized counties in the whole district, Baker County, Oregon, Boise County, Idaho, and their county seats and sheriffs were 200 miles apart, and in one year of the worst period, Sheriff Pinkham of Boise County was murdered by a bad man and the Sheriff of Baker County, Parker, was killed by the Indians while in discharge of their duties.

In the country at this period there was nothing to interfere with the work of the bad element. Gangs of them made their headquarters where they pleased. It was only an impromptu gathering of the better class that would, once and awhile, cut short some extra outrageous action on the part of the bad men.

But as we look over the conditions confronting the early settlers and settlement of this country we find there existed the following bad elements: the gambler who coolly dealt cards from the bottom of the deck or any other dishonest way, who had his six shooter by his side ready to put a bullet through his antagonist who he might detect in a similar act. This type which was often in trouble was a distinct class. The second type was the thief who went on the range and rustled your horses or cattle and took them to a market of his own. Then there was the more honorable bad men who had the bravery to meet you on the road and demand your "money or your life" and ran the risk of getting a bullet through his own hide. This type never got anything much better than an even chance, for we know many of the poor devils who bit the dust in such an effort.

One of the gangs of bad men made their headquarters at the Washo Ferry on Snake river at the mouth of the Malheur and extended their operations from Horseshoe Bend on the Peyette to Powder river, Oregon. With this gang were Jack Carter, Limerick Jim, Chas. Stewart and Boggs Greenwood. Greenwood was really the head man, and as they frequently gathered at our cabin at the ferry many times did we hear accounts of their different efforts.

During the stay of this outfit at the ferry, it drove the travel off our road and ruined our business.

But a general breakup of the gang occurred when Boggs Greenwood and Charley Stewart went on their raid up Burnt river in which they killed John Kinnear, robbed R.A. Pierce and shot a Mrs. Durkey in the arm because she was too slow in getting them something to eat. A posse had organized by freighters and packers at Miller's Station near where they had killed Kinnear and was after them, and soon after the Durkee affair, came up with their trail and followed them up the road and in a few miles ran them into the brush on Pritchard Creek, where they caught Greenwood and hung him to a tree. Stewart made his escape.

But along with all these bad elements to contend with there was another element which was always on the road killing settlers, stealing stock and pack trains, that was the Indians of the Snake and Burnt river countries. They killed many travelers, freighters and packers, and one family Scott and his wife; but the two children belonging to this couple were rescued by some freighters who met them as Mrs. Scott came running her team to their camp on Burnt river with the dead body of her husband and a mortal wound in her body from which she died in a few hours. Two little children were alive in the wagon having been covered by some blankets. The Scotts had been to a mining camp with some produce.

The foregoing story was written not so much to tell of individual bad men and their works, as to let the present generation know something of the none too pleasant conditions under which our fathers, the old pioneers, labored when they were developing and doing the best they knew how to build homes in this beautiful Inland Empire.

M.C. Seek

Mr. Seek was one of the first settlers
to come to the newly opened Inland Empire in 1858.

"I don't think there were over fifty people here when I came, outside of the fort people. Women? I do not remember of but one woman, outside of the garrison. Her name was Mrs. Moore, I believe."

"They platted Walla Walla in 1859 and gave any man two lots provided he would build on one of them. I went out and started a ranch on Dry Creek, at what is now the Sam Kees place, and sold oats to the government at four cents a pound.

"Nobody was allowed here in 1858 without a special permit from the government. General Harney gave me one. I heard that the country was thrown open for settlement in November and left The Dalles at once.

"The place where the old fort was build still had the old buildings, three or four of them, in 1858. But at that time only one of them, the suttlers' store, was being used. The rest of the fort had been moved to its present site.

"The only streets in Walla Walla then were Main and Second streets, and they were little more than trails.

"There was no city government of any sort in 1858. Everybody was peaceable then. The bad times began in 1861 and 1862. Then you could hear shooting at almost any time.

"It was a common thing for a man to come in and sit down with you to eat in the morning and say: 'Well, we have got somebody for breakfast again.' Everybody carried a pistol and a knife, as a rule."

Mr. Seek remembers well an encounter between Bill Bunton, the famous desperado, who was afterwards hung in Montana, and Jim Buckley, who kept a saloon on Main Street.

There had been a row between these two men. Buckley walked from his own place, where the Union Savings Bank now is, across the street to where Bunton was standing in front of his saloon, where Tallman's drug store is now located. Both men drew guns as Buckley came walking across the street, but Bunton held his down at his side. As Buckley came across the street, Bunton said: "You take the first shot, Jim." That was too much for Buckley. He backed clean out and went back to his own place without another word.

"Many, many times I have seen a thousand, yes, two thousand Indian ponies running loose, anywhere above town up to three or four miles, and from one to thirty or forty Indian lodges. This used to be a great camping ground for them.

"The Indians were peaceable enough around here generally, but when you went off a ways you had to be careful.

"I could tell you many good Indian stories if I could get them together. Why, when I came up here from The Dalles, I was stopped below Umatilla by the Indians. They were awful sassy and demanded matches and tobacco. But Bob Wright, an old Indian fighter, was with me, and he bluffed them off then and there.

"Another time a drunken Indian grabbed the lapels of my coat with his left hand and flashed a big knife right in front of my face. The only way I could save myself was to tell him that he was not a brave to tackle a man who was not armed. He let me go."

C.G. Cunningham

Harvard graduate hears 'call of West',
and in the goldfields "witnessed the execution
of some 70 or more men",
the desperadoes of the Northwest.

C. G. Cunningham soon after graduating from Harvard law school, heard the 'call of the West' and came to the Pacific northwest where he engaged in packing to mining camps. He came here and wintered his packtrain at the "forks of the river" as he expressed it, west of the town, in 1865.

H.E. Johnson showed him a cut of the lower story of the Baker-Boyer bank, the oldest bank in the state, in 1869, "That's it" he said, "where is it?" When told it was a bank and had merged into the present National bank, "Baker and Boyer were always bankers," he said. "My partner and I left $700 in gold-dust with them during our stay here."

Mr. Cunningham was a witness to the shooting of Ferd Patterson, one of the early pioneer tragedies. Ferd Patterson came to Walla Walla with a reputation that caused the law abiding citizens to consider him an undesirable. He was a sure shot and had a record of killing a sheriff at Boise and a captain of an ocean steamer plying between San Francisco and Portland.

His coming was during the early history of the "vigilance committee" which came into existence as a result of the state of lawlessness existing at that time and was composed of men who were dissatisfied with the reign of lawlessness tolerated by the authorities and took the law into their own hands. It is generally believed that his death was instigated by this committee. He was in a barber chair, in the Bogle shop, being shaved, when night watchman Donahue walked in, revolver in hand. Approaching Patterson, he said:

"Patterson, I shoot you or you kill me," and fired. Patterson was mortally wounded but was able to get out of the chair and go into the saloon next door, where he got his revolver and attempted to return but fell dead on the street.

Mr. Cunningham witnessed the execution of some 70 or more men whose presence had caused terror to the inhabitants of the northwest. Among these were Bill Bunton and Cayuse George, both well known in Walla Walla in the early 60's. The former has the distinction of having a creek in Walla Walla county named for his calling, Whiskey creek, where he sold whiskey to wayfarers. The place was characterized as a "very tough joint." Bunton shot a man at an evening gathering, where he was an uninvited guest. The shooting was considered unprovoked and had Mr. Bunton not succeeded in a quick get away, there is no doubt but that he would have been executed here instead of Montana.

During this conversation of reminiscences, Miles Moore, former Territorial Governor of Washington, told of one of his pioneer experiences, which certainly contained thrills.

He with a friend were coming from Montana to Walla Walla on horseback and having heard that Magruder, a successful miner was going to the same place, made a call on him. He would not be ready to start on the journey for at least two weeks, so Mr. Moore and friend started and when they arrived at Lewiston, Idaho, they were greeted by a number of citizens. They wondered why they should be thus honored. Magruder was expected at this time and these were mostly friends coming to welcome him. Mr. Magruder was murdered on his way to Lewiston and had Mr. Moore and friend waited to accompany him there is no doubt but that they would have shared the same fate.

Magruder's friends watched for his coming but had no fears as to his safety until one day some one told Hill Beachy, an old friend, then living in Lewiston, that Magruder was in town. Mr. Beachy said: "No he is not here."

"Well his saddle is," was the reply.

This news aroused Mr. Beachy's suspicion that all was not well with his friends and he looked up the saddle and recognized it as Magruder's.

An investigation followed and revealed that Magruder and helpers had been murdered and robbed. The murderers were traced to San Francisco, brought back to Lewiston and hung.

James W. Watt

*Pioneer packer tells of
his experiences in the goldfields
of the Northwest. Mr. Watt begins with
an account of the Magruder murder.*

Well, as I started to say, along with the hordes came the unscrupulous gambler, the bandit, road agent and murderer and the usual camp following of dancehall girls, and citizens of the underworld that preyed upon both the miner, the merchant and legitimate laborer. At first we had no courts, or any means of law enforcement and early in the discovery of placer gold in the Clearwater, the Salmon river, and the Boise and Upper Missouri river watersheds this latter law-breaking element reaped a rich harvest. For a time in the absence of any organized peace force the honest men in camp hesitated to take any individual stand against them, and incur their ill will, so the criminal element carried on their operations in each camp for a short time with apparent impunity.

It was somewhat difficult in those days for law abiding men to know just whom to trust among their neighbors and acquaintances in camp. In the end the situation in nearly every camp became so bad that the better element finally had to band themselves together in a secret body to enforce law and order. These organizations were named "Vigilantes." I never knew why they called themselves by that Spanish term. I suppose that the earlier organizations in California first got the name there. These bodies of courageous citizens soon helped to make the mountain trails and pathways safe for the honest miners, merchants and packers. A few hangings in a community were usually sufficient to check the graver crimes of murder and robbery. Life in those days was lightly valued by some, and the deeds of these road agents and of the vigilantes for a few years in the early 60's beat beyond comparison any dime novel or present day fiction of the wild and woolly west I have ever read.

I was intimately acquainted with most of the people connected with the Magruder murders. I knew Hill Beechy well and was often a guest at the Luna House. Magruder was a packer and trader with headquarters at Lewiston. He was married to a girl named Arthur, a sister of Sam Arthur, one of the early hotel men at Spokane Falls. Magruder's wife lived in McMinnville, Oregon, and as a young fellow I knew both her and her sisters. Magruder himself I knew and had often associated with as a fellow packer. He packed out of Lewiston.

People about Hill Beechy's livery stable in Lewiston knew Lloyd Magruder's mules and equipment and this was the first clue of the murders. Dan Dwight later long in the mercantile business at Lewiston associated with his brother Henry Dwight, was one of the guards over the murderers in bringing them up from Portland. It was freezing weather when they were brought into Lewiston. Bill Page, who stood "state's evidence" and made a full written confession of the crime was released and afterwards did chores about Beechy's hotel at Lewiston.

In October 1863, Magruder, who had been on a packing trip to the Beaverhead Mines, sold out his goods and part of his pack train at Virginia City, Montana, and was returning to Lewiston with considerable bullion. It was said he had between $16,000 and $20,000 in gold dust. En route back, he and some companions, Charles Allen, William Phillips and Robert Chalmers, were brutally murdered in the Bitter Root mountains in the most cold blooded manner by men who had accompanied Magruder from Lewiston in the guise of packers for the sole purpose of robbing him. The murderers were "Doc" Howard, Christ Lowry, J.P. Romain and Bill Page. Their capture and trial is a part of the history of those days.

The murderers had hung around The Dalles and Lewiston for some time before their departure with the Magruder party in August 1863, and I knew them. Daniel Howard was a well built, good appearing man who had evidently studied medicine at some time and he was generally known as "Doc". James P. Romain was an idler and gambler and acted as cook on the fatal trip. Christopher Lowry was a man from down in Oregon, or rough and reckless disposition. He was a blacksmith by trade and had been with Capt. John Mullan on his road-building expedition a few years before. William Page was a worthless, no-account fellow, easily led. He came from over in the Klickitat country, in Washington territory.

Hill Beechy used to say that he had dreams of the murder of his friend, even before the murderers appeared in Lewiston. There was some suspicion of them at that time and they were questioned some, but there being then no suspicion or evidence of a murder or other grave crime, they were permitted to go and soon made their way down to San Francisco. One of the murderers, Christopher Lowry, had been a schoolmate of Mrs. Magruder's down in Oregon. After his arrest she went to the jail and asked him what he and his companions had done with Magruder. He afterwards told his jailers that he didn't ever want to see her again. This man Lowry, himself, had killed Magruder with an axe.

Bill Page, who had turned "state's evidence" was killed a couple of years later at Lewiston by Albert Igo. Al was a tough worthless character himself, and of a very bad reputation. Page at the time was reduced to the job of carrying water from the river up to the house where Igo was then staying. Igo had been drunk the night before and in a quarrel had been "beaten up" by Bill Page. He was in an angry mood the next morning and when Page entered the house carrying a pail of water in each hand, Igo blew his head off with a shot from a shotgun. This was on December 25, 1866. Al Igo immediately fled Lewiston, but was followed by his brother, Bill Igo, who overtook him and persuaded him to go back with him and stand trial.

Everyone in Lewiston thought the killing of Bill Page was a good act, and after some pretense at an investigation, Al Igo was turned loose. Many years ago a man named Chapman wrote up the history of the Magruder murders. "Doc" Howard, Lowry and Romain were executed at Lewiston on March 4, 1864, after a short trial.

This Magruder murder trial was the first case we ever tried in the courts of the new territory of Idaho. It was tried before Judge Samuel C. Parks, judge of the Boise county, or second judicial district, who held a special term of court at Lewiston for that purpose. The defendants were found guilty on January 20, 1864, and sentenced to death. A detail of soldiers from the Fourth U.S. infantry at Fort Lapwai formed a guard around the gallows at the hanging on March 4, 1864. Hill Beechy's expenses at running down and bringing back the murderers were something over $6,000 and later the Idaho territorial legislature passed a special appropriation bill to reimburse him. Hill Beechy later sold out his hotel and livery stable in Lewiston to the Dwight Brothers and moved to the Boise basin where he operated stage lines to Nevada and California. He died in San Francisco about 50 years ago.

My cousin, D.M. Jesse, of Dayton, was one held up by road agents on this side of the Clearwater river, about 25 miles out from Oro Fino, on a return trip to Lewiston. Jesse was on the alert, and when he met the holdups he shot at them and chased them into the brush. Pack trains were frequently held up on the Boise trail.

I was acquainted with most of the master packers and I worked at one time or another for most of them. D.M. Jesse and H.H. Snow were in partnership as D.M. Jesse & Co. They had a large pack train, Jesse had charge of it, while Snow handled the mercantile business. When the packing business fell off in 1866-7 they sold out their train and Mr. Jesse went into the stock business in Walla Walla, while Mr. Snow went into business at Lafayette, Oregon. His son Wilbur is in the bank at Dayton, Washington.

Old Andrew Lafevre was a partner with "French Louie" in a train of 65 or 70 mules at Walla Walla operating into Helena and on the Boise road in 1864-5. George Dacres of Walla Walla had a train of 45 or 50 mules. I went with this train to Helena in the fall of 1865. Charlie White, his "boss packer" who lived at the mouth of Dry Creek, left him at Helena and I took his place. I was then 22 years old. I handled the train for two years. Frank and Mat Lowden at the mouth of Dry Creek, near Walla Walla, also owned a train of about 125 mules and packed into the various camps. They were likable and popular men and Frank Lowden was later elected county commissioner of Walla Walla county.

Jones and Dalton ran a pack train of 125 packs out of Lewiston. Bludsoe and Creighton also ran a train of 65 to 70 packes out of that place. D.M. Jesse and John Thompson had a train of 40 packs running out of Lewiston and Pierce City. Bob Grostein also ran a train of 100 mules out from Lewiston. Virgo Little was boss and packmaster of a train of 40 or 50 mule teams running from Umatilla into the mines. Bill Sperry and his brother also ran a train out of Walla Walla. Later they sold out and went into the flour milling business at Pendleton. Their brother-in-law, Manse Chrip, located the first farm above what is now Pendleton. Part of his original holdings are in the present townsite.

Most of the large packing outfits had their headquarters at Walla Walla, but they packed out of Wallula, Umatilla, Walla Walla, or Lewiston, wherever they could get the freight. One trip might be into Florence or Warren or Mormon gulch over beyond Burnt river. The next might be to Helena or Virginia City. Our next trip into the Kootenai or Columbia River mines, some 400 miles northeast across the international boundary line into British Columbia, or south into the Boise Basin. In my 10 years on the trail I packed into every good sized mining camp of the Northwest.

Lize Dove and his brother had a train of about 25 mules running from Lewiston into Elk City and Florence. I worked with this train in 1864 and made one trip into Florence. Lize died in Spokane about five or six years ago, while his brother Tim died down in the Palouse country years ago. At one time they were large landholders there and had wealth, but they "went busted" in the hard times of 1894.

In packing days I worked with Johnny O'Hearn's pack train from Walla Walla, also with George Williams' train from The Dalles, packing into the military posts. O'Hearn had the contract for Camp Hearny supplies.

The highest freight we ever received was around $1.25 a pound, received when we went into Bannock, Idaho, after the fire. The lowest freight received from Umatilla into the Boise basin was 20 cents a pound for the 300-mile pack. Pack trains used to be of all sizes, from a small train of but five or six animals up to large trains numbering 100 or more animals. It all depended on the amount of business. Some pack train proprietors had several hundred pack animals on hand and kept a number of pack trains in a constant and regular operation on a fairly regular schedule from outfitting points into the various mining camps.

An average pack train into the larger mining camps would average say about 25 pack mules. Trains of 25 pack animals were easier to handle than larger trains on account of the greater convenience of making camp and finding feed. The size of the trains was increased or reduced, or additional pack trains placed on the route, as the immediate traffic needs of a mining camp required.

Packing was a trade which called for both skill and strength. In loading and unloading we usually worked in pairs. One was on each side of an animal. Each man had to swing his half of the heavy pack up from the ground onto the animal's back, and hold it there on one side of the pack saddle with one arm, despite the kicks and bites and protesting lunges of the mule, until he and his partner had it securely lashed there by means of a diamond or other hitch. To round up, saddle and load and unload 25 such packs a day and to meet all the emergencies of the trail was a real man's sized job. If a mule got down, you'd have to get him up. Sometimes you'd have to unload, other times the mule would succeed in unloading for you. Some mules got real mean and tricky and would try to rub their packs off against trees or would lie down and try to roll them loose. It took a good tie to stand such treatment, even if you rode up at once and started the animal along with the train again. If straps and ropes broke you had to splice them, you had to mend your pack saddles, sometimes you had to shoe the mules. Sometimes animals got sick and you had to nurse them. Worst of all sometimes the packs broke or sprung a leak, and you had to devise means-- way out alone in the wilderness--to save your cargo.

Talk about roads and trails. Principally there weren't any. We penetrated into the most remote and inaccessible places, over all kinds of country and in all kinds of weather conditions. At the head of the trains long before you met them you could hear the tinkle of the bell on the bell mare. For convenience in locating stray animals, we sometimes used to hobble new pack horses and mules at night, unless a corral was handy to put them in. We sometimes placed a bell on animals that were given to straying away for convenience in locating them when turned out. On all ordinary occasions the "bell mare" kept the pack animals together.

Heavy snows in the mountains usually forced us to quit our packing ventures along in November. Then when we returned from our last trip we drove the pack animals down to winter at some ranch in one of the lower, warmer valleys along the Columbia River where there was plenty of good feed and water.

This packing business called for both skill and strength, the lifting of heavy weights, sometimes a barrel of whiskey--right up from the ground to the pack saddle required a young, muscular man with a stout back and good arms and shoulders. In addition to taking care of the freight and animals a man had to prepare camp and cook his own meals and act as his own valet and wash and mend his own clothes. We often camped out in rain and snow and severe cold without even a tent. With the larger pack trains one man was usually taken along as cook.

Besides all this work we had to be on the alert to preserve our own scalps. On the trail there was always more or less danger from attacks by hostile Indians, and murderous road agents. If they didn't kill you they might run off your horses and mules or rob you of your freight. It wasn't an easy life by any means.

At first there weren't any trails and we often had to strike out over virgin country and find our way with no one to inquire of in case we got lost. When we came to bad places we had to work our train around them, cutting a way through fallen timber, working around or across a bad rock or slide or detouring impassable cliffs. Often there were no bridges or ferries, when we came to streams we sought to ford. If there was none we swam our animals across. If there were no boats available we built a raft and rafted our outfits and goods across. Sometimes when a spring freshet had made a stream impassable we had to sit down and wait until the high water passed.

The whole packing business called for courage, hardihood and endurance and that wasn't all. You had to have skill, daring, initiative, gumption and loyalty.

Rev. J.V. Crawford

Former Pastor of
Christian Church in Prescott, Washington,
remembers a story about Joaquin Miller.

"The first time I ever set foot in Walla Walla was on July 1, 1861. There was not much of a town here at that time. Only a few business houses and some residences. It was rather a winter quarters and supply point for the Idaho mines and there were always a lot of miners either coming or going from the various eldorados.

"We spent the morning that Fourth of July in visiting around among the business houses, principal among which was Kyger's. In the afternoon we all went out to the races which were being pulled off just East of where the Union office is now located. The particular thing that impressed me at the time was the appearance of Sheriff Bill Bunton on the scene when he declared that the races must be conducted 'according to law.' To emphasize his declaration he pulled one of his big heavy revolvers from the scabbard and flourished it authoritatively above his head. He was dressed in buckskin clothes, with the usual sombrero and red handkerchief. He was a picturesque character, but the next I heard of him was after the vigilantes of Montana had celebrated a necktie party in his honor for engaging in the road-agent business.

"The following winter Joaquin Miller, now known as the 'Poet of the Sierras,' was riding between Walla Walla and Oro Fino for Mossman's express. A bunch of road agents chased him into Walla Walla one day and it was by the merest chance that he escaped with the express matter and his life. As it was, he rode down Main street on the dead run, flung the express bag, containing a large amount of gold dust, through the door of the express office, tied his horse and returned to stand guard until it could be placed in the safe. That night Miller was surrounded by the road-agents in a saloon and only escaped by drawing his gun and standing them off until some miners, who happened to be playing cards at a nearby table, came to his rescue.

"When the future poet explained the situation the miners took the road-agents to the edge of town and gave them to understand that their space was more desirable than their presence. The miners realized that if the gang were permitted to remain in the vicinity some of their hard earned gold dust would have to be 'given up' at the point of a gun."

-229-

Joaquin Miller

*The "Poet of the Sierras"
was a pony express rider
in the Idaho goldfields in the 1860's.
His story is entitled,
'A Race With Idaho Robbers.'*

Now that the President has signed the bill admitting Idaho into the Union, the forty-fourth star in our glorious constellation of States, it may not be out of place for one who, if he did not really give the name to this new State, first put that name in print, to record a page or two of its early history, and recall an incident that still makes his nerves tingle as he tells it.

Gold was first found, in that vast and trackless region now forming the new States of Washington, Idaho, and Montana, in the spring of 1860, by a small party of prospectors led by Captain Pierce on the spot where Pierce City now stands.

The writer, although not then of age, had read law and been admitted to practice under Judge Geo. H. Williams, afterwards President Grant's Attorney General. And when news of the discovery of gold reached Oregon, I gathered up one law-book and two "six shooters," and set out on a ride of many hundred miles through the mountains for the new placers.

But as gold was not plenty, and there was no use for the law-book, because there was no law; and as there was an opening for a good and hardy horseman to carry letters and money to and from the new mines, the writer and a young man by the name of Mossman soon had nailed up over the door of the only store as yet in all that wild region, a sign which read: "Mossman and Miller's Express."

It was two hundred miles to the nearest post-office at Walla Walla. The lover of pretty names will easily trace this Walla Walla back to its French settlers' *"Voila! Voila!"*

No man can look down from the environment of mountains on this sweet valley, with its beautiful city in the center, whose many flashing little rivers run together and make it forever green and glorious to see, without instinctively crying out *"Voila! Voila!"* It is another Damascus, only it is broader of girth and far, far more beautiful. In this ride of two hundred miles there was but one town, Lewiston. Get your map now, and as you follow the story of the ride, fix the geography of this new empire in your minds, for it will be a grand land.

Lewiston, you observe, is at the head of navigation on the "Shoshonee" or Snake River, by way of the Columbia River. This word Shoshonee means snake. I fancy you can almost hear the rattle of the venomous reptile as you speak this Indian word. The accent, as in nearly all Indian names, such as

Dakota, Iowa, and so on, is on the middle syllable. In reading Longfellow's poems you will find he has preserved the proper pronunciation of Omaha by putting the accent where it belongs. And more than once this learned man reminded me that Idaho must be pronounced in the same soft and liquid fashion: I *da* ho.

In these long, long rides we changed horses from five to ten times daily, and we rode at a desperate speed. We used Indian ponies only, and usually rode without escort, with pistols ready at hand. Indians were numerous, but our fear was not of them, but of white men. In fact, the Indians were by far the most peaceable people we had to deal with. They always kept our "Stations," that is, the places where we changed horses and drank a cup of coffee. These Indians were of the Nez Perce tribe. It may not be generally known that these noble Indians were nearly civilized long before the renowned Chief Joseph (who fought the whole United States for half a year not long ago) was ever heard of. These Indians, under the direction of good old Father Spaulding, published the first newspaper that was issued west of the Rocky Mountains. They also printed some portions of the Bible in their own tongue, including many Psalms. Keep these facts of history as well as the geography of this great region in mind; and we will now get to the robbers.

As before stated, we did not find gold plenty at first, and the "Express" did not pay. We two boys worked hard, took many desperate risks, and lived almost literally on horseback, with little food and with less sleep for the first few months. But suddenly gold was found, as thick as wheat on a threshing floor, far away to the east of a big black mountain which the Indians called "I-*dah*-ho," which literally means, "mountain where light comes." I happened to be in Lewiston, on my way to Pierce City with the Express, when the ragged and sunburnt leader of the party that had made the discovery beyond the Black Mountain came in. He took me into his confidence. I sent an Indian on with my Express; and branching off a hundred miles to the southeast, reached the new mines, took up "claims," and opened an Express Office before a dozen people knew of the discovery which was to give State after State to the Union. You will find the place on the old maps, and some of the new ones, marked "Millersburgh." But there is no town there now.

The gold lay almost in the grass-roots, in the shallow surface, like grains of wheat. It was a high bleak place, densely wooded and intensely cold as winter came on. Greater discoveries lay further on and in kindlier climes, and broad valleys and rich cities receive you there now. But our story is of the snow and the stony steeps of Mount I-dah-ho.

Returning to Lewiston with saddle-bags nearly full of gold, I wrote the first published account of the discovery; and the new mines were naturally called in that publication, as they were called by all that excited mass of people from Lewiston on their way to the mines beyond the Black Mountain, the "Idahho Mines." The name, however, like that of Omah-ha, soon lost in the mouths of strangers its soft, sweet sound.

California now emptied her miners, good and bad, gamblers, robbers, desperados, right in upon our new mines and the roads thither.

My young partner, a daring and dashing boy, who, as I write, is visiting me here after thirty years, had many desperate encounters.

Suddenly, as winter came on, the rivers closed with ice, and horses could not go and steamers could not come.

I was lying ice-bound at Lewiston. Men wanted to send money below to their friends or families; merchants, anticipating the tremendous rush, must get letters through the snow to Walla Walla. Would I go? *Could* I go?

The snow was deep. The trails, over open and monotonous mountains, were drifted full. Could any living man face the drifting snow and find his way to Walla Walla? At first the merchants had tried to hire Indians to undertake the trip and deliver their letters. Not one could be found to go. When the storm abated a little, the men who kept the ferry across the Shoshonee River scraped off the snow, and cutting down the upheaved blocks of ice made it possible to cross with a horse.

I picked out a stout little iron-gray steed, with head in the air, an eye like an eagle, and a mane that tossed and tumbled like a thunderstorm. At first I meant to carry only letters. But having finally consented to take a little gold for one merchant, I soon found I should lose friends if I did not take gold for others. The result was that I had to take gold worth nearly ten thousand dollars. And ten thousand dollars of dust you must know means nearly fifty pounds!

A few muffled-up friends came down to the river bank to see me off. It was a great event. For two weeks we had not had a line from the outer world. And meantime the civil war was raging in all its terrible fury. As I set out that bleak and icy morning, after I had mounted my plunging pony I saw in the crowd several faces that I did not like. There was Dave English, who was hung on that spot with several of his followers, not forty days later; there was Boone Helm, hung in Montana; Cherokee Bob, killed in Millersburgh; and also Canada Joe. This last lived with some low Indians a little way down the river. So when he rode ahead of me I was rather glad than otherwise; for I felt that he would not go far. I kept watch of him, however. And when I saw that he skulked around under the hill, as if he were going home, and then finally got back into the trail, I knew there was trouble ahead.

But the "Rubicon" was now behind. My impetuous horse was plunging in the snow and I was soon tearing through the storm up the hill. Once fairly on my way, I looked back below. Dave English and Boone Helm were bidding good-by to two mounted cowboys at the ferry-house. Ten minutes later, as I looked back through the blinding snow, I saw that these two desperate fellows were following me.

True, there was nothing criminal in that. The two highwaymen had a right to ride behind me if they wished. And Canada Joe had just as good a right to ride ahead of me. But to be on a horse deep in the blinding snow and loaded down with gold was bad enough. To have a desperado blocking the narrow trail before you with his two friends behind you was fearful!

I had two six-shooters close at hand under the bearskin flap of my saddle-bag where the gold was. I kept my left hand in my pocket where lay a small six-shooter warm and ready. Once, as the drifting and blinding snow broke away up the mountain, I saw Canada Joe with his head bent down in the storm still pushing on ahead of me at a safe distance. A few moments after, as I crossed and climbed the farther bank of an ugly canyon, the two robbers came close enough to hail me. One of them held up a bottle. They evidently intended to overtake me if they could, and profess to be friendly. This I must not allow. I urged my ambitious horse to his best. But, to my dismay, as I hastened up a narrow pass I found that I was not far behind Canada Joe. This low-browed black fellow was reported to be the worst man in all that country. And that was saying he was bad indeed.

I was in a tight place now, and had to think fast. My first plan was to ride forward and face this man before the others came up. But I was really afraid of him. It seemed a much easier task to turn and kill the rear men and get back to town. But, no! No! All this was abandoned almost as soon as thought of. In those days, even the most desperate had certain rights, which their surviving friends would enforce.

I remember that I fell to wondering what the murderers would do with my body. I had a horror of being eaten by wolves. I then thought of the true and trusting men who had sent me forth on my responsible task, and I took heart.

I was now but a few hundred yards behind Canada Joe. So far as I could find out, the robbers were closing in on me. But we had ridden over the roughest part of the road and were within a few miles of the high plateau, so that the wind was tearing past in a gale, and the drifting snow almost blinded me.

Suddenly, I had a new thought. Why not take to the left, gain the plateau by a new route, and let these bloodthirsty robbers close their net without having me inside? I rose in my saddle with excitement at the idea, and striking spurs to my brave horse, I was soon climbing up the gradual slope at a gallop. Ah, but I was glad! Gallop! gallop! gallop! I seemed to hear.many horses! Turning my head suddenly over my shoulder, I saw my two pursurers not a hundred yards behind me. They shouted! I was now on the high plateau and the snow was not so deep. Gallop! gallop! gallop! Canada Joe-- thank Heaven!-- was away to the right, and fast falling behind. Gallop! gallop! gallop! I was gaining on the robbers and they knew it. Fainter and fainter came their curses and their shouts!

And then: Whiz! Crack! Thud!

I looked back and saw that they both had thrown themselves from their saddles and were taking deliberate aim. But to no purpose. Not one shot touched me or my horse, and I reached the first station and, finally, rode into Walla Walla with my precious burden, safe and sound.

Hon. Thomas H. Brents

*Judge Brents, who served
several terms in Congress,
recalls the days when he was
plain old Tom Brents,
pony express rider.*

Sitting next to me in the grandstand at Pendleton was a dignified gray
haired, gray bearded stranger. I sized him up and decided that he was a New
Englander--well to do. Probably a banker, who had stopped off on his way
east to see the round-up. I made a mental bet with myself that he would ask
me if the Indians were real Indians, and if the horses hadn't been trained to
buck. Having thus catalogued him, and disposed of him to my entire
satisfaction I turned my attention to the scene before me.

It certainly was a picture--one that would delight an artist. How Frederick
Remington, or Russel, the cowboy artist, or Sharp, the painter of Indians,
would have revelled in the varying western types with their picturesque
costumes and their vivid color schemes! In the arena, cowboys, lean of face
and figure, lithe and sinewy, quick as cats, tough as wet buckskin, sat on
their horses with sure and easy grace. With their broad brimmed, gray Stet-
sons shading their cleancut bronzed faces, knotted silk handkerchiefs about
their necks, blue flannel shirts, bearskin chaps, high heeled boots, jingling
spurs and their happy-go-lucky, improvident, reckless ways, they are
typical of the old days and of the old west.

Bull doggers, rope spinners, broncho busters; squaws, with a king's ransom in elk teeth on their jackets; braves, gay with mink and otter, beads
and bearskin, paint and eagle feathers, with their war bonnets priceless in
value, handed down from father to son for generations, made before the
coming of the white man; outlaw horses, rearing, plunging and fighting as
the rope settles over their necks; longhorns from Texas, charging the men
on foot or when pursued, leaping over the fence like deer; teepees, smoke
stained and dingy against the background of vivid green; curling smoke and
quivering leaf; hills bare and brown, or yellow with stubble, a sky cloudless
and blue, and over it all the yellow sunshine, the smell of sweaty leather, of
smoke tanned buckskin of sagebrush and campfire--where could a setting
for such a picture be more perfect?

The megaphone swung slowly and came to rest with its open work
countenance pointing toward our section of the grandstand. Lee Drake, the
official announcer, whispered his message into the small end of the horn,
and like a 13-inch gun the announcement boomed out of the big end. "The
next event will be a pony express race for the championship of the world."

In a moment the riders were off and suddenly, and to me as unexpectedly as if Mount Hood had burst into eruption, the dignified old gentleman on my right exploded into a series of blood curdling whoops. "Give her the quirt, get there, you man with the red shirt. Whoopee!! That's the stuff. Come on in now." He turned to me saying, "Watch that man in the red shirt win. See him change horses. Isn't he chain lightning? Just watch his horse stretch out coming around that turn. Here he comes. He's ahead! Did't I tell you so?"

Evidently I had another guess coming as to my staid and dignified neighbor in the grandstand. I concluded I would have to hedge on my bet with myself, I said, "You seem very much interested in that pony express race."

"I am," he responded, with glistening eyes. "Fifty years ago I was a pony express rider, and for a moment that race had me back in the old days. This country is my old stamping ground. I knew it in the days when you could ride where you would, and never, in a week's journey, see a fence. I passed through here in the fall of '52. The old emigrant road ran not far from the round-up grounds here.

"The next event will be a cowgirl's pony race," came the megaphone announcement.

"Come up to Colonel Raley's home tonight, where I am staying, and we will talk over old times. Just ask for Tom Brents."

"Are you a relative," I inquired, "of Judge Thomas H. Brents, who served several terms in congress?"

"I guess I will have to plead guilty as charged," Mr. Brents responded. "However, I am going to tell you of the days when I was plain Tom Brents, pony express rider."

"To begin at the beginning," said Judge Brents when I saw him that evening, "my people started from Pike county, Illinois, for the Willamette valley in the spring of '52. My sister had married when she was 17 years old, and had come out to Oregon in 1849. We joined a wagon train bound for Oregon. There were nearly 100 in our party. I was a little chap, about 12 years old, and the events of that trip stand out very vividly in my mind. Near what is now the city of Lincoln, Nebraska, but what was then called Loop Fork, the Asiatic cholera broke out in our party. Five died the first day. Some of them were sick less than an hour and died in agony. Thirty-one of our party died during the next few days, and then the plague left as suddenly as it had come. We saw numerous shallow mounds beside the road--grim reminders that other parties had also lost some of their numbers. In our party one entire family was wiped out with the exception of a baby. We took it on to Oregon. It was a little boy named Sam Taylor. I saw him 25 or 30 years later in eastern Oregon.

"The vicinity of Pendleton was particularly impressed on my mind because just east of here one of our oxen played out. Ben was his name. We had made a regular pet of him. The hard work, scanty feed and the heavy pull over the mountains was too much for him, so we had to abandon him. I was mighty fond of Ben, and didn't like to leave him, so when they left him I stayed behind, thinking I might be able to bring him into camp if he rested a while. I succeeded in getting him to come along for a few miles, and then he laid down and wouldn't get up. It was about dark and I didn't know how many miles ahead our party had made camp. Some Indians came up and offered to trade me a peck of potatoes for old Ben. I hadn't seen nor tasted potatoes for months, and my desire for those potatoes proved stonger than my regard for old Ben, particularly as I felt pretty sure that he couldn't come on without several days' rest, so I swapped Ben for the spuds and got into camp that night pretty late with my booty.

"Our camp was on the Umatilla river near where Pendleton is, and that same night our sorrel mare got away and went up the old Nez Perce trail. I spent most of the next day trailing her. I met some Indians, who told me that she was up the trail at least 15 miles, and that they would go and get her for $1. A dollar, however, was a pretty large sum in those days, so I told them that I would go and get her myself. I overtook her a few miles up the trail and brought her into camp that night.

"From The Dalles there was no wagon road on to the Willamette valley, so my father and brother swam our cattle and horses across the Columbia river and took them down on what is now the Washington side to the mouth of the Sandy river. The rest of us went down the Columbia river in a flat boat, I earned my fare by bailing the boat, which was very leaky. We met the men folks at the mouth of the Sandy, and from there we drove to the home of my married sister at Oregon City.

"My father took up a donation claim in the valley. Provisions were very short. Dried fruit and beans and similar articles were imported from South America and cost 50 cents a pound. The high cost of living was just as much a problem then as it is now. In fact, it was so much of a problem that my father named the district where he settled 'Hardscrabble Neighborhood' and called the post office 'Needy.' While the occasion for these names has long since gone by they still retain the old names. That winter I went to school in Oregon City to Professor Port, who was in charge of the Baptist school there.

"After a year or two of schooling my money ran rather short, so I went to work in Dr. McLoughlin's grist mill at Oregon City. Dr. McLoughlin sympathized with my efforts to get an education and allowed me to work from 6 o'clock in the evening until 10 o'clock, paying me what were good wages for that time.

"A year or so later I went to Portland, going to school to Professor C.S. Kingsley and wife at the Portland Academy and Female seminary, a Methodist school. I remember in the fall and winter of 1858, when I was 17 years old, Levi Ankeny was one of my schoolmates. I had no idea at that time that we were to be so intimately related in business as well as socially in later years.

"My father developed tuberculosis in the spring of 1858, dying from it. A little later my brother and two sisters died from the same cause. In the winter of 1859 I also became affected. The doctor told me that my only hope was to live out of doors entirely. On the principle of being killed or cured. I took a job as cowboy and helped drive a herd of cattle up to the Yakima valley. I worked for an Irishman by the name of Bill Murphy. I went up there in February, 1860, and for the next year or two I was out of doors most of the time. The Indians had been pretty troublesome in killing cattle and running off stock in the past, so Murphy told them that I was the son of Colonel Wright and that if a single steer was lost or taken the soldiers would come up and kill all of the Indians' horses. It was only a few years before that that General Kelly, in the pursuit of the Indians, had overtaken them and killed over 700 of their ponies. I didn't lose a single steer through the entire winter. The Indians scoured the hills and brought the steers in sometimes from 15 or 20 miles away.

"We drove the cattle up into British Columbia, where they were sold, and I came back to the Willamette valley. In the fall of 1861, George Byers and the two Hall boys, Henry and William, and myself, drove a herd of milch cows up to the Walla Walla valley. The winter of 1861 and 1862 was a record breaker, the thermometer going down to 30 below zero. The snow stood three feet on a level and stayed that way for weeks. Our herd of dairy cows met the same fate that thousands of other cattle did that winter, dying from exposure and lack of feed. Early in the spring of 1862 the Hall boys and I started for the newly discovered mines on Powder river.

"We went to the new camp near Baker City, which was named Auburn. In the latter part of May, Henry Hall and myself came back to Swift's Station, as Pendleton was then called, to get supplies. I happened to be there on election day early in June, and there is where I cast my first vote. I voted for Gibbs for governor. We heard there of the discovery of gold in the John Day country, so a party of us went into that district. We found gold on what was called Canyon creek, and I helped build the first cabin there. The settlement which sprang up there was named Canyon City, so I guess you can call me one of the founders of Canyon City.

"The miners were anxious to send letters to their homes in the Willamette valley or California and to get news from the outside, so my partner, Nelson, and myself, got a few horses together and borrowed a mule from the outside, and started a pony express route. It was called the Brents & Nelson express. The Dalles was the nearest settlement at the time, and our first trip took us six days to go from Canyon City to The Dalles. It was about 225 miles distant, and of course there were no trails except Indian trails in the country. We followed these Indian trails, and when they bore off to one side, we cut across the country. In trying to find a short cut we got lost in the Box canyons on the John Day and lost a good deal of time before we got out and headed in the right direction again. At first we had to ride one horse clear through but we soon established relay stations every 25 or 30 miles, where we changed horses. A little later an opposition express company started. The rate for carrying letters was 50 cents each, and we had many letters to carry out, as well as gold dust to take out for the miners. The Civil war was in progress, and the miners were eager for newspapers giving particulars about the battles being fought. We got the Willamette valley newspapers at The Dalles for 10 cents each, and the Sacramento Union, which would be about 10 days old, we got for 25 cents per copy. Naturally, the man who first reached Canyon City could sell at 50 cents all the papers he took in, while the one who got beaten had his papers left on his hands and was lucky to get cost out of them. This made pretty keen competition between the two express companies.

"I remember of having ridden a race in June, 1863, with the express rider for the opposition company. I rode the 225 miles in 28 hours and beat him out. Those were pretty stirring times.

"The Dalles was the county seat of Wasco county and Wasco county extended eastward to the summit of the Rocky mountains, including a part of what is now Wyoming.

"The miners, with their vigilante law helped out the regular law when they thought it was necessary. The carrying out of gold dust encouraged the highwayman so that an express rider did not lack excitement. I remember one night hearing several horses coming up the trail at a fast clip, back of me, I rode into the brush and held my hand over my horse's nose so he wouldn't whinny. They rode on and when they had gone beyond hearing I struck off the trail and went around them. They had stopped, thinking they were ahead of me. It was Jim Romaine and Howard, two notorious characters at that time. A few months later Romaine killed McGruder in Montana and was hanged for it.

"I remember another time in the spring of '63 when I was coming out from Canyon City with about $4,000 worth of gold dust in my cantinas. Before the establishment of the relay stations we used to camp where dark hit us, provided there was good grazing for the horse and water and wood to make camp with. Dusk had overtaken me but I decided to ride on until I came to a good camping place. I saw the light of a camp fire at the camp I was making for so, being glad of company, I rode into the firelight to camp with them. Too late, I recognized Jim Parton with Berry Way and Berry Way's woman. It was too late to back out so I rode up to camp and dismounted. Berry Way was an escaped convict from California. As I unsaddled, Berry said, 'What have you got in your cantinas, gold dust?' I laughed and said, 'I wish I had, it's heavy enough. They're saddle irons that I am taking out for Lockwood's pack train.' I threw the cantinas carelessly aside in the grass and after we had supper together I rolled in my blanket, being apparently utterly indifferent to them. However, I put my six shooter under my head and in those days the slightest movement would awaken me. However, they took my word for it, particularly since I was so careless and indifferent about my cantinas and they didn't bother them. Next morning I pulled out for The Dalles. I had only gone a few miles when I met the sheriff of Wasco county with a posse. He asked me if I had met Berry Way. I told him I had camped with him last night. 'The Hell you did,' he responded, 'we're after him for murder. Some men camping on Fifteen-mile creek saw him washing some bloody blankets in the creek and after he had gone they looked around and found a man named Gallagher dead under a Juniper tree a little way back from the trail.' The sheriff and his posse rode on and overtook Berry Way and his party. They took him to Canyon City, putting him in the log jail there. He was brought back to Canyon City and again placed in the log jail. I belonged to the vigilantes, as did most of the better element. The vigilantes talked the matter over and being afraid that Berry Way would get out of jail again they went to the log jail and took him out to one of the hills overlooking the city and hanged him.

"In June, 1863, we sold out our express business. I was appointed Canyon City's first postmaster. When Wasco was formed, the county being named after General Grant, I was made the first county clerk. Some time before that I had borrowed Kent's Commentaries from Orlando Humason. In the early days some of the mining camps were long on vigilante law and pretty short on legal lore. My knowledge of law resulted in my being appointed justice of the peace.

"I remember one of the attorneys who practiced in my court was Heine Miller or, to give him his full name, Cincinnati Heine Miller, and who is known to literary fame as Joaquin Miller, the poet of the Sierras. In those days we called every one by his first name or a nickname. Everyone called me Tom or Tom Brents, and we always used to call Miller, Heine, sometimes Henry. His wife's name was Minnie Myrtle and I remember she used to write some excellent poetry. Heine used to come around once in a while or, rather, twice in a while and that was pretty often, to read poems to us, claiming that he was the author of them. I remember one that struck me particularly was a poem called 'Gettysburg.' We talked it over among ourselves and decided that Miller was something of a fraud and was palming off his wife's poetry as his own. However, as he continued to turn out poetry after his wife left him we came to the conclusion that the work was probably his own.

"In 1869 I went to Oroville on the American river and from there I came up by stage to Hubbard, Oregon to visit some of my relatives. In 1870 I went to Walla Walla. I used to attend court in Pendleton, La Grande, Baker and Malheur City, making the rounds on horseback. In 1878 I was sent to congress where I served three terms.

"Looking back at it now, I don't know but what I like the old days about as well as these more modern days with all their improvement. Living out of doors cured me of the consumption and dodging Indians to save my scalp and holdup men to save the gold dust I was carrying, kept me busy and interested. Lots of men who have made their mark in the history of the northwest handled the pick and shovel, the gold scales or the butcher cleaver in those early days at Canyon City, Orofino and Florence."

William Polk Gray

The son of W.H. Gray,
a missionary who came to Oregon in 1836,
tells about his experiences
boating on the Columbia and Snake rivers.

"My father named me William Polk Gray. I remember when I was four or five years old someone asked me what my middle initial stood for. Father said, 'I named him after President Polk. When I named him, the president had taken a strong stand of "54-40 or fight". Polk reversed his attitude on that question and I have been sorry I called my boy after him ever since. Sometimes I have a notion to ring the youngster's neck, I am so disgusted with President Polk'."

A prospecting trip near Roslyn, B.C., failed to pan out as well as expected, and Gray started a ranch on the upper Okanogan river. Then he determined to build a boat, go down the Okanogan and Columbia rivers to the miners. Gray said:

"We had practically no tools, and of course no nails. We went into the mountains, whipsawed out the lumber, hauled it down to the water, and father, with the help of us boys, built a boat, fastening it together with trunnels or wooden pegs. We built a boat 91 feet long with 12-foot beams, drawing 12 inches of water. The next thing was calking her, but I never saw my father stumped yet. He hunted around and found a big patch of wild flax. He had the children pick this and break it to use as oakum to calk the cracks in the boat. We also hunted all through the timber and found gum in the trees, which we melted up for pitch to be used in the calking. We had no canvas for sails, so he made some large sweeps. He launched her on May 2, 1861, and started on his trip down the river on May 10th.

"To give you an idea of the determination of my father, he sent that boat, without machinery, sails or other equipment except the sweeps, through the Rock Island rapids and through the Priest Rapids, both of which he negotiated successfully. He left me to bring the family down and I certainly had a very exciting time doing so."

Accompanied by A.J. Kane, Young Gray started down the river on horseback, with his mother and two sisters and two brothers. On their way they learned that the Indians had killed a man and his wife near Moxee Springs, so they crossed the Columbia and started down the east bank. Kane had been injured and could scarcely ride.

One night the Snake river Indians drove away their horses, and young Gray started out on the trail of the Indians. He followed their trail to near the present site of Pasco. Entering the camp, he rode up to a large tent where he heard the sound of tom-toms and dancing.

"Some years before, General Wright had inflicted punishment upon the Indians by killing a large band of their horses. On the spur of the moment, I decided to put on a bold front and demand the return of my horses. I rode up to the tent, dismounted, threw the teepee flap back and stepped into the entrance. The Indians stopped dancing and looked intently at me. I talked the Chinook jargon as well as I did English, so I said, 'Some of your Indians have stolen my horses last night. If they are not back in my camp an hour after I get there, I'll see that every horse in your band is shot.' There was utter silence."

As Gray rode back to his camp, four Indians rode after him, whooping savagely, and when they got to him surrounded him. He did not look around. One Indian rode directly into the trail ahead of him. Gray spurred his horse and raised his quirt. The Indians gave away before his bluff of appearing perfectly fearless.

When he got back in camp, he sat down to a delayed breakfast. In a few minutes his horses were driven in. He led his party to an Indian camp.

"I again rode up to the large tent, opened the flap and said in Chinook, "I want one canoe for my women and children to go to Wallula and three canoes to swim my horses across. You have delayed us by driving my horses off, so I want you to hurry.' They looked as impassive as wooden statues. One of the chiefs gave some command to the others. Several of the young men got up, went down to the water and got out the canoes.

"My mother and the children got in and the Indians put in our packs to take to Wallula, 11 miles distant. My brother, Albert, went in one canoe and I went in the other, while one of the Indians went into the third canoe and we swam our horses across the river. Albert and I rode on toward Wallula, where we arrived at 10:00 o'clock that night and rejoined the rest of the family."

Gray put his family in the adobe fort. He herded stock for J.M. Vansyckle until his father returned from Deschutes with their boat, now rigged with sails and loaded with supplies, for the new Orofino mines. The freight was to be hauled to the mouth of the Clearwater, and he had mortgaged his entire property to purchase the boat load.

At Wallula the entire crew deserted, since they had heard that it was impossible to navigate the rapids.

"Father finally secured another crew of seven men, and on September 20, 1861, we left Wallula. It took us three days to reach the mouth of the Snake river, a distance of only 11 miles. The prevailing winds were directly across the current, so that it was necessary for us to cordelle the boat almost the entire way.

"Another boy and myself took ropes in a skiff up the stream, found a place where the rope could be made fast. We would then come down stream bringing the rope to our boat where the rope was made fast to the capstan and the rope would be slowly wound up. We had a difficult trip to Lewiston and before we got there my comrade and myself in the skiff had demonstrated that there was not a single rapid in the Snake river that could not be swum. It was October 30 when we finally arrived at Lewiston.

"Provisions were getting short at the mines and father sold his flour for $25.00 a sack or 50 cents a pound. Beans also brought 50 cents a pound. Blankets were eagerly bought at $25.00 a pair and we sold all of our bacon at 25 cents a pound. Father had made a very profitable voyage, and had not only carried out his plan, but came out with a handsome profit."

After some time in Portland, young Gray quit school to help his father on the river. They were carrying freight in their sailboat between Deschutes and Wallula. The elder Gray decided to build a steamboat at Columbus, on the Washington side of the river.

Gray, then 16 years old was put in charge of the sailboat after it was bought by Whittingham and Company of Wallula, and he strove earnestly to make a record with his first command.

"During the month of July, I made five round trips between Deschutes and Wallula, which was not only a record trip up to that time, but has never been broken by sailboats on the river since."

Through his exertions the new owners paid for the boat and all operating expenses in one month.

The elder Gray launched his steamboat, the Cascadilla, in December, 1862, and the next spring took it up to Lewiston. It ran on the Clearwater and Snake rivers. An interesting incident of his story is that of the transfer boat, Frederick Billings, which carried Northern Pacific railway cars across the Snake river (Pasco, Washington) before the bridge was completed. The boat took cars from Ainsworth to South Ainsworth. It was 200 feet long with a 39-foot beam, had a square bow and stern and a deck house 25 feet high and 165 feet long. Of this craft Gray said:

"It was the consensus of opinion that it would be impossible to handle her in strong winds. No one was anxious to handle the job. The very difficulty of handling such a Noah's Ark of a boat appealed to me and I applied for the position and was given the job before I could change my mind."

He transferred as many as 213 cars in a day with this boat, and when the bridge was completed in 1884, took it to Celilo to be overhauled. The boat was then used to transfer cars from Pasco to Kennewick.

Gray secured 80 acres of land and filed a plot of an addition to Pasco before the original townsite was plotted. When the railroad wanted to cross his land, he stood off the grading crew with a shotgun until the higher authorities of the Northern Pacific agreed to pay him $500.00 for the right of way.

W.J. McConnell

*A former Idaho governor
and Vigilante Captain
tells the story of the notorious badman,
Ferd Patterson.*

The discovery of new placer fields in British Columbia and Oregon caused a large influx of miners and camp followers to flow into those regions during the years 1861-1862, taxing the steamers plying between San Francisco, Portland and Victoria, to their utmost capacity. On one of the regular voyages between the California port and the two last named cities, the passenger list, which was a large one, included a party of so-called sporting men and women, who, after the vessel had cleared the harbor and was fairly out at sea, took possession of the cardroom and began to ply their trade, three-card monte and other games being introduced, while in the social saloon orgies were enacted which drove all the other passengers outside. Among these bacchanalians was a man named Patterson, who wore without attempt at concealment a large ivory-handled revolver and a formidable bowie-knife to match.

He seemed to be the recognized leader of the party, and the woman who passed as his wife was equally as proficient as he in dealing three-card monte--which seemed to be their specialty. They were a couple to attract attention in any place. He was in height above six feet, with a well-knit muscular frame, weighing over two hundred pounds, without any appearance of being stout or fleshy. He had sandy, or red hair, and a florid complexion, which bore marks of dissipation; heavy, bushy eyebrows partially concealed a pair of restless blue eyes, which never seemed to center on one object, but shifted as if expecting some kind of hostile demonstration. He wore a pair of high-heeled boots, which fitted his shapely feet to perfection, and a pair of plaid trousers which had been reinforced, or foxed, with buckskin, after the manner of similar garments worn by cavalrymen in our army. He also wore a cassimere shirt, a fancy silk vest, across the front of which dangled a heavy gold chain, made from specimens of native California gold. A long frock coat of heavy pilot-beaver cloth, trimmed with the fur of the sea-otter completed a wardrobe typical of the man who wore it. He was about forty years old, and being destined to play a prominent part in the then unborn history of Idaho, the foregoing description is given.

The woman who claimed recognition as his wife was perhaps twenty-eight years of age, though dissipation and the continued use of cosmetics had caused her to appear older. She had a figure to which even the modern mantua-makers' art could add no line of symmetry, a brunette in complexion and in form a Venus, tall and willowy in her movements. Mate to such a man as Patterson, they were the observed among the observers. The steamer arrived abreast the Columbia river bar too late in the evening to cross in safety and the captain concluded to lie off and on till morning. Complaint was made to the officers of the ship during the night, by a committee of passengers, who demanded that the boisterous conduct and the profane language being used in the presence of ladies and children be stopped. Whereupon the captain visited the card-room, where he found the sporting fraternity assembled and addressing them courteously, requested that they retire, as the hour had arrived when the lights must be extinguished. To this request Patterson, who had probably been drinking more than was his usual custom, replied in an insulting manner, causing the captain to threaten to put him in irons if he did not behave. The party then dispersed, Patterson saying that he would see the captain after the ship landed in Portland.

The vessel crossed the bar the following morning, and after discharging freight and a few passengers at Astoria, proceeded on its way up the river to Portland, arriving there during the night. After the ship was docked and secured in her berth, although the hour was late, the passengers, weary of being confined, went ashore and were soon distributed throught the city. The following morning after the crew, under the direction of the second and third officers, had begun to discharge the ship's cargo, the captain proceeded up town to call on some of his late passengers who had gone to the Cosmopolitan Hotel. That old time hostelry was then the best in the city of Portland, or for that matter, on the northwest coast, and stood on the north side of Stark street between Front street and the river. The main entrance was into the office, or large reception room, which occupied the first or ground floor fronting on Stark and Front streets. There being no hall or elevator, access to the hotel parlor, which was located on the second floor, was gained by ascending a broad spiral stairway which arose from the office floor; hence no visitor or guest could come or go without their movements being noted by the bookkeeper or landlord, one of whom was always present.

The captain, after arriving at the hotel, sent his cards to those he desired to see, and was at once shown up to the hotel parlor. A few minutes later Patterson entered the office door and proceeding to the clerk's desk inquired for the captain and upon being told that he had gone up stairs but would soon come down, he took a seat directly opposite the stairway, remarking that he would wait. But a short time elapsed before the captain and the friend he had called to see, appeared at the upper landing of the stairway, and after good-bye had been said, he began to descend. Patterson had been watching the parting of the friends from where he sat, and when the captain had descended about half way down the stairs, he arose and shot him dead, the limp body bumping from step to step until it reached the office floor. The murderer surrendered to a policeman, who entered at the moment the shot was fired, but too late to prevent the tragedy. It has often been said that none other than Deity can foretell the verdict of a jury, and such was the case in the trail which followed the death of the captain. He was shot by a ruffian in revenge for an imaginary insult and a jury of "good men and true" exonerated the murderer and turned him loose on society to seek other victims, the first of whom was the woman he had flaunted as his wife on the incoming voyage of the steamer. Suspecting her of disloyalty, he became enraged, and seizing in one hand the coil in which she always wore her hair, drew his bowie-knife, which was as sharp as a razor, with the other, and attempted to cut it off close to her head at one stroke, but aiming too low, when the hair came off in his hand a large piece of scalp clung to it. A policeman, hearing the woman scream entered the house and placed the offender under arrest. Again Patterson was in the hands of the Portland authorities, and again as quickly released. He then made his final departure from Oregon, vowing vengeance on the officer who had arrested him for scalping the woman. The foregoing biographical sketch is pertinent to this narrative only for the reason that its hero, Patterson, after leaving Oregon went direct to Idaho, where he soon became a prominent luminary among the bravos who controlled the body politic of that territory for years.

From the time the first county officers were appointed in Boise county, until after Lee's surrender at Appomatox, civil government presented a strange anomaly. The territory, for judicial purposes, was divided into three districts, to each of which was appointed a judge by the then president of the United States, Abraham Lincoln, and for the territory at large was appointed a United States marshal, who in turn appointed a deputy in each judicial district. The officers thus appointed were Union men, while the sheriffs and their deputies, as well as all other elective officers in the territory, were usually adverse to the government and the laws which they were expected to enforce. Especially was this true in Boise county, which embraced Boise Basin.

There were in Boise county during the foregoing period a few men who were as staunch and loyal to the government as others were disloyal; men who never hesitated to declare themselves and who always were prepared to meet emergencies as they might arise; men who, in fact, courted the danger of conflict. Prominent among this class was a man named Pinkham, who was the first sheriff by appointment in Boise county, serving only until an election was held and his successor qualified. He was one of Nature's noblemen, six feet two inches tall, with the frame of an athlete. Although he was yet in the prime of vigorous manhood, his hair and beard were almost snow-white, while his cheeks were as rosy as a boy's. Not only physically, but mentally, he was a leader among men, and although he had been marked from the first for the bullet of an assassin, the seasons there as elsewhere came and went for more than two years before a man could be found to undertake the desperate enterprise. Finally, Ferd Patterson who had gained notoriety in Portland, Oregon, by killing the captain of the steamship and scalping his erstwhile mistress, and who had been a sojourner in Idaho since that time, expressed a willingness to add another nick to the handle of his revolver by killing Pinkham, provided the "boys" would stand in and secure his acquittal by being present when the killing occurred and testifying afterward that Pinkham drew his weapon first, or attempted to do so, thus showing that Patterson acted in self-defense.

An arrangement was accordingly made one Sunday during the forenoon, accompanied by those who were to appear at the anticipated trial, Patterson went down to the Warm Springs, a bathing resort located on the Boise City stage road about one mile below Idaho City. Prior to their starting, however, they knew that Pinkham had been invited to ride down to the Springs by a Boise City man who was there with a team and buggy. As he had planned, Patterson and party arrived first at the Springs. At once they repaired to the bar-room where liquors were dispensed.

The building in which the bath rooms were located was erected above the road on ground which sloped into the gulch, or ravine, which carried into Moore's Creek the overflow from a large hot spring, which flowed out of the side of a steep hill above. Along the front of the house which was the end of the building, ran a porch, or piazza, and it being elevated above the ground except at one end, was surrounded by a railing as a precaution against accidents, while entrance to the house was made via the porch, access to which was gained by means of a short flight of steps at the end where it was near the ground. The room which was entered from the porch was used as a bar-room and a door in the rear of this room opened into a hall which extended the entire length of the building, and on both sides of the hall were bath rooms, while above the house on the hillside was a swimming pond filled with warm water.

The foregoing explanation of the premises is necessary that the future reader who may not have visited this resort will more fully understand the tragedy which was enacted there. When the buggy in which Pinkham rode arrived at the Springs he alighted and entering the bar-room found Patterson and his party there. Having had no previous intimation of their presence, accustomed as he was to the methods of Patterson and his friends, it doubtless flashed on his mind in an instant that the crowd was there to murder him. Patterson began an attempt to start a quarrel, but Pinkham, realizing that he was alone, among unscrupulous enemies, would not be drawn into a difficulty and remarking "That's all right Patterson," brushed past him and entered one of the small bath-rooms and closed the door. Patterson and his friends soon afterwards went out through the hall, and on up to the swimming pond, where they all proceeded to take a swim.

Patterson related the succeeding events to a friend who made the story public after those who were parties to the affair left the country.

Patterson said that he and his companions were so long in the swimming pond that he thought Pinkham would be gone before they returned to the bar-room, and he hoped he was gone, as he knew that if he did not continue his efforts to force a quarrel the men who were with him would think he had weakened, and he said that he knew that if a quarrel was precipitated, he must get Pinkham quickly, or Pinkham would get him; so upon entering the hall he drew his revolver and carried it cocked in his hand as he entered the bar-room, and Pinkham not being there, he walked directly to the open door leading to the porch, and found Pinkham standing waiting for the hack which conveyed passengers to and from the Springs; raising his pistol, he said, "Will you draw, you Abolitionist son of a b----?" And as Pinkham turned his side toward him he fired. The smoke of his pistol, he said, partially obscured his view, and dropping on one knee, he leveled the pistol across his arm and fired the second shot, both bullets taking effect, although the first shot caused a mortal wound. Pinkham instinctively reached for and drew his weapon, evidently cocking it by the same motion, and as he was falling, it discharged into the ceiling. The murdered man fell to the floor and immediately expired. Thus was completed the mission on which they came.

Arrangements having been made for his speedy departure, Patterson at once mounted a horse and started to leave the country, but Pinkham's former deputy, Rube Robbins, followed by the sheriff, were soon in pursuit, and the murderer was overhauled by Rube who came up on him first before half the distance to Boise valley was covered. His arrest was accomplished without difficulty, when, joined by the sheriff, they started back to Idaho City, and making a detour to avoid difficulty with a large force of miners who had assembled and were threatening to hang Patterson, they arrived at the county jail and succeeded in placing him behind the bars without interference, although at least a thousand men were clamoring for his blood.

But the danger-point had been reached. Meetings were quietly assembled in all the mining towns for several successive nights and couriers were kept continually on the move, carrying news from one point to another. Men gathered in whispering groups on the hillsides and in the miners' cabins. A spirit of mystery and secrecy pervaded the atmosphere, culminating finally in a delegation from all the mining towns being sent to Idaho City for the purpose of holding a conference, looking to the organization of a vigilance committee similar to that which had accomplished such effective work in the Payette valley. The conference was held in a large fire-proof cellar used for storage purposes, and it was concluded that before perfecting an organization a messenger should be sent to the captain of the Payette Vigilance Committee, and if possible, secure his attendance at a subsequent meeting which would be called in Idaho City at such time as would be convenient for him to attend. Orlando Robbins, or Rube Robbins, as he was generally known, was accordingly dispatched to find the captain and if possible persuade him to come to Idaho City at once. Robbins was successful in his mission and two days afterward returned with his man.

Arrangements were at once made for a meeting consisting of a few reliable men to be held the succeeding night in the fire-proof cellar which had heretofore been used for meetings. As secrecy was to be observed until an organization was perfected the cellar was wisely chosen. Ten o'clock that night was the hour named, and when the time arrived approximately two score of the most prominent men in the Basin were present, to whom was introduced the captain, who upon being informed of the object of the gathering, at the request of the chairman, gave those present an outline of the constitution and by-laws of the Payette committee, stating that it was the fault of the citizens of Boise Basin that conditions such as had heretofore prevailed were allowed to continue. In the aggregate the men who had committed all the crimes in Idaho were few in numbers, and he thought the time had arrived for the people to put a stop to such atrocious murders as had been of frequent occurrence in the past. He stated that as the first object of the proposed organization was the punishment of Patterson, the murderer of Pinkham, he would like to be present when that event took place, and assured them that while his own affairs would prevent him from becoming a member of their organization, he would come to Idaho City at any time on receiving notice that they were ready to act.

The meeting then proceeded to organize on the same lines as the Payette committee had followed, adopting for its name "The Idaho City Vigilance Committee." A blacksmith who had a shop on Buena Vista Bar was chosen as captain, and an executive committee of five elected who were to have entire control of the organization, issuing their orders direct to the captain whose duty it was made to carry them out. A committee on enrollment was also appointed, the duty of which was to enroll as members all persons who would be willing to act with the organization in suppressing crime and punishing murderers and robbers.

At the meeting a Methodist minister presided and none of those present ever forgot his opening address; and while the average minister is generally considered out of place in mining camps where the Sabbath is respected no more than any other day, his bold stand in favor of suppressing the lawless class did more to elevate the churches in the minds of his hearers than all the sermons they were likely to hear. Among other things he said "He could fight or he could pray, as occasion required." The man was Reverend Kingsley, who became a permanent resident of Idaho and lived many years of usefulness to his fellows and when his final call came took his departure, loved and respected by all.

Two weeks were consumed in preparation, at the end of which time a membership of nine hundred were enrolled. Among the number were two men who had served in the navy and were familiar with explosives. They were detailed to prepare a number of hand-grenades which were intended to demolish the gates of the prison. It had been determined by the executive committee that the entire force would advance to the door of the jail where Patterson was confined and demand that he be delivered up to them, and if denial was made then the walls were to be scaled and the place captured by assault.

For the purpose of carrying out the foregoing plan, the members were notified to appear fully armed at the city cemetery at two o'clock on a morning named, it being the object to advance on the jail at daybreak. The cemetery was located but a short distance above the jail but it was doubtless chosen as a rendezvous not solely on account of its contiguity to the object of their attack. The leaders apparently counted on the effect which the newly-made graves, and they were all comparatively new, would have on the friends of the murdered men who slept beneath those sodless mounds, as it was well known to the executive committee that many of those who slept their last sleep in that hallowed ground had died from the knife or bullet of an assassin, and from the hearts of a hundred friends, those who were assembled in the haze of that star-lit morning, meeting around those silent mounds, arose a cry for vengeance. At least an hour before the time named in the call the men, in groups of two, three or more, began to arrive, and by two o'clock nine hundred men were on the ground awaiting the order to advance, while on the side nearest to the jail, an emergency field hospital was improvised, with two surgeons in attendance, showing that the serious nature of this enterprise was fully understood by all.

The assembling of so many men could not be accomplished secretly even in the night time--in a place like Idaho City, where many of the inhabitants were night-hawks, men who worked on the night shift, and, while doing so, worked the other fellow. Consequently, as so many men were noticed slipping out in little groups, it was readily surmised that their object was an attack on the jail, so the sheriff was at once apprised. It is more than probable that the news of the intended movement had leaked, and that he was informed in advance. Consequently, in line with his duty, he had garrisoned the jail with practically all the thugs and tin-horn gamblers in the city, and was prepared to defend his prisoner, Patterson. Thus a comical side was presented by even the serious condition that existed at that moment, and this was, that the majority of the men whom the sheriff had engaged as defenders of the jail, and consequently of the law, were many of them, for the first time in their lives, its defenders. But the sheriff was unquestionably right in employing such help as was at hand, it being clearly his duty, as an officer of the law, to protect his prisoner.

The men who were expected to defend the jail from assault were ensconced behind its walls and were provided with arms, besides, judging by the yells and pistol shots, they were also furnished an ample supply of nerve tonic, "the cup that cheers." Immediately prior to the time set for the advance, a man who had been reclining on the ground, well to the rear of the others, arose, and threading his way carefully toward the center of the cemetery, mounted a log and in a voice that could be distinctly heard by all present, said, "Gentlemen: You all know me--at least by reputation; I am the man whom the Payette Vigilance Committee calls captain; I am here tonight upon invitation of your executive committee. Up to the present time I have taken no part in advising, or managing your affairs, but the time has arrived when human lives are in the balance, and I feel that although there are many older and, doubtless wiser men here than I, yet I feel that at this critical moment that it is due you that I should express my views, and whether you concur with me or not, my duty so far shall have been performed.

You have assembled here for the purpose of demanding from the sheriff and his deputies in charge of the jail, their prisoner, Patterson, your object being not only to punish him for the murder of Pinkham, but in so doing, impress upon the lawless classes the certainty that, hereafter, no murderer shall escape. The only object you could have in assembling here in the night and advancing on the jail at daybreak was that you might surprise the guard and capture them without resistance, but as is evident, your plans are known and the sheriff has made provisions for the defense of his charge. You can storm the place and take it by assault, but in so doing many lives will be lost, and I cannot see the philosophy of sacrificing perhaps forty or fifty good men's lives to hang one criminal. A mistake has been made in calling out so many men; I can take Idaho City with ten men; I would go through it like a cyclone, and take whomever I wanted."

Some one in the crowd immediately spoke up and said "That is the man for our captain." The words were scarcely uttered when they were repeated by hundreds of voices. The man who had been in charge up to this time was a blacksmith who worked at his trade on Buena Vista Bar. He at once came forward and asked the Payette visitor to take charge, stating that he was "not qualified for such work."

To this he replied: "Gentlemen, under the circumstances I will assume the responsibility and issue my first orders now. They are that you all go home. When I want any of you, I shall let you know. Before you separate, however, I desire to say that Patterson killed my friend, and the earth is not big enough to hide his murderer."

The crowd at once began to disperse, and when day dawned there was no evidence that such a gathering had taken place, except the trampled weeds and ground in the cemetery.

Thus ended the first crisis in the history of Idaho. Had an attack been made on the prison many lives would have been lost in the battle that would have followed, and it would not have ended until vengeance had been wreaked upon every man in Boise Basin who had unlawfully taken human life.

It was Saturday morning when the gathering dispersed. During the day following business was practically suspended. Men gathered in groups in the streets and in the miners' cabins, the one subject of their discussion being what was likely to occur now that a new leader had been chosen. It was generally believed that a way would be found to punish Patterson, but how was it to be accomplished? No one seemed to be informed on that subject.

During the day warrants were issued for the arrest of Rube Robbins, Elder Kingsley and one other, and they were placed under arrest. It was generally believed that the arrests were made under the impression that the new captain would undertake to rescue the prisoners, in which event it was probably planned that he would be shot by some one concealed for the purpose. But he paid no attention to the matter, in fact did not appear in the crowd that immediately gathered. The prisoners were at once paroled by the federal judge who was in the city. Thus, under high tension, passed that day and the succeeding night. That the leader had formulated some plan which was known to not more than two or three persons, was considered certain. But what was the plan? All was shrouded in mystery. Sunday afternoon he and Rube Robbins appeared on the street, both mounted, and rode across to Buena Vista Bar and down the road past the warm springs toward Boise City--the cynosure of all eyes. Soon afterward a group of miners and others began to assemble at the blacksmith shop on Buena Vista Bar, owned by the former captain, and when the assemblage had grown to such a size as to attract attention, the sheriff approached and demanded that they disperse within thirty minutes, or he would arrest them all.

They were doing nobody any harm, being there on the public road, each one being intent to learn all he could concerning the probable outcome of the pending difficulty. Some of those present were doubtless members of the Idaho City Vigilance Committee, but many were not, and as the observations of all alike had caused them to have but little respect for sheriffs and their deputies as peace officers, they did not propose to be ordered off the public highway, or arrested, because they did not see fit to go. So they at once began the erection of barricades along ditches that crossed near the shop. John C. Henly, an attorney, happening along on horseback, took in the situation at a glance, and at once galloped down the road after Robbins and the captain. Fortunately, he met them on their way back to town, and spurring up their horses, they were soon at the scene of the proposed hostilities. From here could be seen the sheriff and his deputies assembling their forces on a sawdust pile near the jail, preparatory to making a descent on the miners. Attracted by the unusual sight of a large force of men tearing down ricks of cordwood and building barricades, many persons had congregated, who knew nothing about the approaching conflict. Among this number was a company from Payette Valley, consisting of, approximately, twenty men, all of whom were members of the Payette Vigilance Committee, who had come to Idaho City to look for their captain, fearing something had happened to him. On their arrival they had placed their saddle animals in a feed-yard and started out in quest of the object of their search, arriving at Buena Vista Bar in time to meet him at the barricade. A hurried conference followed, in which he requested them to take no part in the coming conflict, if one occurred, but to remain where they were, and they could probably see the prettiest fight they had ever witnessed.

-251-

He told them his plan was to draw his men off to the other side of Moore Creek and take possession of a large dry ditch which girdled an ox-bow point, and there make a stand, since the ditch was a breastwork already prepared, and, furthermore, if a battle ensued, it was far enough removed from town or dwelling houses to insure the safety of non-combatants. He would listen to no remonstrance, but turning from them to the trenches and barricade, sang out, "Boys, this is no place to make a stand; I will show you a better one; follow me," and immediately started across the creek bottom for the ditch on the opposite side. Arriving there he instantly threw his men into line and dividing them into three squads, placing Rube Robbins in charge of one, and Al Hawk another, while he took command of the third, placing them in front at the apex of the bend, sending Rube to guard one flank with his men and Hawk the other. By the time these dispositions were made the sheriff had started his men on the double quick from where they were assembled, to make an attack. When they reached Moore Creek they were halted by the captain, and told "if they had an officer to send him forward to talk matters over, and if not, they had best come no nearer." A man who was mounted on a horse at once rode out and across to where the captain stood awaiting him, and on gaining speaking distance, exclaimed, "The only terms I have to propose to you is that you stack your arms and disperse, or the last divvil of you will be kilt." To this salutation the captain responded: "The h--- you say. What is your name?" the answer being, "My name is German; I am under-sheriff." The captain then said: "Mr. German, you had better return to the ranks; you and I cannot settle anything--send your chief up here. I will talk to him." Mr. German quickly complied with the suggestion, and within a few minutes the sheriff approached, exclaiming as he came near, "My God, cannot this be stopped?" To this the captain replied, "It is stopped. I've stopped right here. Don't you think I've got a good place? If you had wanted to arrest me, or any of my men, we respect your duty as an officer, and would submit to your authority, as was done yesterday; or, if you had needed a posse, and had secured one composed of respectable citizens, I or any of my men would surrender to you, but instead of such a possee, you come with all the cut-throats in the country." To this the sheriff answered that "when he chose man with a fight in view, he picked fighting men." The captain replied that there had always been a doubt in his mind "as to whether blow-hards and murderers could fight better than decent men. We have a chance to settle the matter now. The responsibility rests upon you--fire the first gun and not a man of you will ever cross that bar alive."

The sheriff then proposed that "they all deliver up their arms to him, and he would pledge his word of honor that in thirty days they would be returned, and the men could all go home." The captain in reply said, "I have a very pretty gun here; it was sent me by a friend in Centerville when he learned that these boys had chosen me to be their captain. He thought, when he sent me the gun, that I would not surrender it while I lived, and he was not the least bit mistaken.

"You have sent Holbrook around with a body of men to get in my rear, and I have sent some boys over there who will hurt him, and we shall be obliged to hold another election. You had better send men to call him off at once, and you go back to town with all your force, and try to make them behave. I am not going to attack your jail. You may rest easy on that score-- for I would not sacrifice the life of even one man for the sake of hanging a murderer. You may give Patterson his trial without hindrance, and, since the evidence has been arranged to secure his acquittal, he can go forth into the world, but the world is not big enough to hide him." Thus ended the second crisis. The sheriff withdrew his force and left the captain and his men in undisputed possession of the field.

A calamity was happily averted, for, had a single hostile shot been fired that day, the few decent men who were with the sheriff's party would have paid the penalty for being in bad company, because it would have been impossible, in the battle which would have ensued, to distinguish them from their allies; and as a force even larger than that with the captain had assembled on Buena Vista Bar, and joined the company from the Payette, the sheriff's force would have been between two fires--meaning their total extermination. The promise made to the sheriff, not to attack the jail and allow the trial to proceed, became generally known during that and the following day, hence the excitement subsided and business was resumed.

A short time afterward court convened and the trial of Patterson began, culminating as he had prearranged, in his acquittal. That he would eventually receive punishment for his crimes merited, no one doubted; but when or where he was to pay the extreme penalty was known only to the executive officers. He took his departure from Idaho City soon after his acquittal, going to Walla Walla, where there happened to be, at the time of his arrival, the man who was on the police force in Portland when Patterson scalped his paramour, and whom he had threatened to kill for arresting him. The ex-policeman having faith in Patterson's intent, as well as ability to keep pledges of that character, was on the lookout for him, and seeing him enter a barber-shop soon after his arrival in Walla Walla, followed him in, and finding Patterson seated in a barber-chair, shot and killed him instantly--after the same manner he had been in the habit of killing his victims. Thus ended a career of crime, relieving the Idaho City committee of the task they had set for themselves.

The writer of the foregoing narrative was the captain of the Payette Vigilance Committee, hence he was in a position to know the details of what transpired during those turbulent days and nights.

Daniel Hayes

*Chore boy for James Hamilton
comes west and witnesses
the killing of Ferd Patterson in 1865.*

Daniel Hayes was born at Galberstown, Tipperary, Ireland, December 12, 1840 and came to America in 1853. A sister and brother had preceded in his coming, and met him at New York. He came with neighbors, who looked after him, and the journey was made in a sailing vessel, which arrived in the New York port in August, just five weeks and three days after leaving the home port.

His brother sent him to Williamsbridge to work, soon after his coming and from 1854 to '57, he was chore-boy for James A. Hamilton, brother of Alexander Hamilton. He was a very small boy and had gone to school but little. Mr. Hamilton's daughter, Angelica, took a great interest in him, and during these three years, gave him private lessons at night, and he never went to school afterward. Mr. Hayes has ever cherished such feelings of gratitude for Miss Hamilton, on this account he named one of his daughters, Angelica.

Mr. Hamilton lived in a beautiful colonial home on the Hudson, near Dobb's ferry. He was wealthy and had in his employ two coachmen, a butler, waiters and five servant girls.

Mr. Hayes remembers skating across the Hudson in 1855 and says the river has never been frozen, to that degree since. A steamer that plyed on the Hudson at that time was frozen solid in the ice, in front of the Hamilton home for a month.

The Schuyler family, of which Mrs. Schuyler was a daughter of James A. Hamilton lived near the Hamiltons. The French governess of the Schuyler's became engaged to one of Mr. Hamilton's coachmen. This romance was, indirectly a factor in the life of Mr. Hayes, for it was responsible for him leaving his home of every comfort, and good friends for a life in the far west among strangers. The coachman left his New York home to try his fortunes in the west, going to San Francisco, where he succeeded beyond his expectations. The governess wanted to join her lover and persuaded "little Dannie" as he was affectionately called, to accompany her as she did not want to make the long journey alone.

The Hamiltons did not want him to leave and offered many inducements to him to remain, but the governess continued her persuasions, which prevailed. He resorted to strategy to get away, he said which did not work, so he "just left."

The journey was made by the way of the Isthmus of Panama. From Aspinwall he wrote a letter to Miss Hamilton, which was the first information she had of his whereabouts. She answered it immediately, giving him much good advice, and it reached him at San Francisco. They were met at the steamer by the former coachman and two days after the arrival the couple were married.

After spending two weeks in San Francisco, Mr. Hayes journied to Benicia and went to work for the government in the quartermaster's department. Eleven months later he came to The Dalles with Captain Jordan. In the spring of 1858 when on the way to Ft. Simcoe with a government train of forty wagons, at the present site of Prosser, news of Col. Steptoe's defeat in the battle near the present site of Rosalia, was received.

He returned to The Dalles where Col. Wright fitted out troops and moved to the mouth of the Tucannon river on the Snake river, where Ft. Taylor was built. It was built of rocks and was named in honor of Captain Taylor who was killed in the battle between Col. Steptoe and the Indians. The battery of Ft. Taylor consisted of two canon. Here Major Wise stopped, where ammunition and supplies were stored to be forwarded to troops when needed and where sick soldiers were brought who were unable to continue the march north. Mr. Hayes was the driver of the ammunition wagon. The other wagons bringing the supplies returned to Walla Walla. Major Wise remained at Ft. Taylor until the return of Col. Wright's expedition when it was abandoned.

Mr. Hayes continued work in the quartermaster's department until 1859 when he went to Ft. Benton with a crew surveying the Mullan road. On his return he went into the employment of the government again.

In 1861 he went to the Orofino mines and "made some money," he says. Later he engaged in packing, but in 1873 bought the farm owned by James O'Donnell on Spring Branch, nine miles east of Walla Walla.

Mr. Hayes entered the service of the government, during the Nez Perce Indian war and also served as a government packer in the Modoc and Bannock wars. He also went to Cuba in 1898, in the government employ.

Mr. Hayes well remembers the killing of Ferd Patterson, one of the tragedies of Walla Walla, when it was a frontier town, and about which there is apparently a wide diversity of opinion in the minds of pioneers of that time. The shooting occurred in 1865, when Mr. Hayes was a packer. He was sleeping at the time in the City Hotel which was near the Bogle Barber shop, where the tragedy occurred.

"I heard shots at 7 o'clock in the morning and rushed out to see what was going on," he said. "I asked what had happened and was told Ferd Patterson had been shot."

Mr. Hayes went into Dick Barrett's saloon next door to the barber shop. Patterson lay on the mat in the front of the bar, where he had fallen dead.

"Patterson was in the barber chair, being shaved, and was unarmed, when Donahue, a night watchman, entered through the back door of the shop, with pistol in hand. He spoke to Patterson, then shot at him five times, all shots striking but one," is Mr. Hayes' remembrance of the event as told to him by those present at the shooting.

Mr. Hayes helped carry Patterson out of the saloon. There were no undertaking parlors here at that time and the body was carried into the back of some business house where it remained until taken away for interment. Mr. Hayes says there was considerable difficulty in securing a minister to officiate at the funeral.

Patterson was considered an undesirable citizen at the time of his coming as he had a record of killing two men before coming here and his killing was supposed to be sanctioned by the law and order league of that time. Mr. Hayes contends that Patterson was not a bad man, but was a quick tempered Southerner. When war issues came up, he lost his temper, which was somewhat fiery, and in both the murders done by him, there had been heated arguments on the war and the south.

H.L. Wells

Mr. Wells, one of the principal writers of F.T. Gilberts' 1882 book, Historic Sketches, *writes about vigilante times in the Inland Empire.*

The great rush to the Idaho mines during the few years immediately following their discovery, in 1860, carried with it some of the most lawless and desperate characters which the peculiar conditions of the Pacific coast had drawn hither. There were murderers and desperadoes who had fled from justice in the Eastern states, outlawed "Greasers," from Mexico, and "Sidney Ducks," from the penal colonies of Australia, and, in fact, outcasts from nearly every land beneath the sun. Their naturally vicious characters had been developed almost abnormally by the disordered condition of society in the California mines, and emboldened by numbers and exemption from punishment, they carried things with a high hand wherever they went. Generally denominated "Sports," they were of all grades of humanity, from the well educated to the ignorant, from the most gentlemanly and honorable gambler, so far as honor can be said to appertain to so degrading a business, to the most depraved and vicious of the human species.

Walla Walla was on the route of travel to and from the mines, the last great supply point before reaching them, and was a favorable and favorite place for hundreds of them to spend the winter season, whose rigors in the mines they were anxious to escape. With such an element among its population, the repression of crime and enforcement of law were always difficult, and often impossible. Lawlessness was rampant, and the officers struggled against it in vain. Thousands of men roamed round the country embraced in Idaho and Eastern Oregon and Washington Territory, having no permanent abiding place. Every town and mining camp was overrun with a transient element, of whom it was impossible for the officers to keep track. Miles of unsettled and unclaimed land stretched out in all directions, offering secure range upon which stolen cattle could be grazed; and strangers with bands of horses and cattle were constantly coming in, whose title to the property had to be assumed as good. Camped along the routes of travel and in the shanty hotels of towns and mining camps, were hundreds of men whose sole visible property was a roll of blankets. In such a condition of society there was little chance for the detection of criminals, and but little hope for their punishment when caught; for the migratory habits of the people generally carried the witnesses beyond the jurisdiction of the court long before the case came up for trial. Only when men were caught in the act of robbery, or when shooting occurred as the result of a sudden quarrel, and in the few cases where it was easily ascertained who were the guilty parties, was there any hope of inflicting punishment, and then it was but slight.

The plea of self defense was a very flexible one in those days, when men went armed and looked to themselves alone for protection. Disputes were settled with the revolver and knife, a custom not wholly dispensed with at the present day, and in the many quarrels that arose it was not difficult for the survivor to prove that he was defending his life. Sometimes there was no survivor, and in many instances this was a very satisfactory condition of affairs. Very little crepe was worn by the community at such times, and so long as the sports confined themselves to mutual extermination, all bade them Godspeed in their good work; but when good citizens suffered at their hands the case presented a different aspect.

During the winter of 1861-2 a gang of men made their headquarters on the Touchet, Whiskey and Copei creeks. Their ostensible means of support was the precarious one of gambling and selling whiskey to the Indians; but they were generally credited with much of the horse and cattle stealing so prevalent at that time. Among them were Brocky Jack, or Winter, George Ives, Clubfoot George, or George Lane, Bill Bunton, John Cooper, John Turner, Dave English, Peoples, and other well known desperate characters who inflicted their presence by turns upon Walla Walla, Auburn, Boise City, Lewiston, Oro Fino, Florence and all the old mining camps of this region. Nearly all of these met their death within a few years, many of them at the hands of vigilance committees in various places.

The vigilance movement was inaugurated in the fall of 1862, when the citizens of Auburn hanged two Spaniards and shot another, the latter for firing into the crowd during the ceremonies incident to the taking off of his two companions. Brocky Jack came to his death at the hands of A.I. Chapman, at Slate Creek, in December, 1862. He attacked Chapman with a knife, and received a blow from a hatchet that terminated his earthly career. The vigilante spirit first came to the surface at Walla Walla among the farmers and stockmen living near the city. In May, 1863, sixty-six of them signed a remonstrance because no effort had been made by the authorities to capture Bill Bunton for a murder committed by him a few months before, and a month later offered a reward for the capture of Bunton, Clubfoot George and John Turner.

In February, 1864, a vigilance committee in the Bannock mines hanged thirteen men, some of them the most noted desperadoes of this region. They were George Ives, Henry Plummer, a desperate character from Nevada City, California, and at the time of his sudden taking-off sheriff of the county, Ned Ray, Buck Stinson, John Wagoner, or Dutch John, Spanish Frank, Jack Gallagher, Reed Brown, George Lane, or Clubfoot George, Haze Lyons, Boon Helm and Frank Parish. A month later Bill Bunton was disposed of in the same manner at Beaver Head, and in July vigilantes near Burnt river hanged a halfbreed named Greenwood, a son of Old Greenwood, the trapper. These incidents show how universal was the feeling that citizens must rely upon themselves for protection, and that crime could only be suppressed by the concerted action of all, unhampered by the machinery of the courts.

A list of the willful murders committed in and near Walla Walla would be a long and black one, and yet the records fail to show that any punishment was inflicted, or, in many cases, that the least effort was made to bring the offenders to justice. Highway robberies and cattle stealings were so numerous that the officers paid no attention to them whatever. Added to this was the fact that the jail at Walla Walla was so poor a structure that the majority of prisoners broke out of it within a few days after being confined. With but little chance for a prisoner remaining until his trial came off, and with no secure place to confine him if convicted--for in the absence of a territorial penitentiary each county had to take charge of its own convicts-- what encouragement was there for the officers to arrest wrongdoers? The reader cannot fail to appreciate the chaotic state of society. Robbery and murder were committed, and the perpetrators went unwhipped of justice; the pioneer farmer, laboring to establish himself in a wilderness as yet unsubdued to the yoke of the plow, saw his horses and cattle disappear and no one held responsible; teamsters and packers on the roads, passengers and expressmen on the stages, and travelers on the lonely mountain trails, were robbed, and often murdered, with but faint chance of punishment for the offenders; theft was committed in the streets of Walla Walla in broad daylight; men were garroted in their own places of business; nothing seemed secure from the bands of plunderers who infested both city and country. In four years, but one man was convicted of murder, and the unexpected verdict so displeased him that he took an early opportunity to escape from the jail. The people found themselves overrun with thieves, gamblers and desperadoes, and no protection through the law was to be hoped for. Men began to say to each other that it was about time something was done to bring about a better condition of affairs and the idea of a vigilance committee became very popular, especially among the farmers.

This idea was made a living reality by the quiet circulation of a pledge for signatures. A month was consumed in perfecting the organization, and then the leaders announced themselves as ready to execute all business in their line with neatness and dispatch. It is claimed that at this time the organization numbered eight hundred men, and carried on its roll the names of a majority of the business men and honest citizens of Walla Walla, while the farmers joined it almost to a man. The sports and the few law abiding citizens who were opposed to mob law in any form, were the only ones not connected with the organization or who did not approve its actions during the first few months of its existence.

The committee began its active career early in February, 1865, by requesting a number of characters who had no visible means of support, and who were suspected of horse stealing and other kindred eccentricities, to find a more congenial abiding place ere the week closed. Many of them complied with the request with an alacrity highly gratifying to the committee. Hearing that a few of these had gone to the ranch of a man named Gondon, on Mud creek, a select party paid that gentleman a nocturnal visit, but finding no one there but the man himself, gave him a week's time to settle up his affairs and find another abiding place. They then proceeded three miles up the Walla Walla, to the ranch of one Beauchemin, where they captured a halfbreed named Chas. Fancy. This man was conducted a mile down the stream, where a vote was taken upon the question of hanging him. By a majority of three votes his life was spared, but nine o'clock the next morning was fixed as the hour when his further presence would be exceedingly disagreeable. They then went home to bed.

A few days after this, Robert Waddingham and Six-toed Pete knocked a man down near the jail and robbed him of $40.00. They were captured and lodged in the county jail, but friends of Waddingham aided them to escape from that frail institution a few nights later. As soon as this became known, the vigilantes scoured the country in search of the fugitives, and soon found them in a school house near Milton, busily employed in freeing their limbs from the irons with which they had been secured. Upon their return to Walla Walla, an exciting time ensued. Many of the vigilantes wanted to hang them in a summary manner, while the friends of the prisoners, and the sporting class generally, insisted that they be turned over to the authorities again. Armed men of both parties promenaded the streets, and a bloody conflict was imminent; but after keeping the prisoners under guard a whole day, the committee finally turned them over to the officers. The men were tried, convicted and sentenced to prison for life, and in default of a territorial prison, were confined in the county jail. Waddingham was soon declared to have been innocent by his companion in misery, and was pardoned by Governor Evans. Unable to endure the lonliness of his lot after his fellow prisoner's departure, Pete took an early opportunity to make the usual nocturnal exodus, and was seen in the valley no more.

Early in April, 1865, a party of vigilantes paid a visit to Fred Swartz, commonly called Dutch Fred, on Walla Walla river, and hanged that gentleman to a tree for a brief time, to force him to disclose some information they desired. In this they were unsuccessful, and the next day the outraged man went to town and swore out warrants against five of the men, but was unable to have them punished. The demonstrations of their earnestness of spirit and their power to enforce their commands, had their effect, and great numbers of bad characters departed for a more inviting field of operations.

There existed, at this time, a band of cattle thieves, who were herding stolen beef cattle a few miles below the city. A couple of butchers were in the habit of slipping out "in the silent midnight watches," and procuring a supply of beef for their stalls, at rates much below the market price, to their great financial advantage, and the injury of their more honest competitors. These parties stole sixty head of cattle from John Jeffries, on the Umatilla river just below the site of Pendleton, and the owner tracked them to this robbers' range, near Walla Walla. It was about the first of April when he came to the city and procured warrants, which the sheriff and a posse undertook to serve. One of the gang, called Doc Reed, who lived in the city, learned of the intended raid, and hastened to warn his comrades of their danger. When the posse arrived on the ground, they found the robbers in full flight, and gave instant chase. Doc Reed and Thomas Arnet were so closely pursued, that they hid in the brush along Mill creek, to let their pursuers pass by. Reed secreted himself beneath the overhanging bank, one of the posse passing directly over his head, the pursuer's life being spared because a pistol shot would have brought others to the spot. One of the gang, named McKenzie, or Reynolds, was captured near the old race track, three miles above the city, and immediately hanged, cursing his executioners with his last breath. A party of the vigilantes followed the cattle trail in the direction of Wallula, and soon found the stolen animals in charge of William Wills and Isaac Reed. They summarily hanged these two and took charge of the cattle. Of the gang of six, three were thus disposed of, and Doc Reed, Arnet and Sage Brush Jack escaped and never returned to the valley.

A few days later the committee executed a negro, known as Slim Jim. He was one of the hard characters whom they had requested to depart from the city, but who had failed to comply with their reasonable demand. At a secret meeting, a sentence of death was voted, and that same night he was taken from his bed, conducted nearly a mile south of town and hanged upon a tree, which is still called "hangman's tree." It is claimed by some that Slim Jim did not deserve this fate, and that personal enmity was the cause of his delivery into the hands of his executioners. The committee met in secret, the accused not being present or allowed opportunity to make a defense; and upon what evidence the verdict of death was based, can never be fully known. It is certain that he was given ample warning and failed to heed it.

The next demonstration was made on the night of May 23, 1865, when an old man, named Saunders, was taken from him cabin by four of the committee, and in spite of the piteous appeals of himself and his aged wife, was perforated with bullet holes. His body was found next day near the mouth of the Tumalum. The reason assigned for this outrage was that Saunders had threatened the lives of some of the committee; but it soon transpired that the whole affair was the result of a family quarrel, and that the old man had done nothing to entitle him to punishment. A majority of the committee disapproved this hasty act of a few of their number, while many of them at once severed their connection with the organization, desiring to have nothing to do with a society whose members could use it to settle their personal or business quarrels. Men who did not belong to the committee were much excited and alarmed at the prospect of such a powerful secret organization summarily disposing of men who had committed no crime, and every one who had a personal enemy in the committee had fears that he, too, might receive an unwelcome midnight visit. Of course, the secrecy and mystery connected with the affair tended to exaggerate it in the minds of those not familiar with all the facts. The truth was, that members of the committee having done the act, the others felt obliged to sustain them; and though a number ceased thereafter to act with the organization, others, just as good and substantial citizens, believing the object of the society not yet accomplished still persevered in their efforts to rid the country of its horde of thieves.

July 21, 1865, a negro named Green had some difficulty about a land claim, with a man named Wells, whose arm he nearly lopped off with a drawing-knife. The vigilantes captured him after a long chase, and strung him up to the limb of a tree at the foot of the mountains. The result of this act was to discourage the prevailing idea that a man was justified in carving or shooting every one with whom he had a personal controversy.

In the fall of 1865, a stage was robbed near Burnt river, and a gold bar and quite a sum of money secured by the highwaymen. When one of the passengers arrived in Walla Walla, he claimed to recognize one of the robbers in the person of William H. Lamar, a plasterer, who had resided in the city for some time. A strict watch was kept upon the suspected man's movements, to see if he would not, in some way, furnish evidence that would convict him or give a clue to the hiding place of the treasure. Finally, the vigilantes were satisfied of his guilt, and decided that it was useless to delay action longer. Late in the evening of October 31, 1865, Lamar was decoyed to the edge of the city, near the brewery on Second street, upon the pretense of examining a job of plastering. Some of the vigilantes secreted themselves in the bushes along the stream flowing past the brewery. As the party came to the foot board across the stream, Lamar's companions halted and allowed him to cross alone. As soon as he stepped out upon the board, six or seven shots were quickly fired from the bushes, and his dead body fell over into the water.

For several months thereafter, the committee confined itself to quietly notifying undesirable parties who came to the city, to take their departure again, and no overt act was committed.

In February, 1866, Ferd Patterson, for years one of the most noted desperadoes on the coast, came down from the Boise mines. He expressed great contempt for the committee, and publicly insulted the head of the organization. Thomas Donahue, one of the night police, had once arrested Patterson in Portland, for the crime of murder, and when the latter saw him here he expressed an intention of killing him. Donahue heard of this threat, and decided to do the killing himself. Early in the morning of the fifteenth, he entered Bogle's barber shop and shot Patterson, who was sitting in a chair and being shaved. The wounded man jumped up and ran into Welch's saloon, whither Donahue followed him and dispatched him with two more shots from the revolver. After Donahue's arrest, the excited sports threatened to take him from the jail and hang him. Because Patterson was on their black list, the vigilantes endorsed the act of Donahue, and declared their intention of protecting him. The excitement was great, but the committee was too powerful to be resisted, and four months later they aided the prisoner to escape. In September he was arrested in San Francisco, but the vigilantes again came to the expenses of releasing him from the toils of the law in that city.

On the 9th of June, 1866, the committee published a manifesto, calling attention to the result of their efforts, and announcing that arrangements had been made whereby it would be rendered still more effective than in the past. A month later they made their last midnight raid. A man named Richa was accused of having attempted an outrage upon the person of a little girl, and he was seized by them and tried for the offense. The family who were said to have suffered at his hands appeared at the trial and testified that he had done nothing beyond the making of an improper proposal to the young girl's mother. Richa was acquitted of the charge and released from custody by the committee, and for a time it was generally supposed he had taken his departure from the country; but on the morning of July 14th, 1866, his headless body was found under a tree on the bank of Walla Walla river, the head being still suspended from a rope secured to a limb of the tree above. It then transpired that four of the vigilantes, being displeased, for personal reasons, with the acquittal and release of Richa, had taken him from the farm house where he was employed, and hanged him, the body remaining suspended until it had been severed at the neck.

This was the last act of the committee, and it was fitting, that, when members could so take advantage of their connection with the organization to commit such outrages upon peaceful citizens with impunity, it should disband as having lived beyond the period of its usefulness. Thereafter the committee used its power only for the protection of its members, and to prevent any official investigation of its conduct. In the times of its greatest strength, both political parties had been brought under its complete control, and it dictated the election of county and city officers, and the selection of grand juries too blind to see these unlawful acts. It still maintained this political ascendency, the people gradually arraying themselves into two factions, vigilante and anti-vigilante.

In 1867, the law and order citizens called a mass meeting, nominated an independent ticket, and succeeded in electing the sheriff. The district judge advised no investigation, and thus the matter ended.

Levi Ankeny

Account books and letters of
an early Lewiston business man, mayor and
later U.S. Senator, tell of conditions
in a mining supply town in the 1860's.

Pioneer days of Lewiston, Idaho, were vividly brought to the minds of old timers recently by the finding of a lot of private letters, bills (receipted), book accounts and papers of more than 40 years of age in the Martin Meuli building, which has been razed to make room for a three story brick hotel. Most of the documents were the property of Ankeny & Son. Mr. Ankeny is now United States senator from Washington. The accounts were those of Hexter & Braiter, who did most of their trading with San Francisco.

The finding of the papers created no little interest and many examined the papers and books, which had been brought to light by the workmen.

All the notes, which had been cancelled, bore the civil war revenue stamp, the number depending upon the amount involved. Many of the letters were written before postage stamps were plentiful in what is now Idaho, it then being a territory, and in lieu of the stamp the postmaster wrote on one corner of the envelope "paid," showing that the envelope had a right to be transported through the mails. Some of the envelopes were of the pattern of 1855, when the government so cut the paper from which the envelope was folded that three black lines showed through the front, to assist the writer in writing the address straight across the face of the envelope.

That greenbacks were not worth their face value in this section of the country then was shown by some of the accounts. They were accepted as legal tender at a discount of 45 cents on the dollar. Gold dust was used in great quantities, as the accounts showed, credits being given on bills for so many ounces of the yellow metal. That firms in those days did an enormous credit business is attested by the size of the account books. Everybody seemed to buy on credit. And in those days when Lewiston's population was largely floating, people going to and from the mining camps beyond, it would be thought that giving credit would be a risky piece of business, the chance being taken of a man passing through and never returning. But the fact that almost all the accounts were at one time or another closed by payment of discounted greenbacks or gold, shows that honesty existed then.

An interesting feature of the accounts was the prices that were paid for goods in Lewiston in those gold excitement days. Flour was worth 13 cents per pound. Hams and bacon never sold for less than 40 cents a pound. These prices prevailed between 1863 and 1865. No accounts were found later than the latter date. Garden seeds brought $2.50 a package. The variety and size were not shown by the notation in the sales book or receipted bill. Sugar sold for 50 cents a pound, the retail bills showing that it was not used in large quantities. Miners' shovels which were sold in large numbers, one or two at a time, were worth $6 each. Pick handles brought the same. Beans were sold in vast quantities at 30 cents a pound, and rice at 40 cents.

There were oysters here at that time, not in bulk, but in cans, and they sold readily at $2.50 a can. Rubber boots were worth $15 a pair, and mustard, pepper and similar spices sold at $1 a box. Tea sold for $1.15 a pound.

Many of the envelopes addressed to Levi Ankeny & Son were in stamped envelopes of the 3-cent variety, upon which the Wells, Fargo & Co., had printed their notice to the effect that the charges--usually 50 cents--for delivery to points where Uncle Sam did not go had been paid. Some of the letters were delivered by Ramsey & Co.'s express at a charge of 50 cents above the postage, and others bore the printed statement "Hunt & Hart's Warrens Express, Paid 50 cents."

Barney Owsley

A Missourian,
not content with Civil War strife,
heads for the gold fields of Idaho in 1861.

I was born March 29, 1847, in Cooper County, Missouri. In 1861 we started from Missouri, heading west to the Northwest Territory, as conditions were not comfortable in Missouri due to the Civil War. We thought there would be better opportunities in the far west. We had four yoke of oxen when we started and reached here with three head. I walked all the way from South Pass. The last house I saw was on the Loop Fork of the Platte. The first one I saw on this side was the Indian Agency at Umatilla. By the time we reached La Grande our food was gone and we waited there until our scouts went ahead to the agency and returned with supplies.

We left the wagon train at Umatilla, and started for Walla Walla, the straggling village on Mill Creek. There we learned that we could get work up the Touchet. We followed the trail as far as a wagon could go. That brought us to "Stubb's" place where he had built a cabin and lived there with his squaw. His real name was Schnebley and the land afterwards became the townsite of Dayton. "Stubbs" was killed in the Okanogan country, while running government horses across the border.

Davis and Whetstone had located in what is known as Whetstone Hollow, and father hired out to him to get logs from the Blue Mountains to put up their cabins, so we went up in the mountains and built a cabin of logs where we spent that first winter, which turned out to be the most talked-of winter in the history of this country.

We had been told that the winters were mild and we could work outside in our shirt sleeves. It began to snow and kept on snowing. Our cabin was completely covered. We had to keep shoveling the snow away, but we got along some way.

During the following April, when my father, brother and I started for the Florence mines, we went up over the Alpowa hills. They were covered with ice from the snow that had packed there during the winter. We dropped down into the Snake River Valley, to find the grass green and Indians camped at the mouth of the Alpowa. That was Chief Timothy's home. Many a time in later years I was to see this encampment and accept the hospitality of the friendly chief, who never lifted a hand against the whites.

We found ten thousand men in the Florence mines, and the good claims all staked. They were taking out $6,000 a day with rockers. We didn't stay long, but went down to the Salmon River Valley and spent the winter. Flour was $2.50 a pound and bacon the same.

I was 16 years old in the spring of 1863; my brother, Dick, was older. He killed a big elk in the Salmon River Valley, and we packed that to Florence and sold it for $1.00 a pound. That kept us going for awhile. The woods were full of huckleberries, so when they got ripe we sold them for $5.00 a gallon. I could pick two gallons a day.

Two men whipsawed some lumber for father, and he made a skiff and we crossed the Salmon and went south. We drifted around, hearing of diggings here and there and finally returned to the Pataha.

Two miles above the place where the trails crossed the creek, a man named Sunderland had located. I went up to the mountians and got out logs for him and helped build his log cabin, the first on the site of the present Pomeroy, but the town started a long time after that.

I started packing to the mines and stayed with it six years. In 1863, Colonel Craig put his ferry on the Snake river between the present sites of Lewiston and Clarkston. The former was not long in becoming a town, but Clarkston was only a horse pasture for a long time. A man named Greenfield had a horse ranch on that side of the river. John Silcott had a ferry on the Snake river. His wife was Chief Timothy's daughter, Jane. When I'd go to Montana with a pack train, I would stop there. She was a good friend of mine.

Every kind of merchandise needed at the mines was packed in on the backs of mules; mining machinery, tools, tables for the gamblers, food and clothing. Expert skill and judgment were required to prevent over-loading and the wrong kind of packing. Flour was one of the most difficult articles to pack. Three hundred and fifty pounds of merchandise were considered a good average load for a mule. Each pack train was led by a bell horse with a rider. The rider was also the cook. Forty-five mules was a five-man train, and twenty-three a three-man train. Sometimes we would be gone for months. President Lincoln was assassinated a year before I heard of it.

I packed to Fort Colville and to the Coeur d'Alene mines, through the Palouse and Spokane countries, stopping at George Lucas' on Cow Creek. Many a time we played checkers together and George always won. At the forks of the Palouse, where the town of Colfax was later founded, there was nothing but brush.

While operating a pack train into the Idaho mountains, during the Chief Joseph war, I brushed into the retreating Joseph and his warriors. I discovered my dilemma in time to escape with a whole skin, but I deserted my pack train to do it. When Chief Joseph had passed, I went back and found horses and cargo largely intact, though Joseph's men had tapped a whiskey barrel and consumed considerable of it. This episode was one of my big moments.

The moderate climate of the lower Grande Ronde river and the Imnaha canyon attracted me. I moved my herd to that region, where in cold weather the stock grazed on the river bank and moved up on the hills in summer time. At the very point where engineers are now building the Shumaker grade, I found abundant pasture. I should have stuck to it, as it was a great stock country.

I crossed the Spokane river on Joe Herron's ferry, seven miles above the falls, often stopping there to fish. I could have owned the site on which Spokane was built. The townsite of Lewiston was offered to me for thirty dollars. It was traded by the owner, Mr. West, for a horse. Mr. West was homesick for trees, so he crossed to the Washington side and rode on and on until he sighted the feathery tops of pines against the skyline.

By 1866 enough farmers had located in the Touchet Valley to call for a grist mill. It was built at Long's, now the site of Long's Station. The method of threshing and winnowing wheat was primitive. I remember seeing Elisha Ping at his ranch on the Patit above Dayton, cleaning his grain in an old fanning mill, after tramping it out with horses.

I took grain to Long's mill in 1866 and had it ground and packed a whole train to Boise and another to Orofino. My uncle, Jesse Day, lived on the Touchet, and raised a lot of hogs. He made bacon, which I packed and sold for a dollar a pound. Uncle Jesse took the money and bought the land of Schnebley where Dayton now stands. Schnebley had a log house where travelers stopped for meals and to spend the night.

Archie and Frank McCrearty were here when we came. So was James Bower. He owned the site of Pataha City. "Parson" Quinn had a squatter's claim on Pataha Creek. Billy Freeman and "Aunt Ellen" ran the stage station on Alpowa Creek. I stopped there many a time. Aunt Ellen was a famous cook.

I knew Jerry MacQuire, said to be the first permanent settler on Asotin Creek. He was a big Irishman, handy with his fists. His wife was a squaw, yet Jerry had a lot fights with Indians. The hills were full of Jerry's horses, at least a thousand of them. His brand was a horse's head.

One day while in the hills, he ran into a band of hostile Indians. They were sixteen to one, but Jerry had the advantage. Beside him was a pile of rocks, apparently made to order. These he used with such unerring aim that the redskins fled.

Indians wintered in the Asotin where it empties into the Snake, as well as at the mouth of the Alpowa. The apple trees planted for Red Wolf by the missionary, Rev. Spalding, were still there on Chief Timothy's ranch. Many a time I enjoyed their fruit. The trees grew from seedlings, so the apples were small and of inferior quality, yet they were a treat in the early days, when fruit was scarce.

The Nez Perce was a fine type of Indian. When I first knew Timothy, he was about thirty-five years old. His wealth consisted of horses. It was Timothy who saved the Steptoe expedition from utter failure. He crossed the Steptoe command over the Snake River under cover of darkness and they went on to Walla Walla. I heard Timothy preach a number of times.

This was a stock country at first. Newton Estes, on the Deadman Creek, had a lot of cattle. J.M. Pomeroy brought in the roan Durham. Truly, there were "cattle on a thousand hills." The farming was all done in the valleys along the streams. Then it was discovered that wheat could be raised on the hills. From that time farmers turned their attention to wheat raising, especially after Dr. Baker's road was finished.

Steamboats ran on the Snake River and several shipping points were established. There was one at New York Bar, another at Grange City. Almota was a lively little shipping point in the early days.

When the government built the road over the Lola Trail, I packed to the 200 men at the construction camps. There I saw Col. Craig. He had settled on land on the Idaho side in the 30's, later taking it as his donation claim. Col. Craig, Doc Newell and Louis Raboin came from St. Louis to trap for the Hudson's Bay Company. They were all "squaw men." Col. Craig established the first ferry on the Snake river. Doc Newell became Indian agent at Lapwai and Louis Raboin, or "Marengo," as he was known, settled on the Tucanon, just three miles over the hills from the site of my ranch in later years, and I knew him well. He was there in the 50's when Governor Stevens and his party of surveyors passed that way. Later the town of Marengo was named for him. He was always fighting mosquitoes when he was trapping in the Pend Oreille country and his companions named him

"Maringouin," French for mosquito. Spelling it the way it sounded changed the name to Marengo.

In 1869 I settled on Pataha Creek, four and one-half miles from the present site of Pomeroy. I homesteaded and bought land and my farm covered three thousand acres, part of it being the "Parson" Quinn place. I had loaned him some money and one day he appeared and insisted upon giving me a deed.

The Grange put up a rough lumber building on my ranch and held their meetings. Other meetings were held there and later the building was used for a school house.

Game was always plentiful. When I ran out of meat I took my pack-horse and went up into the Blue Mountains, returning very soon with a deer. There were thousands of prairie chickens along the Tucanon; they fed on birch buds in the winter. Grouse hatched along the Tucanon in the spring.

In 1874 there was talk of dividing Walla Walla county. Elisha Ping was in the territorial legislature at that time and he used his influence to form a new county with Dayton as the county seat. He wanted the county named Ping, but Columbia seemed more suitable to the majority, so in 1875 the new county was sliced off. Some wanted Marengo for the county seat, but Dayton received the most votes.

Practically all conspicuous Indians of an early date were on speaking terms with me, and I had frequent intercourse with them, over the poker table, or in a business sense. Red Elk, Mox-Mox and even Long John, the renegade, are listed in that respect. Long John's checkered career has in it ample material for thrilling western history.

And there was Cherokee Bob! Of that man I have vivid recollections. Cherokee Bob was a Georgia "breed" who came to Walla Walla when that place was wild and wooley, and Bob was not long in spinning a web of troubles about himself. During a theatrical production, some soldiers persisted in annoying the actresses. Cherokee Bob may have been a "breed," but he had a sense of chivalry not understood by some westerners. Cherokee Bob warned once, then shot. Six soldiers "bit the dust" and Bob scooted for Florence. Soon he was in trouble there, and again over a woman. In the shoot-off which followed, with a man named Jack Williams, Bob's weapons having been tampered with by the woman over whom they fought, Bob's finish was foreordained. His remains lie at Florence, now a city of "bats and ghosts," under a rapidly disintegrating plank marker.

I engaged in stock-raising and sold my cattle to Dooley and Kirkman of the Figure 3 ranch. I homesteaded and bought land until I had 3,000 acres where I raised these cattle and part of my herd was raised in Asotin county.

In 1877 a buyer came in and I went with him to drive the cattle out. On the way back I heard that Chief Joseph was on the warpath and his warriors were killing the whites. Families were rushing from all parts of the country to forts that were being hastily constructed. At first I couldn't believe it. Chief Joseph was a friend of mine, a highly respected one. He had never made any trouble, asking only that he and his tribe might dwell in the valley which was his birthplace.

I joined the company that was organized, and did scout duty, going as far as Kamaia. Joseph retreated, entered Montana, kept up a running fight and retreat which lasted three months. Finally he surrendered to General Miles near Bear Paw Mountain.

The trouble started over the possession of the Wallowa Valley, the land given to Old Chief Joseph in the treaty of 1855. There they lived happily and peacefully for years. It was an ideal place for anybody, white or red. Wallowa lake was full of sockeye salmon. Worlds of elk and deer came down from the hills in the fall and roamed along the river. There was small game of every description. In the spring there were roots of all kinds, and berries in the summer. It was sheltered in winter, cool in summer, and nothing more was needed or desired by the Indians.

White men coveted this Paradise, and the land was taken by them. Chief Joseph blamed Lawyer, saying, "If I had a horse and you wanted to buy it and I said 'no,' and you went to another man and he sold my horse to you, would that be right? That is just what you have done. You have sold land that did not belong to you."

When the young men of the tribe became restless in 1873, President Grant again turned the valley over to them, but in 1875 the order was revoked. From that time there was trouble. The Indians refused to leave. Stock was killed. Soldiers sent to reinforce the order of removal were ambushed and killed and the war was on. Chief Joseph was never allowed to again look upon the valley where he was born.

Returning from the war in 1877, I found that a grist mill was being built. Ben Day built a store. Carnahan had a saloon. The town of Pomeroy was starting.

The skeleton of an old mill marks the site of the first town in what is now Garfield county. That was Columbia Center, a thriving little village of the '70's. A man named Stimson, miller and mill wright, built the mill, also building one on the Alpowa. In 1876 he and his family entered the Asotin country, settling at Anatone. It was there I met his daughter, Harriet, when I went into the Grand Ronde Valley to raise cattle in 1878. We were married in 1879 and spent a year on Joseph Creek right across from Old Chief Joseph's ranch.

My cattle range was where the Grande Ronde empties into the Snake. When we were living on Joseph Creek, I was coming along the trail through the alders one day, when I discovered a cave. I explored it and found plenty of room for a good-sized camp, so I moved in. It extended far back and I chose a good place for my fire where the smoke drifted out through a crevice.

My father and another man visited me there at times and we cooked our meat and sourdough over the fire, using forked sticks. Years after I had abandoned the camp, the newspapers carried the announcement that a cave had been discovered that bore evidence of having been occupied in pre-historic days. It seems the cave-men had left forked sticks, ashes and a moccasin. These were sent to the Smithsonian Institute.

On the homestead on the Pataha, now known as the Wesley Steele place, we had a race track for training and race meet purposes. Some of the finest horse-flesh of the period capered over that track. Of all the horses I owned, Bob Mill, sired by Jim Miller, out of a strain of Kentucky runners, brought to Salem, was the favorite. Faster horses then than now? Sure. More interest and better horses.

For many years beginning with 1869 the Pataha homestead was headquarters for our family. When we came out of the Grande Ronde Valley in 1884, my farm on the Pataha was in Garfield county, the new county cut out of Columbia county in 1881. I paid taxes on the same piece of land in three counties.

In 1883 Asotin county was formed from the eastern end of Garfield. Each time there was a division I wondered whether the new county would ever "stand alone" but the past fifty years have proved that no worry was necessary.

I might say that I have voted during 73 years, voting the first time at the mines when I was 18 years old, with two guns held over me.

Chapter **6**

Building and Civilizing

"I remember when Seattle
boasted of being as large
as Walla Walla."
W.H. Kirkman

*G*old provided the wealth necessary to bring more settlers to the Inland Empire. Blacksmiths were needed to shoe animals, leather workers for making harness, and farmers to till the soil. Merchants, packers, tinners and all sorts of men and women moved to the new country, hammering, sawing and working hard to civilize the new land. Small towns soon formed, scattered at the base of the Blue Mountains.

As the gold miners moved further east into Montana and were able to get cheaper supplies from the Missouri River drainage, the mining supply business gradually declined in the Inland Empire. Fortunately, another discovery was made that would prove to be more valuable than that of gold. It had been thought that wheat would only grow in the rich bottom lands of the river valleys, but the enterprising farmers found that wheat would grow on the rolling hills that extended from nearly one end of the Inland Empire to the other. This grain growing area, the Palouse, provided the wealth to extend the building and civilizing of the region.

Small towns like Walla Walla kept growing and as the merchants prospered, churches were built and schools were opened. Railroads were first dreamed about and then built. The first railroad in Washington Territory was finished in 1872 and operated between Wallula on the Columbia River and Walla Walla, twenty-nine miles inland. With the completion of the railroad and its feeder lines into the wheat country, freight rates dropped and more wheat was produced.

Life on the frontier wasn't easy--lots of hard work was necessary just to get by. Many of the newcomers prospered however, and those without family sent for their sweethearts and all settled down to raise families. Each year saw more emigrants heading for the Northwest. After 1860, most trains heading for Oregon split in the Grande Ronde valley and part of the settlers came to the new Walla Walla country. Let's join one of these settlers, Andrew Jackson Evans, who chose to come to this country because of what he called "vegetable talk".

Andrew Jackson Evans

1861 wagon trail arrival
finds work hauling freight
between the Columbia River and Walla Walla.

Andrew Jackson Evans was born September 2, 1842, at Portsmouth, Ohio, son of Mr. and Mrs. George Evans, and was one of a family of ten children.

Mr. Evans, senior, was a stone-mason, and on account of the small wages he received, and large family to provide for, he decided to come west where he and his sons could take up land and not have to depend on the wages of their native state for a livelihood. The sons, as soon as old enough, used to spend most of the time during the summer in the fields, hoeing corn, receiving a wage of 10 or 15 cents per day.

The start west was made in 1860, when the journey was continued as far as Sidney, Iowa. The teams consisted entirely of horses. At Sidney, Mr. Evans was told that he did not have the right kind of an outfit for "crossing the plains." He then decided to delay his trip until the next year and in the meantime make the necessary changes in his equipment for the long journey. One of the changes was replacing the horses with oxen and cows; the latter were yoked with the oxen and shared the burden of drawing the wagons.

The spring "round up" of emigrants rendezvoused at a point on the Missouri river and the start was made May 16, 1861. At Platte these wanderers joined with more westward bound travelers, increasing the train to thirty-six wagons.

Mr. Evans, senior, started for California, but changed his mind at Raft river, Wyoming, at the forks of the continental road, one branch going to California the other going to the Northwest.

At this point they fell in with William Babcock who had settled on a part of the William Reser place southeast of the city, and was returning from a trip east, bringing his family.

He spoke in glowing terms of the fertility of the soil, the fine bunch grass, the fat cattle and great amounts of vacant land of the Walla Walla Valley, dwelling at length on the fine vegetables growing his garden.

The "vegetable talk" Mr. Evans believes was the most convincing of Mr. Babcock's arguments, as it appealed with great force to the travelers who had not tasted vegetables for months. Mr. Babcock concluded his argument with, "come with me and I will kill a fat beef and give you a feast."

Some of the undecided ones remained up all night discussing the California or Northwest question. One man said:

"Well, I can't decide this question."

Picking up a stick and holding it up on the ground, he said:

"Whichever direction this falls I go."

Removing his hand, the stick fell toward California. "Well," he remarked, "I'm going the other way anyhow," and he did.

The next morning a train bearing sixty-four people, led by Mr. Babcock, started for the Walla Walla Valley. The country traveled through was not in the least attractive until La Grande was reached. When the train arrived at the point in the Blue Mountains where travelers got a view of the valley for the first time, "It looked good to us," Mr. Evans said, "and there was great rejoicing among the weary immigrants, realizing that the long journey was so near the end."

Mr. Babcock piloted the train to his home where the travelers camped and rested. He made good his promise of the feast, when these tired wayfarers were served a bountiful supply of good fat beef and fresh vegetables, the first food of the kind they had eaten in more than three and a half months.

After a rest here, Mr. Evans, Sr., rented the Winnett home, east of the city on Mill Creek, now known as the McWhirk farm. The building was a log cabin, about 16 x 20 feet and here the entire family with the exception of one son and family lived.

The boys went out in every direction looking for work, to earn dollars which were much needed. Work was scarce. Mr. Evans' first work was in harvesting a small field of grain which included the present site of the Dement mill. For his work here, he made $15.00, $1.50 per day and board. He says he felt rich when he received that amount of money.

The favorable impressions made on the minds of emigrants by the Walla Walla Valley received a rude shock when winter came. A few days before Christmas, snow fell; then cold weather; then more and more snow and cold weather until the snow was three feet deep and in some places much deeper and had a heavy crust on it. How low the temperature was then, no one knew, as there were no thermometers here then.

Mr. Evans' father and older brother urged the other boys of the family to go to California. "They would not," Mr. Evans states, "and the father could not, so the question was settled." Mr. Evans' reason for not complying with his father's wish was that he liked the country and saw a bright future for Washington, and he has never been sorry he remained.

When spring came the boys went out in search of work. "Any kind just so it was work." Mr. Evans secured employment on the Dan Sheets farm Northwest of Walla Walla.

As soon as the cows and oxen took on sufficient flesh to give them strength to work, Mr. Evans and brother, Edmund, yoked the six survivors of the winter to a wagon and went to Wallula to haul freight. The load they brought back was the first freight to arrive for the Schwabacker Bros., the largest mercantile company in Eastern Washington at that time. This business has been purchased by Gardner and Company, of the present time.

The young men, (Mr. Evans was not twenty-one then), had some remarkable experiences. On the way down, the Touchet river was normal and was easily forded by the team. When they returned the stream had risen to such a height that the drivers did not consider it safe to attempt a crossing with the freight in the wagon, so they took it all out and carried it across the river on a footlog. Freight at that time was packed in small bundles, instead of boxes as at the present time. The oxen swam across the swollen stream arriving safely on the opposite side with the wagon in perfect condition ready to continue the homeward trip. The load weighed a ton and a half and the price received for it was 2 cents a pound.

Mr. Evans and his brother increased their team to twelve oxen. The animals were brought here from Oregon. Their scope of activities extended to Colville, Ft. Colville, Lewiston and Boise. They also hauled freight for the Schwabacker firm to Colville; for this freight they received four and five cents per pound. Sometimes the trip for the freight was made to Umatilla. Other teams went as far as The Dalles.

"We made good money," Mr. Evans said. "We did not have to feed the oxen through the summer. Whether at home or on the trip they lived entirely on the bunch grass and thrived on it."

The freighting business was continued for seven years when Mr. Evans rented a small farm, four miles east of Walla Walla on Mill Creek, and March 24, 1867, was married to Mrs. James Evans. Mr. and Mrs. Evans are the parents of Attorney Marvin Evans of this city and Mrs. Evans is the mother of Emmett Evans of this county.

In 1871 Mr. Evans took a homestead of 160 acres a short distance north of Dry Creek. This land has been added to until it is now more than twelve hundred acres, and on this, which is six miles north of the city, Mr. and Mrs. Evans make their home.

Mr. and Mrs. Andrew Evans moved to the city many years ago and in 1886 built their present home which they have occupied ever since.

Mr. Evans accompanied his brother, James, who was sick, to San Francisco on the way to Honolulu, for the benefit of the latter's health. The sick man was taken to one of San Francisco's prominent physicians, who pronounced the case incurable and advised Mr. Evans to start home at once with him. The return trip was made on the first north bound steamer, but a delay of several days was caused by the schedule at that time. James Evans did not survive the trip, passing away at Portland.

The ocean trip south was made on the steamer Brother Jonathan. On the return trip it was lost with all on board.

During the stay at San Francisco, news of the surrender of General Robert E. Lee was received. There was great rejoicing, parades, many demonstrations. Cannon had been brought up in the city and a national salute fired in honor of the victory. Following this salute, news of the assassination of Lincoln arrived. All demonstrations of joy ceased.

The authorities had learned of the intention of bands of Southern sympathizers to start an anti-demonstration, with mob violence, and the city was put under martial law for three days. Mr. Evans says those were the longest three days of his life, as he was not allowed to leave the hotel for that length of time.

"The population of Walla Walla was about 300 when I came here," Mr. Evans remarked, "and it would not have been that large, if it had not been for the mines."

There have been many changes since Mr. Evans arrived here. Washington was at that time a territory and extended to the Rocky Mountains, including all of northern Idaho and a part of Montana. Walla Walla was the largest town in the territory and Walla Walla county extended from the present western boundary to the eastern territorial line, a distance of more than 300 miles, which is greater than the distance from the western boundary to the coast. Olympia, the capital, was the largest town on the west side.

R.R. Rees

An ardent suitor pleads his case
in the court of love, hoping for
an affirmative answer and soon, please!
Miss Ward lived in Portland, Oregon in 1863.

Walla Walla, December 27, 1863

Augusta:

"Consider well before you make a promise," is an old and a wise proverb. This you have placed yourself in a position to do with reference to my proposal to you; and while I freely admit that I respect you all the more for doing so, I acknowledge that this waiting between doubt and uncertainty is by no means pleasant to me. Feeling thus, I have sat down to-night to write to you, and, if possible, to give you something more of an insight as to "what manner of man" I am so that you may be able the sooner to make up your *verdict*. However I am not going to assume the position of an attorney and plead my case, but simply intend to "talk" with you. Our intercourse has not been of such a nature as to allow us to become *lovers* in the sentimental sense of that term, though we have been intimate enough and long enough acquainted to have obtained a very general idea of each others' leading characteristics--to know, at least, that each is capable of experiencing the emotions of the "divine passion." But as I am not an adept either in writing or talking love, I drop this question with the remark that while I believe in matrimonial alliances, it should be the *first* consideration, I by no means think it should be the *only* one. You said today that you "did not think you would suit me as a wife," etc. Well, such a one as I want I think you would make, and it's easy told what kind of a one I would and would not like. First, I should not like such a one as is described in the song of "I Should Like to Marry--the beauty of the ballroom, the dandy of them all." As your namesake, 'Artemus' says, "Not by no means" would such a one suit me. But I should want her,

> "The darling of *my own home*
> The tidiest of them all"

a *woman* competent to superintend such a place, and one who would study her husband's best interests in superintending it. Not a plaything, to meet me with a frown at every mishap or when I failed to call her 'pet names' every time I went home tired and care-worn from my business; but a *woman* who could love me for *myself* and could never imagine that I loved anyone else better than her. "Now, my dear," as Mrs. Candle says, "don't you think you would fill the bill?"

I believe I told you, or at least attempted to tell you, my circumstances. I will repeat: a little more than two years ago, having lost the hard-earnings of five or six years by a bad land investment, I came here more than five hundred dollars in debt, and my partner was in a like situation. His history and fate you know. Under the adverse circumstances that surrounded me in consequence of his sickness, during my first year here, by constant application, I managed to save enough to pay our indebtedness. Since then, in conjunction with my brother, we have made enough to purchase the building we occupy. So, I own half the office and building -- and out of debt, and have nearly enough to buy and furnish me a *home*. This I intend to do before I get married, and if no misfortune befalls me, will be able to do. So long before this time next year, by practising economy, I can make a good living, and perhaps a little more. Still, my possessions are in such a shape that I am liable by accident, to lose them in a day; and if I should, I can only do as I have done before: commence, with my hands as my only capital, and climb the hill again. Could I not do it as well with a 'helpmate' as I have done it without one? and would you shudder at such a prospect? If so "consider well before you promise." This much for my pecuniary affairs. It sums up that I am not rich and have only myself to offer you. I don't know what else I can say in relation to myself, save what, perhaps any of my acquaintances could say for me. I have no intemperate habits worse than smoking and chewing, neither of which I consider particularly bad, nor yet at all commendable.

I may add here, while upon the subject of appetite, that I have a fondness for *good dinners*, and could love the individual equally well who cooked them, *provided she was my wife; though I wouldn't eat her*. Now, don't lay too much *stress* upon those words "equally well." Of course, when you have "considered well" in this matter, it is your duty *first* to consult your parents before giving me a definite answer; for they are the *best friends* you ever had. You will pardon my trick, but to ascertain whether you had done this was what I wanted to find out today. Next to being a first choice as a husband, I should want to be that as a son-in-law; for I should expect to regard them as parents and should expect to be esteemed by them as a son.

I said in the beginning of this that waiting in uncertainty was unpleasant to me. It is not so because I am in a hurry to get married, for as before indicated, I should prefer to wait awhile; but if your answer if favorable I could feel that I had a better and more welcome right to come and see you, and that my visits were acceptable to your parents as well as to yourself. If your answer is to be no, I would rather have it now than after awhile. But I have written enough, and will conclude by saying that I believe I could make a good husband to a good and true wife.

Hoping you will reply to this, I subscribe

Yours truly,

R.R. Reese

Miss Augusta M. Ward

The matter of my asking you to become my wife was not from the impulse of a moment, but from months of consideration.

R.

Cora Clark

*There were
good and bad times
setting up a household
on the frontier.*

I was born in 1863. My father crossed the plains in 1852 and settled in the Willamette Valley. He served in the Rogue River war in 1855-56. Mother crossed the plains in 1859, coming straight to Walla Walla. Father brought his cattle up from Oregon and located on the Walla Walla river two and one-half miles from Touchet in 1859. He was attracted by the fine pasture land and the stream. Our nearest store was at Wallula. Father's timber claim was where the penitentiary now stands. My father was a government surveyor and my husband was the city engineer and engineer for the O.W.R. & N. railroad.

Walla Walla river was a much larger stream when we played along its banks in the 1860's and 1870's. We had a row boat. Our only playmates were two quarter-breed children. Their father was a white man. I was eight years old before I ever saw a white woman excepting my mother. Father's surveying duties kept him away quite a bit of the time, and mother and us children never had a way of traveling, and there were Indians prowling around.

We had a one-room log house with lean-to and a loft, reached by a ladder, where the boys slept. We cooked in the fireplace. Mother made the most delicious scones, dropping the dough in a frying pan which she placed in front of the fire. We hung our kettles on a crane.

One of the best meals my mother ever cooked, we had to run away from. It was in the year 1878. Our first new potatoes and peas made part of that dinner which I shall never forget. Father had brought down two wild ducks that morning and mother dressed them; then made a currant pie. Just as everything was on the table, a man dashed up on his horse, shouting, "Three hundred Indians on the warpath!"

Mother snatched a few trinkets and valuable papers and she and us children joined the procession of settlers on their way to the fort. Father refused to leave his place, but hid the most treasured possessions in the old dug-out which had been his first home. It was overgrown with grass and vines, so he felt it to be a safe hiding place. We met the soldiers, but no one turned back. There was no battle, and in a day or so we returned home.

We were near the old camping ground of the Indians. In the fall they came for choke cherries and black and red haws. They dried this fruit and from the farmers they bought or begged pumpkins, and stewed them and dried the pulp.

Frenchtown was not far away, where many of the French Canadians who were with the Hudson's Bay Company, had settled with their Indian wives.

The cattle trail went past our farm and the cowboys always bedded down on some vacant land near us, so they could be near water. They would come to the house and get milk and other provisions. One of the most wonderful sights of my childhood was 10,000 head of cattle being driven to Cheyenne.

Father drove his ox team to Wallula for provisions. He always bought in quantities. He bought calico and domestics by the bolt; coffee, tea and sugar and other necessities in large quantities. One time he drove the ox team to Wallula and "fast freight" had just been unloaded from a boat. It had to be in Walla Walla by sundwon. Freighters had horse teams at that time and they refused to take it, as it was a 32 mile drive with a heavy load. Father agreed to do it, and left Wallula at 4 o'clock in the morning. That evening, just as the sunset gun was fired at the fort, he pulled into Walla Walla with the load of freight.

We had no school when I was a child and never any church services, Sunday school, or anything of the kind.

Miles C. Moore

*Washington's last territorial governor
tells about his journey west in 1863
and the search for his "pile of gold."*

In thinking of my personal experience there always comes to my mind a letter written by Mark Twain in response to an invitation to attend a banquet
to be given in New York city to a few California pioneers. Mark Twain was
at that time living in Connecticut.

His letter expressed regret at his inability to be present but he said "in
order to satisfy you that I am eligible to membership I will relate that in the
early sixties I packed my blankets from Virginia City over the mountains to
Nevada City, a California mining town. There I found a job feeding a
quartz mill—and wished to God I was a quartz mill and had somebody to
feed me."

There were no quartz mills in Walla Walla at the time of my arrival and I
had to feed myself.

Most of us, I fancy, hoped to better our fortune in what seemed to be a
land of opportunity. Some of us heard "the call of the wild," another name
for the migratory instinct that is implanted in the breast of the average
human being. Curiosity to see what lay behind the horizon; to see the
wonderland of which I had read in tales of travel fired my youthful im-
agination, jarred me loose, as it were, from old associations and led to the
breaking of home ties. Gold discoveries in Idaho and Montana in the early
'60's lured many from their original habitat. As I was not quite 18 when my
journey began and had never been thrown upon my own resources, I did
not fully realize how important a substance gold was in the general scheme
of things, but was not long in learning.

Our little party consisted of a college professor, an uncle, a cousin and
myself. We set out with a four mule team and a canvas covered wagon
laden with provisions for the long journey to Montana. At Omaha, we attached ourselves to a train of emigrants traveling with ox teams and our
progress was not rapid. We left the Missouri river in May, 1863, and it was
August before we reached Bannack, a new mining town in Montana.

Looking backward, I can see this ox train of canvas covered wagons moving in slow procession up the Platte river over interminable plains, through
the South pass in the Rockies, through long stretches of sage brush country
beyond, and finally north on the road leading from Salt Lake to the new
mines in Montana. All this occurred in what was known as the "old whoa
haw times." No railroad had been built west of the Missouri river, the Pony
express and Ben Holiday's stage lines having been but recently established.

The first mining camp we visited was at Bannack, a little town on

Grasshopper creek, Montana, where gold had been discovered the previous year, 1862. After a few weeks spent there and having found out there was much dirt mixed with the gold, and having discovered how hard it was to dig, the professor, a young Chicago business man we had met on the plains, and myself started for Oregon. We were homesick for civilization but we were, as we used to say, "two thousand miles from home and all the way up hill," too far away to retrace our steps that year. A packer from the west side who camped near us told us of the attractions of the Willamette valley, describing it as "a land of big red apples and rosy cheeked girls, a white man's country." We decided to go to this paradise and were not long in making the necessary preparations. We hitched our two mules to a light wagon, bade farewell to my uncle and my cousin, to whose care I had been consigned, and turned our faces again to the westward.

A few days travel over a frightfully rough road brought us to Fort Owen. Major John Owens, for whom the post had been named, told us that he had just come through from Walla Walla, the timber was burning in the Coeur d'Alene mountains, that the bridges were gone, and that it would be necessary to exchange our wagon and harness for cayuse ponies. This was done. Pack saddles for the mules and Indian riding saddles for the ponies were procured. Hair ropes were utilized for bridles. After two days spent in learning the art of packing, throwing "the diamond hitch" and in fitting out, we left Fort Owens on our journey to Oregon. At Hell Gate, now Missoula, Montana, we found a trading post conducted by Captain Higgins, who had been a wagon master for Captain Mullan when he built the Mullan road. We purchased a few articles there and continued our journey along the Mullan road. This road we were informed ran to Walla Walla. The timber was burning and the bridges were gone as were told. A pack train returning from the mines had passed just ahead of us and by following its tracks we were able to find our way through the smoke.

Coming to the Coeur d'Alene mission, of which we had no previous knowledge, we were delighted to find that we could buy fresh meat, milk and vegetables and could sleep on the new mown hay in a barn. This was a luxury never to be forgotten and for which we were forever grateful to the good padres who conducted the mission. Two days later we arrived at the Antoine Plant ferry on the Spokane, a few miles above the present city of Spokane. We expected to go to Lewiston, having been told that steamboats carried passengers from there to Portland.

An Irishman whom we met there told us if we would wait until the following morning he would show us the Lewiston trail on the other side of the prairie. Accordingly we waited and in the early morning rode across the prairie.

We came to Indian trails, 20 or 30 of them running parallel. Our friend said "That is your trail, you cannot miss it," then bade us good-bye.

After traveling half a day we found ourselves again on the Mullan road, at a point not far beyond the present town of Spangle. Realizing that the

Mullan road ran to Walla Walla and fearing we might not find the Lewiston trail again we decided to go on to Walla Walla. We knew no one at Walla Walla, nor for that matter no one west of the Rocky mountains.

The loss of our trail was the circumstance that brought me to Walla Walla 56 years ago.

"The pebble in the streamlet scant has changed the course of many a river." The losing of the Lewiston trail changed the whole course of my life.

I used to tell my good wife that but for this circumstance I should not ever have had the pleasure of knowing her.

We continued on the Mullan road, crossing Snake river at the Silcott Ferry, now known as the Lyons Ferry, crossed the Touchet at the old Ben Flather's place, Dry creek at the John Sheet's place. Arriving at Walla Walla, we tied our horses in a clump of willows where the house of Mrs. Thomas Quinn now stands. I was asked to go down town and buy some beef steak while the Professor and Buchanan were to unpack the mules and make camp.

The bakery was conducted by O. Brechtel and was located on the site of the Strand theater. I asked for a loaf of bread and in payment laid on the counter a twenty-five cent "shin plaster" as fractional currency was called. Mr. Brechtel looked at it contemptuously and said "What's that?" I said that was government money and passed current in the country I came from. "Well," he said, "it doesn't go here." Fortunately I had a little gold dust and was able to pay for the loaf of bread. Mr. Brechtel was a very good man and I came to know him quite well, but never quite forgave him for the contempt he showed for my money.

We afterward put our mules and cayuse ponies in Tom Tierney's feed and sale stable. The mules were sold to James Truit, an old timer, who said, "being good Republicans, I suppose you boys would just as soon have greenbacks as gold in payment." But we replied, "If we were in a civilized country that would be all right, but we've been told that greenbacks are worth only about sixty cents on the dollar and we would like to have gold." He laughed and handed us 15 twenty dollar pieces which certainly looked good to us.

A few days later we were introduced to Captain John Mullan who had built the Mullan road from Walla Walla to Fort Benton. He took some interest and asked of our plans and invited us out to his country home, now the Harry Lasater place, the next day to dinner. We were very glad to accept the invitation. After dinner the following day, being Sunday we sat out under the shade of some locust trees and talked on various topics. During the conversation he told us that he was going in a few days on a prospecting trip to the lower Pend 'Oreille river and that if we cared to join the party, he would be glad to have us do so. He related that on Christmas day about 1862 he was taking dinner with some of the Jesuit missionaries, among them the Father De Smet--that during the dinner the conversation turned on the recent gold discoveries at Orofino and Elk City. He said, "In your wanderings around the mountains it is surprising that some of you did not find gold." A young priest said "We did," then waited for consent to proceed. He told how down at the old mission on the Pend 'Oreille river, 17 years before this, the Indians were digging a ditch and seeing some shining particles in the gravel, set up a shout, calling for the padres in charge to come down where they were. Fearing the discovery of gold would cause excitement and bring whites in great numbers and that would destroy their influence with the Indians, they were told to fill up the ditch.

Captain Mullan said he made a mental note of this and resolved when the road was completed he would go up there and rediscover the gold find.

This story, of course, greatly interested us and we accompanied the small party to the old mission. To shorten the story, the shining metal proved to be mica or fool's gold. A more disheartened and disgusted party than ours would be hard to find. Buchanan, the youngest member, and myself were utterly discouraged.

Returning to Walla Walla, I found that the Professor had opened a private school and had used the $200 I had left with him for safekeeping in buying desks and benches. Not feeling quite certain that he could ever repay me, I felt quite disconsolate and practically broke. I went every day to the postoffice hoping for letters from home. One day Alpheus Kyger of the firm of Kyger & Reese, an uncle of our townsman Dan Kyger, accosted me on the sidewalk saying, "Well, my boy, where are you from?" I replied from Alder Gulch, Montana. He asked what were my plans and I told him I was going to the Willamette valley. He then said "Don't go to the Willamette valley. I have lived there. You are in the best country in the world right here." A few days later he again spoke to me asking if I had found a job. When I said no, he said, "Well, bring your blankets up to our place Monday morning and we will try you out. If you please us you can stay here until you are greyheaded. If not, we will probably fire you in a couple of weeks." This was the beginning of my business career in Washington, about October, 1863.

In the few weeks spent with Captain Mullan, I became quite well acquainted with him and learned something of his history. He was born in Maryland and educated in West Point. He was with General Stevens' expedition when Stevens came to Washington as its first territorial governor. The expedition made a preliminary survey for the Northern Pacific railroad. He afterward had charge of the construction of the military road from Fort Benton, the head of navigation on the Missouri, to Walla Walla.

Points on this road where the present highways touch it, have been marked by suitable monuments in Montana and Idaho and our State Historical society is also moving in the matter. This is of much historic interest and will no doubt be favored by our Pioneer associations.

This road was supposed to be a military necessity, the idea being to connect the head of navigation on the Missouri at Fort Benton with the head of navigation on the Columbia, so that if Pacific sea ports were blockaded troops could be moved over this interior route. Fortunately there never was occasion to use it for the movement of troops--but packers and miners did find it a convenience.

Captain Mullan was a Southerner and a Southern sympathizer during the war of the rebellion. He told us one evening, sitting around our campfire while on the prospecting trip, that when General Stevens tendered his services to the government he had written him a letter saying he could give him more honorable employment on the road he was building, wielding a pick and shovel, than he would find in fighting his fellow countrymen. Having been brought up in the Republican faith this did not appeal to me as very good sentiments.

At another time when we were somewhere in the Spokane country an Indian came into camp. Captain Mullan filled up a plate with bread and bacon and beans and passed it to the Indian, saying "Did ever white man enter Logan's cabin hungry and he gave him not meal."

This was a graceful act that much impressed me. Mullan resigned from the army and never re-entered it. He was a man of considerable attainments but his career was clouded by his resignation from the army in time of war.

He visited me in 1889 at Olympia during my term as governor.

Mrs. (Pomeroy) St. George

Mrs. St. George and her first husband,
J.M. Pomeroy, ran the stage coach stop called "Pum's"
between Lewiston and Walla Walla in the 1860's.

"A quarter of a century or more ago there were two famous eating houses on the stage road between Walla Walla and Lewiston, houses which were the occasion of many heated arguments between those who had been over the road as to which was the better, houses at either of which the traveler, tired and sore from the lurching of the stage, was sure of a substantial meal, the memory of which, as it flitted through the brain, lingered and made the mouth water. These were the houses which the familiar, all-pervading, time-serving drummer contracted into 'Pum's' and 'Freeman's.' The former was located near what is now the center of the thriving City of Pomeroy; the latter was on the Alpowa, about half-way between 'Pum's' and Lewiston. Coming passengers dined at Pomeroy's'; going took breakfast at Freeman's. Possibly stage passengers have eaten better cooked meals and sat down to more attractive tables than those found at Freeman's and Pomeroy's, but they never said so while at either place, or elsewhere.

Delicious bread, fresh from the oven, that which was properly seasoned by age, sweet butter, thick cream in genuine coffee, meats done to a turn, chicken fried or stewed, vegetables in their season, fruits, pastry, each and all 'fit to set before a king,' were provided in profusion in both places. In winter huge fires in equally huge fireplaces thawed out the frozen traveler. In summer cold buttermilk cooled his heated blood and washed the alkali dust out of his throat."

Walla Walla Union, 1894

"I came from Salem, Oregon, where I had lived with my people for eighteen years, being four years old when my folks crossed the plains, among the early pioneers of Oregon.

"I was married at the age of fifteen years, and, for a while, lived in Salem with my husband and two small children.

"I came up the Columbia River by steamer to Wallula, took the stage for Walla Walla, with twelve other passengers, on April 6, 1864. At Wallula I found a great rush of travel, many on their way to the reported gold strike at Orofino, Idaho.

"I had two pairs of fine blooded pigs in a small box, two dozen fine chickens, but no baggage except a suitcase with a few things for my children. My trunks had been left at Portland and came the next day.

"My husband was coming overland with a band of fine Shorthorn cattle and about twenty head of horses. He had been driving stock for about four weeks, and I had remained with my mother for awhile, so we would arrive at Walla Walla about the same time. Arriving there with my little ones, a stranger in a strange land, with very little money, and board and lodgings at the City Hotel twenty-five dollars a week, and no letter from my husband awaiting me, I did not feel very much at home.

"But soon we met the man with whom Mr. Pomeroy had made arrangements for the place where we were to live until we could look about and select a piece of land for our homestead. We were to stay that summer on the ranch two miles east of Dayton, belonging to Mr. William Rexford, in a small log house with a fireplace, and there, in September, Mrs. McClung was born.

"We were as poor and hard up for money as any one that ever came to this country. In the month of July Mr. King, who at that time carried the mail, express and passengers from Walla Walla to Lewiston, made me a proposition to keep a stage stand and feed his hungry passengers every day, and very soon I was giving two dinners each day to the coming and going travelers.

"I had told Mr. King that I had nothing to work with, no stove, table or dishes; nothing to cook and I did not see how I could accommodate him. I had been helping to break some of the young heifers to milk, and made some butter to sell, having no other way to make a dollar. I sold all the butter I could spare for one dollar a pound; but soon winter would come on and then what would we do with no money, no sale for what little stock we had? Something had to be done. We had made a garden soon after we settled and by this time we had some nice vegetables, which were a great treat to the travelers coming out of the mines.

"Mr. King told me to make a list of what I needed for my house so I could feed his passengers, and, finally, after much urging, I did so. He took my list to Walla Walla, had the bill filled, put on a freight team the next day and brought me a big, nice cookstove with all the things belonging to it; lots of dishes and linen, and said I could pay him when I made the money and could spare it.

"The very next day I gave a dinner to ten passengers, and, oh, didn't they brag on that dinner. I never will forget all the nice things they said.

"I kept the stage stand there until December 10th, when we bought this place, where Pomeroy now stands, or rather the improvements on it, consisting of a large house, a log barn and corral.

"Then the daily stage service was discontinued to once a week, with this station as a night stopping place, where all that traveled the road always got their meals. Our house became the famous stopping place between Walla Walla, Washington and Lewiston, Idaho.

"When the travel was heavy we made some money, and when the travel was light I had to work outdoors milking cows, making garden and all kinds of hard work. My little children almost raised themselves, taking care of the baby, and helping me in many ways. Working, always thinking of how to make nice things to eat for the traveling public, and how to keep expenses paid.

"Walla Walla was our trading place, for everything was high at Lewiston. But if I had anything to sell I sent it to the latter place.

"There was one family living on the Pataha besides us, two or three squaw men and some bachelors living where the King boys now live, and for a little while a family was located on the Alpowa Creek. There were some Indian ranches on that creek at that time. No one lived below on the Pataha, till you came to the old 'Parson' Quinn place, eleven miles down, then farther on were two or three cattle ranches--Rice and Montgomery, Platters, and later Archey McCrearty. There was no settlement on Snake River except at Almota, no one living on the Deadman, nor anywhere over there, and no settlers between the Pataha and the mountains.

"I helped my husband to stake the roads to the mountains. There had been a road up the Benjamin Gulch, which was so badly washed out it could not be traveled. We staked a road across 'Dutch Flat' for our own use, as wood and fencing had to come from that direction.

"There was scarcely enough brush along the Pataha to make a camp fire. The Indians would burn the grass every year along Pataha, thus killing the tender willows.

"In those early days the Indians were very plentiful. I have seen as many as 100 or more pass by our place in one day, their destination being the

Camas and Kouse districts, as Camas Prairie was then called. Then, later in the season, they would go to a lake at the head of the Yakima River, high up in the mountains, where the squaws would fish, and the men hunt deer, which were plentiful.

"During these camping periods, horse racing was the principal amusement; the Indians had many fine, fast horses, and the several tribes wagered many dollars and trinkets on the merits of their race stock. During this racing season many unscrupulous white men, or 'renegades,' would arrive, camping close by, winning the money of the Indians and selling them liquor.

"The Alpowa Indians were very friendly, and the squaws would work for me; I would hire them to work in the garden. They would take potatoes for their pay and pack them on their ponies. If not watched, they would steal some of the vegetables, but most of them did an honest day's work and were satisfied with what I gave them for their labor.

"Sometimes I could buy huckleberries from the Indians and dried antelope hams during the first few years we lived here. There was an old Indian called 'Squally John,' who would catch salmon on the Snake River and bring them to us. They would catch hundreds of them and dry them for the winter and would also get plenty of venison in our mountains.

"I was afraid of the Indians for a few years, but got over that feeling. It was slow work for one or two men to make a farm. Not a furrow had ever been plowed when we came, no fencing. Barbed wire was not known then, and Mr. Pomeroy had to haul feed for his team, and seed grain from the Touchet; and that, with the timber hauling from the mountains kept him busy, which left the cows and the chores and all kinds of outdoor work for me to do with one hired man and the help of the children.

"I was a very busy woman, although I did find time to teach the children to read and write, and the first lessons were learned at home. There was a school taught at Dayton the summer of 1869, and we sent Clara and Ned there. This was a four months' term. The next year we sent Clara to the sisters at Walla Walla, then, in 1872, Bishop Wells started the St. Paul School, and Clara was one of the pupils there, until she finished her schooling and was married to Eugene T. Wilson, on Christmas Day, 1877.

"In the meantime we had opened a school at the Owsley place, and our two children attended school there, going five miles in a buggy. There were ten pupils the first year. The country was settling up everywhere by this time; many had settled on the Pataha Prairie, and Alpowa, and over in the Deadman country and along the Pataha Creek.

"When the flour mill was built, a man wanted to put in a stock of goods, then others came, and a town was laid out.

"Then there was no more frontier."

James H. Purdin

*He made his "poke" in 1864,
selling vegetables to the miners
in the Boise Basin.
Later, a farmer in the Wenas Valley near Yakima,
he tells about raising tobacco
and making his own furniture.*

A terrific thunder storm was breaking just as we reached the Platte River. Heavy rains had already swollen the river, so the crossing was delayed while the men removed the wagon beds and caulked them. They lashed them together, end to end, and floated them across, carrying families and goods, the oxen swimming.

By this time we found that our provisions would not hold out, so a trade was struck with a man returning east. He was driving a team of horses and was willing to pay "boot" for the Purdin ox-team. With this money enough food was purchased to enable us to reach Boise.

Reaching Boise in November with less than a dollar in my pocket, I turned our horses out to seek their living on the range. Boise was a mining town. Bacon was $1.00 per pound, flour $4.00 a sack, coffee $1.00 per pound, and everything else in proportion. I must have work, and I found it, mauling rails from bull-pine at 75 cents per day. The small wage could not keep pace with mounting expenses. My employer, a kind-hearted man, befriended us, providing for us through the winter and in the spring when our son, Hugh, was born.

In order to pay the debt incurred, it was agreed that we rent fifteen acres of land of our employer and raise vegetables to supply the demand of the miners.

Fortune favored us from the very beginning of our venture. During the winter our thoughts often turned to the faithful team turned out to wander in the hills. One day in May a band of wild horses passing through the village attracted my wife's attention. She immediately recognized the two horses we had driven all the way from the Platte. Following each was a lively colt. Calling me, we separated our team from the band.

Our garden grew and thrived. Miners' fare that summer included luxuries from our garden. By the first of October, enough gold dust had been weighed out in exchange for vegetables to enable us to settle up with our landlord and leave Boise with $1,500.00 of dust in a little buckskin pouch. In October, 1865, we set out for the land of our dreams.

We reached the Willamette and homesteaded, but our plans for an or-. chard never materialized, as the rainy weather affected my health, undermined as it was by the hardships of war.

Relinquishing our homestead, we drove back up the Columbia river, crossed over and settled at Dixie, twelve miles from Walla Walla. We resided there seven years, raising horses and cattle. Yakima Valley was the cattleman's Paradise in those days, and in 1874, we again crossed the Columbia with our four sons, Hugh, Owen, Lloyd and Lee, our herds and other possessions. We entered the beautiful Wenas Valley, preempting 160 acres, released by a man named Perkins, some of this land being under cultivation. Here, Wallace and Walter were born February 24, 1879, the first twins born in what is now the Yakima Valley. Later came Charles and Ralph, making eight sons to grow into manhood and help settle and develop the sage brush wilderness, and transform it into the productive and fruitful valley that it is today.

There was a small log house of two rooms on the farm. Being handy with tools, I made furniture of the black birch growing along the creek. The chair seats were made of strips of rawhide. I have always kept one of these chairs for myself. The legs are worn down considerable, but I always said it was the most comfortable chair in the house. I made a rocker for my wife. I remember that later I brought her a rocker from The Dalles, 90 miles away.

These freighting trips were made only once a year. If the coffee gave out in the meantime, parched wheat made a fair substitute. This was ground in a mill attached to the wall. The hopper held about two quarts. The mill was also used for grinding flour corn, a variety of white corn with dentless kernels. The cornbread and mush made from this meal are still remembered as the most delicious ever tasted anywhere, before or since.

I grew my own tobacco. I burned willow switches over a small tract, worked the ashes into the soil, mixed the seed with sand and sowed it, later thinning out the plants. When it came time to harvest, it was pulled and hung upside down from poles in the shed. After it was cured, I made it into "hands." There was a good supply for the old meerschaum.

Before the railroad came, cattle-raising was the most profitable industry. Cattle were driven over the Naches Pass to Seattle and shipped down the coast.

Our ranch was a stopping place for the stage operating between The Dalles and Ellensburg. Mail was distributed here for the settlers. Later a justice court was held there when I was elected justice of the peace.

One of the three commercial orchards in the Wenas during those days was on our ranch. When it came into production, we marketed the fruit in Ellensburg and Cle Elum, driving over the old state road and up the Shushuskin Canyon.

Our boys and the neighbors' played games in the old crumbling stockade on the L.C. Rice farm adjoining. There was a circular embankment enclosing the space where the sod forts were built, one for each family. The enclosure held the stock.

In 1873 a log schoolhouse was built near the creek between the Longmire and Albert Lotz farms. Logs were split for the recitation benches, the legs being wooden pegs. The furniture was manufactured in the same crude way. Among the names in the old school register may be found Hugh, Owen, and Lloyd Purdin. The schoolhouse was used for the debating society, where many very important questions were settled.

Elections were held in the schoolhouse. The most exciting, according to my recollection, was the year of the "Cross of Gold" presidential election, ushered in by torchlight parades, noisy rallies and much oratory.

I recall with amusement the Fourth of July celebrations, with their marvelous parades, the display of flags, lemonade stands, patriotic speeches, and last but not least, the "plug uglies," clowning through the streets.

Christmas was observed with religious entertainments in the schoolhouse.

Thanksgiving was more reverenced than it is today.

All the lumber used in the State Fair buildings was sawed from logs brought down to John Cleman's mill. Lloyd Purdin hauled all the lumber. The road taken by the early Wenas settlers crossed the ridge to Lower Naches, down past the old Nelson place, over the Nelson bridge, from there the trail crossed the rocky land and sage brush flats now covered by the Fruitvale orchards. Traveling this road one day with my father, I remember that we went out of our way in order to see a wonderful sight. Yakima City was being moved through the sage brush from the "Old Town" to the place known as North Yakima until 1917. Business was transacted as usual while the buildings were en route; merchants sold goods over the counter, boarders ate their meals in the hotel, church services were held.

Mrs. Brewster Ferrel

Mrs. Ferrel came west
in the "short haired train" of 1864.
She portrays a vivid image of travel
on the overland trail in the 1860's
and life on the frontier.

W e started from Corydon, Wayne County, Iowa, to travel the wild and desolate plains and seek a home in Walla Walla, Washington. This is a true story, but before you get through reading it you will not wonder at the people out west calling us green immigrants.

My husband and I and our little boy, who was two years old, and my husband's brother, were all that came in our wagon. We had a good little mule team. I have had a kind regard for mules ever since I took that trip.

Did not know a mule could learn so much.

The first day was a sad one going past our relatives and old neighbors' homes and stopping to say good-bye. Our people gave us little presents, tokens of love, and lots of good advice, such as, "be careful and don't let the Indians get you," or, "be a good girl and come back some day." Well, we did come back twenty-four years after, but not with a mule team.

The first night we stayed at a house. Next morning the good woman said, "I will give you some pickled meat." So she went out in the meat house to get it, and there was a skunk drowned in the brine. We thanked her and got our meat at another place.

The next night we camped out, the first I ever slept out of a house, and when bedtime came our little boy cried, oh, so hard to go home, but we got him quiet and slept well; that was one thing we could do on that trip.

Woman-like, I was very much afraid of the bad roads. We had all of our belongings piled in that wagon, and among other things were our firearms. We came to a very bad place in the road. I took our little boy out of the wagon and we were walking behind when a shotgun that was lying in the wagon went off and the shot came very near us. Then I concluded in the wagon was the safest place and soon got so I was not afraid to ride over any kind of road.

We traveled alone till we got to the Missouri River. Then we came to a string of wagons about a mile and a half long. They were waiting to be ferried over the river. We came there in the forenoon, and took our place in line and moved up as the wagons went over. We stayed there all that day and camped there that night. Next morning we got over.

Then we traveled with a train and the Indians came around our wagons; some of them begged for food. One day when we sat down on the ground to eat our dinner about a dozen big red-faced fellows came and stood around with tomahawks in their hands. I did not want any dinner that day, but they went away peaceably, and we traveled on over good roads and through beautiful country up Platte River and on and on and soon got used to seeing Indians. Sometimes they would follow our wagons and some one would throw a piece of bread out to them and they would run after the wagon and pick it up; then throw another piece, till they would look like little chickens after an old hen.

Fuel was very scarce in that country. We had to burn sage brush, dead weeds, or anything we could get. Sometimes my husband would keep feeding the fire while I baked the flapjacks, as we called them.

The men folks were all the time looking out for good grass and water for the stock, which they would herd on the grass till late at night, and then tie them to the wagon wheels. In the morning they would take them out again and herd them until starting time, which was pretty early, as we wanted to hurry through to Walla Walla. We gave our mules all the scraps we had left from our meals and they relished it very much and would hunt in the wagon for the dinner box and look and wait for their lunch.

There were some mean people crossed the plains. There was a man and his wife and three grown daughters traveling in our train. One day when we lay over we heard a commotion, and looking toward a tent we saw a girl pitch out of it and a man's boot and foot up in the air. The girl said her papa kicked her out because she had forgotten to water the horses. One other time we had stopped to rest and I heard a woman cry and swear and pray, first one then the other. I said to a friend, "Let us go and see if we can help her;" but she said "No; it is a woman with a very loathsome disease and the man that drives the team was kind to bring her out west." The man would cook a little food and hand it to her and then go away.

Well, the people were not all bad; we found some very dear friends on our trip. I never will forget them. It was a trying trip on us all. We had some dangerous streams to cross. We would come to some that looked impossible to cross. We would stop and plan and try the depth in every way possible and then block up the wagon bed to the top of the standard, then tie them fast to the wagon, then cautiously drive in almost holding our breath. We had four mules and the leaders were small. Sometimes we could not see much of them but their heads. Our little boy would laugh and enjoy the excitement, but I took many a cry when I thought of where we were taking him. We had started and must get through. I had about forgotten to mention the weather, which was very stormy. It rained and snowed and blew our wagon sheet off and everything we had got wet. Our flour got musty; we had to eat it; we could get no other.

By this time we were getting pretty well up Platte River, and did not see many Indians, but were hearing a good deal about their committing depredations, and commenced to corral our wagons of nights. That was to drive in a circle, unhitch, then the men would pull them close together by hand, and after herding the stock would bring them in and tie to the outside wheels of the wagons for the night.

One day our train came up to a corral of this kind and the women were sitting around crying and the men were standing in groups talking very earnestly, and not a hoof in sight. We soon learned their troubles. They had left their stock out a little way from the wagons to feed without any guards and the Indians had seen their opportunity and run between them and their stock and run them off. What those poor people did we never learned. We had to travel on.

One morning a few days after this sad scene we passed a train which had not started out yet, and came upon another sad scene. Two men had left their train in the evening and drove about a mile ahead, in order to get better grass for their horses. Just at dusk they were sitting on a log near their wagons when eight Indians came behind them and commenced shooting them with arrows. The men jumped for their guns, but before they reached their wagons the Indians had them both down. They left them for dead and then took the four horses and guns and ammunition and $800 in money and everything else they wanted out of the wagon, and left. But one poor fellow was not quite dead. After the Indians left he crawled a little way off in the brush and lay there till next morning. When we came along he crawled out and told us all about it. We stayed with him till his train came up, then helped him to bury his partner, and then went on. I was pretty homesick for a few days.

We were getting into the mountains and the roads were bad, and so were the Indians. We were very cautious; two men stood guard every night, taking turns.

The weather was getting warm and pleasant after all, and through all of our hardships we had some pleasant and amusing things happen. There was a good many jack rabbits along the road. We had a rabbit pot-pie pretty often. One day about a half-dozen men got after a rabbit and were running past our wagon and shooting with their pistols. My husband was walking by our wagon and said, "Hand me the shotgun;; and I handed it to him. He shot and brought down the rabbit, then gave it to me. That ended the race and raised a laugh.

Once in every two days we would stop a day and rest, lay over, we called it, to do our washing. We would take a bucket and camp kettle and go to the creek; that was all the utensils we had to wash with. When the clothes were dry they were ready to put on--no ironing on that trip. We saw irons, tubs, washboards, and a good many other things that people had thrown out of their wagons because their teams were giving out. We did not dare to pick them up and haul them for fear our own teams would give out. I knew one woman that had a cook stove in her wagon and she was so anxious to bring it through that she would get out and push on the wagon when it was going up hill, but she had to give it up and set it out and go on without it. We were beginning to find out how dependent we were on our teams.

Before we left home our neighbors and friends gave me a lot of nice pieces and helped me make a keepsake quilt. I prized it very highly. One day I put it out to sun and some fire blew on it and burned it up. Then I shed a few tears. Much as we needed everything we had we would lose and leave our things at the camps. We lost our axe and coffee pot and our comb. Then we tried to borrow a comb, but found out there were but few in the train. So we women got together and had our hair cut off. Then we were called the short-haired train.

The health of our train was pretty good. Sometimes a family would get very sick from eating too many wild weeds they would gather and cook for greens so as to have a change, as variety of wood was getting scarce.

We brought a keg of sorghum syrup with us, and would have had plenty to last through, but one day our little boy was missing, and looking in the wagon we saw him. He had found the matches and was just putting the last bunch in the syrup keg, so we had to without sorghum.

One night we stopped near an old fort where some men were staying. So I felt pretty safe, but before morning we found out they were worse than Indians, for they had whiskey to sell and some of the men in our train got some whiskey and got drunk, then fought and quarreled all night. Next morning when a few wagons were ready to start the men that had been drunk were asleep. Another train came along and we drove on with them. It seemed a trip where every one had to look out for self. We did not dare to stop long to help the unfortunate or we would not get through ourselves. We did not start out to die on the plains. We passed many a new made grave.

At this time it was as disagreeably hot as it had been cold on the start. One time we tried traveling at night to avoid the extreme heat, but that would not do.

I have not given many dates, as I have forgotten most of them. Am writing this mostly for my children and grandchildren to read and want it to be as near true as I can remember.

We learned that the main thing on that trip was to keep on moving. As we got near and into the mountains the weather got cool and pleasant. But, oh, such mountains and roads, sometimes they would seem almost perpendicular, but we would climb and get up most all of the wagon walking, then slide down on the other side, then up, then down, and soon day after day some of the mountains seemed almost solid rock.

One day we came to a beautiful little stream. Someone that was walking dipped up a cup of water and said, "Will you have a drink?" I took the cup. Imagine my surprise when it almost burned my lips. Those were the first hot springs we had ever seen. Then we came to a place that looked like it was covered with ice and frost, but it proved to be salt. We picked up some pieces and used it for cooking.

We began to hear more rumors about the Indians and could see signs of their mischief. So we corralled our wagons very carefully and went to bed and were sleeping soundly when all of a sudden we were awakened with hearing screaming and very rapid shooting. I jumped out of bed and said, "The Indians have attacked us." My husband got up and said, "I will go and see what the trouble is." Then I got all of the guns and ammunition to the front of the wagon ready for battle, and was piling the sacks of flour and bacon around our little boy, who was yet asleep, when my husband came back and said it was coyotes yelping and the guards were shooting at them. So we went to bed again and were soon asleep. That was one thing we could enjoy on that trip.

Well, we finally got over the Rocky Mountains. You need not be surprised if I tell you that our shoes were getting thin and pretty badly worn. We did not start with an over supply and our clothes were wearing out fast and we were looking pretty rough and sunburnt.

We came to some more deep rivers and had to block up our wagon beds so we could cross. Then we came to a country infested with crickets. I never saw anything like it; they were almost as big as a mouse and could chirp and jump in such big bands. Our mules shied at them. Well, we were glad to get out of that country.

One day looking ahead in the distance we saw something coming that looked like covered wagons, but as it drew near we could see it was actually coming the other way toward us, something we had not seen for hundreds, yes, thousands of miles. Well, they came on and passed us. It was a pack train, wonderful sight for us. They frightened our teams in their weak and half-dead condition. Then someone said those were cowboys.

Then we came to where some men were camped. They were excited over losing a lot of mules and horses. They were driving a band out west. The Indians had stampeded them and run a lot of them away. We saw several dead horses which the men had ridden to death trying to get the band together again.

We traveled on and came to some timbered mountains. Now we could have plenty of wood to cook with. It was a treat to have plenty of wood and water at the same time.

One evening after we had corralled our wagons and the guards had taken the teams out to grass one of the men came running back and said, "Get your guns quick; there is a drove of elk right among our stock." The men hurried out with their guns, fired, and brought down two big elks and dragged them into camp. I remember it so well, they looked so much like one of our little mules. The men skinned them and cut them up and then decided that my husband had fired the most fatal shot; so we had first choice piece. The meat was fine.

We came to a desolate looking place. It was in a deep canyon and we had to stop over night. There were some old bleached bones and a lot of tangled hair. Someone said it was human hair and bones and that the Indians had massacred a train and their bodies had never been buried. We did not know how much of that was true, but at that time we could believe almost anything. After all, our Indian troubles were mostly scares, but as the old saying is, you had as well kill a person as scare him to death.

By this time we came to some more awful hills to come down. We all got out of the wagons and the men tied ropes to the hind wheels and held back while the teams and people slid down. Well, we all got down and went on our way rejoicing, and finally got into some pretty country and laid over to let our teams rest, and do our washing.

That day I took a stroll down by the creek and saw a big fish lying in some shallow water in a little island. I very cautiously slipped around between it and the main creek and put my hands under it and threw it out on land. Then I wrapped my apron around it and went carrying it into camp. It was alive and weighed about eight pounds. We would not eat it for fear it might be sick, but some of the boys wanted it, so I gave it to them. They cooked it and ate it and said it was very good. Next morning we hitched up and traveled on.

The weather was pleasant and we began to see signs of civilization and met another pack train which was loaded with flour, bacon, whiskey, and tobacco. I should not have said signs of civilization. But we saw better things further on. Some of our people tried to buy some provisions of them, but they would not sell; said they were taking them to the mines and expected to get a dollar a pound for what they had. Our money was pretty scarce and what we had was greenbacks and only worth fifty cents on the dollar out West.

Then we came to a little garden and a cabin back in the brush. We could see the green lettuce and onions through the fence. Some of our boys said they would make a raid on that garden, but when they got on the fence they saw a tree on the other side and a man hanging by the neck from a limb of that tree. Then they said, "We don't want any garden sass." We learned later that it was only a paddy stuffed with straw. Our provisions were getting scarce and our teams were getting weaker, and we were very anxious to get through.

We finally arrived in the Grande Ronde Valley and then we spent the last cent we had to buy a beef bone and some fresh vegetables. Then all got together and made a big dinner. All sat down and ate together. After dinner we all shook hands and said good-bye. Then each one went his own way.

We started to cross the Blue Mountains and one of our mules got sick. We had urged him too much. He seemed to be asleep on his feet, held his eyes shut, and wanted to pull all the time. Well, he pulled through. I had almost learned to love those mules, they had been so faithful.

We arrived in Walla Walla, Washington, footsore and weary, in just three months from the day we started.

When we arrived in this beautiful little valley without a dollar and scarcely any clothing and no provisions we had a pretty hard time. Now, when a family gets their house and everything they have, burned, the people around get together and help them, and it is right they should in this land of plenty; and when a criminal leaves the penitentiary they give him a suit of clothes and some money. But there was no help for the green immigrants, as we were called, and I suppose we were, at least in some respects.

We did not understand the western slang and Indian talk that we heard so much. It was something like this. A man that had been out West about five years was eating dinner with us, said, "That is hiu mucka muck." He was referring to something on the table. We asked him if he liked this country. He said, "You bet your life!" We said, "Why do so many men out West wear revolvers on their belts and big knives in their boot legs?" He said, "It is necessary to keep order; we have a man for breakfast quite often."

Then we would hear the remark, lots of men out West are made to bite the dust with their boots on; and then, you sabba, or savvy, and many such expressions. Well, we finally got initiated. And the people were very kind to us. We never saw a time when we appreciated our neighbors so much. They were friends in need and in deed.

This country was covered with bunchgrass, flowers, Indians, coyotes, and grasshoppers. A few white people were living along the creeks in little huts. Some were growing a little wheat and others small grain and gardens.

Everything was very high priced. Wheat sold for a dollar and a half a bushel. There was scarcely any fruit to be had at any price. When I go through this beautiful valley, now a little less than forty years after, and see wagon loads of delicious fruit going to waste it makes me think of those times.

Well, we went to work; had to rustle, kept at it from early morn till late at night. But we would jump from one thing to another. There seemed to be too many chances. First we would settle on one piece of land, then on another. There were thousands and thousands of acres of good unclaimed land all about us, but people thought none but the sloughs would grow anything. After two or three years of changing about we finally bought eighty acres of land and settled down. Paid eight hundred dollars for it. We gave thirty dollars, a horse, and our only cow to make the first payment. At this time we had two children in our family.

Before we had any wheat to sell it came down to fifty cents per bushel. The country up to this time had been settled mostly by men; only some of them had Indian women for wives. The families that settled this country first were nearly all new married people and a baby came to almost every home in less than two years for a dozen years or more.

One day I went to visit a dear neighbor and I was complaining of hard times and she said, "We have been living on boiled wheat for several days." I believe there were a good many others doing the same thing. Those hard times seemed to bind neighbors close together. Three or four of us would get together and go two or three miles to get some wild gooseberries and elderberries and red haws and fix them up for fruit. They were pretty good when there was nothing better.

I will now mention some of the Indian scares that we had to endure. We had been warned by the newspapers to look out for the Indians, as they were on the war path and had murdered some of the white settlers and had mangled them terribly. So one Sunday the people were holding a meeting on Mill Creek in a little school house when a little girl came running in, crying, and said, "The Indians are killing my mama and papa." Some of the men hurried to the house, which was about a mile away, and the young boy preacher got on a horse and away he went as fast as his horse could go to warn the people at their homes that the Indians had broken out. He stopped at our house and asked for a fresh horse, as his was about run down. We did not have any, so he went rushing on and stopping at every house to give the alarm. My husband and several of the neighbor men had gone from home that day. Imagine the scene. We were running from one house to another; each one of us had three or four little children. After about a dozen of us got together we decided to go to a log cabin that was near and wait for the Indians to come. There was one man in the cabin and he was getting ready to shoot out through the cracks between the logs. When a man came from the seat of war and said no one is seriously hurt, it was a drunken row and only one Indian was killed, we all went home and the boy preacher got over his scare and has been long since a good and noted preacher. And the Indian that was supposed to be dead came to life again. Some of the men took him to town and had a trial and the jury sentenced him to wash his face. Well, this is one of the many such scares as some others can remember that are yet living.

I will relate one more incident. At this time there was a saw mill at the head of Mill Creek and there were several families living at the mill. The men had built a fort for the women and children in case the Indians should attack them. One day some men who lived in the valley took their teams and wagons and started to go to the mill, but when they got in the mountains they saw a band of Indians coming down the trail beyond the mill. The men at once stopped, unhitched from their wagons, and jumped on their horses and used the tugs for whips and came down the mountains on double quick and reported to all the people along the road what they had seen, and the people were soon leaving their cabins and running for the brush. And those at the mill saw the Indians coming and they went running to the fort. Some one relating the scene said the men could run faster than the women and children and got into the fort first. Well, the Indians came and were friendly and very much surprised when they saw the people running and said they had been back in the mountains hunting and fishing and did not know that there was any war going on.

The health of a people in a new country is usually good, but we would sometimes get sick. Would hardly dare think of sending for a doctor. There was no money to pay one and there could hardly be one found. But there was a woman who lived in our neighborhood that had a good doctor book. It was Doctor Gunn's work. She went by it in her own family, and the neighbors sent for her. She would take her doctor book under her arm and go to visit the sick. Then they would read and study together and use the simple remedies prescribed in that book and get along pretty well. In that way she got into quite a large practice. She often rode a little blue pony. People would sometimes make the remark, "I think there is someone sick at a certain house. I see the blue pony tied at the gate."

This woman officiated where more than a hundred babies were born. She was very successful, never lost a mother or child while she was taking care of them. She most always went back every day for a week to see the patient and wash and dress the baby. And most of the time she had one of her own to take with her. She made no charges, as she did not have any license. But she received a good many presents, and is sometimes yet pleasantly reminded of by-gone days. Just a few days ago she received a photo of five large, stalwart men and a letter from their mother saying these are pictures of your boys; see how they have grown. Then another time a picture came from a distance of two large twin boys and a girl and a word saying, see how your boys have grown.

I have not made mention of any names in this sketch, thinking it would be just as interesting without.

Well, I must get back to my pioneer days that I started to write about. Schools and churches were scarce. One woman taught a school in her home of two rooms. She had about a dozen scholars. About one-third of them were part Indian children. As I said before, some of the men that came out West first came alone and took Indian women for wives. People called them squaw men. We remember another woman that taught school in her home of one room. At noon when the children were out playing she would cook dinner and the family would eat, then she would take up her school again.

We would sometimes go three or four miles to church in a home of one room where three or four persons lived. The preacher would stand up in the corner between the table and fireplace and preach, while the congregation sat around on the beds and benches and boxes. Every corner would be full. Many a one received a blessing in those humble meetings. But we did not have to do that way very long. People with such energy soon built school houses and churches.

Building material was hard to get. When one man worked for or sold another man anything he would often pay him in gold dust. They used that a great deal. We would take our little sack of gold dust and go to town to buy things, and the merchants would weigh and blow and spill it till we would not have much left. I said go to town; there was not much town to go to. It was not like the town the little boy said he could not see for the houses. One would hardly know it was a town by the houses. At the time there was about a dozen, mostly business houses, scattered around in Walla Walla.

Tall Tale

*Our anonymous storyteller
must have had a little experience on the
hurricane deck of a wild cayuse
to produce this fanciful tale of Western horsemanship.*

"The fust thing I wanted when I went into the cattle business," said the lonely pilgrim, "was a good cow pony, one of these tame plugs thet'll hunch along behind a cow critter and bite her to make her travel. Then if the cow turns sudden the pony goes too, and sows the rider over about a half-acre of prairie.

"The Injun pony is about as ornery a critter as can live an' stay healthy. He is a cross between a jackrabbit an' the crack of doom. I never could guess what makes thet little hoss so irritable.

"I hed seen fellers, ridin' past on Injun ponies, an' I goes and gits me one.

A nice little yeller cuss he was, with a white face thet reached to his shoulders almost, an' one blue eye an' one pink eye. O, he was a sociable-lookin' plug, I don't think. The feller I bought him of said he'd never been broke, said it was all right, and jest to put on a good, strong saddle an' get on, an' when you was good an' on to stay there.

"I hed tied Mr. Cayuse up short in the stable, so I takes the saddle an' goes in. Pony gives a snort like pullin' a nozzle off a fire hose in action. I takes another step. Pony braces his feet against the side of the barn where the rope is tied, bows his back like a caterpillar, gives one yank an' pulls the whole blame side outen the barn. Over the wreck he goes like a dog after a rat, makes two good jumps an' lands on his back on top of the pieces of barn thet was hangin' to him.

"Before he could git up I had the bridle on him. Then I hed him good. He stood like a genuine angel till I hed got his saddle all cinched up.

"Ol' Bill was there at the time. He claimed thet he hed saw people break ponies. 'Why,' sed he, 'you blame fool tenderfoot,' says he, 'you can't ride thet pinto,' says he.

" 'Why not?' says I. 'I've rid my ol' mule, Dock, an' he's as ornery an ol' critter as ever was made.'

" 'All right, go ahead,' says Bill. 'Ye ain't got no relations, an' I'll jest bury you here,' says he.

" 'Shucks!' says I. 'Any one could ride thet little thing. Even if I do fall off, he ain't very high,' says I.

" 'Ye won't fall down,' says Bill; 'ye'll fall up.'

"But I wouldn't listen to him. I jest walked up an' put the rein over the pony's head, then I gave a jump an' landed a-straddle of him.

"O, the joy of feelin' your own hoss under you! Yes, then right away I seen my own hoss under me, but I didn't feel him none. He was too far under. Gentelmen, I don't care a whoop whether you believe me or not, but I went up 250 feet in the air if I was an inch. Then the pony went back for a fresh start. Come up an' met me half way. You see, I was comin' down. We met in the air an' it didn't seem to hurt the pony none. When we lit, we lit runnin'. Also kickin', squealin', an' doin' sky hops on the side.

"I got a strangle hold on the saddle horn, an' the rest of me floated out behind. Every time the pony would do a sky hop my legs would snap at the ends like a whiplash. Both heels was all frazzled out. Away we goes over the dry creek bed, through the prairie dog town, over the buttes, whoopity-split, tail over the dasher! I hung on to the circus.

"Then the ol' pony got annoyed. He started over the prairie like greased lightnin', straight running'. Then he stopped quicker 'n a wink, an' was half a mile in the other direction before he turned 'round. An' me! I stayed with him, gentlemen, but I didn't have one cussed rag left on my back. I jest jerk-ed me plumb outen clothes, boots, socks, an' most of my hair.

"Well, ol' Bill started fust off to be skeered for me; then he laughed hisself lame, then he got tired of the show an' went to sleep.

"Me an' the pony kept up the game till along in the afternoon. Then the pony seemed to lose interest, too. He stopped an' began eatin' bunchgrass.

"I noticed a mighty queer thing about then. Though I still hed hold of the saddle horn, an' the saddle was in place on the pony, I was away off on the prairie about 15 feet. I pretty soon studied it out. My arms hed been stretched till they were 15 feet long. Yes, sir, 15 feet!

"An' it was all of 10 years before they got back to their right length again."

Joseph Frisco

Mr. Frisco relates his early life
of poverty and war in Europe
and his adventures on the east coast
before he and his wife joined an emigrant train
heading for Oregon in 1865.

M r. Frisco does not know his exact age, but has been assured by relatives that he was born in the early months of 1821, hence is 93 years of age and is hale and hearty and remarkably well preserved for that age.

He is a native of Hungary and was born at Kakacza Szend. His father died when he was but six months of age. His mother remarried and four children were born in the second union. When ten years of age his mother and her four small children all fell victims of the cholera in one week and his step-father died one week later of the same scourge which devasted whole cities in Europe that year.

Thus at the age of ten he and a sister, two years older, were left alone in the world. Mr. Frisco remembers an uncle who was kind to him but his wife prevented in any way possible any kindness to the nephew and later facts prove that she succeeded in carrying out her will.

His sister obtained work in the home town as a helper but he was not so successful. He walked to a neighboring town and secured work at cleaning out barns and yards and eked out a meager existence but sickness came upon him and the man with whom he made his home not wishing to be burdened with such a charge took him back to his uncle. The journey was made in mid-winter in a sleigh. The boy was unconscious most of the way. The weather was extremely cold and both of his feet were slightly frozen. Although unconscious most of the time, he remembers distinctly that on arriving at his uncle's home his aunt would not permit him to be brought into the house and his uncle very much against his will took him into the barn where he made a bed for him and there with little care he remained for weeks, he does not know how many, and apparently due more to a kindly fate, than care, recovered. His uncle visited him once each day and brought food to him without the knowledge of his wife. He had one friend however, a maiden lady, a friend of his mother, who came whenever she could and covered him up when he tossed the bedding aside in his delirious moments. She was poor and had duties that left little time for such attention.

Some one remarked to Mr. Frisco that such conduct was not like the American treatment of an orphan boy.

"No," he said, "they would hang such people here."

When he recovered sufficiently to leave his bed and went out to the neighbors, he was invited to eat at every house and he was so starved and hungry, he says, that he could have eaten at every one and there were many. His feet have never been normal but have served him well considering the freezing they received.

Life had not offered anything but the lot that falls to the poor orphan boy except such small jobs as he could get until he arrived at a maturer age. When the Hungarian Rebellion broke out he at once made up his mind to join the volunteers if he could. Before making application, he set out to visit his sister who was working in a city many miles distant. The entire journey was made on foot. She begged him not to join the volunteers but stay in this city near her as there were but two of them in the whole wide world they ought to be together. The desire to be near his sister was strong but his answer explained the impossibility of such a companionship, however desirable.

"I am going because nobody wants me."

He never saw his sister afterward, nor heard of her.

Later he was accepted as a volunteer and under the command of General Paschel he fought in thirteen battles, some of one day's duration and some of five.

When asked if he were taken prisoner in any of the engagements, he said: "Only in the last one."

In the last battle of the war the Hungarian forces were opposed by 120,000 Austrian troops and the defeat of the Hungarians was the close of the war. Kossuth, commander of the Hungarian troops fled across the Turkish line with a bodyguard of 1,300. All those not killed and who did not run away were taken prisoners. Mr. Frisco, with 1500 others were taken prisoner to Buda-Pest. Here they were placed in a building where the cavalry horses were exercised during the winter months. There was no floor nor any heat and the suffering of poorly clad soldiers was terrible as it was mid-winter. Bread, the only food was thrown into the enclosure to the prisoners as feed to hogs. The body of a dead soldier served Mr. Frisco for a pillow during his first night in captivity.

After three weeks the Emperor picked out the best soldiers and sent the rest home. Mr. Frisco was one retained as a good soldier, just the choice he did not like, for he would be sent into Italy to fight the friend of the Hungarians, Garibaldi. The soldiers were an unhappy lot. They did not want to stay in Austria nor did they want to fight their friend, Garibaldi. A mania of suicide seized the troops. Every morning large numbers were found dead. Many deserted. Mr. Frisco deserted and was captured fifteen miles from headquarters. He with 300 other deserters received as punishment a brutal whipping. The men's feet were tied together and so were their hands, then they were lashed on their bare backs with a whip. The punishment was of a severe and brutal kind but did not in any way effect the result desired. There were deserters every day and Mr. Frisco was among the number. The second time he succeeded in getting across the Swiss line and forever bid farewell to his country and Austria. Later he went to Paris and continued the journey to London, Liverpool and to New York where he arrived with seven companions, all Hungarians, July 4, 1850. The city was in holiday attire, bands were playing, the scenes were so different from any Mr. Frisco had ever witnessed that he thought surely no one would ever die in America. But the next day, things seemed different. Nevertheless he has never regretted coming to America.

The company of eight had but eight cents when they landed, one man had all of that and but one of them could speak any English. Even his vocabulary was very limited. He could speak German better than English.

All went to a German hotel and asked for work. A man a short distance from the city wanted eight laborers to work in a garden and they were employed at $6.00 per month, board was included. Mr. Frisco said it was the finest board he had ever had in his life and he liked his home, but the rest of the party did not fancy weeding onions in a July sun at a $1.50 per week and decided to leave when they received their first payment, which they did, returning to New York. He received more than the others, but felt that he must go with them as he could no speak English.

Mr. Frisco's next work was in a brickyard in the vicinity of New York where he received a salary of $12.00 per month and board. The moulder became sick and he was promoted to his place at a salary of $25.00 per month. This seemed a very large salary and was received for over two years, when a position on a railroad at Cumberland was secured and Mr. Frisco had accumulated what seemed to him a small fortune.

One of his Hungarian friends heard of it and immediately made a trip to Cumberland and persuaded him to come down south where it was warmer. In a few weeks after coming to Baltimore, meeting his old comrades who were out of money, his savings of more than two years had dwindled to a mere pittance.

He drifted back to New York, his first American home and went to the hotel that sheltered him on his arrival. Later he went to West Point, walking the whole distance, about 50 miles. Here he announced that he was a soldier of Kossuth's and the commander took him in and gave him a supper of which he ate until he was ashamed to eat more and still was he hungry.

After supper the commander took him over to the barracks and called the soldiers out, saying:

"There is something here that you have never seen, one of Kossuth's soldiers," at the same time taking his cap and putting a five dollar piece into it and passing it around. Two hundred and fifty dollars and some cents were the contents of the cap at the end of the passing and this was presented to the distinguished soldier.

The following day the commander asked him to give an Austrian drill to the American soldiers. This was so well received that the cap was passed again and $100 was taken up.

"It was just like stealing money," Mr. Frisco said.

After a week's stay there he went to New York receiving a free pass to the city. Here he struck some more Hungarians and the West Point donations soon melted from view.

A brick yard was sought again not far from New York and a good place with good wages secured. All went well with the wanderer for a while. Here it was that Mr. Frisco had his first romance. The lady he says was a good woman and the alliance was highly favored by the landlady at whose boarding house he lived. There were obstacles in the way however. The girl's face was covered with large freckles, a blemish unknown in his native land. He did not have the courage to become a benedict and he said when some preparations were going forward for the wedding he decided that Hungarian and Irish would not do, and without giving out any information, beat a hasty retreat to New York.

Philadelphia was the next place visited and work at unloading flat boats was obtained but this was too strenuous to suit the wayfarer and he interviewed the landlord of the boarding house in regard to some other kind of work after a week. He was sent to a Catholic priest to be his hostler. Short of funds he walked out to the church, a distance of thirty miles. The priest received him very graciously but there was some kind of a church festival in progress when he arrived and no mention was made of supper. As Mr. Frisco had had no meal since breakfast, supper was the uppermost thought in his mind. Seeing no prospects of supper he walked back to Philadelphia without eating and told the landlord not to send him to any more priests.

The next work offered was unloading coal from boats.

"After a look at this slavish work," said Mr. Frisco, "I beat it back to New York, my last visit to New York."

It was during this stay that the first trouble came to him. At the German hotel that had so many times sheltered him, a bully engaged in a quarrel with a half intoxicated man of about 200 pounds weight. A fight ensued. The bully retired gracefully through the back door and the brunt of the battle fell on those in no way responsible for the trouble. A policeman was called and Mr. Frisco was arrested and locked up in jail. His friends interceded for him and he was released on condition that he leave New York within 24 hours. Chicago was selected by him and his friends bought a ticket to that place and he left his first American home forever.

He went to work on a railroad between Chicago and St. Louis at a good salary.

December, 1854, Mr. Frisco was married at St. Louis to a lady from Bohemia, and Missouri was the home of the couple until they left for the West eleven years later.

Mr. Frisco fought with the federal forces in Missouri during the rebellion and had some narrow escapes. When asked if he were ever captured, he replied, "No, I had a good horse."

Mrs. Frisco's father had a very narrow escape from being hanged by the confederates.

May, 1865, Mr. and Mrs. Frisco joined an emigrant train of 280 wagons, for the West. This was an exceedingly large train. Several trains combined for protection against the Indians who were hostile at that time.

At North Platte some Indians visited the camp and tried to pull the six-month old baby of Mr. and Mrs. Frisco out of the back of the wagon.

The Indians had murdered many people ahead of them and had taken some prisoners. A girl about sixteen years old and several men, all scalped were found by the train and buried. Several fresh made graves were also found. The remains of nine partly burned wagons were found by the road side.

A man seriously wounded by the Indians had reached Ft. Laramie. His wife and two children were taken prisoners by the Indians. She escaped from the Indians and arrived on the opposite bank of the Platte from the Fort. Her cries for help were heard and she was brought across the river but not in time to see her husband alive.

Mr. Frisco decided that whenever he found a settlement of white people he would stop. Such a condition was found at Baker City and he with seven other families stopped. The first night spent there was a happy one for in a sense the long perilous journey had ended. The sage brush was cleared off of what is now the main street of Baker. Mr. Frisco got out his violin and dancing on the common continued till a late hour. This was a happy occasion for the residents who were mostly bachelors as there were no ladies in that vicinity.

Mr. and Mrs. Frisco's total of worldly belongings consisted of a wagon, four oxen, camping outfit and five dollars in currency worth at that time three dollars.

A cabin was offered them for the winter. The dimensions were about 10 x 12 feet. The floor was of earth and the roof was of straw, but it had a fire place and served for heating and cooking purposes.

Nine belated freighters applied to Mr. Frisco for board until spring.

"Well, there's the hotel," said Mr. Frisco, pointing to the cabin, "if it suits you, all right."

It suited for it was a camp for months in the deep snow for their shelter. They had their own beds and constructed bunks one above another on the wall of the cabin from parts of the wagon beds. Mr. and Mrs. Frisco had one corner with bedding hung around it for their sleeping apartment. The table, a dry goods box stood in the center of the room and space was at a premium.

Mr. and Mrs. Frisco kept a way station for three years, the cooking was done on the fire place. Later they moved to Rye valley where they engaged in dairying.

In 1872 they came to Walla Walla and bought a farm near Waitsburg where they lived two years when they moved here. Mr. Frisco bought four acres of Mrs. Jane Singleton for $750.

A.H. Harris

A tribute to the
faithful oxen
who pulled the first traces of civilization
across the western plains.

But for the big-eyed, patient, faithful old ox and the vigorous, sometimes boisterous man with the goad and the long whip the country west of the Mississippi would still be marked on the maps as the great American desert and the buffalo would be dodging nothing more dangerous or deadly than a flint pointed arrow tossed at him by a painted savage.

It was the "whoa-haws" that pulled the first evidence of civilization across the arid western plains; that furnished the gold stampeder with his flour and bacon, with his pick, pan and shovel. It was the ox that could always be depended on to move steadily onward through the mud and slush with wagons loaded to the limit; never faltering at either swamp or swollen stream, and never demanding provender other than such as he could gather as he labored through the country.

The big, long-horned ox, with his hide pricked with the steel of the goad stick or cut into fantastic brands by the buckskin popper of a long whip, that is entitled to all of the honors that have been appropriated by the pioneer, who but for the ox would still be grubbing corn beyond the Platte. Gold seeker, doctor, business man and ruffian alike were dependent upon this humble, plodding animal.

The best drivers could handle the whip so dexterously that he could flick a fly off the hip of an ox twenty feet away or cut out a T-bone steak, and his swearing was of wide range and quite poetic. Drivers have been known to turn 22 yokes of oxen hitched to three trail wagons in the main street of a frontier town without mishap.

Next to the ox his driver is entitled to the credit for wresting this beautiful, sunkissed country from the tribes of Indians and peopling it with a God-fearing, Christian population. The good bullwhacker was always a man of more than ordinary intelligence, rough looking and somewhat coarsely vulgar, though he was. When a wagon boss was needed it was always the best driver that was named, and he it was who drove the lead wagons.

One of the most necessary qualifications for a good bullwhacker was a complete vocabulary of "cuss" words. The bullwhacker who could not or would not swear when occasion seemed to demand it or would only use a few common words of condemnation of the off bull on the swing team in a half-hearted way was given the rear team with the light mess wagon. To be a real driver it required an inventive genius who could say the right thing at the right time in words that were perfectly understood by the oxen, although perhaps not reported by Noah Webster. This fact was so well recognized by everybody in the early days that even the preachers--good, earnest Christian men every one--realizing the absolute necessity of it either only mildly rebuked or failed to hear the flow of profanity.

One of the reasons for the popularity of cattle during the early freighting days in the west was the fact that under all conditions and all circumstances they were reliable. Oxen seldom strayed away from the wagons and one man, who understood his business, could yoke up a long string of well broken oxen while a mule "skinner" was putting a saddle on the near wheel mule.

An average ox when driven to the freight wagon would seek his place in the team at the driver's mere suggestion. When the yoke was raised he would lower his neck and step under it. It took but a moment for the driver to put in the bow and key and thus proceed until the whole team was ready to stretch the chains for the long weary journey.

Ox-teams brought the first immigrants to the "Oregon Country" three-quarters of a century ago. For many years the only conveyance across the Plains was the plodding ox team. The hardships of the trip were such that no other animal could have withstood them. All along the old trail bleaching bones of the faithful burden-bearers were strewn when the locomotive first broke the death-like stillness of the desert.

Ox-teams moved the freight, the logs and the lumber. They drew the crude wagon in which the family rode to the village or to the house of worship. Ox-teams pulled the ore from the mines and the supply of bacon and beans to the workers who dug in the bowels of the earth. No pioneer activity could have been carried on without the unrewarded assistance of the ox.

In the mining districts of Idaho and Montana an average ox team consisted of 20 to 25 yokes of cattle -- 40 or 50 head. Never less than three trail wagons and sometimes four carried the freight. The average number of miles made every day, Sunday included, was about 20, although it was not uncommon to make 20 when the roads were good.

Different wagon bosses had different methods, of course, during the long, hot summer days some of them made a practice of making an early and a late drive, allowing the cattle to rest and feed during the heat of the day, others made but one drive during the day, aiming to make some good camping place for the night. Feed for the cattle was always the main thing, although wood and water was also considered.

Some of the great men of the west drove bulls across the plains. Hundreds of the most able lawyers, doctors and business men formed the plans that resulted in their future success and greatness between lurid oaths violently thrown at the faithful cattle.

The ox, real pioneer of the west, has vanished. True to every trust imposed upon him, unrewarded even in memory for his great service to the west, the plodding ox was compelled to give way to more rapid if less certain methods of transportation. The mad rush of civilization has swept him from the land, without a monument to his memory, with scarcely a word of sadness at his going.

Palouse Falls Trip

*A sightseeing trip to
Palouse Falls,
one of the wonders of the west,
in 1867.*

Palouse Falls -- A party of our citizens consisting of Judge Wyche and family, Mrs. Sexton, Dr. Stevenson, Mr. Boyer and family, lately made a visit to the Palouse Falls and we publish an account of the Falls in this issue from one of the party. The Falls are well worth a visit and a stereoscopic view of them may be seen at Shupe's gallery.

The Falls are some fifty-five miles from Walla Walla and you go on the road to the Snake river ferry (Silcott's) at the mouth of the Palouse; and if you go for pleasure and want to take it leisurely along, you drive the first day, seven miles beyond the Touchet, where you will find a nice spring, with fine grass, surrounded with interesting hills, now rejoicing in their robes of green...

The next day you start early to go down the long canyon on the way to Snake river before the heat of the day; Silcott will put you over the Snake river here, about a quarter of a mile wide, on his well arranged ferry run by a wire and pullies, in four minutes by the watch and then you keep on the Colville Road about four miles to the north end of a series of buttes and there you turn off and as there is no road, by picking your way, and looking for the most practicable ground and driving easterly for two or three miles you can drive your carriage directly to the falls and camp on the banks of the Palouse with the roar of the waters in your ears. If you are on horseback, follow the trail up the Palouse from the ferry to the falls.

The drive from the Walla Walla to the Falls is highly interesting; a succession of hills of all sizes and proportions greet you on all sides. From the summit on the divide, between the waters of the Touchet and Snake rivers, you have an extended view back to the Blue mountains and ahead to the Snake river and the hills and country far beyond and just before descending the Snake river hill your eye rests on the grateful green bottom of the Palouse with its clear and pure waters, flowing into the turbid Snake and after ascending the Snake river hill to the northward and eastward the eye sweeps over a vast extent of country rarely surpassed in rugged desolation and wildness.

The Palouse, for miles above the Falls, and below, is confined to a narrow canyon and at the Falls, the water making a sudden turn to the west, leaps over in one sheet, a rocky ledge falling from 150 to 200 feet into a large and nearly circular basin below. The exact height of the Falls is not known. There is a sketch of the Falls in "Mullan's Military Road Report" and he estimates the height at 100 feet and Castleman, who took a photograph of the Falls, calls them 190 feet; probably they are not less than 150 feet or more than 200. The river near the Falls is hardly excelled by the Falls itself. The banks are of solid rock and perpendicular and the water rushes along from 200 to 300 feet below, so deep down as hardly to be seen and making one giddy as standing on the brink he looks down. How the river has made its way through this rock must be left to the geologist to determine.

The basin below is nearly circular and from 300 to 500 feet across. To get a good view of the Falls and to see its real beauties, you must descend into the basin and get directly under the Falls. To do this you go down the river about three hundred yards and descend a chasm over piles of rocks to the bottom below; the way down is not easy but practicable and then you go over and under and through a dense mass of bushes and undergrowth, some 200 yards up to the Falls.

H.E. Holmes

*Setting up business on the frontier
was an adventure in itself.
Mr. Holmes talks about the early drug business
and tells a humorous story of "sponges to fill."*

In the 'fifties and 'sixties the upper Columbia river country and points in Eastern Oregon were as remote as the Yukon is today. All freight was by boat up the Columbia, portages having to be made at the Cascades and at The Dalles, and taken by teams from Wallula to Walla Walla and the interior points, and distributed again by more freight teams and pack trains to the verges of civilization. Ice and low water closed the Columbia river to navigation about December 1st, and no more freight could be carried up until the early spring, so all stocks for four months had to be in by the middle of November and stores and warehouses would be filled to overflowing with goods. Portland was the distributing point for the upper country and it took a week or more to get returns from there for the small express packages that could be brought through on stage. There was no stocking up; no "hurry up orders"; what was in stock could be sold; what ran short had to be waited for until spring. Freight was charged on a basis of measurement of forty cubic feet per ton. The freight on a barrel of lamp chimneys or lamp black was the same as on a barrel of rosin, and on a case of empty bottles the same as if they had been packed with merchandise. Straw and sawdust packing cost 75 cents to $1.00 a cubic foot freight, and to avoid paying this it was not unusual for retailers to direct some merchantable commodity to be used as packing as 'linseed meal to pack,' 'Epsom salt to pack,' 'sassafras bark to pack.' The writer remembers an order sent to a well-known eastern house with directions to 'use carriage sponges to fill.' On arrival of the shipment it was found that the order had been heartlessly 'stuffed' with sponges, for there were boxes and barrels and cases 'filled' all right, each with few drugs and-much sponge. There were piles and piles of sponges taken out as each succeeding case was opened, and in the midst of the avalanche the writer stood appalled and paralyzed. But there they were. The order had been given 'sponges to fill,' and apparently it was interpreted to mean sponges to fill the store instead of the packing cases. They nevertheless had to be cared for and so they were stored away in a damp basement, and behold, in a fortnight's time they had swelled up and crawled all over and filled that basement. That was over thirty years ago, but there are some of those sponges still in Walla Walla.

The only towns in Eastern Washington in the 'fifties, 'sixties and early 'seventies from the Oregon boundary to the north pole, were Walla Walla, Dayton and Waitsburg. The site on which the thriving city of Spokane stands had not been discovered, and Colfax had not been founded; and in all that fertile country, a big empire of 40,000 square miles, now checkered by railroads, cross-sectioned by irrigating districts and alive with prosperous people, the many towns and cities now dotting the map were then undreamed of and were to be future realizations. 'Virginia Bill' held one trading post on Columbia river, and 'Wild Goose Bill' had another, and there was a long reach to Fort Colville and another 200 miles to the Kootenai, and then the untrodden wilderness to the frozen north.

The first drug store that can be definitely determined was that of Dr. J.H. Day, at Walla Walla. Just the date of his coming cannot at the present writing be stated, but quite likely it was in the early 'sixties. He was a practicing physician, well educated and a close student. He took up assaying and did a thriving business in purchasing and melting gold dust -- Walla Walla being in those early days the center for the Kootenai, Colville, Orofino and Boise mines. Dr. Day practically had a monopoly of the drug business in Eastern Washington well into the 'seventies. He carried what was then a large stock of drugs and did a large and profitable outfitting business for the mining districts tributary to Walla Walla. In 1873 or 1874 he built one of the first brick buildings in Walla Walla, and put in the first soda fountain that was installed in Washington. Dr. Day was a central figure in Walla Walla and his sturdy eccentricities gave him a distinction of which he was apparently all unconscious. He lived a bachelor to his death and the poverty of his life was the absence of the riches that shower on a home blessed with wife and children. The history of Day's drug store would not be complete without mention of Mr. Ryan, who is affectionately known through the whole Walla Walla Valley as "Mike" Ryan. Little "Mike" went into Day's drug store a wee bit of a lad, hardly big enough to look over the top of the counter, early in the 'seventies, and has been in that one store ever since. Forty-one years in one store is a long time and "Mike" certainly holds the record for continuous service. Mr. Ryan is deservedly a favorite, and the money he has made for others would fill a wagon.

Dr. C.J. Taft, now a retired capitalist, of North Yakima, had a small stock of drugs opposite Dr. Day's drug store in the early 'seventies, but gave most of his attention to the practice of medicine, and it might be added that he dearly loved a good horse.

Dr. Shoue also had about the same time quite a pretentious drug store at the location now occupied by the Green & Jackson Drug company. He was a German physician and his temperament was not calculated to succesfully master the details necessary to make a success out of a pioneer drug store and his business was closed out about 1875.

In 1873 Mr. Newby, from Oregon, opened a small stock near the corner of Third street. After about a year he was succeeded by Mr. Gray, a former clerk of Mr. Day's, who in turn sold the store to Henry Cock. As Mr. Cock was not a druggist, and quickly discovered that the way to a quick fortune did not lay through a drug store he got "cold feet" and turned the store over to the writer, whose assets consisted mostly of courage and self confidence, in consideration of his assuming the liabilities against the store. The store room was only eleven feet wide and had no show window, the only light being through an ordinary sash door, yet it was big enough and light enough in which to make friends. I recall a remark made by Dr. Day, the proprietor of the big bright drug store that had held the drug business of the inland country for years against all comers: "Give that fellow rope enough and he will hang himself." Well he did -- he hung on. That was thirty-seven years ago and he has been hanging on ever since. Somehow business kept coming; a move was made across the street to the location formerly occupied by Dr. Shoue; later the stand was purchased; then a wife and babies came hanging on and a modest home was paid for. The story is told. I have always been profoundly thankful for the liberal supply of rope my good friend permitted to be used.

The first drug business in Waitsburg was started in 1867 by Dr. Parkinson, who continued to 1870, when he sold to J.A. Brown, who in 1875 sold to J.W. Morgan, who still owns it and gives it his personal attention. The drug business at Dayton was started by Dr. J.H. Day, of Walla Walla, as a branch of his Walla Walla business, and shortly after was sold to his brother, Jesse N. Day, who was the founder of the town, and placed in charge of the latter's son, J.H. Day, Jr., who is familiarly known as "Joe." He took a course and was graduated by a college of pharmacy and has since successfully conducted the business, having been in charge some 30 odd years, during which time he has served as president of the state association and on the state board of pharmacy.

The people of those days may not have lived the simple life, but there is no doubt that they lived simply. The transformation of the pharmacy found in that oracle of the primitive drug store, the dispensatory, to the pharmacy of the pharmaceutical patents, of the copyrighted and scientifically mysterious labels, of the wondrous mixtures with still more wondrous names that are given to the latter day saints of the dispensing case, has not been made. The pioneer druggist came to his place of business betimes in the morning, cleaned his lamp chimneys, shook up his macerations, took a few packages to the early stage or boat, glanced at the little weekly paper that had the latest news from the "states" and waited for the tingle of the coin that would make up the day's business. He had no "full lines" of ready made stuff -- not he.

Oh, halcyon days, there were none! And cut rates! Why, I grow generous when I think about it: the smallest change was a dime that passed as a "bit" of 12 ½ cents. No nickles; nothing sold for less than a "bit." Everything was based on a gold standard and silver and currency were both taken at a discount, a roll of silver ($20) or a $20 bill passing at from $18 to $19 according to the premium on gold in the "states." The changes that have been wrought by the coming of the multitude and by the introduction of modern methods have kept the Pacific Northwest actively abreast of the best of the East, and today we in Washington can well be proud of our two schools of pharmacy, one at the State University and one at the State Agricultural college; of our State Board of Pharmacy, which sets a high standard of requirement for registration; of our State Pharmaceutical association.

With these achievements of the present before us let us hope that there are none who "mourn for the days that are gone."

O.F. Canfield

A Portland horse racer, Joe Crabbe, gets outsmarted by Indian Chief Howlish Wampoo.

When Howlish Wampoo, the famous Umatilla chief, was the ruler of his tribe he had many horses, some fine racing animals. There was a great horse racer at that time named Joe Crabbe, living in Portland. Crabbe had known of Howlish Wampoo's fast horses and was anxious to get up some races and incidentally clean up some big bets. Going to Umatilla he finally engineered a big meet with the Indians. The crowning event was to be between Crabbe's champion and anything that the Indian chief could bring on. Howlish Wampoo was very crafty. He might have been a Teuton diplomat of the present. He brought out and made a great parade of a spotted horse which he said he was going to run, and then innocently put the horse in a corral very handy to the white men. Crabbe's hostlers took the horse out in the night, no Indians being in sight, and tried him. They found that he was nothing extra fast, and so they made all their plans in the light of that discovery. The next day came the great race. Everything was excitement, and betting went to a great pitch. Crabbe finally put up $1,500 on his horse and at last even his silver mounted saddle and spurs. Howlish Wampoo accepted the bets with seeming reluctance and Indian stoicism. When the horses were brought out Crabbe saw with some suspicion that the spotted Indian racer looked a little different and stepped a little different from what he did the day before. As he told Canfield in relating his experience he "felt a sort of cold chill go down his back." But it was too late to back out. Off they went, a four mile race, two miles to a stake, around it and back again. The Indian horse was evidently not the same horse. He went like a shot out of a gun and reached the goal post so much ahead that his rider turned back to run again with Crabbe's champion, and then beat him into camp. The Indians made an awful clean up on the white men's bets. Howlish Wampoo, with just a faint suspicion of an inward grin on his mahogany countenance, told Crabbe that he might have his saddle and spurs back again, and enough money to get home on.

Afterwards Crabbe made great offers to the Indian for the spotted racer, wishing to take him East or even to Europe, for he was satisfied that he could beat the world in a four mile race. But Howlish Wampoo would never sell the pet racer.

P.B. Johnson

The editor of the Walla Walla Union
and Secretary of the board of the W.W.& C.R.R.
tells the story of the construction of
Doc Baker's Rawhide Railroad in 1872.

Take any map of the United States -- one issued free by either of the great transcontinental railroads will do -- trace out on it the boundaries of the state of Washington, and see if you have not traced the outline of a big jar lying on its side with its mouth toward the Pacific ocean. That jar is typical of the resources of Washington. Look again at the map and trace out that portion of Snake river which runs through Washington to its junction with the Columbia, and down that stream to the Oregon line, and you have, south of the river, a large portion of what is known as "the Walla Walla country" located, a designation which covers a goodly slice of Oregon south of the state line, as well as of Washington. This region is noted for its great fertility, and gives the name to a variety of wheat known in the markets of the world as "Walla Walla." It is noted in the history of the Pacific Northwest as the scene of the labors and massacre of Dr. Marcus Whitman, the man who made a memorable midwinter ride on horseback from Walla Walla to Washington city, nearly 60 years ago. This famous region was thrown open to settlement in the spring of 1859, and for several years afterwards was regarded as fit for stockraising and nothing else.

To this stock country went many men with their herds and flocks. Among the first to enter was Dr. Dorsey S. Baker, a native of Illinois, who, having graduated from one of the medical colleges in Pennsylvania, had migrated to the Willamette valley, in Oregon, where his money-making instincts led him to abandon the saddlebags of a country doctor for the more lucrative horse furniture of a stockraiser and dealer. He took with him to the Walla Walla valley a large band of cattle and a small stock of general merchandise. The cattle were turned into the vast sweeps of succulent bunch-grass which began in the streets of the little town, started on the boundary line of the military post called Fort Walla Walla, and extended in all directions more miles than an eye could survey during several days of travel. The merchandise was offered for sale to the scattered cattlemen in the valley, and hangers on of the garrison at prices which were fabulous in their magnitude.

When gold was discovered in northern and eastern Idaho, Walla Walla became the outfitting point for the hardy miners and the place they resorted to pass the winter. The store opened in Walla Walla by Dr. Baker and his brother-in-law, John F. Boyer, became noted all over the Pacific Northwest, and was regarded as reliable in all things it undertook. Hundreds of miners deposited in the iron safes of Baker & Boyer their buckskin purses filled with gold dust, and left them there for months, serenely confident that the sacks, with their contents untouched, would be delivered up to them on demand. Never was this confidence ever betrayed.

As the mines gave out the cattle began to be a small value, owing to their rapid increase and the distance to market, it being necessary to drive them almost to Chicago before a purchaser was found. People began to investigate the capabilities of the soil of the Walla Walla valley, and in a short time with satisfactory results, and the problem was changed from how to get flour into Walla Walla to how to get wheat out. At that time the only way to get Walla Walla wheat to the market was to haul it with teams 30 miles over a sandy, alkali road to the Columbia river, to the wharfboat of the Oregon Steam Navigation Company, at the old Hudson's Bay town of Wallula, where it was put on a steamer and carried to Celilo, some 120 miles down stream, where it was transferred to cars and hauled 16 miles around The Dalles, and then transferred to another boat and carried 50 miles to the Upper Cascades, where it was put on another railroad and hauled six miles, past the blockhouse that marks the scene of Sheridan's first battle, to the Lower Cascades, and then put on another boat and carried 10 miles to the mouth of the Willamette and 10 miles up that stream to Portland, where it was put into warehouses and then into deep seagoing ships bound for England and other markets. For putting the grain on and taking it off of and carrying it on three steamboats and putting it on and off and transporting it over two railroads, the Oregon Steam Navigation Company charged $6 a ton. All the wheat had to be shipped in sacks to permit easy handling from boats to cars and from cars to boats as well as for shipment on the ocean, the shipmasters fearing to undertake the long voyage around Cape Horn with a cargo of wheat loaded in bulk.

Teamsters charged all sorts of prices for hauling wheat from Walla Walla to Wallula and merchandise back. Many farmers hauled their crops to the wharfboat. As much as $13 a ton was charged to haul wheat by team over the excessively dusty alkali roads on the 30 miles between Walla Walla and the Columbia river. In addition to this heavy charge teamsters were frequently paid by the hour to keep their teams harnessed up and in line at Wallula, so as to get their loads on the wharfboat at the earliest possible moment.

When you know that the mighty Columbia, above The Dalles, flows over a rocky bed, that its banks are high ledges of basalt rock, or long stretches of drifting sand; that the tillable soil begins several miles back from the river, and that grain and other farm products are not raised on the banks of the Columbia as they are on the banks of the Ohio and most Eastern streams, the reason for hauling the wheat so many miles is evident, and the necessity for a railroad becomes as plain to the reader as it did to the people who raised wheat in the Walla Walla country. To meet this great necessity a company was organized in 1871 to build a railroad between Walla Walla and the Columbia river. Dr. Baker, by reason of being the richest man in the valley, became the principal stockholder. The company, or rather Dr. Baker, decided to build a narrow-gauge railroad, beginning at the Columbia river, to Walla Walla. He selected a landing place on the Columbia, about a mile above the old town of Wallula, built a steam sawmill there, and began to cut up logs cut in the forests of the Clearwater section of Idaho and rafted down Snake river, and cut in the heavy timbers on the headwaters of the Yakima, driven down that stream to the Columbia and rafted down to the mill. He went into the field and assisted the engineers in locating the line of the road; he personally superintended the grading and tracklaying; in short, he "bossed" the construction of the entire road from the throwing of the first shovel of sand to the driving of the last spike, and personally superintended the operation of the road until he sold it. Not only did he direct all the work of construction, but he furnished the money to purchase rails and other supplies without mortgaging a mile of the road or issuing a bond. The road from the Columbia to Walla Walla, as built by Dr. Baker was 31 miles long, and cost a little over $10,000 a mile. He built a branch 14 miles long into Umatilla county, Oregon, to tap the great wheat fields there.

Dr. Baker built the first 10 miles of his railroad out of wood. That is to say he laid red fir rails sawed at the mill, in mortices cut in the wooden crossties, by spikes driven through the rails. Over this primitive railroad freight was hauled by little eight-ton engines, which carried water in tanks on their boilers and burned wood. The next year the road was extended a few miles and the wooden rails given a coating of strap-iron spiked to their surfaces. The next year Dr. Baker extended the road to a point five miles west of Walla Walla, and laid on all the road 25-pound iron T rails, bought in England and landed in Portland at a cost of nearly $100 a ton. It cost $15 a ton to have them transported by the Oregon Steam Navigation Company from Portland to Wallula. The first terminus of the road was almost on the spot where Dr. Marcus Whitman and a dozen others were murdered by the Indians in 1847, and was named Whitman. There Dr. Baker said the railroad should end; that he would not build it to Walla Walla. The people of Walla Walla held a mass meeting and appointed a committee to induce Dr. Baker to build the road to Walla Walla, where he owned more property and had greater interests than any 10 other men in the place. The money was raised and the road extended to Walla Walla.

The nature of the country is such, the down grade of the first 12 miles west of Walla Walla is so heavy, that a train will make the distance going west without other motive power than gravity. From there to the river were one or two short heavy up-grades but most of the way from the city to the river is down hill, Walla Walla being 600 feet higher than the Columbia at the end of the road. The worst thing to contend with in operating a railroad from Walla Walla to the Columbia is several miles of sand, which frequently causes blockades worse than snow blockades, the wind driving the sand between the tracks in such quantities and with such force that it is necessary laboriously to dig the track out with pick and shovel. This difficulty existed from the laying of the first tie, and is as bad today as it was then. It is now to some extent obviated by the use of sand fences and the constant vigilant labor of a large gang of men.

Returning east from the Columbia, the little blanket engines had to climb the 12 miles of hill, and it made them cough and snort to do it at a snail's pace. The rest of the equipment of the road was on a par with the engines. Freight was carried on flatcars, and passengers in a "homemade coach," a flatcar on which a house was built, with windows in the sides and a door at each end, and seats on the sides. It was like a bobtail horse car, though not as comfortable. This car was attached to the end of a freight train, and accompanied it on its slow trips to and from the river. Coming up, the little engine occupied from five to ten hours, depending on the amount of freight. Going down from Walla Walla to the Columbia took almost as much time, because of the very heavy grade where it was frequently necessary to cut the train in two and haul part of it to the summit and go back after the rest. It is recorded in the papers of that time that the train which carried Senator Morton and party to the Columbia made the trip in the "extra-ordinary time of two hours." The fare was $5 either way. The charge for freight was $5 a ton, without regard to classification or direction. It was $5 a ton on wheat going to market and $5 a ton a drygoods, groceries or millinery going to Walla Walla.

One season the farmers were very anxious to get their wheat to market so as to obtain the then prevailing high price. They appointed a committee to confer with Dr. Baker and see if some way could be devised to expedite the movement of wheat over the road. At the meeting of the committee and Dr. Baker, it was agreed that he would haul, as "fast freight," all wheat offered, provided $1 a ton more was paid on it. Those who did not take kindly to the extra dollar-a-ton idea insisted that, "when Dr. Baker made up a train, he put the 'fast' wheat on the forward end of the train, and the slow, or $5-a-ton wheat, on the hind end of the same train."

While Dr. Baker was operating his narrow-gauge railroad, the grangers were trying to run the country and all things in it to suit themselves. The order reached Walla Walla in due time, and, among other things, it attempted to reduce the price on horseshoeing and other blacksmith work. With these ends in view they rented a shop in Walla Walla and installed a crossroads blacksmith in it, who sang through his nose as he burned the iron in the fire and strove to shoe horses for less than the expert city smiths charged. Of course, the shop soon failed to pay, and was closed up by the poorer if wiser promoters. Not long after the shop closed a committee from the local grange, composed principally of the managers of the closed blacksmith shop, called on Dr. Baker to induce him to reduce the freight charge on wheat. Dr. Baker listened patiently to all they had to say, meanwhile rubbing his long nose with his forefinger, a familiar habit of his, indicating strict attention to all that was going on. When the committee finished Dr. Baker rose and said: "All I have got to say, gentlemen, is you had better learn how to run a blacksmith shop before you undertake to run a railroad." The committee departed much crestfallen.

Pondering over the physical characteristics of the Columbia basin where the banks of the navigable rivers are either sharp basalt rocks or shifting sands, and the tillable land begins miles back from the rivers, rendering it necessary to haul the products of the country to a few convenient points on the rivers, over long distances by team or steam, Dr. Baker formulated the axiom: "He who owns the approaches to the river owns the river." Some time after he had reached this conclusion Dr. Baker went to Portland and had an interview with the officials, who were also the owners, of the Oregon Steam Navigation Company, a powerful corporation which owned all the boats on the Columbia above the Willamette, and the railroad portages around the obstructions to navigation at the Cascades and The Dalles. During this interview Dr. Baker proposed to sell his road to them. To this offer they replied they did not want it; that it would be better for them all for Dr. Baker to keep on operating the railroad, to bring them freight and let them haul it to Portland; that they did not care to leave the river and branch out in railroading.

Dr. Baker replied that he was going either to sell out or put boats on the river and build narrow-gauge portage roads around the obstructions.

"When I have built my portages and put on boats where will you get your freight?" asked the doctor. This was a stunning question and the steamboat men asked time to consider. When next they met the steamboatmen agreed to buy the road at a good round price, possession to be given the first of the year, Dr. Baker to have the income of the road till then. Crops in the Walla Walla valley were light that year and Dr. Baker grumbled at his hard luck.

The writer is reliably informed that Dr. Baker sold a six-seventh interest in his road to the Oregon Steam Navigation Company for $321,000, and the profits to follow its operation for six months; that he afterwards sold the remaining seventh to Henry Villard for $100,000, taking in payment stocks that he sold for $175,000.

The first year the road was operated by the Oregon Steam Navigation Company it carried 75,000 tons of freight, principally wheat, out of the country, and 10,000 tons of freight into the country. All of the freight paid $5 a ton, and the expenses of operation were about $50,000.

Nettie M. Galbraith

Bishop Lemuel Wells' daughter
tells about the operation of a girls' school
on the frontier in 1872.

The words, "My brother, you are going to a new work and a new country, and I would advise you to bend much of your energy in the founding of schools and other institutions," expressed by Bishop Morris, made a profound impression upon the young missionary, L.H. Wells, at his consecration. Reflecting upon this advice as he rode on horseback through the country, he decided that schools, as well as churches, were needed. "I will found a school for girls," he declared, and a letter to his parish in New Haven followed this decision.

Twelve hundred dollars was the immediate response and a school building was erected. At first this building was used for religious services for St. Paul's, by which name his little mission was known. Soon a church was erected next to the school.

St. Paul's School for Girls was opened in 1872 with three boarders and twenty day pupils. Traditions and history of this school date back to the frontier days when gold dust and nuggets, cattle and wheat or flour, were used as mediums of exchange or barter.

A pair of gold scales was kept in the office to weigh the dust which fathers brought to pay for their daughters' board and tuition. The first boarder lived in a little village where the missionary came to hold services. In the family where he spent the night, he saw a pretty little girl and he asked the parents to send her to his boarding school soon to open in Walla Walla. The farmer told him that he couldn't sell his cattle and he had no money. "Give me cattle, then" replied father. So the two men rode out to the range and the missionary selected the cattle. The farmer agreed to keep them on the range. When they were sold several years later, they, with the increase, brought enough money to build an addition to the school.

Potatoes paid for another boarder. There was no place to store two wagon loads of potatoes, so a big hole was dug for them. One girl came to school the first day perched on the top of a load of flour drawn by six mules. "Here comes the flower of the family," said one of the teachers, as the wagon was halted before the school. Another came riding a mule in a mule team, all the way from near the Alaska line in British Columbia, where provisions had been taken.

The teachers had a difficult time with one little girl, trying to teach her to say her prayers. Before she had acquired the habit, a new girl arrived and was given her as a bedfellow. That night cries and shrieks were heard and a teacher rushed to their room. The new girl was declaring, "I won't sleep with a heathen. I won't sleep with a heathen! She won't say her prayers." The little heathen soon became a Christian.

Long years afterward the first boarder wrote to Rev. Wells. She said: "I consider it a glorious privilege to have watched the development of the West during the last half century and to feel that I have been a part of it." She expressed her appreciation for the value rendered by St. Paul's school as a center of intellectual and spiritual culture when the West was new and crude and there was so much need for what the school could offer.

In 1872, a recipe book, "Choice Receipts" was published in New England to benefit the girls' school opening in the Walla Walla frontier. The book's preface page and first recipe are included here.

PREFACE

All of the following "choice receipts" have been thoroughly tested; and the most of them taken from old family manuscripts.

The first edition of this little book, issued in 1872, for the benefit of Christ Church Fair, sold so rapidly, that the demand far exceeded the supply; and in order to accommodate a large number of subscribers, it is deemed advisable to put forth a second and revised edition, containing a number of additional receipts--the proceeds of which have been donated by the compiler toward the erection of a Girl's School at Walla Walla, Washington Territory.

RECEIPTS

Calf's Head Soup -- Boil until the meat cleaves from the bone; cut in pieces the size of an egg; strain the liquor and add to the meat; also one dozen large onions chopped fine, and fried with butter. Season with black pepper, cayenne, and salt, one large spoonful each of marjoram, thyme, cloves, and mace, (powdered.) Save the brains and boil in a cloth by themselves, then mix them with browned flour, two ounces of butter, and add to the soup, to thicken it. For Balls, three or four pounds of veal, chopped fine, with quarter the proportion of salt pork, and half the quantity of onions. Season the same as the soup, with the addition of two eggs, and two crackers pounded fine. Fry in lard. Add catsup and wine to the soup, also slices of lemon and hard boiled eggs after it is dished.

Order the calf's head from market with the *skin on.*

Chapter **7**

Indians' Last Stand

"The wild Indian is gone;
his trails that wound over the hills
and through our valleys
are obstructed by barbed wires
and the last trail vanished long ago."
Miles C. Moore

R ailroads, schools, churches, wagons loaded with sacks of wheat, barbed wire fences -- these were all marks of civilization. It seemed as though the wild west had been subdued, if not tamed, in the Northwest. Law and Order was extended to all areas of the Inland Empire as the land became populated. It was hoped that Indian troubles were a thing of the past. But fate had one or two more uprisings in store for the settlers.

A band of Nez Perce Indians who had refused to move to the Reservations established in 1855, lived in the beautiful Wallowa Valley in northeastern Oregon. Chief Joseph, the tribe's leader, was told in 1873 that they must leave their homeland and join the other Nez Perce on the Reservation. This order was appealed by Joseph, and a Presidential order allowed them to remain in the Wallowas until 1875 when increased pressure by white settlers convinced the President to rescind it. In 1877 a council was held at Lapwai by General O.O. Howard where Joseph was told he had thirty days to round up his livestock and get them and his people onto the Reservation. While Joseph favored leaving the Wallowas, a few restless young braves murdered some white settlers and the Nez Perce War was off and running, not to end until Joseph delivered his famous surrender speech in the mountains of Montana.

The last of the Northwest Indian Wars were fought in eastern Oregon (1878 Bannock War) and central Idaho (Sheepeater War, 1879). Both of these uprisings were supressed by General Howard's troops and since that time the Indians have been mostly at peace.

By the 1870's, emigrants had new ways available to reach the Northwest. Some took the transcontinental railroad to San Francisco and then traveled by boat to Portland and from there up the Columbia to their destination. Let's join one of those pioneers as he recounts his impressions of his new home.

Daniel Williams

Sixteen year old lad emigrates in 1873
with his parents to Washington Territory
where thirteen members of his family had
a 16 x 20 foot log cabin
for their first home.

It was in 1873, back in Hardin County, Iowa, that my father decided to come to Washington Territory. Neighbors had made the journey, and sent back glowing accounts of the mild winters, the hills covered with bunch grass where stock roamed the year round, making it unnecessary to provide winter feed.

The route my father chose was by train to San Francisco, then by boat to Wallula. I was a lad of sixteen years, and I found the trip most interesting. There was the ride on the steamer to Portland, then up the Columbia, portaging twice before reaching Wallula. At this place our belongings were transferred to freight wagons and the long tedious ride to Waitsburg was begun.

Dr. Baker's famous strap-iron road was then being constructed, but was finished only as far as the Touchet. Stages were running between Walla Walla and Lewiston. Mines were active in central Idaho and stage travel was heavy. There were several stage stations; one of them being where Dayton now stands, one at Marengo, one at Pataha and another on the Alpowa. Stages had no springs. The body swung on heavy straps as the cumbersome vehicle jolted along through clouds of dust.

The only roads were the old Indian trails. Some of them are still visible five miles east of Pomeroy; the same trails that Lewis and Clark followed when Indian guides led them through here in 1806 on their return from the mouth of the Columbia River.

In 1874 my father located his land. He bought a relinquishment from John Rush, who had filed a preemption. There was a log cabin 16 x 20 feet in size, and thirteen of us to occupy it, as one of my sisters was married and lived with us. There was a tiny cabin built to smoke meat, that accommodated two beds, while trundle beds were used by the younger children.

Soon we were building a roomier house, hauling the logs from the Blue Mountains. We hewed the logs and made the floors of lumber hauled from the Eckler mill on Eckler Mountain. We made the sash for the doors and windows ourselves, getting the window-glass from Waitsburg. There were two rooms, with a sort of gallery between them, where we often ate in hot weather. There were rooms upstairs, so we were not crowded.

In 1881 we built a really good house. There was a planing mill at Pomeroy by that time, so we brought lumber from the sawmill and had it planed. Windows and doors were shipped up the Snake river and we hauled them from New York Bar.

About the first article manufactured in this locality was a chair. Hartrode made the first chairs, using native maple which grew along the creeks and gulches. The seats were made of rawhide strips. We still have our set, made more than fifty years ago.

There was a lot of game in those days, although the Indians had killed off many of the deer. There were no elk. Prairie chickens and grouse were here by the thousands. The first elk were brought into the Blue Mountains by the Game Commission, which sent to Montana for two carloads, and turned them loose in the mountains.

There were no bridges. I used to watch the stage horses, lathered with sweat, plunge into the ice-cold streams, the stage coach dropping down the bank a foot or two, jolting the passengers unmercifully. Four miles east of Waitsburg a man named Star lived on the banks of the Touchet River by the stage crossing. The road commissioner, Mr. Fudge, decided that the time had come for a bridge. My brother-in-law, Thornton, and my brother and I were given the contract for its construction. It was a simple affair, but a real blessing to travelers and horses. We cut down trees along the Touchet River and so came into being the first bridge between Pomeroy and Walla Walla. This was called Star's Bridge.

The first school east of the Tucanon was on Pataha Flats. It was built in 1874 by a man named Sharpneck, who had a little sawmill at the edge of the Blue Mountains. We met there for spelling school, literary and debating society, and the usual gatherings typical of the frontier days.

I recall going to Marengo in 1875-76-77 to attend Fourth of July celebrations. We had a picnic dinner, singing and speaking. Ernest Hopkins, a pioneer teacher, was the orator of the day. I knew Louis Raboin, the Hudson's Bay Company trapper. He lived with his Indian wife and children at Marengo, the place having been named for him.

I was well acquainted with Jerry McGuire and the Hopwoods, who settled in what later became Asotin County. I knew Chief Timothy well, and heard him preach on Pataha Flat. The site of his village at the mouth of the Alpowa later became the home of David Mohler. I have stayed there over night and gathered apples from the trees planted by the Rev. Spalding.

Where Pomeroy now stands were fields of wheat. The McCabe cabin stood near where Main street is now. The first wheat was hauled to Wallula; then to Walla Walla. As soon as father raised enough wheat to sell, we hauled it twenty-five miles to New York Bar using four to six horses to a load. In 1878 a mill was built at Pataha by Mr. Houser. Garfield County was organized in 1881.

The country was full of peaceful, blanketed Indians. They wintered at the mouth of the Alpowa and the Asotin. Spring found them journeying to the camas grounds. Over in the Wallowa Valley, Chief Joseph lived with his tribe on the land which his father, Old Chief Joseph, had demanded as a part of the treaty grant in 1855. The treaty had been broken once by the whites, but in 1873 it was again restored to the Indians, but only for a short time.

The valley was the hunters' paradise. There were deer, elk and mountain sheep; wild fowl by the thousands and a lake full of fish. There were berries and roots, everything the Indians desired, summer or winter. It was here that Chief Joseph was born. When an attempt was made to drive the Indians out, they fought to keep their home. Soldiers were ambushed on Whitebird Creek. I was at Lapwai when they brought in the wounded.

When a company of volunteers was organized at Pomeroy, I joined and got the contract to haul military supplies for General Howard. I freighted as far as Mt. Idaho, fifteen miles from the Clearwater. From there, pack-horses and mules were used.

Chief Joseph retreated and kept up a running fight for three months before surrendering to General Miles. He was taken to the Indian Territory and kept there for seven years, then transferred to the Colville reservation in Northeastern Washington, where he died an exile from his old home. There is a monument at the foot of Wallowa Lake marking his grave.

George Christopher Johnston

Mr. Johnston had experiences
in practically all areas of the West
before he married and settled down in 1873.

George Christopher Johnston was born in New York, March 3, 1835. His mother died when he was a mere child and he was left to the care of two step-brothers and a step-sister. His father left New York after his wife's death, never returning, and the family never heard from him. Mr. Johnston has no memory of his father. It was a custom in that part of the country to bind out children to work. The age varied from as low as six years to twenty-one. Mr. Johnston was bound out to a family in New Jersey, by his older brother, when he was eleven years old. Here he remained three years, when an event, seemingly most unfortunate, changed the plans of his brothers and in all probability resulted in his journeying to the Pacific coast. One day while engaged in spreading lime on the farm land, the wind blew lime dust into his eyes. A cold added to his eye trouble. Every old woman in the vicinity had an unfailing remedy for such a complaint, and "I tried every one of them," he remarked, "with the result that I became blind." His brother, Dick Gilbert, took him to Dr. Wallace, a celebrated eye specialist of New York City. Two operations were performed on the left eye and one on the right. The operations were successful; Mr. Johnston has wonderful eyes. he has never worn glasses and he says, "I have never needed glasses; at the age of 84 I have no difficulty in reading without them." His brother sent him a pair of the green goggles from San Francisco during the period of this treatments. He wore them one day when he saw the doctor. "My boy," said Dr. Wallace, "take off those glasses; more eyes are ruined by wearing glasses than from any other cause." In 1855 Dick Gilbert decided to bind out his ward to a friend of his to work in a foundry. The ward was not at all pleased at the prospect. The result was a visit to Dr. Wallace. "Don't do it," Dr. Wallace said. "All that I have done for you will be for naught. The heat of the furnace will make you blind. Why don't you go west?" "It costs something to go west," was the reply. "Study the matter and if you decide to go, come bid me good-bye." The decision was made to go west, to San Francisco, to live with brother James, who was both a father and mother to him. When he told Dr. Wallace of his decision, he seemed very much pleased. When he bid him good-bye he dropped a twenty dollar gold piece in his hand.

Charles Minot, superintendent of the New York and Erie railroad at that time, gave him a pass to Chicago. Mr. Minot was a friend to him and offered to educate him and make him his secretary, but his brother did not want to disappoint his friend who wanted him at the furnace and would not give his consent. Mr. Johnston and a chum who was going as far as Chicago, decided to run away. The fact was confided to Mr. Johnston's sister who informed the brother. He started in haste for the depot. Mr. Johnston saw him coming and hid behind the car. When his brother had gone through the car, he climbed in and followed behind him. When his brother jumped off, Mr. Johnston went to the window as the car started and shouted good-bye to him. A stay of three years was made in Chicago. Mr. Johnston secured work on the Chicago Tribune as mail clerk. The Tribune was at that time a paper of four pages. He was also mail clerk on the Northern Christian Advocate, Prairie Farmer. "I must have made $110 or $120 per month," he said, "and spent most of it." After three years stay in Chicago he went to St. Louis. Just looked over the town and went to Hannibal, Missouri, where work was secured on the Hannibal and St. Joe railroad, selling books and papers. The baggage master left. On leaving he said to Mr. Johnston, "Why don't you take it?" He filled this position for about six months.

In November 1858, he bought a wagon and four mules and with two other men started on his trip westward, traveling to Colorado. They remained at a point on the Arkansas river until February, when the journey was continued to Denver, which at that time did not have more than a dozen houses, and was a characteristic mining town. Mr. Johnston prospected for gold and found some good prospects, but they were not paying ones. He became ill and was taken back to Fremont, Nebraska, for medical treatment and remained there until the next spring, 1860, when he made another start for California, arriving at Placerville in September, where he was met by his brother, who made most of the journey from San Francisco by stage. His brother did not recognize him while he knew his brother the moment he saw him. When they parted, the brother was a grown man and he was a small boy. The two brothers journeyed together in the emigrant wagon to Folsom. There the brother took a train for San Francisco and Mr. Johnston continued his journey to Sacramento and later went to the Elkhorn ranch where he left his mules and went to San Francisco to spend the winter with his brother. The following spring with a team of 12 horses he began hauling freight from Sacramento to Carson, Virginia and Silver cities in Nevada. It proved to be a very remunerative business and was continued until he went to Salt Lake City. Mr. Johnston sunk a well in Nevada, where water was very scarce and took a contract to furnish the residents of this vicinity with water at five cents per gallon. He made the deliveries and sometimes made as much as a hundred dollars in a day.

Later he continued his journey to Montana where he again encountered the pioneer mining conditions much as they prevailed in Colorado. After a short stay here he returned to Salt Lake City where he entered the employment of Ben Holliday as stage driver from Millersville to Green River. In 1865 he went to Salt Lake City. The Mormons had intended to take the land on which Warm Springs were located, but a gentile, Dr. Robinson, got ahead of them and located there first. This was considered an unfriendly act. One night Dr. Robinson was called to set the broken leg of a man. When he came out of his house he was instantly killed. Later he saw John D. Lee when he was brought back from Beaver, Utah. The officers who went after him hired Mr. Johnston's wagon and team for his transportation. When Lee was arrested he said he was glad of it for he had had no peace of mind since the Mountain Meadow Massacre. Later Mr. Johnston went to Pioche, Nevada, where a new mine had been struck. Here he met Miss Ida F. Robinson and they were married, November 18, 1873, and in 1874 Mr. and Mrs. Johnston came to Walla Walla. At one time they owned the residence at the corner of East Rose and Idaho streets. Mr. Johnston's first work here was taking charge of the Short livery stables on Main street between First and Second streets. Later he engaged in carpentry, painting and papering and at the age of 84 he still does this work and does not spend many idle hours.

A.H. Harris

*Opium smuggling
was a flourishing trade
in the Northwest in the 1870's.*

When Walla Walla straggled along a cow trail following the meanderings of Mill Creek, used as the only thoroughfare between the old garrison and the few one-horse trading establishments located on the banks of the unmanageable stream, a colony of shacks appeared at the rear of a saloon built of logs on the land which the Greater Baker-Boyer bank building is arising. The colony of shacks gave way about five years ago, when the Odd Fellows' erected a spendid temple facing on Alder Street. The history of those old dilapidated was never printed, as a matter of fact it is not known to anybody; the historian had no time to gather the facts. Unless a man spoke the Chinese language it would be impossible to get much history, and even if it were gotten there would be doubt of its credibility.

Pioneer draymen will recall those old shacks with considerable pleasure, for good business was gathered there at times, and, entirely unwittingly, the hard-working express drivers assisted a band of wise celestials in plying their trade and coining fortunes in a small way. In reminiscent mood, draymen have told of hauling "trunks" to and from the alley between Main and Alder Streets, connecting Second and Third, and wondering why the burden always seemed so heavy and so dead. Yet Chinamen were uncommunicative, and draymen cannot pry into matters too far.

Over at Victoria, about thirty years ago, was established a plant for the manufacture of opium into the merchantable product, ready for the pipe. For some reason the plant was established in Canada, and about the same time the United States saw an opportunity to make revenue from the business and promptly placed a tariff of $12 per pound upon the product of the factory. With Victoria but a few miles from the American border it was natural that a smuggling business would grow quickly, and as Walla Walla was becoming the home of the Chinamen, and the outfitting place for the celestials who had been lured to the mining camps of Idaho and Eastern Oregon, a natural distributing point was easily located.

The depot for the reception of the drug, for its sale and distribution, was quietly opened in the basement under the old dingy shacks, where prying eyes seldom went and were never wanted. Thousands of dollars worth of the sleep-producing drug passed through the dark recesses of the old underground "fence" during the years when smuggling flourished, and even up to the time of the demolition of the houses a few years ago.

Opium could be bought outright in Victoria at prices which made splendid profits to the importer even when duty was paid, but the allurment of the smuggling business has gotten hold of many men and caused them to stare the penitentiary in the face while they were trying to land tins of the condensed poppy. By purchasing the drug, smuggling it across to the San Juan Islands in the night time, there having "fences" where the cans could be secreted and later taken to the railroad and sent to places of sale, saving $12 per pound duty demanded by the Government, the business offered immense profits. And the profits induced many men to undertake the task of eluding revenue officers and finding sale for the drug.

Naturally Chinamen were selected to handle the sales of the business among their countrymen, even if they were not directly responsible for the smuggling of the drug and its concealment from the beginning. Usually white men were charged with the smuggling, and perhaps the celestials took advantage of that fact and made away with the booty quite as often as their palefaced brethren. At any rate when the contraband drug reached Walla Walla it was accompanied by a Chinaman. He watched it on its trip from the railroad station to his shack, carefully unloaded it from the expressman's wagon and carried it down the rickety steps himself. No Chinaman ever quibbled with an expressman about his charges for carrying one of the old-fashioned "trunks."

Opium is packed in half-pound tins or taels, and in this form can be shipped in any climate. The drug is heavy, and a few hundred pounds of it can be packed in a comparatively small space. Chinamen usually travel with a crude box of "stuff," or with a bag or two of clothing and other belongings. Once the drug was across the line it was easy for a celestial to "load" himself and bring it across the State, landing at Walla Walla with $1,000 to $2,000 worth without detection. Frequently the drug would be packed in old tea boxes or other trunk-shaped contrivances, but always within the baggage limits of the railway company. A Chinaman seldom, even if carrying nothing contraband, offerd the railway campany a parcel for checking that weighs within a few pounds of the limit. He would prefer to carry a good-sized load himself.

Far below the level of the street, or better the alley, "rooms" and alleyways were excavated under the old shacks. When workmen removed the buildings to make way for the secret society temple they unearthed a more perfect secret society's remains than could ever occupy the temple of brick and stone. Here were evidences of men having lived, eaten, slept, and died in the dingy depths of the earth, with no outlet for air save a narrow stairway from the inside of the buildings, and no possibility of sunshine having penetrated the dark recesses. Here is where the smuggler had his day; here is where he saw his business wane and finally die out. Encroaching progress drove him to the daylight, and no man ever smuggled successfully when the sun was shining on his actions.

How much opium was smuggled into Walla Walla? Nobody knows and nobody ever can know. The business flourished for many years, and during much of the time the demand for the drug was tremendous. Thousands of

Chinamen followed the early placer mining camps, and not one of them is recorded as having lost his appetite for the drug. Among white men the drug habit has grown with alarming rapidity. So strong has it become that the Government receives in duties millions of dollars annually, and it is not recorded that the last smuggler has quit business yet.

Near the international boundary the opium smuggler has his night. Hundreds of miles in the interior, secluded among friends and clear of suspicion, he had his day. And a long, bright day he had in Walla Walla.

William H. Kennedy

Mr. Kennedy corresponded with his family
on a journey from Pittsburgh to Washington Territory
in 1875. These letters cover his trip
from Helena, Montana to Walla Walla, Washington.

Missoula, Montana. October 17th, 1875

Dear Thomas:

I arrived here last night after a ride of three and a half days, the distance from Helena is one hundred and fifty miles. About ten miles from Helena I crossed the main range of the Rocky Mountains, and since then have been on the western slope. After crossing the mountains I followed down the Blackfoot, a tributary of the Columbia River to where it joins the Bear River, and the two form the Hell Gate River which I followed down to this place, they call it the Missoula River here but Hell Gate is the name on the maps. The first half day of my journey I only crossed the mountain and stopped at a house a short distance from the foot. I shot a grouse in crossing and it was well I did so, as it and a little bread and butter was all I had for supper and breakfast next day and for that and feeding my horse they charged me three dollars. The second day out just as I was going to stop in the middle of the day to let my horse eat some grass, I came to a beaver dam and shot three beaver, but I did not get any of them as they dived to the bottom and did not come to the surface again. I was sorry for this as I would have liked to have got their skins. About dark I stopped at the house of a Missourian and got a good supper and breakfast.

The next day, shortly after I started, I saw a wolf and shot at him three times, wounding him the last time but he got away. At night I stopped at the house of a man named McCarty. He gave me some supper but had no spare bed so I spread my blanket on the hay in the stable and slept with my horse. In the morning I saddled up and rode on ten miles when I got a good breakfast and some oats for my horse at a ranch or farm, and about six in the evening arrived here, and after dinner today I will start on and ride twenty miles and stop at a place called French Town. From French Town, I will likely have to camp out at nights most of the time for several days to come as the country is almost uninhabited.

I suppose it will take from ten to twelve days for me to reach Walla Walla. I have to cross a very high range of mountains, the Coeur D'Alene, and the snow may be several feet deep on them. If it is I will have to go very slow as I will have to break my own path. In coming here, I have had to cross the River four times and the water was deep enough to come up to the middle of the body of my horse. From here to Walla Walla I will have to cross it again thirty-six times, so you can judge how crooked it is.

I have a very good horse, a Broncho. He is an elegant buggy horse as well as a saddle horse. I do not know whether I can sell him for much when I get to Walla Walla. He cost me sixty dollars. If Mr. Wells needs a horse I may perhaps give him to him, and then Aunt Lidie could drive him when she wanted to. He is very gentle and any one could drive him. If I could get him home I would like it very much as I would give him to you, you could ride him easily.

If you would see me now you would not know me when I am riding along. I am riding on a California saddle which has leather thongs attached to it to tie things on. I have a large roll of blankets tied on behind, cantinas (a kind of little saddle bag) in front, a tin cup and a long rope to tie my horse tied on in front of my saddle, a pair of revolvers and a Bowie knife in a belt around my waist and a rifle hung to the horn of my saddle. With all this to carry my horse will go for hours at a lope or slow gallop, and will carry me sixty miles a day, and one day on the trip I expect to go eighty miles. You could hardly get one horse in all Pittsburgh that could do as much and yet my horse is quite small, hardly more than a pony.

The scenery so far has been beautiful. Most of the time I have been travel-ing in a narrow valley shut in by high mountains. The valleys are devoid of trees except a few cotton wood, quaking asp, and Balm of Gilead trees near the streams. The soil is rich and is covered with grass. The mountains are covered with large pine and spruce trees. In places you will see immense masses of granite and porphyry rocks entirely bare of soil or vegetation, and in some portions of the journey I rode close to the foot of mountains composed entirely of broken rock which looked as if a touch or even a breath of air would cause the rocks to slide down and crush you. I tried to climb one of these piles of rock to shoot a 'fool hen' but had to desist as the rocks began to slide down as I climbed over them. Some of these mountains are covered with snow the whole year round.

You will not hear of me again till I get to Walla Walla when I will write to little Annie. With love to all at home, I remain as ever,

Your affectionate Uncle,
W.H. Kennedy

Dear Little Annie:

When I last wrote home I was in Missoula in Montana. After putting my letter in the Post Office I got on my horse and rode to French Town, a miners' camp, containing a half dozen log houses where I stopped all night. The next day, Monday, I rode about fifty miles down the Missoula or Hell Gate River and slept at night under my blankets with my horse tied with a long rope near me. On Tuesday morning I got up early and rode all day down the river bank and at night I crossed it and slept on the bank on the other side. Just before I camped, I shot with my pistol a fine deer and had nice venison steak for my supper to eat with my bread and onions which was all I carried with me. On Wednesday I did not start until about half past twelve as the grass was good and I wanted my horse to fill himself with grass as from the river crossing I was beginning to ascend the Coeur D'Alene Mountains, and could not get good grass for my horse except at two points, one twenty-five miles from the river and one eighty miles, and the eighty miles was almost too far for my horse to go in one day after I had ridden him as hard as I did from the start.

After eating my dinner I rode twenty-five miles and camped about dark. I shot, on the way, with my pistol some fool hens and a pheasant, and had a nice supper broiling them and some of my venison. I saw thousands of wild geese but did not shoot any as I did not need them and I never like to kill anything unless I want to use it for food. After I laid down to sleep I was awakened by a lot of wood rats which bothered me a good deal, smelling my ears and nibbling my hair. I got up and tried to chase them away and took a large piece of bread which I had cut and stuck it against a tree, pinning it there with my butcher knife. The rats bothered me all night. In the morning when I got up I found the rats had some way got my bread down from the tree and had gnawed it all over and spoiled it. Luckily I had more in my cantinas. The rats had also carried off my onions and dirtied all my salt so that I had to throw it away. After a breakfast of bread and venison and birds without salt, I started on and rode over the mountains about fifty-five miles and camped on the other side of the mountains. After eating my supper of bread and birds I had shot during the day, I spread my blankets at the foot of a little mound and after heaping wood on my fire, I prepared to go to bed, when I noticed a stake driven into the ground at the end of the mound and on examining it I found that my mound was a grave, and the stake was for a monument. As my fire was made and my blankets were spread, I concluded I would not change and laid down with the heaped up grave for a pillow and went to sleep, but I did not sleep long for it soon began to rain and by twelve or one my blankets and clothes were all wet and I was lying in a puddle of water several inches deep. I stood it as long as I could and then got up and stood by the fire till morning. On Friday morning I started early and rode all day through a drenching rain and made about forty miles. I camped early as I came to a place under some enormous cedar trees where it was perfectly dry and near which was good grass for my horse. After I camped I shot three pheasants (and could have shot a dozen) and collected an enormous pile of wood and built a roaring fire, where I dried all my clothes and blankets. I had an elegant supper. I toasted some bread and broiled two pheasants and ate nearly all of both. I had no salt but they tasted very well. I slept splendidly although it rained the whole night I did not get a particle wet, the trees keeping off all the rain.

On Saturday morning after cooking and eating my other bird, I started on in the rain and rode till about noon when I arrived at the Coeur D'Alene Mission where I got my dinner and stayed until the next morning. The priest and lay brothers treated me very kindly and gave me the best they had, which by the way, was poor enough. This Mission was established by Father DeSmet, a Jesuit priest, many years since for the purpose of Christianizing the Coeur D'Alene Indians. They have succeeded tolerably well. The Indians live in log houses and cultivate the ground a little, but they are still very poor, very dirty, and very miserable, but they attend church and repeat the Latin prayers and response just as well and know just as much about the meaning of them as the most of those that go to the Cathedral in Pittsburgh, and that is nothing at all. I went in the evening to the church and heard the priest preach to them in the Indian tongue, and heard the Indian women and men sing and chant the same words and music they do in the settlement, the execution as you may guess was not of the best. On Sunday morning, I started in the rain although the Priest wanted me very much to stop another day, and rode forty-five miles to the Spokane River, a tributary of the Columbia River where I stopped all night and slept on the floor of the house of a trader with the Indians. Here for the first time since I left Pittsburgh I found bank notes would not go except at a discount, the currency in Washington Territory being gold and silver. On Monday I crossed the Spokane and rode to a place called Pine Grove; there is only one house in the place, and the reason I suppose they call it Pine Grove is because there are no pines or any other trees within sight of it. On Tuesday when I got up it was raining torrents but I pushed on and rode till dark. When I arrived at the ranch or farm house of an old bachelor who got me the dirtiest supper I ever ate. But my horse got a good feed of oats. On Wednesday morning I started early and rode forty-four miles and arrived here at about eight in the evening and went to the hotel. In the morning I hunted your Uncle James up. I met him on the street and said, "Well, how are you?" He said, "I beg your pardon, I have forgotten your name though I know your face." I soon told him where we had met and then he took me up to his house, and in the afternoon your Aunt Lidie came up and we had a pleasant time. Mr. Wells called on me and I have been to a guild party at the church building and had a very nice time. Your Uncle has not done a bit of work at his office since I have been here, and every one has tried to make it pleasant for me. Next week I am going down the new railroad (which is just finished) to the Columbia River with Dr. Baker. I will leave here likely in the latter part of the month. With love to all at home, I am as ever,

Your Uncle,
W.H. Kennedy

P.S. I will write a little more as I am waiting till your Uncle James comes in to go up home with him. Your Aunt Lidie lives the most of the time at the church building where she has a very nice and well furnished room. She teaches from nine to two. I think she likes it very well although, of course, she misses you all. She has an Indian girl in her class. She is very much liked here and they all like her to stop with them. She stops a good deal at Mr. Boyer's. Today Mr. Boyer drove Lidie and me out to show me the country which is very nice.

Your Uncle is going to keep my horse which is a very good one. He will send him out to a farm this winter.

I nearly forgot to say that Aunt Lidie told me to send her love to all of you. She started to write yesterday but did not finish her letter. She will write soon. James is waiting for me so I will say good night.

W.H.K.

Susan M. Stringer

Alone with her children on their ranch,
Mrs. Stringer has a confrontation
with Chief Joseph and his band
at the beginning of the Nez Perce hostilities in 1877.

Mrs. Susan M. Stringer, pioneer of the Inland Empire, relates her sensational experience, struggles and hardships of the early West. Mrs. Stringer came to the Pacific Coast by way of the Isthmus of Panama, in the year 1864, where she joined her husband who was a meat contractor in the Union Army. They went from California to The Dalles, Oregon, and then to Fort Lapwai, Idaho. Here she had the pleasure of gazing upon the real red skins, as the savages were about all the inhabitants there were in that neck of the country in those wild days. Her husband, the late R.J. Stringer, turned his hand to farming, taking up a homestead where the prosperous city of Pomeroy now stands. The country was a howling wilderness; and owing to the depredations of the Indians, cowboys and outlaws, they were forced to give up farming and come to Walla Walla where more peaceful conditions prevailed.

Mrs. Stringer's story of crossing the high hills of the Tucanon would make one shiver; the road was only a deer trail; the men held the wagon from capsizing and dashing her down the hill into the valley miles below. Coming through where the agricultural city of Dayton now stands, she was compelled to hold her baby son, (Wm. F.) down in the wagon bed to keep the brush from tearing out the child's hair.

Reaching the Garden City, Mr. Stringer started into the meat business and conducted a market for some time. Getting the farming fever, once more the family took to the wagon route, their destination this time was on the Tucanon at the base of the Blue Mountains. Mrs. Stringer's neighbors consisted of wild animals, rattle snakes and other varmin, the first social call she received from her neighbors was a visit from a giant panther. The beast crawled under the house and remained all night. Just what his mission was, the family never ventured out to learn, but barricaded all the doors and windows and kept up a roaring fire in the old fire place all night so that the tiger could not climb down the chimney and devour the whole family. She was a prisoner in her own house all night. The next day, Mr. Goodrich, a hunter, happened along killing the tiger, and liberating the Stringer family from an animal siege. Mr. Stringer bought an old musket as a preventative from further invasions of ferocious animals. His battles with them when they would come into the yard to carry off the chickens, to say the least, were sensational. The timber gray wolf was a mighty dangerous animal to take chances with; this animal will just as soon eat a human being as kill a calf. Mr. Stringer became County Road Supervisor, and when the Nez Perce Indians went on the war path, Mrs. Stringer was living in the war zone. The men of the district were poorly armed; they asked Mr. Stringer if he would not go to Fort Walla Walla and secure them arms and ammunition with which to defend their homes. He consented to make the trip which was a long one. The Indians were supposed to be out on Camas Prairie, which was some distance from the Tucanon; however this was a mistake; for the second evening after his departure, a large troop of the redskin warriors appeared on a long winding ridge that would bring them to her very door step, and there she was with her children left to the mercy of the savages.

They came on down the ridge in single file as that was their mode of march in war time, swinging rifles, bows and arrows, and the favorite weapon, the tomahawk, over their heads and singing their favorite war songs. As the Western sun cast its last golden shadows on the valley of the Tucanon and its last shades stole up over the bunch grass covered hills, it looked like the last setting of the sun on Mrs. Stringer and her offspring. The game little woman gathered her children around her and told them that they were the Lord's people and the Indians were good Indians and would not harm them. The red warriors with the feathers dangling from their hair came on down the ridge, crossing the Tumalum single file, pitching their camp but a few rods from her home. Things looked mighty blue now for the little woman of the mountain range.

A short time after they had made camp a strapping Indian appeared at the door; he had a string of feathers that reached from his head to his feet, his moccasins and legging were all bedecked in beads, and his face was painted a scarlet red. He said in a loud clear voice, "I am Chief Joseph, Chief of all the Nez Perce Indians, and I have come to notify you that your family will not be molested by my warriors." He was a man of his word. Mrs. Stringer asked the handsome big chief what he was fighting for. He told her before he would let the whites plow up the graves of his forefathers he would cut off his right arm and let his heart's blood drop into the sands. The chief told Mrs. Stringer not to be afraid, for none of hers had never harmed the red man, and they would not harm her. Bidding her good evening he went back to the wigwams. The next day they moved out of the Blue Mountains by way of the head waters of Cumings Creek and the Tumalum; coming out of the thick timber they were attacked by the troops under command of Gen. O.H. Howard, and the long and bloody Nez Perce war was on. Gen. Nelson A. Miles came to Gen. Howard's assistance and Chief Joseph, the greatest Indian general of his day, was captured.

Mrs. Stringer witnessed one of the most sensational duels of the frontier between two young bucks. Two tribes of the Snake River Indians were camped on the banks of the Tucanon. One of the tribes boasted a beautiful maiden. As a rule the young bucks selected their cluchmen from their own tribes; however, this young maiden attracted a young buck from a foreign tribe who possessed a large herd of ponies. The custom was for the lover to buy his girl from her father and ponies were the monetary consideration; the chiefs were the potent power. When they met to settle the love affair, the young buck of her own tribe became crazed with jealousy, drew a large hunting knife, called to his rival to come and fight to the death. The young invading lover was game; no sooner had the challenge been issued, than he sprang to his feet, and drawing a huge knife made for his opponent. The other Indians rushed in and separated them, but not before they were both seriously wounded. The Indians brought the disabled lovers to Mrs. Stringer who was called the little medicine woman by the redskins, as she always kept a supply of liniments on hand for the care of her children. She dressed their wounds and was assisted by the young maiden, and it was plain to be seen that the poor Indian girl's heart was with the young buck of her own tribe. They both recovered from the knife wounds, and the buck of her own tribe had a clear field from that time on and bought the girl from her father without further opposition.

Once more the Stringers moved back to civilization, locating in Walla Walla where they have since resided. Mrs. Stringer was born in Wexford county, Ireland, 73 years ago, coming to America when she was a young colleen. She was married at Dubuque, Iowa, June 9th, 1858. After enjoying 56 years of happy, sensational and romantic life, her husband departed from this life last October, 1913. There were ten children born to the happy union. Mrs. Stringer likes to talk of the early days especially about the Indians. As she never saw one of the red tribe until she came West, they were a great attraction to her blue eyes.

W.S. Clark

Volunteer companies
were raised in various communities
to aid Idaho settlers in fighting
the renegade Nez Perce Indians.

On the morning of June 19, 1877, a courier reached the city of Walla Walla bringing the sad news of the engagement on Camas prairie between the Nez Perce Indians and Col. Perry's troop of cavalry in which one half of Perry's troop were killed. The news caused a great deal of excitement. Word also came that the citizens of Lewiston were in danger of a raid by the Indians and that the settlers were pouring into town from all sides and help was much needed.

Thomas P. Page, county auditor of Walla Walla county started to work raising a volunteer company. At one o'clock in the afternoon a meeting was called at the court house where the facts were presented and resolutions were passed promising to go to the aid of the people of the Lewiston district. One hundred names were set down on the roll and all who could get horses were to start that night. The quartermaster at the fort gave us rifles and sixty rounds of cartridges apiece. At six o'clock that evening the following party left Walla Walla en route for Lewiston:

A. Reeves Ayres, John Agu, Ike Abbott, A.L. Bird, Charles Blewett, W.S. Clark, Lane Gillam, H.E. Holmes, Albert Hall, Jake Holbrook, Frank Jackson, John Keeney, J.H. Lister, Henry Lacy, Wm. McKearn, S.H. Maxon, Alec O'Dell, C.S. Robinson, J.S. Stott, Ben Scott, Albert Small, Frank Waldrip, T.P. Page, L.K. Grimm, J.F. McLean.

We arrived at Dayton at one o'clock that night and put our horses in the livery stable and ourselves to sleep in the haymow overhead. Next morning we breakfasted at the hotel, A.R. Ayres, H.E. Holmes and Tom Beall were missing. We traveled on to Marengo where a short stop was made and the troops under Col. Whipple came up. We volunteers took the Indian trail across the hills, the regulars followed the wagon road. We stopped two hours on the Pataha and then traveled on to Dan Favor's ranch, which was about fifteen miles this side of Lewiston. Here we waited about three hours for supper, there being some misunderstanding about it. The troops camped at the same place.

On the morning of the 21st, after paying out bills we traveled on to

Lewiston, leaving our horses on this side of the river we crossed over to the town where we met Major Spurgeon, the commander at that place, who gave us to understand that the settlers nearby were in no immediate danger, and that if we cared to go on into the Indian country we could be of good service, but would have to be under the command of the military authorities. We re-crossed the river to our horses, got dinner and signed our names to report to Gen. Howard for eight days service. We then elected our officers as follows: T.P. Page, captain; L.K. Grimm, lieutenant, and John F. McLean sergeant. We again crossed over to Lewiston, this time with our outfits, and were regularly mustered in for the eight days of service. Up to this time Ayres, Holmes and Beall had not caught up with us. Some thought that they had backed out and gone home, others that they would yet come up.

Major Spurgeon directed us to Fort Lapwai to report to Gen. Howard where we arrived at six o'clock in the evening. Here we had supper and after drawing on the post commissary for rations, retired. It rained on us all that night. The morning of the 22nd we spent in repairing and fixing up our outfits. At one o'clock we were again on the march as Gen. Howard's guard, the troops going in advance. There were three companies of infantry, two of cavalry and one company of artillery, and our little company of volunteers.

As we were starting off from camp we were surprised, as well as pleased to see Doc Ayres, Doc Holmes and Ike Abbott, coming up. They were forgiven on our learning that they had got lost, being led astray by Beall, whose horse gave out, and then he went back home. They joined us in the march without waiting to secure any dinner. While we were going up Craig Mountain Ike Abott's horse got away from him and he did not catch him for several hours. On the evening of the 22nd we made camp on the Craig mountain, putting our horses out with those belonging to the troops and Sergeant McLean detailed J.H. Lister, Frank Waldrip and myself to guard the first part of the night, and Lane Gilliam, A.L. Bird and Frank Jackson for the latter part. This was our first guard duty. I thought that night that upon me rested the entire burden of herding those three hundred head of horses.

On Saturday June 23rd we started early and traveled along the mountain until after noon we reached the great Camas prairie. I was very much surprised to see the extent and richness of the prairie. I am told that timothy hay will grow here anywhere. We passed the place where our former citizen Lew Day was first attacked by the Indians and we later came to Ben Norton's place on the Cottonwood where we camped. Owing to the fact that we were in advance of the command Captain Page put a guard on the house and barn. Captain Page had placed Henry Lacy as guard over the barn and after the command came up Captain Wilkinson started to enter the barn and Henry stopped him. The captain told Henry who he was, still it did no good, and the captain turned and went off. Henry and Charley

Blewett were the youngest members in the company.

On Sunday morning June 24th, Alec O'Dell, Lane Gilliam, Al Hall, Jake Holbrook, Ben Scott, Ike Abbott, Wm. McKearn and W.S. Clark got up early and started for Mount Idaho nineteen miles distant. We passed the place where Lew Day, Mr. and Mrs. Norton and Hill Norton, Joseph Moore, John Chamberlain, wife and two children and Miss Bowers were overtaken by the Indians. We also saw the place where a load of goods for Mount Idaho had been captured by the Indians. We passed through Grangeville and on to Mt. Idaho where we arrived at about twelve o'clock. We hitched our horses to the fence of a resident who gave them some hay. Mr. Brown of the hotel told us that dinner would be at four o'clock. We told him we were hungry and couldn't wait. He wasn't long in getting us something to eat.

During our stay here O'Dell and one or two others had their horses shod. I went into Volmer's store and wrote a letter home. Mr. Scott the manager of the store, showed us many courtesies. He and Mr. Volmer were formerly from Walla Walla. Mr. Scott said that all who could were preparing to leave for Salmon river. We were given an invitation to dinner which we gladly accepted. Here we received the following information in regard to the depredations of the Indians. Joseph's band from the Wallowa and the Salmon River Indians, under White Bird, had been camped on Rocky canyon and White Bird creek. The outbreak was on the afternoon of June 13 by a small party of Indians, killing Richard Divine, an old man living alone on Salmon river. The next morning, the 14th, Henry Elfers, Robert Bland and Henry Beckroge were killed between six and seven o'clock. Shortly after Samuel Benedict was wounded while out hunting cattle and managed to reach his home where the Indians followed and put him to death. The same day on White bird they wounded J.J. Manuel and his little girl, killed James Baker and at the same time a Frenchman named August Bacon. On the fifteenth Mrs. Manuel, William Osborne and Henry Mason were killed and in this Joseph is said to have participated. On word reaching Mt. Idaho of these depredations people were fearful of the Indians.

The settlers on Camas prairie shared a similar fate. According to Mr. Scott, Lew Day left Mt. Idaho to place the settlers on the prairie on guard and give notice to the troops at Lapwai. The Indians overtook Day two miles beyond Norton's house. They immediately fired on him hitting him twice in the back. Lew turned and went back to Norton's place and found Norton and his family just getting ready to go to Mr. Idaho. Norton with his wife and boy, Joe Moore, Miss Bowers, Mr. and Mrs. Chamberlain and their two children and Lew Day all got into the wagon and started for town, the Indians following and firing on them. Four miles this side of Grangeville the party all got out of the wagon and Hill, Norton and Miss Bowers made their escape and came into Grangeville bringing the first news of the slaughter. The team of horses had been shot when they got out of the wagon. Norton was killed, Joe Moore had been hit twice, Mrs. Norton had been shot through both legs. Chamberlain and his boy were killed, the child's head being crushed between the knees of a powerful Indian. Mrs. Chamberlain was shot in the breast with an arrow and a portion of their child's tongue was cut off. They both later recovered. Theodore Schwartz was wounded. Day died a few days later and Moore some six weeks later.

We started back to camp about six o'clock that evening and arrived at nine. On Monday, June 25, we left our camp on the Cottonwood and continued our march where we camped. On the road we passed the place where about one hundred lodges of Indians had been camped at the lakes, on the rocks in the canyons and on the prairie before the outbreak. On the ground of Col. Perry's retreat Captain Page picked up some twenty cartridge shells within a distance of fifty yards. At Johnson's we were given a camping ground to the right of the main column about half a mile from wood and water. The boys were dissatisfied and we got permission to camp within the enclosure at Johnson's house. H.E. Homes, Ike Abbott and C.S. Robinson were put on guard.

After breakfast on Tuesday morning we left camp to reconnoiter. We were in advance of the command that day. Almost on the start we came across a dead soldier about two miles from camp. Here we rested to give the infantry time to come up. We reached the summit looking down on White Bird creek about 12 o'clock. During this morning's ride most of the soldiers killed in Col. Perry's fight with the Indians were buried. For several miles we kept coming upon dead bodies.

In the afternoon, with Chapman as guide, we rode along the top of the divide between Salmon river and White Bird. It was rough and tiresome riding. We saw fresh tracks and Chapman told us we were liable to meet Indians anywhere. Presently we discovered three Indian spies across the river and soon after we saw the whole band moving further up the mountain. We fired a number of shots toward them but they were too far away.

Next we left the ridge and went down on the bottom to Manuel's on White Bird. We went inside the gate and looked at the ruins of the fire. A few of the soldiers strayed down to the creek and what was their surprise to see sitting in a little shed, which the Indians had spared, a white man whom we all soon found to be Jack Manuel, whom we had reported as among the killed. He had been wounded in the back of the neck with an arrow and had also been shot in the hips. Our next task was to get him out and away to safety. We soon fixed a pole in a broken buggy that was standing near and by fastening what spare ropes we had to the buggy and to the pommels of our saddles we succeeded in getting him away. Finding that we were not making headway fast enough our captain sent to Captain Miller for two pack mules which we soon had. Then, turning the pole into shafts we soon got to camp where we turned Mr. Manuel over to his friends who were to take him to Mount Idaho the next day. It had rained all day and we had had a hard day's work.

On June 27th we broke camp and marched to White Bird, the soldiers burying those they had not had time to bury the previous day. It was here on the White Bird side that the terrible battle had taken place. That night we were within a short distance of the Salmon river which we intended to cross the following day to fight the Indians on the other side. We could see them for hours that afternoon riding their horses, and swinging from side to side in all kinds of capers. After making camp we got instructions to escort the pack train back to Lewiston where they were going for supplies. On reaching Lewiston the eight days for which we had enlisted were up and believing that the army of General Howard was fully able to meet and conquer Chief Joseph and his band we returned to our homes.

The day after our return came word of the ambushing of Lieut. Rains and ten volunteers of the regulars and the killing of Blewett and Foster.

Colonel Whipple says of this:

"I marched to Cottonwood, July 2, and on the following morning sent two citizens named Foster and Blewett to examine the country in the vicinity of direction of Craig's ferry, the place where Joseph and his party swam the river, for indications of the presence of the Indians. Toward evening Foster returned rapidly to camp and reported that he had seen Indians about twelve miles distant coming from the direction of Craig ferry; that they had fired a shot or two at him; that he last saw his comrade about that time. I directed Second Lieutenant S.M. Rains of my company with ten picked men and the Scout Foster, to proceed at once to the point where the Indians had been seen for the purpose of ascertaining the strength of the enemy and to aid young Blewett. I particularly cautioned Rains not to proceed the command too far, to keep on high ground, and to report the first signs of the Indians. The command was in motion very shortly after the detachment had started and firing was soon heard on our front. A rapid gait was taken up and after a couple of miles Indians were discovered about half a mile distant, and on approaching nearer it was found that they were in large force and that Lieutenant Rains and every man of his detachment had been killed.

General Howard writes: "These were dreadful tidings. This young officer was of the same mould as the famous Winterfield of history who was killed in just such fashion under Frederick the Great, prompt, loyal, able without fear, and without reproach. Frederick lost many brave leaders but only one Winterfield. We lost one Rains."

The citizens of Walla Walla came to know and to admire Lieut. Rains very much. Blewett had been killed further around the mountain undoubtedly after a run for his life. Blewett had been my next door neighbor for a number of years. We were students together in old district number one and also at Whitman seminary. We had all regretted leaving Charley but he wanted to stay and Colonel Whipple said he would look after him and take him into his own mess. He was a likeable boy. As soon as conditions would allow we had his remains brought home and given a military funeral.

Adam Crossman

*Indian fighting from the deck
of the steamer,* Spokane,
*on the Columbia River during the
Indian uprising of 1878.*

Elisha P. Ferry, then governor of Washington territory, wrote a letter to Justice of the Peace J.D. Laman of Walla Walla to raise a company of 40 volunteers to aid the United States troops in fighting these hostile Indians (the Nez Perce). A call was made for a public meeting for Sunday, in July, 1878. The meeting was held at the appointed time at the court house then located at the southwest corner of Third and Alder streets.

The governor arrived to be present at the meeting. When the call was made, there seemed to be a hesitancy on the part of all to sign the roll. Governor Ferry had done a favor for Mr. Crossman in the past, and he asked if Adam Crossman were present. Mr. Crossman came forward.

"Come and sign up," said the governor. Mr. Crossman complied with the request. After he signed nearly every young man in the house came up and signed. W.C. Painter was elected captain, Dr. J.M. Boyd, first lieutenant and surgeon and F.B. Morse, second lieutenant.

The captain was instructed to take the company to Umatilla and meet Major Kress, captain of ordnance, from Vancouver. Major Kress, with 16 regulars, arrived on the steamer *Spokane*, of which he was in command, with Captain Gray, now of Pasco, captain. Major Kress supplied the volunteers with arms and ammunition for the expedition. Its object was to prevent Indians who were coming from the Wallowa Valley from crossing the Columbia river.

The steamer *Spokane* used as a gun boat to patrol the river went up the river on the south side of Long Island, now Blalock Island, which it was learned later the Indians had reached. When the boat later reached the north side, most of the Indians had crossed to the north bank of the river and reached a high bluff from which they began firing into the steamer which was met by a return fire from the steamer that caused them to retreat.

One amusing circumstance Mr. Crossman remembers, was of a very tall Irishman, a fireman on the boat who was standing against a post laughing and making fun of the regulars and volunteers, because they did not kill more Indians. A bullet struck the back of the post, he ducked with great speed and was not seen again during the battle.

Major Kress ordered all the horses shot. Mr. Crossman and his pal asked Major Kress if they could capture a horse for each and take them home. They got permission. Each soon was in possession of an Indian pony. The volunteers were returned to Umatilla and informed the "war was over."

Their guns were returned to Major Kress, who dismissed them and journeyed back to Vancouver.

This was Tuesday and the boys had had nothing to eat since Monday morning. They went to the hotel, but were refused, the management fearing supplies would run low on account of the war. Dr. Boyd and Crossman announced they were going to have something to eat and walked into a store and helped themselves to a can of canned salmon and crackers enough for a meal.

A company under command of Captain Kelly had arrived from The Dalles, Oregon, Governor Chadwick with them. Mr. Crossman went to Captain Kelly and asked if the remaining volunteers could get a cup of hot coffee. The captain said he had only enough provisions for his company.

All of the volunteers, except five including Mr. Crossman and his pal had started home. This party did not consider traveling over a route where they might encounter hostile Indians, safe, and especially since they had neither guns nor ammunition, Mr. Crossman asked Governor Chadwick if he would furnish an escort for them to Wallula. He replied, "You have horses, you can ride across the country."

A steamer came along at this time carrying United States troops with Captain Wilkinson in command and Captain Stump, pilot. The stranded volunteers lost no time in making their way to the boat, but Captain Wilkinson refused to let them come aboard on account of the horses. Captain Stump knew Mr. Crossman and recognized him.

"Is that you, Adam?" the captain called out from the pilot house. When the reply was "yes," he ordered the gang-plank put out for the horses.

Captain Wilkinson, at this point said: "The horses cannot come aboard."

"I am the master of this craft," said Captain Stump, "and those boys can bring their horses on the boat," and they did.

The steamer landed at Wallula at 6 a.m. Here the stranded party met Dr. D.S. Baker, owner of the railway from Wallula to Walla Walla.

"Doctor, we are just back from the war and want to get home," Mr. Crossman said.

"All right, just go aboard," the Doctor replied.

"We have two horses, too," Mr. Crossman's pal ventured. The Doctor ordered a box car for the horses, and the party was conveyed home in safety.

The horse that caused Mr. Crossman so many anxious moments, he sold later to Frank Scholl, still a resident of this vicinity for six dollars.

Mr. Crossman stated, "I never received any pay, never was discharged and don't know whether I am a soldier or not a soldier. If I am a soldier, I have arrived at an age, that I should be retired. I at least consider that I am entitled to an honorable discharge."

The record given below may be the only one in existence in regard to the organization of the volunteer company: "At a meeting held at the court house in Walla Walla, Washington territory, at 10 o'clock a.m. July 13th,

1878, for the purpose of organizing an Independent company of volunteers. The following proceedings were had. Meeting called to order by John F. McLean. On motion Mr. Sharpstein was elected to the chair and Geo. T. Thompson elected secretary.

After the reading of the call and stating the purposes for which the company was about to be organized (which were the protection of the city of Walla Walla and surrounding settlements) the following names were subscribed (names subscribed on schedule). After the enrollment of its members the company proceeded to elect officers and the following named gentlemen were elected: W.C. Painter, captain; Dr. J.M. Boyd, first lieutenant; Frank B. Morse, second lieutenant; John F. McLean, orderly sergeant. The captain then dismissed the company to be marshalled at 8 o'clock on the morning of the 14th inst. Geo. T. Thompson, secretary of meeting; John F. McLean, orderly sergeant of company.

First company of volunteers on Gunboat Spokane; 42 men under Major Kress.

CAPTAIN W.C. PAINTER'S CO. VOLUNTEERS

Hugh McLaughlin, Adam Crossman, E. Stillwell, Ed. Johnson, A.P. Sharpstein, C.T. Warecke, Wm. Stewart, E.J. Lafflin, Thomas Lee, C.D. Laughlin, W.S. Clark. D.J. Coleman, W.C. Painter, F.B. Morse, J. Stevens, Jeremia Clemonts, A.C. Russell, Chas. W. Phillips, J.L. Henderson, J.A. McClure, D.C. Cronan, B. Chapman, J.N. Reynolds, George Wagner, George Anderson, Oliver Diller, Thos. Madden, James Harrington, Alfred Cook, Frank Trullinger, J.I. Harcleive, D.E. Smith, John Murry, K.R. Sutliff, R.I. Dunn, W. Tillard, A. Higgins, Thomas Hall, Solon Moffit, John Deere, David Dunn, Geo. Safford and C.E. Dunn.

From a report, dated, Headquarters department of the Columbia Ft. Vancouver, W.T., March 13, 1879, interesting data is given of the gunboat service in which the Walla Walla volunteers participated.

"Assistant Adjutant General Military Division of the Pacific. Sir: My attention having been called to the fact that I omitted any mention in my annual report of the Volunteers from Washington Territory, who rendered us such good service upon the gunboats on the Columbia river during the campaign of last summer. I desire to call attention to the following telegraphic report from Captain John A. Kress, ordnance department, who was in command of one of the boats at that time.

Umatilla, July 8, 1878, 9 a.m.

To Captain Sladen, Vancouver: Small bands of Indians with large number of horses passed to north side of Columbia simultaneously at daylight this morning at point near North Willow creek, at Coyote Station, at head of Long Island, just above Umatilla. I caught one band in the act at Long Island as reported this morning. Have attacked and dispersed these bands at different points during the day. Had possession of over 200 horses at one time but was not able to keep them.

Had two very lively skirmishes, landing after firing from steamer, and charging Indians successfully up steep hills; no casualties known except wounding one Indian and killing five horses.

Captain Painter and the 42 volunteers from Walla Walla deserve praise for good conduct and bravery, not excepting my Vancouver regulars and Captain Gray with officers and crew of the steamer *Spokane*, who stood firmly at their posts under fire.

Kress, Captain of Ordnance.

All concerned, including Governor Ferry, whose zealous aid you mentioned, have my hearty commendation for good service rendered on that occasion.

I have the honor to request that this communication be made a part of my annual report before referred to O.O. Howard, Brigadier-General, commanding.

In a letter from Major Kress to Mr. Painter, the following excerpts are taken:

"Your letter gave me much pleasure in recalling those incidents of your Indian wars in which I had the honor to participate with thorough appreciation of the patriotism and bravery of the gallant company of men from Walla Walla, who under your command, joined me at Umatilla.

"You represented material that makes the best soldiers in the world and when the time came for me to put you to the test, when bullets flew thickest, not a man was found lacking.

"I am glad to know that Gov. Ferry recognized your praiseworthy share in the campaign by appointing you Lieutenant-Colonel on his staff."

Mr. Painter used to tell of an incident of this war which he considered of invaluable benefit to him. He had suffered an injury to one of his knees which had resulted in lameness, which obliged him to walk with a cane for several weeks.

When he returned to the boat after a skirmish with the Redmen, someone asked: "Where is your cane Captain?" Mr. Painter looked down and for the first time realized that he did not have his cane and he had climbed a steep hill in the meantime. Under the stress of excitement and strenuous exercise his injured limb had become normal.

One phase of this history that readers will note, is the conflict in dates. They are however the dates used in military and civilian official reports.

Col. Frank J. Parker

*A scout for General Howard
during the Nez Perce Indian campaign,
Col. Parker was correspondent for
the California Associated Press and Boise Statesman.*

Col. Frank J. Parker, present proprietor of the *Statesman*, was born in Western England, April 28, 1845. At eighteen years of age he came to the United States, crossed the continent to California, where he arrived in 1864, visited Nevada, passed through Arizona, a portion of Old Mexico, and reaching Fort Union, New Mexico, joined the California volunteers December 9 of the year that he reached the United States. He served through the Apache campaign, was twice wounded in one day, then discharged and returned to California. From there he started for the Big Bend mines at the headwaters of the Columbia river, from where he went to Lewiston, Idaho Territory. For eleven years he followed mining in different camps through the mountains with varied success, until the Nez Perce outbreak in 1877, when he became a scout, bearer of dispatches for General Howard, and correspondent for the California Associated Press and *Boise Statesman*. His letters through the press, and exploits during that war, brought him prominently before the people of Idaho, and his name became as familiar in that country as that of the General who commanded the campaign. It was during this war, that the "Scout's Soliloquy" was penned by him, that, finding its way into the *New York Graphic*, was extensively republished by the Eastern press with many flattering comments. It was the poetic reflection called forth by the appearance before him of a hideous old squaw accompanied by a little three year old naked child, and we give a brief extract from the poem:

SCOUT'S SOLILOQUY
As published in *N.Y. Graphic*

Ah! yet her age her reputation spareth,
At three years old, pert Venus little careth,
She puts her hand upon her hip and stareth.

Could boundaries be neater, posture meeker,
Could bronze antique, or terra cotta beat her,
Saw ever artist anything completer.

Hast thou no notion, of what's before thee,
Of who shall envy or adore thee,

Or the dirty siwash that's to rule o'er thee?

Die young for mercy sake! If thou grow older,
Thou shalt get lean of calf and sharp of shoulder,
And daily greedier and daily bolder.

Just such another as the dame that bore thee,
That haggard Sycorax now bending o'er thee,
Oh, die of something fatal I implore thee!

At the close of the campaign, General Howard gave to Mr. Parker the following in recognition of his services:

HEAD QUARTERS IN THE FIELD,
JUDITH, BASIN, MONTANA, SEPTEMBER 27, 1877.

MR. F.J. PARKER:
Permit me to thank you for the generous service you have rendered the U.S. service during the Nez Perce war of 1877. You have ridden long journeys night and day and worked and fought right nobly. I hope to have the benefit of your services should another Indian outbreak take me into the field.

O.O. HOWARD
BRIG. GEN'L COMMANDING EXPEDITION, IN THE FIELD

The Governor of Idaho, M. Brayman, then gave him the position on his staff of Aide-de-camp, with the rank of Lieutenant Colonel, stating on the commission that it was given as a reward, "For gallant services in the Nez Perce war of 1877." In 1878, during the Bannock outbreak, he served again as scout and courier for General Howard, but this time as exclusive correspondent for the San Francisco *Chronicle*. During the last week in 1878, he took editorial charge of the *Statesman* of Walla Walla, ran it a year, and then assumed full control.

Mrs. J.W. McCrite

Grasshoppers brought her west
in 1876 on the transcontinental railroad.

Mrs. J.W. McCrite is of true pioneering stock, her family originating in Virginia.

In 1856 her father, J.H. Lewis, took up a homestead in Kansas near Topeka, where he built a home of walnut logs for his bride whom he married the following year.

When Mrs. McCrite was four years old she remembers the sky being darkened by a peculiar cloud, which as it approached, was accompanied by a strange humming sound.

Suddenly the ground was covered to a depth of five inches with grasshoppers, the hungry horde eating everything in sight, even riddling clothes.

With the depletion of feed, stock died all over the country and soon most of the farmers were on relief.

Becoming desperate Mr. Lewis joined his brother in Los Angeles and sent for his family a year later.

Selling what was left of the ranch and embarking on an old fashioned emigrant train where families cooked on a common stove and stopped hours on end en route for refueling and what not, Mrs. Lewis and her family of five children journeyed toward the West in 1876.

Men on the train whiled away the hours crossing the plains by shooting at herds of antelope and prairie dogs until an ill-aimed bullet mowing down a Chinese section hand put a stop to the sport.

The railroad of that day was crooked and rough and passengers were cautioned not to rush to one side or the other for fear of tipping over the clumsy affair.

From Sacramento to Los Angeles the trip was made by boat. The entire journey consumed 13 days and the $500 received from the sale of the ranch had all gone for expenses.

In April 1880, after four years in California, the pioneering urge got the upper hand and the Lewis family, the Chastains and Dave Bowman now of Milton, made up a train of 22 wagons and pushed toward Walla Walla which they thought was an Oregon town.

During their journey they were continually beset by horse thieves, and constant vigilance was necessary to save their stock. Even the women in the party took their turn at the night watches and on one occasion warned the men in time to save their animals.

Bridges other than the railroad crossings were few and the smaller streams were forded. To cross the larger rivers they swam the horses and the wagons were trundled across the railroad bridges.

The ties were far apart and Mrs. Lewis, hyterical with fear of the dizzy heights, was blindfolded and tied in a rocker and carried across by the men.

The wagons were heavily laden and the most of the party walked almost all the way.

The swollen streams forced the travelers to pick their way along the foot hills where they encountered quicksand perils. By cutting brush and building corduroy roads, by the hardest labor they were able to cover three miles a day.

Hardship, however, was interspersed with fun and at Red Bluff and Redding the townspeople arranged picnics and parties in honor of the young people in the wagon train. At the foot of Mt. Shasta a lively dance was held in a new barn.

Through the lava beds in the Modoc country a guide led them and though they saw no Indians they saw many prints of moccasined feet.

Mrs. McCrites tells of visiting what was known as Madam Jack's milk house--a cave in the side of a mountain with a peculiar formation making shelves all around the rock walls with a spring in the center.

By the time the party reached Lynn, Oregon, they were about out of food and all that was available was coarse ground corn which they cooked in their Dutch ovens. This was their fare for four days and in a mountain snowstorm on June 9, they went supperless to bed.

Running across an old mountaineer they inquired how far it was to the next town. "About as far again as half," he answered. Gnats were swarming in the air and asking what he called them he said, "I don't call them, they come without calling;" and when asked how long he had been there he said, "When Adam left I came."

They crossed the John Day river on a little ferry and covering the long dusty pull through Heppner, Pendleton, Centerville (Athena) they reached Walla Walla July 5 and camped on Garrison creek near Ninth avenue in a terrific dust storm.

Early days in this valley were hard, too, and the following extremely cold winter gave the Lewis family a struggle for subsistence. Their menu consisted mainly of potatoes boiled with their jackets on; beef tallow gravy and sour dough bread.

Mr. and Mrs. Lewis slept in the one pine bed, and the children on the floor of their three-room home. They had the three chairs they had brought from California and an old stove without legs.

But the family was well and jolly; they had their good times and Mrs. McCrite loves to recall those happy days.

Col. J.W. Redington

U.S. Scout and Courier during the
Sheepeater War
tells of an incident hunting hostiles
"where Man Never Trod Before."

Where did he go?

Why did he so suddenly disappear?

Did the ground swallow him? or was he suddenly sucked into some secret subterranean passage known only to our hostile enemies?

"Hal-l-l-o-o! Hallo there!"

That yell showed that he was still on earth, and had not entirely evaporated.

And when we rushed over to where the yell came from we reached down and pulled Lieutenant Benton out of the hole he had stepped into, and it was over his head.

He was fresh from the east, and had volunteered to go out with Farrow's Scouts, a command comprising 35 Umatilla and other Indians, including the old veteran Cutmouth John, and 25 soldier-sharpshooters from the first cavalry, the fourth artillery and the second and 21st infantry, who were out in the rough Salmon river mountains of Idaho hunting the hostiles of Eagle Eye, Warjack and Chuck--copper-colored free-lances and murderous maurauders who had raided the ranches of the pioneers who were pushing civilization up the Weiser, the Payette and the Boise, and had murdered Jim Raines, and Groseclose, Munday and Tom Healy, besides 37 Chinese miners over on Loon creek and seemed to think the latter a joke, and had near-murdered Threefingered Smith, who dived under a drift at Payette Falls, not to mention Jackass Johnson and many others who had turned up missing.

Farrow's Scouts had been seeking out trails all that long day, up one mountain and down another, and toward evening had dropped down into a most beautiful little mountain valley, with grass knee-high to the horses, and running water from the adjacent snowbanks. Nature there was undisturbed. Not a sign of intrusion of man or beast.

"We are now where man never trod before!" said Lieut. Benton, and all agreed with him. Then he turned loose his horse and said he would look for Indian signs. And he had not gone 50 yards toward the creek when he disappeared. Walking through the tall rank grass, with his eyes on the opposite mountain range for possible smoke-signs, he had stepped right into a big hole--a real prospect-hole dug by the hand of man, and down to bedrock.

Further proof of our mistake in thinking we were where man never trod before were the rusty remains of an old shovel and miner's pick, and near by a few bleached bones--human bones that told their own story.

The prospector had penetrated in there and remained. Whether a victim of hostiles or of one of the big snowstorms that came there every month in the year, no one could tell.

The quiet old blacksmith who was with the outfit was asked what he thought about it, and said:

"Well, you boys think you are explorers and trail-blazers, and perhaps 50 years from now you may be considered such. But now you are all tenderfeet. Why, Miles Moore and Levi Ankeny and other pioneers had their big packtrains in the Salmon river mountains 15 or 20 years ago. They packed in supplies from Umatilla, Walla Walla and Lewiston, to the mines at Florence and Warrens. I was in Florence in '63, and helped bury many of the 48 men who were planted in Boot hill. Joaquin Miller and several other since noted men were there then. Several of the prospectors struck off into these wild mountains, and never again came back. These bones here belonged to one of them. That's plain enough. When a prospector did not come back, we always said that the Injuns got him. He took his chances.

And when this hard campaign was nearly over, and first frosts had turned the tall tamaracks along the higher ridges, and the cottonwoods and quaking-asps along the water-courses from bright-green to old gold, and Major Farrow's command had corralled the hostiles and forever ended up all their raids in Idaho, the Scouts had reached Warren's Diggins, on their way out to Fort Walla Walla and civilization, the old blacksmith applied for a hurry-up discharge. But Major Farrow reminded him of his contract calling for his sticking to the outfit until its return to the fort in the beautiful valley of winding waters.

The blacksmith explained that he had seen strong symptoms of well-mineralized rock both beyond Buffalo Hump mountain and on the edges of the Seven Devils during this campaign, and he was very anxious to go back in there and give the country a thorough testing. He wanted to outfit in Warren's and start back on the trail next day.

Major Farrow reminded him that he might get snowed in or get taken in by the few of Eagle Eye's outfit still scattered in the inaccessible spots, but these things had no terrors for the blacksmith. He was there to take chances. He would work all night, and re-shoe every scout-horse that needed it, and tighten up every shoe in the outfit, and guarantee that they would last to Fort Lapwai and Walla Walla.

And so, with western broadness Major Farrow did not stand on ceremony, and accommodated the old blacksmith with his honorable discharge.

Dr. Foard, one of the whole-souled pioneers of Warren's mining camp, was down to Portland three years later, and I asked him whatever became of the old blacksmith.

"Well," said Doc, "I don't know. I suppose the Injuns got him. When Major Farrow paid him off, he bought a very good prospector's outfit, and started off towards the Seven Devils, but said he expected to eventually swing around to Umbrella mountain and Buffalo Hump. We never heard of him again. Two years later other prospectors found human bones and campfire remains near the head of Elk creek, and also where the battle of Vinegar hill had been fought, but there were no identifying features. The Salmon river mountains are immense. You know, as you have scouted through them. A few dozen prospectors more or less might be scalped and swallowed up there, and would not leave a dent on the atmosphere. But is a grand place to pass in your checks! There are grassy glades as green as emerald, stately spruce and towering tamaracks, bold bluffs and sky-scraping peaks whose duplicates laugh back at you from lovely little lakes in baby-basins far below, with snow--both red snow and white snow--oceans of it, clean and undefiled. No more magnificent setting could be found for the last resting place of the man with lofty ideals as to solitude and natural grandeur."

Epilogue

Miles C. Moore

*The former Governor's speech
to the Inland Empire Pioneer Association
in Walla Walla in 1917.*

Many of you came here long years ago and saw the city in its earliest beginnings; saw it when it was only a frontier trading post--an outfitting point for miners bound to the mines of Pierce City, Orofino and Florence in Northern Idaho and to Boise in Southern Idaho--all new camps. A little later Kootenai in British Columbia, and the mining camps of Western Montana became the Mecca of the gold seeker.

Many of them outfitted here and were followed by pack trains laden with supplies. Many of you will remember the tinkle of the mule bell which the pack mules followed in blind obedience.

All day long these pack trains filed in constant procession through the streets of the busy little city, bound on long journeys through the mountains to the various mining camps.

Indians, gaudy with paint and feathers, rode their spotted, picturesque cayuse in gay cavalcades along the trails leading to town to trade for fire water and other less important articles of barter.

Covered ox wagons laden with dust begrimed children and household goods 'all the way from old Missouri,' ranchmen, and cow-boys in all their pristine swagger and splendor helped to make up the motley throng that filled the streets. The cow-girl who rides a horse astride had not then materialized.

The packers and many of the miners came here to 'winter' as they expressed it in those days. They spent their money prodigally and unstintingly in the saloons, in the gambling and hurdy-gurdy houses, and in the spring would return to the source for fresh supplies of gold.

Some of the more successful would return to the States, and all expected to when they 'made their pile.' None of us had any idea of making this a permanent place of residence or of being found here fifty years later. As youngsters we sang with lusty voices:

> We'll all go home in the Spring, boys
>
> We'll all go home in the Spring.

Later as the years went by and we did not go, there was added by the unsentimental, this refrain:

> Yes, in a horn,
>
> Yes, in a horn!

SOURCE MATERIAL

ABBREVIATIONS

(PML) - Penrose Memorial Library, Whitman College, Walla Walla, Washington
(OWWC) - *Old Walla Walla County*, W.D. Lyman, 1918
(TBTP) - *Told By The Pioneers*, Works Projects Administration, Washington State,
      three volumes, 1937-38
(UTTT) - *Up To The Times* magazine, Walla Walla, Washington

Actor, Charles - *(UTTT)*, October 1913, Pages 5333-5335, by Nellie G. Day.

Ankeny, Levi - *(UTTT)*, April 1907, Page 25.

Berryman, J.E. - (PML), typed manuscript, no date.

Brents, Thomas H. - *Walla Walla Union*, December 15, 1912, courtesy of *Oregon Journal*, by
      Fred Jackson.

Campbell, Martin - *(UTTT)*, March 1918, pages 8117-8119, by Nellie G. Day.
      (OWWC), pages 416-417.

Clark Charles W. - (OWWC), page 455.

Clark, W.S. - *Walla Walla Union*, May 15, 1927, page 9.

Cornwell, James M. - *Historic Sketches*, F.T. Gilbert, 1882, appendix pages 8-9.

Cox, Philip - *(UTTT)*, July 1916, pages 6194-6196.

Crawford, Rev. J.V. - *(UTTT)*, March 1907, page 11.

Crossman, Adam - *(UTTT)*, February 1917, pages 6480-6482.

Cunningham, C.G. - *(UTTT)*, October 1916, pages 6267-6268.

Dement, W.C. - *(UTTT)*, November 1911, page 4756.

Evans, Andrew Jackson - *(UTTT)*, April 1919, pages 9020-9022, by Nellie G. Day.

Ferrel, Mrs. Brewster - *(OWWC)*, pages 447-454.

Frisco, Joseph - *(UTTT)*, April 1914, pages 5699-5703, by Nellie G. Day.

Galbraith, Nettie M. - *(TBTP)*, volume three, pages 197-198.

Gilbreath, Margaret - *(OWWC)*, page 470.

Gilliam, W.S. - (PML), typed manuscript, dated March 8, 1904.

Gray, William Polk - *Oregon Historical Society Journal*, December 1913,
      volume 14, number 4, by Fred Lockley.

Harris, A.H. - *(UTTT)*, August 1910, pages 2736-2737.
      (UTTT), March 1910, pages 2494-2495.

Hawk, Al R. - *(TBTP)*, volume 1, pages 158-166.

Hayes, Daniel - *(UTTT)*, December 1916, pages 6366-6368.

Holmes, H.E. - *(UTTT)*, June 1914, pages 5826-5828.

Isaacs, Lucie Fulton - *(UTTT)*, February 1917, page 6475.

Jacobs, Nancy Osborn - (PML), paper presented to Inland Empire Pioneer and Historical Society.

Johnson, P.B. - *(UTTT)*, December 1918, pages 8797-8801.

Johnston, George Christopher - *(UTTT)*, August 1919, pages 9229-9231.

Kennedy, William H. - (PML), re-typed letter.

Kenney, Michael - *(UTTT)*, December 1906, pages 20-23 and
      (UTTT), February 1916, pages 5901-5904.

Kershaw, James Stott - *(UTTT)*, October 1914, pages 6051-6053.

Kelso, John - (PML), photocopy of manuscript copied from a worn tablet by Miss Gwendolyn
      Watson and recopied by Edna Mae Karnes.

Looney, Jesse - *(OWWC)*, page 427-428.

Lowden, Frank M. - *Portland Journal*, April 7, 1915, by Fred Lockley.

McConnell, W.J. - *Early History of Idaho*, Caxton Publishing, Caldwell, Idaho, 1913, pages 262-287.

McCrite, Mrs. J.W. - *Walla Walla Union-Bulletin*, August 7, 1936, page 4, column 3.

McMorris, Lewis - *(UTTT)*, December 1908.

Miller, George Washington - *Tacoma Tribune*, October 28, 1892, and *Walla Walla Daily Union*, December 7 and 8, 1905.

Miller, Joaquin - *St. Nicholas magazine*, December, 1890, pages 138-142.

Moore, Miles C. - *Walla Walla Union*, June 8, 1917.
(OWWC), page 204.

Myers, Joseph - *Oregon City Argus*, November 24, 1860.

Old Timer - *(UTTT)*, January 1912, pages 4849-4851.

Owsley, Ambrose A. - *(UTTT)*, December 1914, pages 6166-6169.

Owsley, Barney - *(TBTP)* volume two, page 210-217.

Page, Frances Ellen - *(UTTT)*, January 1919, pages 8858-8859, by Nellie G. Day.

Palouse Falls - *Walla Walla Statesman*, June 28, 1867.

Parker, Frank J. - *Historic Sketches*, F.T. Gilbert, 1882, pages 354-355.

Pringle, Catherine Sager - *(UTTT)*, December 1906, pages 7-9.

Provo, Narcis - *(UTTT)*, April 1910, pages 2551-2552.

Purdin, James H. - *(TBTP)*, volume one, pages 54-57.

Redington, J.W. - *(UTTT)*, October 1915, pages 5674-5675.

Rees, R.R. - Private collection, original letter dated December 27, 1863.

Roberts, A.B. - *(UTTT)*, April 1910, pages 1889-1894.
(UTTT), March 1910, pages 2487-2488.
(UTTT), March and April 1911, pages 3288-3292 and pages 3345-3349.

Rohn, J.J. - *(UTTT)*, March 1909, page 1853.
(UTTT), August 1914, pages 5925-5928.

St. George, Mrs. (Pomeroy) - *(OWWC)*, pages 361-363.

Scholl, Lewis - *(UTTT)*, October 1907, pages 531-534.
(UTTT), December 1907, pages 51-54.
(UTTT), January 1908, pages 97-99.

Seek, M.C. - *(UTTT)*, November 1906, pages 13-14.

Shaw, Thomas C. - *(UTTT)*, March 1913, pages 4965-4967.

Smith, Armanda - *(UTTT)*, March 1914, pages 5665-5666.

Stoughten, J.A. - (PML), typed manuscript dated 1899,
(TBTP), volume one, page 73.

Stringer, Susan M. - *(UTTT)*, August 1914, pages 5948-5949.

Sweazea, Charles - *Walla Walla Union*, April 9, 1915, page 4, column 3-4.

Tempany, John - *(UTTT)*, June 1916, pages 6139-6140.

Walter, W.W. - *(OWWC)*, pages 430-436.

Ward, Michael B. - Private collection, Gregory's Express Pocket Letter Book, (3″ x 5″, 48 pages), dated 1851.

Watt, James W. - *Washington Historical Quarterly*, volume 19 number 3, July 1928.

Wells, H.L. - *The West Shore* magazine, Portland, Oregon, November 1887.

Williams, Daniel - *(TBTP)*, Volume two, pages 207-210.

INDEX

-363-

Robbins, G.C. 201-208
Robbins, Orlando "Rube" 247-253
Roberts, A.B. 106, 107-110, 151, 152, 199-209
Robidoux, Antoine (Rubydeau) 25
Robinson, C.S. 337-341
Robinson, Dr. 327
Robinson, Ida F. 327
Rock Creek, (Wash.) 91-92, 126
Rock Island Rapids (Columbia River) 240
Rocky Bar (Mont.) 219
Rocky Mountains 11, 97, 178, 276, 280, 294, 330
Rodgers, John 156
Rogers, Andrew 26-30
Rogers brothers 86
Rogue River 16, 73, 134
Rogue River Indians 124-125
Rogue River Indian Wars 107, 124-125, 133, 278
Rohn, J.J. 128, 129
Romaine, James 225-226, 238
Rosalia, Washington 123, 126, 255
Rose, Bill 183
Rosebud River (Mont.) 141
Roslyn, British Columbia 240
Ross, Ed 187
Rowley, Mrs. Robert 155
Rundel, George "Cayuse George" 136, 216
Rush, John 323
Russel, Charles 135
Russel Creek (Walla Walla) 148
Russell, Billy 150
Russell Diggins, Colorado 162
Russell, George 151
Russell, Green 162
Russell, Lou 98
Russell, Samuel 94
Ryan, Mike 311
Rye Valley (Oregon) 306
Rynearson, Jacob 27

St. George, Mrs. (Pomeroy) 284-287
St. Joseph, Missouri 9, 23, 25, 101, 168, 169, 170, 175
St. Louis, Missouri 145
St. Paul School (Walla Walla) 287, 319-320
Sacramento, California 58, 327, 348
Sacramento "Union" 133, 138, 238
Sacramento Valley (Calif.) 16, 17, 134
Sagebrush Jack 260
Sager family 39-40
Sager, Francis 30, 34, 40
Sager, Hanna 29, 40
Sager, Henry 26, 39-40
Sager, John 40
Salem, Oregon 16, 17, 27, 28, 196, 285
Salmon Falls (Snake River) 98, 99, 179
Salmon River (Idaho) 74, 77-78, 339
Salmon River Indians 339
Salmon River Mountains 351
Salmon River Valley 265
Salt Creek Valley (Missouri) 171
Salt Lake City, Utah 79-81, 94, 124, 133, 135-136, 280, 327
San Francisco, California 21, 57, 58, 62, 70-72, 79, 124, 139, 140, 141, 189-190, 223, 225, 226, 243, 255, 262, 263, 275, 322, 323, 327

San Francisco Chronicle 347
San Joaquin Valley (Calif.)
San Jose, California 186, 187
San Juan Islands (Wash.) 329
Sand Pete, Utah 124
Sandwich Islands (Hawaii) 69-70
Sandy River (Oregon) 73, 111, 236
Sanford, E.L. 216
Santa Fe, N.M. 173
Santa Fe Trail 158
Saunders, L.W. 28-30, 33
Saunders, Mr. 260-261
Saunders, Mrs. L.W. 37-38
Schnebley, Theodore "Mr. Stubbs" 153, 214-215, 266
Scholl, Frank 343
Scholl, Louis 132, 142
Schwabacher Bros. 274, 275
Schwartz, Theodore 340
Scott family 220
Scott, Mr. 26
Scott, Mr. 339-340
Scott, Harvey 187
Scraggy, Mount (Klamath) 71
Seattle, Washington 190, 289
Seek, M.C. 217, 221-222
Seven Devils (Idaho) 351, 352
Sharpneck, Mr. 324
Shasta, Mount (Calif.) 16, 349
Shattuck, Judge 149
Shaw, Judge Thomas C. 38-40
Shaw, Capt. William 39-40
Shedd's Station (Oregon) 111
Sheepeater War (1879) 322, 353-354
Sheets, Dan 274
Sheets, John 191, 282
Shell Creek 96
Sheridan, Phil 125
Shobat, Charley 90
Shorthair wagon train 290-296
Shoshone Falls (Snake River) 99
Shoshone Indians 136, 203, 204
Shoue, Dr. 311
Shushuskin Canyon (Wash.) 289
Sierra Mountains 134
Silcott Ferry (Lyons) 282, 308
Silcott, Jane 265
Silcott, John 265
Silver City, Montana 219
Silver City, Nevada 86, 87, 327
Silverton, Oregon 195
Silvey River (Idaho) 136
Simms, J.A. 150-152
Sinker Creek, Idaho 206
Sioux Indians 141
Siskiyou Mountains 72
Six-toed Pete 259
Skinner, Bill 154
Slate Creek, (Calif.) 51
Slate Creek house 78
Slim Jim 260
Small, Albert 337-341
Small's stable (Walla Walla) 91
Smith, Armanda (Mrs. Sergeant) 191-192
Smith, Capt. A.J. 124, 131, 133, 136
Smith, Daniel 119
Smith, G.W. 118
Smith, "God Almighty" 186

-368-